AF326773

All The Hits All The Hits
All The Time

More Distinctive Rock Memories from the Coffman Collection

Larry Coffman

Library of Congress Control Number: 2025913020
ISBN: 978-1-963851-69-4 (Paperback)
        978-1-968069-35-3 (Hardback)
        978-1-963851-70-0 (Ebook)

Olympus Story House

CONTENTS

All The Hits All The Time

More Distinctive Rock Memories
from the Coffman Collection

Larry Coffman

For Dr. Paul B. Snider — teacher, mentor, friend

I would like to thank Bill Drake and Gene Chenault, producers of The History of Rock & Roll syndicated radio documentary, for inspiring me to write my own three-part history of rock. Thanks to Sally Gordon-Mark, Carol Fischer and Carl Giammarese for not only being part of the history of rock but also for sharing their memories in this book.

Preface

I have a mental picture of the history of rock & roll.

In my mind, I can see a long, long corridor, several feet wide. In the beginning, this hallway was empty. Then, starting in 1951, it started to be populated by images of the singers, songwriters and musical instruments of the people who created the songs that have come to be known as Rock & Roll.

To be sure, this mythical corridor is super-lengthy, because it holds images all of the musicians who contributed major hit songs to the record charts over the years. As I write this book, that would include over seventy years' worth of contributors.

It's an interesting concept, don't you think? A display of statues representing the stars of rock, in the order they hit the charts! It would resemble a wax museum. If only such a conglomeration of images could be assembled!

As long as I'm fantasizing about this corridor, let me add that there would be a console next to each musician or band. If you were to push a button on this console, you could hear every song the artist recorded.

On a smaller scale, however, music fans who have collected recordings for decades have their own form of rock's history. The 33 rpm albums and many 45 rpm singles have come with jackets and sleeves that contain photos of the artists. Regardless of the condition of the vinyl platters, the packaging is valuable because of the photos and sketches contained thereupon.

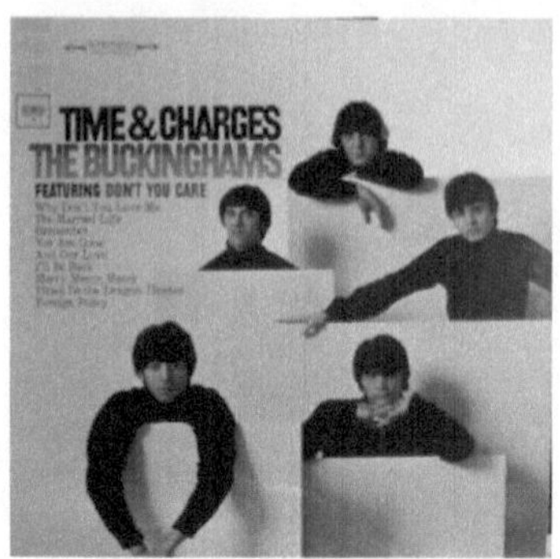

Courtesy of Columbia Records

Courtesy of RCA Victor Records

The tie that binds

One thing about rock music that I particularly like is the fact that people who have embraced the songs and memorized the lyrics have something special in common. That may be the only thing some strangers can share.

Two events in my personal history illustrate this unlikely common denomination. First, one time in the 1990s I was playing golf with my regular foursome on a city course in Phoenix. On the 16th hole, there was a line of houses on the north side of the course boundary. As we rode in our carts to find our golf balls, we noticed a family was enjoying a backyard birthday party. A "Happy Birthday" sign and other decorations tipped us off.

Being the friendly guys that we were, Russ, Paul, Martin and I walked up to the chain link fence and asked the name of the birthday girl. We were told the woman's name was Susan.

Without saying a word, my friends and I looked at each other for a second and then broke into song. We serenaded the party guests with the first verse of "Susan," the Buckinghams' 1967-68 hit: "Susan, looks like I'm losin' – I'm losin' my mind, I'm wasting my time."

The spontaneity of the singing surprised the birthday girl and duly impressed the other celebrants. It was a magic moment.

In 2022 my wife and I were on a cruise ship, entering the Agua Clara locks of the Panama Canal. A photographer was on deck to take passenger photos with the locks as a backdrop, and he instructed us to adjust our stance by saying, "Come together."

Without thinking, I remarked, "Right now."

Another passenger, standing about five feet away, then added, "Over me."

It was the completion of the chorus to the Beatles' "Come Together," pieced together by three strangers in a most spontaneous way. I loved it!

You just never know when you will encounter another person who is on the same musical wavelength as yours.

My good friend Jim, whom I have known for twenty years, definitely is on my wavelength when it comes to music. He has said, "Music is at my core. It's those magical moments in time that get me through this life."

Jim is 11 years younger than I, and it's been my privilege to share with him music from the 1960s and '70s that he was too young to enjoy back then. He eagerly listens as I talk about the old songs from rock's early years that helped form my musical tastes. Rock & Roll is the backbone of our friendship.

On the other side of the coin is my friend Phil, who is my age and attended four different schools with me. He told me the classical and big band music his father played on the home record player influenced his musical tastes, as well as the material he practiced during piano lessons in his youth.

Phil says the artists who were his early musical heroes include Dion, Rick Nelson, Del Shannon and the Rascals. That's a good representation of the talent we heard on the radio when we were twelve to sixteen years old.

The One Note Song

When I was in college, I lived off-campus in a house with several other students. We became very close, like a family. One thing Chet, Gator and I liked to do was play "One Note Song" with each another.

In this game, whenever one of us came home with a new vinyl record album, the buyer would put it on a turntable and choose a track on which to place the tone arm. After a couple of notes played, the owner of the album would lift the needle, leaving the others to guess the name of the song, artist or album. This lighthearted activity bound us together as much as any of the other crazy things we did.

I remember one instance in which I stumped my friends. In the spring of 1970, I bought the Beach Boys' new hits compilation titled *Good Vibrations*. I chose the track "Surfer Girl," which has a four-note electric guitar intro. I pulled the tone arm after the third note played, and the guys were sure it was a country song because of the sound of the guitar. They failed to guess the song title, and they were dumbfounded when I played it in full.

Courtesy of Capitol Records

That's just one instance of rock music enriching my life.

I've been writing books about the history of rock & roll because I want to share with others the passion I have for the music. I enjoy digging up trivial tidbits about songs and artists that my readers may not have already known. If you have bonded with rock music, this probably is important to you.

An idol with feet of clay

There's an old adage that cautions about choosing one's idols carefully, because an idol can have feet of clay. I learned a personal lesson about that when I was a limousine driver in 1980.

I drew the assignment of driving a pop music star around Phoenix for four days. He came to town to play a three-night engagement at a local concert hall. I also drove him to the Turf Paradise thoroughbred race track one afternoon, where a race was named in his honor.

This singer/songwriter was one of the stars who got started in the 1950s. By the early '60s, he was pelting the charts with hit after hit. His career, like many others, suffered a setback in 1964 when the British Invasion changed musical tastes all over the world. In 1980, he was still recording, but he was considered a nostalgia act. The fact that I loved his music and looked up to him had never changed.

But just listening to him converse with his road manager in the back seat of the limo gave me an insight into his personality that I hadn't expected. His remarks about the music business and religion, for example, troubled me. I also was turned off by the distant way he treated me as a contracted employee. After I drove him to the airport at the end of the assignment, I came away with a new perspective of him. I still like his music – but the man, not so much.

Magic is in the music

To me, Rock & Roll is part notes and chords and part magic. The people who write, compose, sing and play the instruments are gifted, talented artists. This is talent that I do not possess, so it seems magical to me.

I remember telling my mother, when I was about seventeen years old, that the Beatles were musical geniuses. She didn't argue with me, but I could tell by the look on her face that she rejected my statement and considered it preposterous. She probably thought of the Beatles more as sorcerers than musicians.

Today, I stand by that statement, and I'll bet I could get more than a few people to agree with me. What the Beatles and other rockers have done to enrich our lives is phenomenal and even somewhat mystical.

In this, my third book, I once again have pulled together songs that share a common denominator to show how those categories have shaped the history of rock. There are other topics related to rock in this book I believe are worth examining.

The radio disc jockeys of yore who proclaimed on air that their stations played "all the hits, all the time" inspired the title for this book. Herein you will find profiles of many hit records from the history of Rock & Roll, along with other related information I hope you will find fascinating.

Join me now as we take another joyous trip down a musical memory lane.

~ Larry Coffman

The Days of Doo-Wop
Major hits of the doo-wop era

Overview: Doo-wop was one of the first genres to pervade Rock and Roll, as it took hold in the mid-1950s. Its roots go back to the 1940s, when youths practiced their acoustic vocals on street corners.

The birthplace of doo-wop was the major cities of the northeastern United States, such as New York, Philadelphia, Washington, Pittsburgh, Chicago, Detroit, Newark and Baltimore.

The genre was all about vocal harmonies, and doo-wop groups varied in size from three members to as many as eight.

The imaginative vocal sounds of the back-up singers gave doo-wop its name. Especially in the chorus, the backing singers would run off an imaginative battery of non-word syllables. This set doo-wop apart from other forms of rock music.

One of the endearing aspects of doo-wop is that singers without instruments or amplification could sing a cappella. In a studio, arrangers and producers could make recordings with minimal instrumentation. Many of the backing vocalists ad-libbed sounds, adding spontaneity to the process.

Most of the doo-wop vocal groups that got recorded and had success on the charts were Black, but White and Latino groups also made their mark. At least one group from Canada had an impact.

The Mills Brothers from Ohio, who got their start in the late 1920s, had greatly influenced doo-woppers with their four-part harmony.

Some of the mainstream songwriters of the 20th century, such as Hoagy Carmichael and Rodgers & Hart, had songs turned into doo-wop hits. Slow tempos and love-song lyrics were the mainstays of the genre.

In 1980, Daryl Hall and John Oates gave a nod to the genre by writing and recording "Diddy Doo Wop (I Hear The Voices)," a song laced with the doo-wop sound.

Concert promoter Harvey Robbins of Massachusetts conceived a Doo-Wop Hall of Fame in 1989, and it eventually found a home in Bellflower, California.

To view the full lyrics of these songs, please log on to www.google.com, enter song titles & artist names and click Google Search.

To listen to these songs, please log on to www.youtube.com and enter song titles & artist names.

"My Prayer" by the Platters
Songwriters: Georges Boulanger, Carlos Gomez Barrara, Jimmy Kennedy
Peaked at number 1 on *Billboard* Top 100 Chart
August 18, 1956
August 25, 1956
September 1, 1956
September 8, 1956
September 15, 1956

The Platters

Tony Williams (April 5, 1928-August 14, 1992)
Herb Reed (August 7, 1928-June 4, 2012)
Zola Taylor (March 17, 1938-April 30, 2007)
David Lynch (July 3, 1929-January 2, 1981)
Paul Robi (August 20, 1931-February 1, 1989)
Formed in 1952 in Los Angeles, California

The Platters: *back,* Tony Williams, David Lynch
front, Herb Reed, Zola Taylor, Paul Robi

The Platters were the first vocal group with a doo-wop sound to hit number 1 on the *Billboard* pop chart during the Rock Era, which began in 1955. They also were the first Black group to top a mainstream chart.

Among their four number 1 singles, the Platters' first was "The Great Pretender," which held the top spot for two weeks in 1956. "Twilight Time" was number 1 for a single week in 1958, and "Smoke Gets In Your Eyes" stayed on top for three weeks in 1959.

Their biggest success was "My Prayer," which followed a success formula of torchy ballads.

According to author Fred Bronson, U.K. songwriter Jimmy Kennedy encountered the Platters' manager/producer Buck Ram on the street one day. Kennedy said he was impressed with the sound of the Platters and offered several of his songs to the group.

The one Ram liked best was a French song originally written as "Avant de Mourir," ("Before Dying") for which Kennedy had written English lyrics in 1939. "My Prayer" was its new title, as suggested by Kennedy's wife.

The Platters' record label, Mercury, refused to release it. But an artist-and-repertoire man at Mercury learned the Four Aces were going to record it. Subsequently, the Platters' version was rushed to market.

A tender love song, "My Prayer" contains the verse: "My prayer and the answer you give, may they still be the same for as long as I live. That you'll always be there at the end of my prayer."

Big band leader Glenn Miller, one of many artists to record the song, had his version reach number 2 on the *Billboard* pop chart in 1939.

Kennedy began service for Britain in World War II, and the song lay forgotten for years. In the 1950s he moved to the United States to continue his songwriting career, according to the *Financial Times.*

In 2017 the television series *Twin Peaks*, which had been revived on *Showtime*, breathed new life into "My Prayer" by dubbing it over two scenes.

"Earth Angel (Will You Be Mine)" by the Penguins

Songwriters: Curtis Williams, Jesse Belvin, Gaynel Hodge
Peaked at number 8 on *Billboard* Best Seller Chart
February 5, 1955

The Penguins

Cleveland Duncan (July 23, 1935-November 7, 2012)
Curtis Williams (December 11, 1934-August 10, 1979)
Dexter Tisby (March 10, 1935-May 2019)
Bruce Tate (January 27, 1937-June 20, 1973)
Formed in 1953 in Los Angeles, California

The Penguins: Curtis Williams, Cleveland Duncan, Dexter Tisby, Bruce Tate

"Earth Angel" was headed for obscurity when Dootone Records tagged it the B-side opposite the single "Hey Señorita" in late 1954.

But fate intervened when a radio disc jockey in southern California decided to play "Earth Angel" on the air. That bit of exposure was all it took for the song to become a doo-wop classic.

Released in its original demo form, "Earth Angel" was a pop smash and a number 1 hit on the *Billboard* R&B Chart. Sales eventually topped 10 million for the song that was recorded in the garage of a relative of Curtis Williams.

Cleveland Duncan sang lead vocal on the track for the Penguins, who had attended high school together in Los Angeles. According to writer Steve Sullivan, "Earth Angel" became the first record on an independent label to appear on *Billboard*'s national pop charts.

When money was slow to come from Dootone, the Penguins hired the Platters' manager, Buck Ram, to guide their destiny. As a result, Mercury Records signed the group in March 1955, and the result was law suits followed by countersuits.

For the Penguins, who took their name from an advertising mascot of Kool Cigarettes, the success of "Earth Angel" was their only time in the limelight. None of their subsequent recordings cracked the top 40 of the pop charts.

"We wanted to be cool, so we took our name off Willie the Penguin, the trademark on Kool cigarette packs," Duncan told a reporter.

Some of the Penguins' thunder was stolen by the Canadian group the Crew-Cuts, who turned their version of "Earth Angel" into a number 3 hit, issued on Mercury.

The hit movie *Back To The Future* introduced the song to a new audience in 1985 when it was included in a scene at the Hill Valley High School dance.

•••••••• ❖ ••••••••

"Why Do Fools Fall In Love" by the Teenagers featuring Frankie Lymon

Songwriters: Frankie Lymon, Herman Santiago, Jimmy Merchant, George Goldner
Peaked at number 6 on *Billboard* Best Sellers
April 14, 1956
April 21, 1956
April 28, 1956

The Teenagers

Frankie Lymon (September 30, 1942-February 27, 1968)
Jimmy Merchant (February 10, 1940-?)
Herman Santiago (February 18, 1941-?)
Sherman Garnes (June 8, 1940-February26, 1977)
Joe Negroni (September 9, 1940-September 5, 1978)
Formed in 1954 in Harlem, New York City, New York

The Teenagers: Jimmy Merchant, Herman Santiago, Frankie Lymon,
Joe Negroni, Sherman Garnes

Doo-wop owes a huge debt of gratitude to the Teenagers and their memorable recording of "Why Do Fools Fall In Love." The song has been a beloved pillar of the genre and helped it gain traction in the formative years of Rock & Roll.

The Teenagers really were in their teens when they pieced together "Fools." It was 1955, and the vocal group was calling itself the Premiers. According to author Marv Goldberg, they auditioned for George Goldner, owner of Gee Records, with a song called

"Why Do Birds Sing So Gay." Tenor Herman Santiago had written it from lines in love letters written to the group.

Goldner suggested some lyrical changes, and Santiago adjusted the harmony to take advantage of Frankie Lymon's soaring tenor/soprano voice.

According to Jimmy Merchant, what happened at the recording session was a combination of "Frankie's singing ability coupled with George Goldner's special ability to bring out the best in Frankie."

The single spent five weeks at number 1 on the *Billboard* R&B Chart, and it hit number 1 on the U.K. pop chart. Worldwide sales topped two million.

"Why do birds sing so gay, and lovers await the break of day," the lyrics ask. "Why do they fall in love? "Why does the rain fall from above? Why do fools fall in love?"

Lymon died of a drug overdose in 1968 at the age of twenty-five, but the world hadn't heard the last of him. In 1998 Warner Brothers released the romantic comedy film *Why Do Fools Fall In Love,* starring Halle Berry, Vivica A. Fox and Lela Rochon. The three actresses played the roles of women in Lymon's life, who claim to have married him and lay claim to his estate. Larenz Tate played the part of Lymon.

•••••• ❖ ••••••

"In The Still Of The Nite" by the Five Satins
Songwriter: Fred Parris
Peaked at number 24 on *Billboard* Best Sellers
October 13, 1956

The Five Satins

Fred Parris (March 26, 1936-January 14, 2022)
Ed Martin (bio unavailable)
Jim Freeman (bio unavailable)
Nat Mosley (bio unavailable)
Al Denby (bio unavailable)
Formed in 1954 in New Haven, Connecticut

The Five Satins

A recording that sounded so divine had to be recorded in a church, right?

"In The Still Of The Nite" was recorded in the basement of St. Bernadette Church in New Haven, Conn., on Feb. 19, 1956, at the suggestion of Father Charles Hewitt. The first recording of the Five Satins' classic had been made in a venue where outside noise spoiled the taping, but the church structure was well insulated.

Vinny Mazzetta, who played the soulful saxophone solo on the record, was a parishioner at the church. The session took place after Sunday mass, and instrumentation included the church piano, guitar, drums and a cello played as a bass.

Fred Parris of the Five Satins wrote the song while riding a train between New Haven and Philadelphia, a route he traveled as a U.S. Army recruit. Shortly after the Five Satins made the recording, Parris was deployed to Japan and wasn't discharged until 1958.

According to *Songfacts*, Parris wrote the lyrics about a former girlfriend whom he hoped would come back to him. The reunion never happened.

The lyrics say, "I remember that night in May, the stars were bright above. I'll hope and I'll pray to keep your precious love."

An up-tempo song titled "The Jones Girl" was intended to be the A-side of the single, but radio disc jockey play influenced public preference for "In The Still Of The Nite."

The spelling of "nite" was chosen to differentiate the song from a song Cole Porter wrote in 1937.

The Five Satins' version had three different chart runs in its original form on the *Billboard* pop charts. It earned a number 3 showing on the *Billboard R&B Chart* in its first release.

In 1987 and '88 it sold ten million units as part of the soundtrack of the hit movie *Dirty Dancing.*

•••••• ❖ ••••••

"Come Go With Me" by the Dell-Vikings
Songwriter: C.E. Quick
Peaked at number 4 on *Billboard* Best Sellers
May 11, 1957

The Dell-Vikings

Clarence Quick (February 2, 1937-May 5, 1983)
Kripp Johnson (May 16, 1933-June 22, 1990)
Norman Wright (October 31, 1937-April 23, 2010)
David Lerchey (December 3, 1937-January 29, 2005)
Gus Backus (September 12, 1937-February 21, 2019)
Formed in 1955 in Pittsburgh, Pennsylvania

The Dell-Vikings: *top,* Kripp Johnson, *middle,* Gus Backus,
Clarence Quick, David Lerchey, *bottom,* Norman Wright

A fluid membership with an interracial makeup were the earmarks of the Dell-Vikings. The original members served in the U.S. Air Force, which made staying together difficult because they could be transferred to other bases from their hometown of Pittsburgh at any time.

Their biggest hit, "Come Go With Me," came from the pen of singer Clarence Quick and was the first of three top 40 singles for the vocal group. It was an upbeat love song.

"Come into my heart. Tell me darlin' we will never part," the lyrics plead. "I need you darlin' so come go with me."

The Dell-Vikings recorded that song and eight others in the basement of Pittsburgh disc jockey Barry Kaye's home.

The recording was an unmitigated success, but the record-buying public may have been a little confused about the artists' name. The record labels and record jackets carried conflicting spellings of the group's name – some had it as "Dell-Vikings" and some as "Del-Vikings."

According to Allmusic.com, there are several schools of thought about the origin of the group's name. One possibility is that Quick had known a basketball team named the Vikings from Brooklyn, N.Y. The other is that the members had read about Scandinavian Vikings in the Air Force base library. Additionally, the members used to read paperback books published by Viking Press. The prefix added an aura of mystery.

The Dell-Vikings were first signed to local label Fee Bee Records. The demand for copies of "Come Go With Me" over-taxed the label's distribution capabilities, and the song was transferred to Dot Records. It achieved million-selling status.

A follow-up single, "Whispering Bells," rose to number 9 on the *Billboard Top 100.*

Dion recorded "Come Go With Me" for his 1962 album "Lovers Who Wander," and the Beach Boys had a number 18 hit with it in 1982.

•••••• ❖ ••••••

"Little Darlin'" by the Diamonds

Songwriter: Maurice Williams
Peaked at number 2 on *Billboard* Best Seller Chart
April 13, 1957
April 20, 1957
April 27, 1957
April 29, 1957 (*Billboard* changed its chart release date this week)
May 6, 1957
May 13, 1957
May 20, 1957
May 27, 1957

The Diamonds

Dave Somerville (October 2, 1933-July 14, 2015)
Ted Kowalski (May 16, 1931-August 8, 2010)
Phil Levitt (July 9, 1935-?)
Bill Reed (January 11, 1936-October 22, 2004)
Formed in 1953 in Toronto, Ontario, Canada

The Diamonds: Phil Levitt, Bill Reed, Dave Somerville, Ted Kowalski

The year was 1956, and singer/songwriter Maurice Williams was about four years away from scoring a number 1 hit with the Zodiacs, "Stay."

But Williams wrote a great song that he recorded with the same band, which was then known as the Gladiolas, "Little Darlin'." They released it in January 1957.

Their version peaked at number 11 on the *Billboard R&B* Chart in April of that year, but it just barely crawled into the pop charts.

The Diamonds, coming off a string of five hit singles, recorded a version that blew the doors off the charts. It spent an incredible eight weeks at number 2 and was only denied the top spot by Elvis Presley's "All Shook Up," which sat at number 1 for nine weeks. *Billboard* rated "All Shook Up" as the number 1 song of 1957, while the Diamonds' "Little Darlin'" was number 3 for the year.

Back in the 1950s it was unusual for cover versions to become more popular than the originals, but that trend would have exceptions later in the Rock Era.

The Diamonds' version starts out with castanets and a cowbell and also features a harp. Both the lead vocal and backing vocals are stronger than those of the Gladiolas.

The lyrics are about a guy who is trying to win back a girlfriend on whom he cheated. "My lover, I was wrong to try to love two," he admits, "knowing well that my love was just for you."

The 1973 movie *American Graffiti,* which triggered a nostalgia craze, featured "Little Darlin'," marking it as a touchstone for the feel of the 1950s.

There would be many more hits for the Diamonds, including the number 4 smash "The Stroll" in 1958.

•••••• ❖ ••••••

"Silhouettes" by the Rays
Songwriters: Frank Slay, Bob Crewe
Peaked at number 3 on *Billboard* Top 100
November 4, 1957
November 11, 1957

The Rays

Harold Miller (January 17, 1931-?)
Walter Ford (September 5, 1931-?)
David Jones (1931-1995)
Harry James (1932-?)
Formed in 1955 in New York City, New York

The Rays

Two music industry up-and-comers who would become prominent in the 1960s wrote "Silhouettes."

Frank Slay, a Texan who moved to New York City in 1951, partnered with Bob Crewe, a New Jersey native, to write the Rays' biggest hit. Slay would move from writing songs to producing the recordings of Freddy Cannon, to owning a record label. His biggest production was "Incense And Peppermints" by the Strawberry Alarm Clock, a number 1 hit in 1967. Crewe later did songwriting for the Four Seasons and a plethora of other artists. He also was a dancer, singer, manager and record producer.

In 1957 Slay and Crewe were co-owners of XYZ Records in Philadelphia. Another local label, Cameo, was their agent for distribution.

The idea for the lyrical plot came to Crewe when he saw a couple embracing through a window shade as he passed while riding a train, according to Dailydoowop.com.

Crewe and Slay gave "Silhouettes" to the Rays, making it their third single for XYZ. The single was their lone top 40 entry on the pop chart. It also peaked at number 3 on the R&B chart.

About two weeks after the Rays' release, the Diamonds issued a competing version of "Silhouettes." Their version, which peaked at number 10 on the pop chart, had "Daddy Cool" as the B-side, as did the Rays' single.

The lyrics tell a story through the voice of a man who goes on a late-night walk and passes his girlfriend's house. Through a closed window shade, he sees the silhouettes of a couple who are in a romantic embrace.

The narrator loses his cool and rings the doorbell, whereupon he finds it is not his girlfriend. He was at the wrong house on the wrong block.

"Rushed out to your house with wings on my feet," he confesses. "Loved you like I'd never loved you, my sweet. Vowed that you and I would be two silhouettes on the shade, all of our days."

Eight years later Herman's Hermits quickened the tempo on their cover of "Silhouettes" and saw their version rise to number 5 on the *Billboard* Hot 100.

•••••••• ❖ ••••••••

"Book Of Love" by the Monotones
Songwriters: Warren Davis, George Malone, Charles Patrick
Peaked at number 5 on *Billboard* Top 100
April 12, 1958

The Monotones

Charles Howard Patrick (Sept. 11, 1938-Sept. 11, 2020)
Warren Davis (March 1, 1939-)
George Malone (Jan. 5, 1940-Oct. 5, 2007)
Frankie Smith (May 13, 1938-Nov. 26, 2000)
Warren Ryanes (Dec. 14, 1937-June 16, 1982)
John Ryanes (Nov. 16, 1940-May 30, 1972)
Formed in 1955 in Newark, N.J.

The Monotones

A lot of radio and television commercials use words or melodies from hit pop songs. But "Book Of Love" was born of a line used in a 1950s commercial.

Charles Patrick, lead singer of the Monotones, heard the line "you'll wonder where the yellow went" in a Pepsodent toothpaste commercial on the radio. This inspired him to pen the opening line to the group's only hit song, which states, "I wonder, wonder who wrote the book of love."

Fellow Monotones George Malone and Warren Davis helped him expand the thought into a full song with a doo-wop treatment.

In a familiar scenario, the song was issued initially by Mascot Records, but the small label could not handle the huge sales demand. Chess Records' subsidiary Argo picked up the distribution and helped "Book Of Love" attain million-selling status.

"Book Of Love" was a number 3 smash on the *Billboard* R&B Chart.

The story line of the song has the narrator talking to his girlfriend. He says he loves her, but he needs to consult the mythical "book" to find out why.

Four chapters are mentioned. Chapter 1: You love her with all your heart. Chapter 2: You tell her you're never gonna part. Chapter 3: Remember the meaning of romance. Chapter 4: You break up, but you give her just one more chance.

In 1974, Protein 21 hair care products produced a radio commercial that used the melody and vocal style of "Book Of Love" to ask, "I wonder, who wrote the book on hair?"

Don McLean's 1971 hit "American Pie" referenced "Book Of Love," as did Led Zeppelin's 1972 song "Rock And Roll."

According to Songfacts, the bass drum smack that appears in each verse was not originally planned. When the Monotones were recording the song in a recording studio, a boy outside the building threw a ball that thumped a window just as the singers reached the end of a line. They liked the percussive feature and did a take with a drum thump at that juncture.

•••••• ❖ ••••••

"Get A Job" by the Silhouettes

Songwriters: Earl Beal, Raymond Edwards, Richard Lewis, William Horton
Peaked at Number 1 on *Billboard* Top 100
February 24, 1958
March 3, 1958

The Silhouettes

Rick Lewis (September 2, 1933–April 19, 2005)
Earl Beal (July 18, 1924-March 22, 2001)
Bill Horton (December 25, 1929-January 23, 1995)
Raymond Edwards (September 22, 1922-March 4, 1997)
Formed in 1956 in Philadelphia, Pennsylvania

The Silhouettes: Earl Beal, Bill Horton, Ray Edwards, Richard Lewis

With the Rock Era in its infancy, the Silhouettes were possibly the most mature vocal group to top the charts in the 1950s. Three of the four members were born in the 1920s.

"When I was in the service in the early 1950s and didn't come home and go to work, my mother said, 'Get a job,'" tenor Rick Lewis told a biographer. "And basically, that's where the song came from." He wrote the song in 1955, and his fellow Silhouettes helped put together the vocal background.

Besides being a number 1 smash on the pop chart and the *Billboard* R&B Singles chart, the song became an icon of early rock and doo-wop music. It was chosen for the soundtracks of major movies like *American Graffiti, Stand By Me and Good Morning, Vietnam.* Sales eclipsed a million.

A doo-wop tag line in the lyrics turned into the name of a pop band years later – Sha Na Na, which became a high profile act after it performed at the 1969 Woodstock Festival.

According to Dailydoowop.com, Lewis joined a church quartet called the Gospel Tornadoes, which became the Thunderbirds. They changed their name after the Rays had a hit with the song "Silhouettes."

Some of the lyrics: "Every morning about this time, she get me out of my bed a-crying, 'Get a job.' After breakfast every day, she throws the want ads right my way and never fails to say, 'Get a job.'

"Get A Job" started its journey to legendary status as the B-side of "I Am Lonely." Disc jockeys on Philadelphia radio stations preferred to play "Job" instead.

The Silhouettes failed to replicate the success of their first hit, and they broke up in 1968. The original members regrouped in the 1980s and performed for a few more years.

••••••• ❖ •••••••

" I Wonder Why" by Dion & the Belmonts

Songwriters: Melvin Anderson, Ricardo Weeks
Peaked at number 22 on *Billboard* Top 100
June 2, 1958

Dion & the Belmonts

Dion DiMucci (July 18, 1939-?)
Angelo D'Aleo (February 3, 1940-?)
Carlo Mastrangelo (October 5, 1937-April 4, 2016)
Fred Milano (August 26, 1939-January 1, 2012)
Formed in 1957 in the Bronx, New York

The Belmonts: Carlo Mastrangelo, Dion DiMucci, Angelo D'Aleo, Fred Milano

The first hit single for Dion & the Belmonts, "I Wonder Why," got the group off to a hot start. Perhaps a little too hot for the benefit of the back-up singers.

After seven top 40 smashes, Dion felt confident enough to begin a solo career in 1960, leaving the Belmonts without a top shelf lead singer.

"I Wonder Why" was a textbook doo-wop recording, heavy on backing vocals and nonsense syllables.

The Bronx singers took their name from the fact two of them lived on Belmont Ave., and two lived near it. Their time with Dion was just one phase of the Belmonts' career, since they had begun without him in 1955.

Mitchell Cohen, in liner notes for a Dion album, wrote, "(Dion) and his friends from the neighborhood earned a reputation as the best streetcorner singers for miles."

"I'd give them sounds. I'd give them parts and stuff," Dion said, as published in *Perfect Sound Forever.* "That's what 'I Wonder Why' was about. We kind of invented this percussive rhythmic sound. If you listen to that song, everybody was doing something different. "It was totally amazing. When I listen to it today, often times I think, 'Man, those kids are talented.'"

The first verse says, "I wonder why I love you like I do. Is it because I think you love me too?"

Later we hear, "When you're with me, I'm sure you're always true. When I'm away, I wonder what you do. I wonder why I'm sure you're always true, always true."

In 1958, after Dion & the Belmonts charted with "No One Knows" and "Don't Pity Me," they went on the Winter Dance Party tour with Buddy Holly, Ritchie Valens and the

Big Bopper. Dion was offered a seat on the airplane that was scheduled to carry Holly and the others from Clear Lake, Iowa, to the next stop on the tour in Moorhead, Minnesota.

Dion declined because he could not afford the $36 required of him. According to author Colin Larkin, that was the same amount Dion's parents paid for monthly rent back in the Bronx.

The plane crashed on Feb. 3, 1959, killing all aboard. But Dion went on to become the preeminent rock soloist for the next five years.

As of this writing, Dion is the only surviving member of the 1959 Winter Dance Party lineup. Belmont Angelo D'Aleo did not go on the tour because he was serving in the U.S. Navy for two years.

•••••• ❖ ••••••

"Little Star" by the Elegants
Songwriters: Vito Picone, Arthur Venosa
Peaked at number 1 on *Billboard* Hot 100
August 25, 1958

The Elegants

Vito Picone (March 20, 1941-?)
Arthur Venosa (September 3, 1939-?)
Frank Tardogno (September 18, 1941-?)
Carman Romano (August 17, 1938-August 2, 2016)
James Moschello May 10, 1938-?)
Formed in 1958 in Staten Island, New York

The Elegants: Vito Picone, Arthur Venosa, Frank Tardogna,
Carman Romano, James Moschello

It wasn't the only time a nursery rhyme was quoted in a pop song lyrics, but it likely was the first when "Little Star" referenced "Twinkle, Little Star."

The lullaby dates back to the early 1800s, when Englishwoman Jane Taylor penned the poem.

In their one million-selling hit, the Elegants started "Little Star" with "Twinkle, twinkle, little star, how I wonder where you are. Wish I may, wish I might make this wish come true tonight. Searched all over for a love, you're the one I'm thinking of."

The narrator of the song appeals to a heavenly star to send him a lover.

The Elegants got a lot of mileage out of the doo-wop line "Whoa oh oh oh oh, ratta tatta too," which is repeated throughout "Little Star."

The late Phil Spector, who would become famous in the 1960s, made this one of his early productions. According to author John Gilliland, Spector described "Little Star" as "an awful good record." It was so good, it hit number 1 on the *Billboard* R&B Chart, as well as the pop chart.

Vito Picone explained the genesis of the song to Newjerseystage.com.

"We were rehearsing one night where we practiced until almost midnight. We were very tired and started to get a little ridiculous. As we were goofing around and getting silly, we started doing 'Mary Had a Little Lamb,' and 'Little Jack Horner,' and then we hit on 'Twinkle, Twinkle, Little Star. How I wonder what you are?' All of a sudden, it seemed to have a certain ring to it.

"We were all exhausted and said, 'Let's go home;' but I said to Artie (Venosa), who lived across the street, 'Artie, come over to my house tomorrow and we'll come up with an idea.' He came over to the house, we sat down, and in 20 minutes we wrote all the words to "Little Star."

Members of the Elegants were still teenagers when they formed.

"We were all going to rehearse at Carman's house and our plan was to come up with suggestions for names, put them in a box, and go from there," Picone said. "On the way to his house, there was a tavern on the corner which was owned by the father of another friend of mine, and in the window, there was a placard that said, 'Schenley, the Whiskey of Elegance.' It was spelled *elegance,* and I liked the name, but I transposed it to elegants and popped it in the box.

"When we pulled the various names out of the box, we looked at them, and nobody really liked anything we saw, so we stuffed the whole box all over again and started going through all the names again. That's when we unanimously voted on the Elegants and kept it."

•••••• ❖ ••••••

"16 Candles" by the Crests

Songwriters: Luther Dixon, Allyson Khent
Peaked at number 2 on *Billboard* Hot 100
February 9, 1959
February 16, 1959

The Crests

Talmadge "Tommy" Gough (October 15, 1939-August 24, 2014)
J.T. Carter (June 5, 1941-?)
Johnny Maestro (May 7, 1939-March 24, 2010)
Harold "Chico" Torres (bio unavailable)
Formed in 1954 in New York City, New York

The Crests: Johnny Maestro *(front)*, Tommy Gough, J.T. Carter, Chico Torres

This doo-wop classic went from the forgotten files to renewed popularity 25 years after its chart run when a hit movie by the same title was released in 1984.

The only problem was that the film's title song was performed by the Stray Cats, not the Crests. Nonetheless, the motion picture established a trend of adopting the name of a hit song. Some of the films that followed suit were *Pretty Woman, American Pie, Dazed And Confused, Can't Buy Me Love, Boogie Nights, Lean On Me, One Fine Day, Stand By Me, Man On The Moon, Sweet Home Alabama and Sea Of Love.*

The dulcet vocal of Johnny Maestro gave "16 Candles" the power to zip up the charts to number 2. His birth name was Mastrangelo, and he also performed under the last names Mastro and Masters. The Crests were another multi-racial group, with two Blacks, a

Hispanic and a white member. A fifth member, Patricia Vandross, dropped out of the group in 1958 because her mother didn't want her to tour with older cohorts.

"16 Candles" is a love song from a guy to his girlfriend, who has reached her sixteenth birthday. " Sixteen candles make a lovely light," the first verse says. "But not as bright as your eyes tonight. Blow out the candles, make your wish come true. For I'll be wishing that you love me, too."

The single sold a million copies and peaked at number 4 on the Billboard R&B Chart. It was featured in the movie American Graffiti.

J.T. Carter, the leader of the Crests, met his future mates while in junior high school. They sang together, sometimes at church benefits, performing their own versions of songs by professional singers, according to the Pocono Record.

"We started thinking up names for ourselves," Carter said. "The others came up with some funny ideas, like The Windows or even The Doorknobs. After we performed at the Wavecrest, I wanted to go with The Crests. That stuck.

"Over the next couple of years, we learned how dirty the record business could be. We and many other artists at that time were taken advantage of and cheated out of the profits of our work. The record companies even went after the leftover pennies we got."

But Carter also got to see some good during his time in the music business.

"We toured in the North and South and saw racial barriers start to come down among the kids who listened to music like ours," Carter said. "I mean, if some of us of different races could learn to sing in harmony, then why couldn't we all learn to live in harmony?"

"16 Candles" was the first hit single by the Crests, but it wasn't their last. They visited the top 40 six more times through 1961.

••••••• ❖ •••••••

"Since I Don't Have You" by the Skyliners

Songwriters: Joseph Rock, James Beaumont, Jackie Taylor, Joe Verscharen, Lenny Martin, Wally Lester, Janet Vogel
Peaked at number 12 on *Billboard* Hot 100
April 13, 1959
April 20, 1959

The Skyliners

Jimmy Beaumont (October 21, 1940-October 7, 2017)
Janet Vogel (June 10, 1942-February 21, 1980)
Wally Lester (Ocober 5, 1941-April 21, 2015)
Jackie Taylor (bio unavailable)
Joe Verscharen (August 30, 1940-November 2, 2007)
Formed in 1958 in Pittsburgh, Pennsylvania

The Skyliners: Joe Verscharen, Jimmy Beaumont, Janet Vogel, Wally Lester, Jackie Taylor

Love triggers intense feelings. A love that is shared brings elation. A love lost brings the pain of heartache. And either of those emotions can trigger creativity.

That's what happened to Joe Rock, manager of the Skyliners, as he was sitting out a red light in his car one day in Pittsburgh. Rock had his heart broken by a secretary he was dating when she left him to attend an airline school in Tulsa.

The situation inspired Rock to formulate the lyrics for "Since I Don't Have You," which would be the Skyliners' first hit song. Lead singer Jimmy Beaumont wrote the melody, and other members of the group also made contributions to the composition.

Rock landed a contract for the Skyliners with Calico Records after thirteen other labels turned him down.

In 1999, the year before he died, Rock told the *Pittsburgh Post-Gazette,* "It was a completely different time. Everything about the music business was so different then. But it was a wonderful time because anything could happen, and it did for us."

The Lenny Martin Orchestra provided instrumentation behind the Skyliners' vocals.

The single reached number 3 on the *Billboard* Hot R&B Sides chart.

The bridge states, "I don't have happiness, and I guess I never will again. When you walked out on me, in walked old misery. And he's been here since then."

The Skyliners followed "Since I Don't Have You" with two other high-charting singles over the next 15 months: "This I Swear" and "Pennies From Heaven."

Don McLean, Ronnie Milsap and Guns N' Roses recorded notable cover versions of the song.

•••••• ❖ ••••••

"Sorry (I Ran All The Way Home)" by the Impalas

Songwriters: Artie Zwirn, Gino Giosasi
Peaked at number 2 on *Billboard* Hot 100
May 11, 1959
May 18, 1959

The Impalas

Joe "Speedo" Frazier (September 5, 1943-April 1, 2014)
Richard Wagner (bio unavailable)
Lenny Renda (bio unavailable)
Tony Carlucci (bio unavailable)
Formed in 1958 in Brooklyn, New York

The Impalas: Joe Frazier, Richard Wagner, Lenny Renda, Tony Carlucci

An Impala was a popular full-size sedan that first rolled off the Chevrolet assembly line in 1958. Its namesake is a breed of African antelope.

With the 1950s being a seminal era in the automotive industry, the doo-wopping Impalas took their name from the car, according to author Jay Warner.

The three original members were all still teenagers when they practiced on street corners and in the back room of a candy store in the Canarsie section of Brooklyn. One day Joe Frazier heard them vocalizing in the store and approached them to offer advice on how to improve their harmonies. Frazier's singing so impressed the others that they invited him to join, making the Impalas one of the first racially mixed groups of the Rock Era.

Their first single on the Hamilton label, "First Date," was a flop. But, with the help of

20

disc jockey Allen Freed, the Impalas got a deal with MGM Records and released "Sorry" on its Cub subsidiary.

The million-selling hit put the Impala's stamp on the doo-wop chapter of rock history, but it was followed by two disappointing singles, "Oh What A Fool" and "All Alone."

The lyrics of "Sorry" are an apology from a guy to his girlfriend for making her cry. "Let's make amends," he tells her, "after all, we're more than friends."

The "uh-oh" uttered by Frazier at the beginning of the song originally was adlibbed because he missed a cue. But it was left in because the group liked the way it sounded. It is intentionally repeated toward the end of the record.

African impala   1958 Chevrolet Impala convertible

•••••• ❖ ••••••

"Hushabye" by the Mystics
Songwriters: Doc Pomus, Mort Shuman
Peaked at number 20 on *Billboard* Hot 100
June 29, 1959

The Mystics

Phil Cracolici September 17, 1937-?)
Albee Cracolici (April 29, 1936-?)
Al Contrera (January 8, 1940-?)
George Galfo (1940-?)
Bob Ferrante (1936-?)
Formed in 1958 in Brooklyn, New York

The Mystics: *front*, Bob Ferrante, Al Contrera;
rear, George Galfo, Phil Cracolici, Albee Cracolici

The Mystics must have thought it was pretty cool to be label mates with a veteran doo-wop group like & the Belmonts at Laurie Records.

Then the whole teammate thing blew up in the Mystics' faces when Laurie yanked "A Teenager In Love" away from them and gave it to Dion and company. Label president Gene Schwartz's rationale was the song would have greater potential in the hands of the more established vocalists.

Schwartz may have been right. Dion & the Belmonts' version went to number 5 on the pop chart. As a consolation prize, the Mystics received "Hushabye," which would become their signature song and only national hit.

"We were very disappointed," Mystic Al Contrera said, as quoted in NewJerseyStage.com. "And Doc Pomus and Mort Shuman were disappointed too, because they wrote 'Teenager in Love' specifically for us. So Doc says, 'We're gonna write another song for you.' And Gene Schwartz said to Doc and Morty, 'Could you write something in the flavor of 'Little Star' by the Elegants?'"

Pomus and Shuman built the lyrics around a lullaby. "Hushabye, hushabye, oh my darling don't you cry," the song begins. "Guardian angels up above, take care of the one I love."

Originally called the Overons, the Mystics had to change their name after they signed a contract with a manager who, it turned out, had mafia ties.

"We actually changed our name because of the mobster who got us into the recording studio," Contrera said. "He had a friend of his who was sort of in the music business, and the two of them realized that we really could sing – we were pretty decent by that time, which was 1957 going on 1958.

"So, the mobster, who made the deal for us to go in and record a couple of songs in a studio for demo purposes, said, 'I don't like the name The Overons, but I've got a great name for you guys.' He said, 'I'm gonna call you The Courtesans!' And at first we said, 'Oh, that sounds decent,' until we looked it up. If you look courtesan up in the dictionary, it means 'woman of ill repute,'

"So, we said, 'We're not gonna use that. We're gonna find ourselves our own name.'"

The group members settled on a plan for each to go home and write down a suggestion for a new name on a piece of paper. The next time the group convened, they put the papers into a hat, and one was randomly drawn. It was Mystics, and Contrera was the submitter.

"I started looking through the dictionary, Contrera recalled. "I just flipped open the dictionary and it went to the M section, and I looked at 'mystic' and thought, 'Wow, that would be a cool name for a group.'"

· · · · · · · ❖ · · · · · · ·

"There's A Moon Out Tonight" by the Capris

Songwriters: Al Striano, Alberico Gentile, Joe Luccisano
Peaked at number 3 on *Billboard Hot* 100
February 27, 1961

The Capris

Mike Mincielli (1941-March 15, 2015)
Nick Santo (1941-December 30, 2010)
Frank Reina (1940-?)
John Cassese (1941-?)
Vinnie Narcardo (1941-?)
Formed in 1957 in Queens, New York

The Capris: John Cassese, Mike Mincielli, Nick Santo, Frank Reina, Vinnie Narcardo

The Capris were on a fast track to nowhere after their outstanding performance of "There's A Moon Out Tonight" was released on Planet Records in 1958. The single sold poorly at first, causing the Capris to break up. But then happenstance took over.

Late night New York disc jockey Alan Fredericks continued to play the record on his *Night Train* radio show, according to author Mitch Rosalsky. This caught the attention of Jerry Greene, an employee of the Times Square Record Store. Greene purchased the master of the recording for $200 and re-released it on his new Lost Nite label.

With well-known disc jockey Murray the K providing exposure on his New York radio show, sales for "There's A Moon" began anew.

Sales for the single grew so fast that Greene soon realized he could not meet the distribution demands. So, he sold his interest to Old Town Records, which satisfied the national demand for the song.

The group had taken their name from the 1957 Lincoln Capri sedan, unaware that there was a Philadelphia group by the same name that had formed several years earlier.

"I didn't know anything about them until 1961, when my mother brought one of their records home, thinking it was ours," the late Nick Santo told Electricearl.com. "But strangely enough, the first song I ever wrote was called 'God Only Knows,' which just happened to be the title of one of their songs (in 1954)."

The Capris made a memorable mistake in their recording of "Moon." It is memorable because it was a good mistake. Seconds before the end of the recording, the five singers did a voice overlay, with each singing the song's title, one after another, a millisecond apart.

"I don't think it was intentional," the late Mike Mincielli told Onehitwondersthebook. com. "It was one of the mistakes – there were a lot of mistakes on that record."

•••••••• ❖ ••••••••

"Blue Moon" by the Marcels
Songwriters: Richard Rodgers, Lorenz Hart
Peaked at number 1 on *Billboard* Hot 100
April 3, 1961
April 10, 1961
April 17, 1961

The Marcels

Cornelius Harp (September 14, 1939-June 5, 2013)
Fred Johnson (1942-March 31, 2022)
Gene Bricker (August 3, 1938-December 10, 1983)
Ron Mundy (April 20, 1940-January 20, 2017)
Richard Knauss (bio unavailable)
Formed in 1959 in Pittsburgh, Pennsylvania

The Marcels: Richard Knauss, Fred Johnson, Cornelius Harp, Ron Mundy, Gene Bricker

In a shocking development, one of the co-writers of "Blue Moon" was rooting hard for the Marcels' version to be a failure.

Composer Richard Rodgers, who teamed with lyricist Lorenz Hart to write the song in 1934, so disliked the doo-wop treatment of "Blue Moon" that he bought ads in music trade publications urging the public to steer clear of the single.

That accomplished little. The record was a number 1 smash in the United States and the United Kingdom and sold over 1 million copies. The Marcels and Colpix Records staff producer Stu Phillips came out smelling like a rose.

Phillips actually stuck out his neck to bring the Marcels into a recording studio. According to author Fred Bronson, Colpix bigwigs gave Phillips orders to devote all his time to develop another artist at the label. But he sneaked the Marcels into the studio after hours when no one could see them.

Three songs were on the slate for the Marcels to record, and they needed one more. "Blue Moon" became the fourth song because one of the singers knew it and was able to teach it to the others.

Eight minutes of studio time remained when the Marcels stepped up to the microphone to record "Blue Moon." They nailed it in two takes.

After a new Colpix promotion man heard the tape, he requested a copy, which quickly went to disc jockey Murray the K at WINS radio in New York City. The popular DJ liked it so much, he played it 26 times on one show. That must have really irritated the 58-year-old Rodgers.

"Blue Moon" became the last doo-wop song to hit number 1 on the *Billboard* Hot 100.

The multi-racial Marcels were forced into a lineup change in August 1961 when they were on a concert tour in the southern United States. Because of racial friction in the South, the white members, Richard Knauss and Gene Bricker, left the group and were replaced by Allen Johnson and Walt Maddox.

The Marcels, who took their name from a hairstyle called the marcel wave, were back in the *Billboard* top 10 in the fall of 1961 with "Heartaches."

The marcel wave hairstyle

•••••• ❖ ••••••

"Tonight I Fell In Love" by the Tokens

Songwriters: Philip Margo, Henry Medress, Mitchell Margo

Peaked at number 15 on *Billboard* Hot 100

May 15, 1961

The Tokens

Hank Medress (November 19, 1938-June 18, 2007)

Jay Siegel (October 20, 1939-?)

Mitch Margo (May 25, 1947-November 24, 2017)

Phil Margo (April 1, 1942-November 13, 2021)

Formed as the Linc-Tones in 1955 in Brooklyn, New York

The Tokens: Mitch Margo, Hank Medress, Phil Margo, Jay Siegel

The Tokens got their start when they were in high school together in Brooklyn, but they were no run-of-the-mill teenage band.

A lineup that once included Neil Sedaka wrote and recorded "Tonight I Fell In Love" in true doo-wop style with lots of "dum doobie dum."

The lyrics are simple. "Tonight I fell in love," the first verse begins. "I want the stars above to know tonight I fell in love. "Oh, what a wonder, this magic spell I'm under. This feeling that I feel, is it really real?"

With "Tonight I Fell In Love" on its way to selling a million copies, the Tokens received an invitation to appear on the American Bandstand TV show. According to writer Colin Larkin, this exposure led to a record deal with RCA Records.

The apex of the Tokens' career came late in 1961 when they recorded a cover version of "The Lion Sleeps Tonight." It topped the *Billboard* Hot 100 for three weeks.

The Tokens later branched out into other endeavors, such as producing recordings for other artists. They formed their own record label, B.T. Puppy, in 1964.

Courtesy of B.T. Puppy Records

•••••• ❖ ••••••

"Those Oldies But Goodies (Remind Me Of You)" by Little Caesar
& the Romans
Songwriters: Paul Politi, Nick Curinga
Peaked at number 9 on *Billboard* Hot 100
June 26, 1961
July 3, 1961

Little Caesar & the Romans

Carl Burnett
Johnny Simmons
Early Harris
David Johnson
Leroy Saunders
Formed in 1959 in Los Angeles, California

Little Caesar & the Romans: Johnny Simmons, Leroy Saunders, Carl Burnett,
Early Harris, David Johnson

The Rock Era was barely six years old when along came a doo-wop song talking about oldies but goodies.

The record-buying public apparently didn't have a problem with the sentiment, sending "Those Oldies But Goodies" into the top 10 of the pop chart. It reached number 28 on the *Billboard* R&B Chart. The song title helped to cement the phrase in the lexicon of disc jockeys and other music industry personnel.

Little Caesar & the Romans began as the Cubans in 1959 but changed their name to the Upfronts after the notorious failed Bay of Pigs Invasion in which Cuban exiles failed to overthrow Cuban dictator Fidel Castro in 1961, according to writer Colin Larkin.

Charles Wright, who would surface as the leader of the Watts 103rd Street Rhythm Band in 1969, played both piano and bass on the track. He was artist and repertoire director for Del-Fi Records in 1961.

The lyrics are sung from the point of view of a guy who remembers his former girlfriend when he hears the good old songs they used to treasure when they were together.

"The songs of the past bring back memories of you," he says. "They always will haunt me although we're apart … forever they will haunt me, but what can I do?"

David Johnson of the Romans told *Goldmine*, "Del-Fi didn't want the typical black sound. They were looking for a white sound to reach the crossover audience."

The group, playing up their name to the hilt, sometimes wore old Roman togas to their performances.

"Here were five Black dudes all dressed up in toga and sandals, wearing wreaths on their heads," Johnson said. "It was a good gimmick, but we hated it at the time. Not only did we hate the togas, we hated the song, too!"

A follow-up single, "Hully Gully Again," fell short of the popularity of "Oldies," as it peaked at number 54 on the *Billboard* Hot 100.

•••••••• ❖ ••••••••

"Rama Lama Ding Dong" by the Edsels

Songwriter: George Jones, Jr.
Peaked at number 21 on *Billboard* Hot 100
June 19, 1961

The Edsels

George "Wydell" Jones, Jr. (October 5, 1936-September 27, 2008)
Larry Green (bio unavailable)
James Reynolds (bio unavailable)
Harry Green (bio unavailable)
Marshall Sewell (August 29, 1937-June 5, 2013)
Formed in 1957 in Campbell, Ohio

The Edsels

As an automobile that was supposed to be the "car of the future," the Ford Edsel was a flop in 1958-59. Supposedly, it was way overpriced, overhyped and poorly made. And it was not much to look at.

The vocal group the Edsels, on the other hand, were successful in their roll out of a song whose title embodied the spirit of the doo-wop era – "Rama Lama Ding Dong."

Like the ill-fated Edsel sedan, "Rama Lama" debuted in 1958. A printing error at Dub Records had the title as "Lama Rama Ding Dong," and the single was lost in the shuffle among other doo-wop releases.

The success of the Marcels' "Blue Moon" sparked new interest in the Edsels' song, which had a similar sound. Twin Records reissued it, this time with the correct title, and "Rama Lama Ding Dong" became a hit in the summer of '61.

The lyrics form a tribute to the singer's girlfriend, whose name is the same as the title. "She's everything to me," he says. "I'll never set her free, for she's mine, all mine."

The song had some unexpected influence. Later in 1961, Barry Mann referenced it in his number 7 hit, "Who Put The Bomp." In 1980, an episode of *The Muppet Show* saw a shepherd and his sheep singing the song in a meadow. The 1973 movie *American Graffiti* also included it on its soundtrack.

The Edsels started out as the Essos, a name they borrowed from the spin-off oil company that was part of Standard Oil until 1911, when the U.S. government sued for violation of the Sherman Anti-trust Act. Little did the Edsels know when they named themselves for a car that it, too, would go bust.

1958 Edsel

•••••• ❖ ••••••

Pretty Little Angel Eyes by Curtis Lee
Songwriters: Curtis Lee, Tommy Boyce
Peaked at number 7 on *Billboard* Hot 100
August 7, 1961
August 14, 1961
August 21, 1961

Curtis Lee

October 28, 1939-January 8, 2015
Born Curtis Edwin Lee in Yuma, Arizona, and died in his hometown

Curtis Lee

In an era dominated by groups, Curtis Lee was an anomaly.

He racked up a top 10 hit, dripping with doo-wop elements, as a solo act.

The Halos, a four-man vocal group from the Bronx, New York, provided uncredited backing vocals on "Pretty Little Angel Eyes." Shortly after Lee's hit peaked on the charts, the Halos had a number 25 hit with "Nag."

Lee was singing at a club in Tucson, Arizona, when he was discovered by recording artist Ray Peterson. In 1960, Lee went to New York, where he was signed to Peterson's Dunes label. He wrote some songs with Tommy Boyce.

Boyce revealed in a book about his career that his publishing company instructed him to write a song for Lee. As Lee departed on a concert tour, Boyce asked him to think of a title. Lee, inspired by a girl he'd met in Florida, responded with "Angel Eyes."

Phil Spector, who already was flexing his magic touch, produced the recording. Within the next two years, Spector's career would skyrocket through his work with Ike & Tina Turner, the Crystals, Ronettes and Righteous Brothers. He also worked with the Beatles and John Lennon and George Harrison as solo artists.

The second verse of "Pretty Little Eyes" reads, "Angel eyes, you are so good to me. And, when I'm in your arms, it feels so heavenly. You know I love you, my darling angel eyes."

Boyce later would form a successful partnership with Bobby Hart, both as a songwriting team and vocal duo.

"Pretty Little Angel Eyes" was only a minor hit in the U.K., but it found acceptance in New Zealand, where it was a number 5 smash.

Lee's follow-up release later in 1961 was "Under The Moon Of Love," which reached only number 46 on the *Billboard* Hot 100. Without Spector's guidance, his hits quickly dried up.

According to the *Yuma Sun*, Lee joined his father in the construction industry in 1969. He died of cancer at the age of seventy-five.

Lee's daughter Stephanie told the Sun, "He will be remembered not only as a local boy who made it big, but as a true family man who believed in the small-town values and roots. He was proud of Yuma and being part of the community."

•••••• ❖ ••••••

"My True Story" by the Jive Five with Joe Rene & Orchestra

Songwriters: Eugene Pitt, Oscar Waltzer
Peaked at number 3 on *Billboard* Hot 100
September 11, 1961
September 18, 1961

The Jive Five

Eugene Pitt (November 6, 1937-June 29, 2018)
Jerome Hanna (bio unavailable)
Richard Harris (bio unavailable)
Thurmon "Billy" Prophet (bio unavailable)
Norman Johnson (1935-1970)
Formed as the Genies in 1954 in Brooklyn, New York

The Jive Five: Billy Prophet, Eugene Pitt, Jerome Hanna, Norman Johnson, Richard Harris

There are two distinct definitions of "jive." One of them is: deceptive, exaggerated or meaningless talk.

Most likely, the members of the Jive Five had the other definition in mind when they chose their name: swing music or early jazz.

Having gotten their start by vocalizing on Brooklyn street corners, they changed their name from the Genies to the Jive Five in 1959. Lead singer Eugene Pitt cowrote "My True Story" in 1961, and it hit number 1 on the *Billboard* R&B Chart.

Repetition of the word "cry," chanted by the backing vocalists, is what carries the song. It's a lament of a love affair that failed.

"Her name was Sue, yes. His name was Earl," the song begins. "His love was Lorraine, she's a wonderful girl. But they must cry, cry, cry whoa, their blues away."

After talking about the anguish of love lost, the lyrics reveal, "names have been changed dear, to protect you and I."

The Jive Five never duplicated the success they attained with "My True Story," but that does not mean their story ended there. Some changes in their lineup and musical direction brought them back to the charts in 1965 with "I'm A Happy Man." The group continued to perform for decades with elements of soul, funk and disco in their repertoire.

The group made its final appearance with Pitt on board in 2016. He died at the age of 80 from complications of diabetes.

•••••• ❖ ••••••

"I Love You" by the Volumes

Songwriters: Willie Ewing, Ernest Newson
Peaked at number 22 on *Billboard* Hot 100
June 30, 1962

The Volumes

Ed Union
Elijah Davis
Larry Wright
Joe Truvillion
Ernest Newson
Formed in 1960 in Detroit, Michigan

The Volumes

It was 1962, and the doo-wop era was on its last legs. But a good record is going to succeed, even if it sounds like it should have been recorded five years earlier.

This was the situation in which the Volumes found themselves. In 1962, their manager, Willie Ewing, and bass singer Ernest Newson wrote "I Love You." It is unknown who produced the record, but a doo-wop treatment was applied to it.

The song is a sweet romantic number, typical of many doo-wop hits. The simple title is a good description of the lyrical content.

"Your love is oh so heavenly, my darling, can't you see?" the first verse begins. "My heart skips a crazy beat. When you're with me, such warmth. When your lips are touching mine, they're sweeter, much sweeter than wine."

Once the single was off the charts, the Volumes quickly became a forgotten component of the history of Rock & Roll. They never had another hit.

••••••• ❖ •••••••

33

"Remember Then" by the Earls

Songwriters: Tony Powers, Beverly Ross
Peaked at number 24 on *Billboard* Hot 100
January 26, 1963

The Earls

Larry Chance (October 19, 1940-?)
Bob Del Din (May 18, 1942-April 8, 1991)
Eddie Harder (December 26, 1942-?)
John Wray (June 19, 1939-November 30, 2020)
Formed in 1957 in Bronx, New York

The Earls: Bob Del Din, John Wray, Eddie Harder, Larry Chance

If doo-wop was on its way out, the Earls were the group that was going to take it to the finish line in style.

The arrangement of "Remember Then" is rife with doo-wop elements. The signature repeated line is "re-meh-meh, re-meh-meh-member." There is also some "oop-shoop" added by the backing singers.

The gist of the lyrics is a guy talking to his ex-girlfriend, reminiscing about how they fell in love. Then he gets a reality check: "Summer's over. Our love is over. To lose that love was such a sin."

In the last verse he exposes his feelings. ""I'm broken-hearted now that we have parted now. My mind wanders now and then.

Remember then." Tony Powers, who cowrote the song with Beverly Ross, said in an interview, "Beverly and I made a plan to try and write something at her apartment. I remember sitting with her at the piano and just riffing on stuff and, somewhere in that process of tossing out ideas, one of us must have hit on 'Remember When' (the original title).

"I'm sure the second we hit on the title, we had the riff: 'Re-meh-meh, Re-meh-meh-mem-ber, Re-meh-meh, Re-meh-meh-mem-ber, Re-meh-meh, Re-meh-meh-mem-ber, When, when, remember when.'

"Either she started the music lick, or vice-versa, and off we went. Once we had that, the song just basically wrote itself. Beverly was doing business with Aaron Schroeder at his January Music (publishing company), so we brought the song there, he loved it, got it to Hy Weiss, and that was that.

"What I do remember vividly, though, was walking in Central Park after it hit the charts and passing someone with a radio. 'Remember Then' was playing. That was the very first time I ever heard a song of mine being played over the air – wow!"

Like so many other urban vocal groups, the Earls got their start singing on street corners. Originally, they were a quintet, but Larry Palombo was inducted into the U.S. Army. He died in 1961 when his parachute failed to open during a skydiving exercise.

The Earls' second tenor, Eddie Harder, recalled to an interviewer, "When the Earls first started singing together, we were always looking for an echo. The Dyre Avenue subway station (in New York City) was a short underground section in the Bronx.

"In the daytime, it was usually empty and quiet, almost creepy for the Bronx. The acoustics were fantastic. With a great echo, it was the perfect place for harmony."

Early releases by the Earls included "Lookin' For My Baby," "Life Is But A Dream" and "My Heart's Desire." But "Remember Then" was their biggest hit.

••••••• ❖ •••••••

"Rip Van Winkle" by the Devotions
Songwriter: Ray Sanchez
Peaked at number 36 on *Billboard* Hot 100
April 4, 1964

The Devotions

Ray Sanchez
Bob Weisbrod
Bob Havorka
Frank Pardo
Joe Pardo
Formed in 1960 in Queens, New York

The Devotions

April 4, 1964, is a red letter day in the history of Rock & Roll.

That's the date the Beatles had the top five songs on the *Billboard Hot 100.*

No other artist or band accomplished that feat, before or since.

April 4, 1964, also is the date "Rip Van Winkle," the final hit of the Doo-wop Era, reached its peak position on the charts.

Mind you, the song was not newly recorded. It had been around since 1961 and was in its third release when it crawled into the top 40 for one week.

From the Astoria section of Queens, New York City, the Devotions had an audition with Delta Records in 1960. They presented doo-wop versions of songs like "Sunday Kind Of Love" and "Life Is But A Dream." The label's owner, Bernie Zimming, gave the quintet a thumbs-down reaction, according to *Oldies.com.* He was looking for a sound that would be more appealing to teens.

The very same day, however, Ray Sanchez of the Devotions wrote "Rip Van Winkle," a novelty song about the adventures of the fictional character created by author Washington Irving.

Zimming approved that song, and the Devotions recorded it in the doo-wop style that was still the rage in 1961. It bombed.

A year later, Roulette Records had acquired Delta, and the larger label re-released "Rip." The result was the same, and the Devotions disbanded.

Early in 1964, with Beatlemania still in its infancy, Roulette included "Rip" on a *Golden Goodies* album series. In its third exposure to the public, the song finally attracted significant attention, and Roulette issued the single.

"In 1964, DJ Porky Chadwick in Pittsburgh boasted he could make any song a hit and picked 'Rip Van Winkle' out of a pile," said Al Vieco, who would join the Devotions after they re-formed. Chadwick helped kick-start the "Rip" revival by playing the song on his radio show. The number of callers asking the radio station where they could get a copy of the record were so great that Roulette began pressing the single again.

Carrying out the theme of the story, the recording begins with the sound of a bowling bowl rolling down a lane and then hitting pins. A high-pitched, elfish voice exclaims, "Wowie, ha ha ha, a strike!" Then the doo-wopping begins.

"He fell asleep in the woods one day," the lyrics begin, "spent twenty years of his life that way. That nagging wife kept all his coin, none of his friends did he ever join."

The prevalent sound of an acoustic bass indeed gives the song a retro feel.

As "Rip Van Winkle" slipped off the charts, the doo-wop era was over. The Beatles would control the trends of rock music for the next six years until they broke up.

One-hit Wonders
For these artists, it was one-and-done

Overview: Let's use 18th century English astronomer/physicist Edmond Halley as an example.

He used historical reports and mathematical calculations to predict a certain comet would return close to Earth after an absence of about 75 years. While he died 15 years before the comet came back into view, his prediction was right – the comet, which now bears his name, makes a loop through the solar system and comes back into Earth view on a regular basis, every 75 years or so.

But what if Halley was wrong? What if all of his expertise in the fields of mathematics and meteorology failed him in his predictions about the comet's return?

Such a quandary has bedeviled talent scouts, producers and record label executives for years after they've found promising musical talent. The singers/musicians have a winning hit on their first try, but there is no assurance of continued success. After one major chart splash, many recording artists have wound up on the scrap heap of history, unable to create a successful follow-up to their first hit song.

We like to call these one-timers "one-hit wonders." They fascinate us so much because, against the odds, they have quickly lost what seemed to come to them so easily on their first visit to the record charts. Their talent is evident from the hit, but subsequent success somehow eludes them.

This chapter will identify some of the most notable and interesting pop/rock musicians that fit into this category. Their stories deserve to be told since, without them, Rock & Roll history would be incomplete and, thus, less compelling.

The source authority for this chapter is the *Billboard* Hot 100.

To view the full lyrics of these songs, please log on to www.google.com, enter song titles & artist names and click Google Search.

To listen to these songs, please log on to www.youtube.com and enter song titles & artist names.

"Summertime, Summertime" by the Jamies

Songwriter: Tom Jameson
Peaked at number 26 on *Billboard* Hot 100
September 22, 1958

The Jamies

Tom Jameson (1937-July 19, 2009)
Serena Jameson (bio unavailable)
Jeannie Roy (bio unavailable)
Arthur Blair (1937-Jan. 8, 2020)
Formed in 1958 in Boston, Massachusetts

The Jamies: *top,* Serena Jameson, Arthur Blair, Jeannie Roy; *bottom,* Tom Jameson

The fate of the Jamies saw their one hit outlast and outshine them over decades.

The song "Summertime, Summertime" itself was a freak of the music industry because it was a single that had two chart runs and peaked in the top 40 both times. The initial release did slightly better than the reissue, which topped out at number 38 in the summer of 1962.

A catchy tune with lyrics extolling the pleasures of the summer season, the record reached its chart peak, ironically, on the last day of the season in 1958.

Tom Jameson wrote and arranged the acoustic recording. His sister Serena, also one of the Jamies, recalled to Thebluegrassspecial.com about the day her brother wrote "Summertime."

"I remember being upstairs while my grandmother lay resting on the couch downstairs," Serena said. "Tom was in the living room, where the piano was, and he composed 'Summertime, Summertime' until every word and note was exactly as he wanted it. He was a perfectionist.

"I thought my grandmother had a lot of patience to listen to it over and over, but she never complained. I think she rather enjoyed it. When he was satisfied that he had written the words and music exactly as he wanted them to be, he asked Jeannie and me if we would sing it.

"Tom was a tough taskmaster as we practiced. Everything had to sound perfect."

The quartet, which included Arthur Blair, was unnamed for months as they rehearsed the song. "It was getting towards summer," Serena reflected. "We practiced with the windows open because nobody had air conditioning in those days. My mother said the neighbors were complaining because we were doing it over and over.

"It seemed like an eternity before Tom was satisfied that we knew it perfectly. He then informed us that it was time to make a demo."

The group recorded the demo in Boston on May 24, 1958. Tom and Arthur took copies to radio disc jockeys in the area in an effort to drum up interest via airplay. One of them, Sherman Feller, offered the demo to the president of Cadence Records, who passed on it. But Epic Records accepted it. Feller became the manager of the Jamies and sent them on a promotional concert tour.

The lyrics say, "Well, shut them books and throw 'em away. Say goodbye to dull school days. So come on and change your way, it's summertime."

Later on there is some sass when we hear, "Well, I'm so happy that I could flip, oh how I'd love to take a trip. I'm sorry teacher, but zip your lip, it's summertime."

Long after the Jamies had been forgotten, their song found inclusion in the 1978 movie *Fingers*. "Summertime, Summertime" also has been used in television ads for the likes of Applebee's restaurants and Buick automobiles.

•••••• ❖ ••••••

"Pink Shoe Laces" by Dodie Stevens

Songwriter: Mickie Grant
Peaked at number 3 on *Billboard* Hot 100
April 13, 1959
April 20, 1959

Dodie Stevens

Born Geraldine Ann Pasquale on February 17, 1946, in Chicago, Illinois

Dodie Stevens

When a singer has her first hit at the age of 13, expectations for a long, illustrious career likely are dancing in the heads of record producers and talent managers.

Such was the scenario when Dodie Stevens zoomed up the charts with "Pink Shoe Laces," a cute little pop song. Fate, however, had other plans.

Having moved to the San Gabriel Valley in California with her family when she was 3, Geraldine Pasquale took dance and voice lessons at a very young age. At 8 she made her first recording and performed the song on the *Art Linkletter House Party* network television show.

Chrystalette Records president Carl Burns saw her on a local TV show and took her under his wing. He changed her name to Dodie Stevens and gave her the song "Pink Shoe Laces."

The record had wide appeal, mostly because of its kooky nature. The lyrics are about the narrator's boyfriend, Dooley, who is quite eccentric in his manner of dress. He wears tan shoes with pink shoe laces, a polka dot vest and a Panama hat with a purple band.

The narrator also claims Dooley takes her deep sea fishing in a submarine and to drive-in movies in a limousine. He must be super-wealthy because he has a helicopter and a yacht.

For the most part, the verses are spoken rather than sung. Stevens did sing the choruses, and the record became a million-seller.

After "Pink Shoe Laces" became a hit, Dot Records signed Stevens to a contract. However, there was no lightning left in the proverbial bottle. A handful of singles failed to crack the top 100. "Yes, I'm Lonesome Tonight" was the best with a showing of number 60.

Stevens appeared in the films *Hound-Dog Man* (1959), *Alakazam The Great* (1961) and *Convicts 4* (1962).

According to editor Colin Larkin, Stevens married at the age of 16 and moved to a farm in Missouri. In 1966, with the marriage over, she tried to rekindle her recording career under the names Geraldine Stevens and Geri Stevens.

She recorded with Sergio Mendes and toured as a back-up singer for various major artists.

According to notes in *Wikipedia*, Stevens has taught singing and stage performance at her studio.

•••••••• ❖ ••••••••

"Sea Of Love" by Phil Phillips
Songwriters: Phil Phillips, George Khoury
Peaked at number 2 on *Billboard* Hot 100
August 24, 1959
August 31, 1959

Phil Phillips

March 14, 1926-March 14, 2020
Born John Philip Baptiste in Crowley, Louisiana, and died in Lake Charles, Louisiana

Phil Phillips

Perhaps Phil Phillips had only one hit record because he was not a singer by trade.

He was working as a bellhop at a hotel in Lake Charles, La., when he recorded "Sea Of Love," a song he had written about a woman he wanted to impress. Her name was Verdie Mae Thomas, and Phillips ultimately was glad he did not marry her.

"I married the right one, though," he told Songfacts. "It's a good thing I didn't marry that Verdie.

"I had my guitar, so I went and wrote this song, 'Sea of Love.' You see, she really didn't believe in me. But I felt if I could sing about it – a sea of love where it's quiet and peaceful – I could really show her how much I loved her and cared for her."

Phillips practiced the song at home on his guitar, and a gas meter reader overheard him one day. The employee recommended that Phillips see record producer George Khoury, who brought Phillips into a recording studio. The result was a surprise hit and a name change from John Baptiste to Phil Phillips.

The record sold so well in Louisiana that Mercury picked up distribution from Khoury's small, independent label.

According to biographer Andrew Hamilton, Phillips claims he made no more than $6,800 from the record.

"Sea Of Love" apparently had peaked at number 15 and had dropped to number 22 when it unexpectedly surged to number 2, where it stayed for two weeks. The single went to number 1 on the *Billboard* R&B chart.

The song inspired the title of the 1989 Al Pacino movie *Sea Of Love* and was prominently featured in the storyline.

The Twilights, who got label credit as back-up singers, were a group of friends Phillips recruited for the recording, according to Songfacts.

Phillips, who died on his ninety-fourth birthday, became a disc jockey in Jennings, La., after his recording career ended.

••••••• ❖ •••••••

"Alley-Oop" by The Hollywood Argyles
Songwriter: Dallas Frazier
Peaked at number 1 on *Billboard* Hot 100
July 11, 1960

The Hollywood Argyles

Gary Sanford Paxton (May 18, 1939-July 17, 2016)
Born Larry Wayne Stevens in Coffeyville, Kansas and died in Branson, Missouri

Gary Paxton

The Hollywood Argyles had one hit, and they were never even a group. The act consisted of one person, Gary S. Paxton, who has one of the most fascinating stories in pop music history.

Paxton broke into the recording business as half of the duo Skip & Flip, who charted with "It Was I" and "Cherry Pie" in 1959-60. When his act with fellow University of Arizona student Clyde Battin dissolved, Paxton went to the West Coast to seek his fortune.

After stops in Oregon and Washington, Paxton drove to Los Angeles, where songwriter Dallas Frazier was one of the first people he met. Paxton eventually formed a music publishing company with producer Kim Fowley. A pay phone in a gas station became their business telephone.

Paxton recorded Frazier's "Alley-Oop" for Lute Records. The song is a playful look at the subject of a comic strip, who is a caveman. V.T. Hamlin created the strip in 1939.

"There were no Hollywood Argyles at the very beginning," Paxton wrote on his website. "I was the only lead singer. Fowley helped me produce it, because we were partners in Maverick Music International/BMI at the time. The background singers were Dallas Frazier, Buddy Mize, Scotty Turner, Diane (a friend) and myself.

"It was recorded at Richard Podolor's American Recorders, next door to Lawrence Welk's Palladium, and across from the Moulin Rouge on Sunset Blvd. near Vine Street. A little bitty street (Argyle Street) was next door to the studio, so I said, 'Let's call ourselves The Hollywood Argyles.'"

After the single became a big hit, Paxton assembled a crew of Hollywood Argyles to make concert appearances.

The lyrics describe the caveman thusly: "He got a big ugly club and a head full of hair, like great big lions and grizzly bears. He rides through the jungle tearin' limbs off of trees, knockin' great big monsters dead on their knees."

Paxton formed Garpax Records in 1962 and was back on top as a producer when Bobby "Boris" Pickett hit number 1 with "Monster Mash."

By the 1970s, Paxton was out of the pop music business and was hosting a Christian talk radio show in Nashville, Tenn., while also writing and recording music in the country and Christian genres.

He survived a 1980 shooting that allegedly was a hit ordered by a disgruntled singer who wanted to escape his contract with Paxton.

After Paxton's death from complications of heart surgery and liver disease, his friend Alex Palao commented, "Paxton's abilities made him a natural to handle whatever genres he chose. He was not only versatile but also, by his own admission, terminally weird."

By his own count, Paxton wrote some two thousand songs.

Alley Oop (courtesy of NEA)

•••••• ❖ ••••••

"Hey! Baby" by Bruce Channel

Songwriters: Margaret Cobb, Bruce Channel

Peaked at number 1 on *Billboard* Hot 100

March 10, 1962

March 17, 1962

March 24, 1962

Bruce Channel

Born Bruce McMeans on November 28, 1940, in Jacksonville, Texas

Bruce Channel

Bruce Channel (pronounced sha-NELL) was only twenty-one years old when his one big hit was released.

"Hey! Baby" was written in 1959 after Texan Channel was introduced to Margaret Cobb by her brother, who was a co-worker of Channel's at the time. Together they wrote twenty-plus tunes, including the song that would become Bruce's signature number.

Delbert McClinton, who is the same age as Channel, provided a soulful harmonica part. The two met in a recording studio.

The gist of the lyrics has the singer telling a woman whom he admires, "I wanna know if you'll be my girl."

When "Hey! Baby" hit the airwaves, it brought a refreshing dose of stripped-down rockabilly that quickly crossed over from country radio to pop stations. Its ascent to number 1 was sure and quick.

It was Cobb's friend Marvin Montgomery who suggested they take their songs to record producer Bill Smith in Fort Worth, Texas, according to author Fred Bronson. Smith changed the intro from guitar to harmonica, and three takes of "Hey! Baby" took 15 minutes to record.

Smith's label, LeCam Records, began pressing copies, and Smith sent a copy to Mercury Records. There was no response but, after the song began to get airplay, Mercury offered to buy it for its subsidiary, Smash. A deal was made for $500 up front. Later the same day, Dot Records offered $10,000, but a contract was already sealed.

"Hey! Baby" sold over a million copies and earned a rating of number 11 for the year 1962.

The song retained its popularity over several decades. Twenty-five years after its chart run, its inclusion on the *Dirty Dancing* movie soundtrack gave it new legs.

"It surprised me then, and it still surprises me now," Channel told *The Tennessean*. "High school marching bands do it. I'm so honored that the different generations have liked it so much. I couldn't ask for more, you know, and I won't. It was too much to ask for anyway."

The follow-up, "Number One Man," peaked at number 52 – but I never heard it on Chicago's rock station, WLS. Channel placed two more songs on the nether region of the Hot 100 before his chart career ended.

•••••••• ✤ ••••••••

"Johnny Get Angry" by Joanie Sommers
Songwriters: Hal David, Sherman Edwards
Peaked at number 7 on *Billboard* Hot 100
July 21, 1962

Joanie Sommers

Born Joan Drost on February 24, 1941, in Buffalo, New York

Joanie Sommers

With a long, illustrious singing career behind her, Joanie Sommers seems a little bitter that she is identified with only one song.

"Twenty albums with some of the greatest names in jazz, and I'm eternally linked with 'Johnny Get Angry,' she said in an interview with Will Ryan in 2001.

Her debut single in 1960, "One Boy" from the musical *Bye Bye Birdie,* peaked at number 54. Two years later she swept into the top 10 with "Johnny Get Angry," a song about a girl with a milquetoast boyfriend whom she would like to see get tougher. The song was contained on an album of the same name.

The song's instrumental middle part features an ensemble of kazoos.

In the 1960s Sommers could be seen on television game shows and variety programs. She acted in an episode of the TV series *The Wild Wild West* (1969). She also did voice work for animated films.

Some of her best known songs never reached the charts – they were jingles for Pepsi soft drinks. She sang on advertising campaigns "Now it's Pepsi, for those who think young," and "Come alive! You're in the Pepsi Generation." She also promoted Diet Pepsi with "Now you see it, now you don't."

Sommers had 18 singles after "Johnny Get Angry," and the most successful was "When The Boys Get Together," which peaked at number 94 in 1962.

•••••••• ✤ ••••••••

"Tell Him" by the Exciters

Songwriter: Bert Berns
Peaked at number 4 on *Billboard* Hot 100
January 19, 1963
January 26, 1963

The Exciters

Brenda Reid (July 20, 1945-?)
Carolyn Johnson (bio unavailable)
Lillian Walker (bio unavailable)
Herb Rooney (bio unavailable)
Formed in 1961 as the Masterettes in Queens, New York

The Exciters: Lillian Walker, Herb Rooney, Brenda Reid, Carolyn Johnson

Like several of the Motown vocal groups of the early 1960s, the Exciters formed when the founding members were in high school.

Unlike most Motown groups, the Exciters issued one big hit and failed to successfully follow it up.

The Exciters originally were a girl group that called themselves the Masterettes. After two lineup changes, the group brought in Herb Rooney and changed their name to the Exciters. Rooney eventually married lead singer Brenda Reid.

According to biographer Jason Ankeny, the group had an audition with famed New York City songwriters Jerry Leiber and Mike Stoller, which earned them a recording contract.

"Tell Him" became the Exciters' lone smash after they recorded it in 1962. Written by Bert Berns (also known as Bert Russell), it originally was written from a male perspective and had the title "Tell Her."

The lyrics advise listeners to be forthright with their boyfriends and "tell him that you're never gonna leave him, tell him that you're always gonna love him ... tell him right now."

Berns, who died in 1967, was an unsung writer and producer who made major contributions to Rock & Roll. He wrote or cowrote hits such as "A Little Bit Of Soap" by the Jarmels, "Cry To Me" by Solomon Burke, "Twist And Shout" by the Isley Brothers and by the Beatles, "I Want Candy" by the Strangeloves, "Hang On Sloopy" by the McCoys and "Here Comes The Night" by Them.

The Exciters' follow-up, "He's Got The Power," fell flat, peaking at number 57. It failed to make the play lists of some major pop/rock radio stations. Four other releases made the Hot 100 without making an impact on the music industry.

Oddly, while the Exciters were unable to forge a lengthy career for themselves, they influenced a singer who became a big star for many years. English vocalist Dusty Springfield was in New York City in 1962, on her way to Nashville to make a country music album with her group, the Springfields.

According to a Dusty Springfield fan website, she was making a late-night walk down Broadway when she passed the Colony Record Store and heard the record "Tell Him" playing in the shop. The song influenced Springfield to change her career path toward rock, pop and soul.

"The Exciters sort of got you by the throat," Springfield was quoted as saying. "Out of the blue, it comes blasting at you – 'I know something about love,' and that's it. That's what I wanna do."

Maybe it was bad timing, but the Exciters recorded an unsuccessful version of "Do Wah Diddy Diddy" about a year before Manfred Mann had a number 1 hit with the song. The Exciters' rendition topped out at number 78.

••••••• ❖ •••••••

"Wonderful Summer" by Robin Ward

Songwriters: Gil Garfield, Perry Botkin Jr.
Peaked at number 14 on *Billboard* Hot 100
December 14, 1963
December 21, 1963

Robin Ward

Born Jacqueline McDonnell on January 1, 1941, in Honolulu, Hawaii

Robin Ward

46

She was a one-hit wonder on the record charts, but Robin Ward had a sterling career as a singer – with practically no listeners being aware of her identity.

After eight-year-old Jackie Ward (Robin's original name) and her two sisters won a talent contest in their home state of Nebraska, their parents moved them to Los Angeles to try to help them break into the music industry.

Jackie was thirteen when she got a job singing on a local Los Angeles television music show, where she sang popular songs for four years.

She enrolled at Los Angeles City College, where she learned to read sheet music.

In 1963 she met what would become her signature song. Writer/producer Perry Botkin Jr. hired Jackie to record "Wonderful Summer" for the purpose of persuading established singers to record songs by demonstrating how it should be done. Her voice might sound better if it were higher pitched, Botkin thought, so he sped up the tape by wrapping splicing tape around the spindle of the machine.

Seagull and surf sounds were dubbed in, and Botkin felt it was good enough to release as a single. Jackie suggested changing her first name to Robin, which was her young daughter's name, because she sounded like a sixteen-year-old on the record. Copies were pressed in the fall of '63.

The lyrics have the narrator gushing to the boy who helped her have "the most wonderful summer of my life."

While the single peaked at number 14 nationally, it got better reception in some local markets. In Chicago, for example, the WLS radio chart had it at number 1 for the entire month of December.

This attention created expectations for Ward, but her follow-up, "Winter's Here," did no better than number 123. The Beatles brought the British Invasion to America in 1964, and songs like "Wonderful Summer" no longer were in vogue.

Ward's career, however, did not end there. She left the pop recording path and became a television singer. According to notes in Wikipedia, she appeared on *The Red Skelton Show*, *The Danny Kaye Show*, *The Carol Burnett Show* and *The Sonny & Cher Comedy Hour*. And she sang jingles on many commercials.

And her work wasn't finished yet. She sang various TV theme songs, including *Flipper, Batman, The Partridge Family, Love American Style* and *Maude*. By Ward's estimate, her voice can be heard in approximately 800 movies. She also did backing vocals on the recordings of several big stars.

As a member of the Ron Hicklin Singers, she sang on practically all of the songs credited to the *Partridge Family*, along with David Cassidy. This kept her anonymity intact.

•••••• ❖ ••••••

"Popsicles And Icicles" by the Murmaids

Songwriter: David Gates
Peaked at number 3 on *Billboard* Hot 100
January 11, 1964
January 18, 1964

The Murmaids

Terry Fischer (April 1, 1946-March 28, 2017)
Carol Fischer (July 20, 1948-?)
Sally Gordon (March 7, 1946-?)
Formed in 1963 in Los Angeles, California

The Murmaids: Sally Gordon, Terry Fischer, Carol Fischer

Three teenage girls from Los Angeles scored a big winner with their first single, but they had nothing to show for it monetarily.

The Murmaids had sung in the Grant High School chorus, and they got their break to record "Popsicles And Icicles" in the spring of 1963. After a slow start, the song shot up to number 3 on the pop chart, but fame was fleeting for Carol Fischer, Terry Fischer and Sally Gordon. They never had another hit – or cashed a royalty check.

"The only money we received was the fee to pay the union," Sally Gordon-Mark said in an exclusive interview for this book. The trio was obliged to join AFTRA (American Federation of Television and Radio Artists).

According to notes in *Wikipedia*, Terry Fischer said, "At that time, we got a statement from the record company charging us an exorbitant amount of money against royalties. Everyone else got paid. Kim Fowley (the producer) got paid. The musicians got paid. We were paid nothing."

The girls got their start in the recording industry when a friend of Sally asked her to substitute in a session she could not attend. "Fowley had written a song called 'Astrology,' and we sang back-up," Gordon-Mark said. More session work soon came their way.

"Kim presented us to Ruth Conte, owner of Chattahoochee Records, who was looking for a girl group. We signed a contract with the label, receiving a royalty of 1 percent, split three ways," Gordon-Mark related.

The Fischer sisters' mother had been a professional big band singer; their deceased father Carl had been a composer and Frankie Laine's accompanist. Sally's father was also a professional musician and assistant music librarian at Paramount Pictures.

"Despite their professional experience, the parents didn't look too closely at the contract in their excitement over us getting what they felt was a great opportunity. Legal consultation wasn't sought by anyone to make sure that our rights were protected," Gordon-Mark said.

With an instrumental track on the B-side of the single, "Popsicles And Icicles" went nowhere. Then a radio disc jockey in San Francisco took an interest in it, sparking airplay around the nation. A different B-side, "Comedy And Tragedy," sung by three different girls, replaced the original.

Sally Gordon-Mark
(2016) Photo by
Tony Mark

The lyrics enumerate the things "the boy I love" likes. They conclude, "If you put them all together, much to your surprise you'll find a bit of heaven right before your eyes."

By the time "Popsicles And Icicles" was climbing the charts, Gordon was away at college. "The only times that recordings and personal appearances could be done were during ... school vacations at Christmas and Easter," she said.

A follow-up single was recorded at Gold Star Studios, "Heartbreak Ahead." Fate did not smile on that release or any subsequent single.

"Fowley, Conte and the recording engineer, Stan Ross, felt that my voice should be brought out more, and I was given small solos," Gordon-Mark said, "which seemed to make the soloist of 'Popsicles' (Terry) jealous, and the sessions became very unpleasant for me afterwards. Terry often pushed me away from the microphone and told me to sing without vibrato, in other words, deaden my voice."

Gordon-Mark added, "I have always respected what (Terry) contributed. I was incapable of singing lead, and so was Carol."

The Murmaids recorded an album at Gold Star, and they tried several styles, including jazz. They made two public appearances – one on the *Lloyd Thaxton* TV show, where they had to dress in matching pink dresses and lip-sync the song, and the second in a roller skating rink.

After the advent of the compact disc era, more Murmaids songs were released to a market hungry for nostalgia. "I was never informed about any releases of our recordings, whether they were in audiocassette, LP or CD form, and never received any royalties," Gordon-Mark said.

"It was great – and over quickly," Carol Fischer told me. "But my sister and I reunited the group with Suzi Robertson, who was not one of the original Murmaids, and loved it. For me and my sister, it really was all about the singing – and singing together."

Popularity of "Popsicles ..." was stunted in Great Britain, where the frozen treats are known as "ice lollies." Hence the record failed to make the U.K. chart.

Terry Fischer died from complications of Parkinson's disease, just days short of her 71st birthday.

"Through YouTube, I've been in touch with fans the last 10 years, and the number of pages posting 'Popsicles And Icicles' there has grown," Gordon-Mark said from her home in Italy. "Friends in the U.S. tell me they still hear it played on the radio and in supermarkets, etc. I'm astounded that the song is still known and that there are so many fans after sixty years!"

• • • • • • • ❖ • • • • • • •

The Boy From New York City" by the Ad Libs

Songwriter: John Taylor

Peaked at number 8 on *Billboard* Hot 100

February 27, 1965

The Ad Libs

Mary Ann Thomas

Hugh Harris

Danny Austin

Dave Watt

Norman Donegan

Formed in 1964 in Bayonne, New Jersey

The Ad Libs

The song carried the DNA of a doo-wop recording, but in early 1965 the Ad Libs put a fresh sound on "The Boy From New York City" to create their only hit.

Lead singer Mary Ann Thomas delivered terrific vocals and was deftly backed by her four mates.

"The Boy from New York City" was released on Red Bird Records' subsidiary, Blue Cat, which was owned by famed New York City songwriters Jerry Leiber and Mike Stoller. Leon Huff, who would form a lucrative partnership with Kenny Gamble years later in Philadelphia, played piano on the track.

"I had the fortunate opportunity to play piano on many Leiber and Stoller recording sessions as a musician in the early days," Huff told Songfacts. "When I had dreams of being a producer, I met Leiber and Stoller in the Brill Building when they called me to play on 'Boy From New York City.'

"I was so nervous, but when I started grooving, that's when I really settled down, because Jerry and Mike cut some really groovy records. That was a great time for me as a studio musician. I'll never forget Leiber and Stoller because they helped me get the knack of the studios."

Huff and Gamble became owners of Philadelphia International Records and, as producers, created the Philly Soul Sound.

Some lyrics from "The Boy …": "He's really down, and he's no clown. He has the finest penthouse I've ever seen in town. And he's cute in his mohair suit, and he keeps his pockets full of spending loot."

After the Ad Libs made a big splash with their first release, things got tough very quickly. "He Ain't No Angel" squeezed onto the chart and peaked at number 100. That would be their final appearance on the pop chart. Their last entry on the R&B Chart would be "Giving Up" in 1969, which hit number 34.

••••••• ❖ •••••••

"The Birds And The Bees" by Jewel Akens

Songwriter: Barry Stuart
Peaked at number 3 on *Billboard* Hot 100
March 20, 1965
March 27, 1965

Jewel Akens

September 12, 1933-March 1, 2013
Born Jewel Eugene Akens in Houston, Texas, and died in Inglewood, California

Jewel Akens

A song purportedly written by a twelve-year-old boy propelled Jewel Akens to his only solo hit.

"The Birds And The Bees," according to Secondhandsongs.com, may have been written by the young son of Herb Newman, the owner of Era Records. It is credited on the record label to Barry Stuart. On copies of the song's sheet music, words and music are credited to Herb Newman.

A lilting, staccato melody goes with the love-song lyrics, and the title is derived from an idiom of the mechanics of sexual reproduction.

Newman's original plan was for the Turnarounds to record "The Birds ..." as a group. But Akens was the only member who was on board with the idea. So, he recorded it as a solo artist. Too bad for the others – the single went to number 3 on the pop chart and number 21 on the Hot Rhythm & Blues Singles chart.

The record was a top 10 hit in Australia, Belgium, the Netherlands and Norway. It sold over a million copies.

At Gold Star Studio in Los Angeles, engineer Stan Ross gave the recording a unique sound by patching the guitar part through the organ speaker.

The second verse says, "Let me tell you about the stars in the sky and a girl and a guy and the way they could kiss on a night like this."

51

According to Waybackattack.com, Akens' mother had been hoping for a girl when she was pregnant with him and decided on the name "Jewel." Though he turned out to be a male child, she still gave him the name.

In the late 1960s, Akens toured with the Monkees. He stayed active in the music business until the mid-1970s.

Akens died at seventy-nine from complications of back surgery.

••••••• ❖ •••••••

"Elusive Butterfly" by Bob Lind

Songwriter: Bob Lind
Peaked at number 5 on *Billboard* Hot 100
March 12, 1966
March 19, 1966

Bob Lind

Born Robert Neale Lind on November 25, 1942, in Baltimore, Maryland

Bob Lind

This artist and his label were caught flat-footed by the success of his one hit and struggled unsuccessfully to follow it up.

Bob Lind's "Elusive Butterfly" wasn't supposed to be a hit, but it created strong expectations for more of his folk rock compositions.

"The record company executives asked me which song I thought we should release as the single," Lind was quoted by Songfacts. "I told them anything but 'Elusive Butterfly.' The execs and (arranger/producer) Jack (Nitzsche) agreed. There was just nothing like it on the charts at the time, and it didn't smell like a hit to any of us."

With its vivid imagery and ethereal production, "Elusive Butterfly" soared into the top five, even though it had been ticketed as the B-side to "Cheryl's Goin' Home." Lind can thank Miami radio station WQAM for playing "Butterfly," which enabled it to rise into the station's top 10 by the end of 1965 and spread to other Florida stations. Liberty Records then reissued the single with "Butterfly" as the A-side.

The first verse begins, "You might wake up some mornin' to the sound of something moving past your window in the wind. And if you're quick enough to rise, you'll catch a fleeting glimpse of someone's fading shadow."

The lyrics describe a quest for love and life's dreams, which can be challenging. Or, in Lind's words, "The magic of the quest, the thrill of searching, even when that which is sought is hard to see."

52

Speaking of his career struggles following "Butterfly," Lind said to Goldminemag.com in 2015, "We're all aware of the iciness of the music business and the fear and shallowness of the people who run it. What's less often talked about is the immaturity of the artist who can't take the industry realities in stride. I was one of those infantile, crybaby artists.

"I could blame it on my drug and alcohol use, but even today, clean and sober thirty-seven years, I seem to be the same stubborn, quarrelsome, inflexible guy I was then."

Of Lind's subsequent singles, "Remember The Rain" charted the highest at number 64. It was his only other release to break into the Hot 100. But who remembers that?

"Black Is Black" by Los Bravos
Songwriters: Michelle Grainger, Tony Hayes, Steve Wadey
Peaked at number 4 on *Billboard* Hot 100
October 1, 1966
October 8, 1966

Los Bravos

Mike Kogel (April 25, 1944-?) lead vocals
Antonio Martinez Salas (October 3, 1945-June 19, 1990) guitar
Manuel Fernandez Aparicio (September 29, 1943-May 20, 1968) organ
Miguel Vicens Danus (June 21, 1943-February 12, 2022) bass
Pablo Sanllehi Gomez (November 5, 1943-?) drums
Formed in 1965 in Madrid, Spain

Los Bravos: Miguel Vicens, Mike Kogel, Antonio Martinez,
Pablo Gomez, Manuel Fernandez

It has been common for foreign bands to become one-hit wonders in the United States. Often, after one release in the U.S., these groups concentrate on selling in markets in their home countries or continents.

According to a story in *Billboard*, Los Bravos formed as an amalgamation of Mike & the Runaways and Los Sonor in Madrid, Spain. Their new name was selected in an audience vote conducted by a Spanish radio network.

When "Black Is Black" reached number 2 in the U.K., number 1 in Canada and number 4 in the U.S., Los Bravos became the first Spanish rock band to have an international hit. Mike Kogel, a native of Germany, sang the lyrics phonetically because he was not an English speaker. His voice sounds a lot like the late singer Gene Pitney.

The song is about a guy who has lost his girlfriend. Although she's not coming back to him, he thinks she might. So, he muses about whether he would take her back, which gives him a choice, in his mind.

"I can't choose, it's too much to lose, my love's still strong," he says. "Oh, maybe if she would come back to me, well, it can't go wrong."

Los Bravos tried to make more hay in the American market, but they couldn't reach the top 40 with subsequent releases. "Bring A Little Lovin'" peaked at number 51 in 1968.

Tragedy befell the band in 1968 when the pregnant wife of organist Manuel Fernandez died in an automobile accident, with Manuel driving. He proceeded to commit suicide.

•••••••• ❖ ••••••••

"Judy In Disguise (With Glasses)" by John Fred & His Playboy Band
Songwriters: John Fred, Andrew Bernard
Peaked at number 1 on *Billboard* Hot 100
January 20, 1968
January 27, 1968

John Fred

May 8, 1941-April 14, 2005
Born John Fred Gourrier in Baton Rouge, Louisiana, and died in New Orleans, Louisiana

John Fred

The year 1967 was a fertile year in Rock & Roll, in large part because of the landmark Beatles' album *Sgt. Pepper's Lonely Hearts Club Band.* Many rock music scholars regard it as the best album of all time.

The album's influence reached a Southern rocker who had been around for a few years – John Fred. He formed a band called the Playboys in 1956, and they charted at number

82 with "Shirley" in 1958. Later they changed their moniker to Playboy Band to avoid confusion with Gary Lewis & the Playboys.

More singles followed, and none reached the Hot 100 until "Judy In Disguise (With Glasses)" charged up the list in late '67. It claimed the top spot in January 1968 by knocking off the Beatles' "Hello Goodbye." It became a million-seller.

The song was a parody of a well-known number from "Sgt. Pepper," the psychedelic "Lucy In The Sky With Diamonds." But "Judy" was far from psychedelic. It sounded more like bubble gum or sunshine pop, but it did have cryptic lyrics.

"Judy in disguise, well that's what you are," the first verse says. "A lemonade pie with your brand new car. Cantaloupe eyes come to me tonight, Judy in disguise with glasses."

Fred told *One Shot Magazine* how he found inspiration for Judy in the crowd of a concert audience. "We were playing in Florida, and the girls at the time had these big old sunglasses," he said. "One of the guys was hustling this chick. She took off these glasses, and her face could stop a clock. "I said, 'That's it.' That's what gave me the idea. I said, 'She's kind of in disguise.'"

The first choice of the girl's name in the lyrics was Beverly. But Fred changed it to Judy since it was easier to sing and more closely resembled Lucy.

A follow-up, "Hey, Hey Bunny," could reach only number 57. Ten other singles failed to chart, and Fred's fame had come and gone.

An athlete in college at Southeastern Louisiana, Fred turned to coaching high school basketball and baseball, and he hosted a radio show. He died at 63 after he encountered complications from a kidney transplant.

•••••• ❖ ••••••

"Angel Of The Morning" by Merrilee Rush & the Turnabouts

Songwriter: Chip Taylor
Peaked at number 7 on *Billboard* Hot 100
June 29, 1968
July 6, 1968
July 13, 1968

Merrilee Rush

Born Merrilee Gunst on January 26, 1944, in Seattle, Washington

Merrilee Rush

She has been identified with only one song for decades, but Merrilee Rush's failure to expand her chart presence was not because of lack of effort.

55

After "Angel Of The Morning" became one of the iconic songs of the summer of 1968, Rush returned to the recording studio, with about 10 other singles resulting. But her magic was used up by one notable hit.

Rush began singing in her native Pacific Northwest in the early 1960s and became friends with members of a band from that area, Paul Revere & the Raiders. They invited her to join their concert tour in 1968. When it ended in Memphis, the Raiders stayed to record an album at American Studios.

Mark Lindsay of the Raiders introduced Rush to Chips Moman, owner of the studios. According to Historylink.org, Rush said, "He asked if I would do a demo for him, just so he could hear my voice. I did a demo, and he said, 'I want you to come back next month, and we'll pick out a couple tunes and cut.'"

One of the songs selected was "Angel Of The Morning," a number that Connie Francis's handlers had rejected because of the nature of the lyrics, according to a story in *Billboard*. Evie Sands was the first to record it, but Rush was the first to make it a hit.

The narrator in the lyrics promises she won't hang on to her man if he decides to end their love affair.

"There'll be no strings to bind your hands, not if my love can't bind your heart," she says. "And there's no need to take a stand, for it was I who chose to start."

It took two years, but the single became a million-seller.

According to notes in *Wikipedia*, Rush's backing band the Turnabouts received label credit, but the musicians who backed Elvis Presley on his late-1960s Memphis recordings played behind Rush on "Angel Of The Morning" and the accompanying album of the same name.

"Angel" garnered a Grammy nomination for Rush, but Dionne Warwick won the award for Best Contemporary Pop Female Vocalist of the Year.

••••••• ❖ •••••••

"Girl Watcher" by the O'Kaysions

Songwriters: Buck Trail, Wayne Pittman
Peaked at number 5 on *Billboard* Hot 100
October 5, 1968
October 12, 1968
October 19, 1968
October 26, 1968

The O'Kaysions

Donnie Weaver – vocals, organ
Wayne Pittman – guitar
Jimmy Hinnant – bass
Steve Watson – drums
Eddie Dement – trumpet
Gerald Toler – saxophone
Formed as the Kays in 1959 in Kenly, North Carolina

The O'Kaysions: (front) Donnie Weaver, Steve Watson (back) Gerald Toler, Wayne Pittman, Eddie Dement, Jimmy Hinnant

It was an upbeat, feel-good song. It spent practically a whole month at number 5 on the *Billboard* Hot 100. And by the time "Girl Watcher" fell off the charts, the O'Kaysions had their only claim to fame.

The band had to abandon their original name because of its similarity to the stage name of New York disc jockey Murray Kaufman, who was professionally known as "Murray the K."

"In order to play in the clubs up North, you had to become a union member," guitarist Wayne Pittman told Rebeatmag.com. "You had to register your band's name, and there was a DJ in New York named Murray the K, and we were told we couldn't register our name because it was too similar to his. So we coined the name O'Kaysions so we could keep it close to that Kays identity we were known by in North and South Carolina, Georgia, and Virginia where we played."

"Girl Watcher" was the band's first recording after their name change.

"We used to play down at Atlantic Beach a lot, and when we got back home people would say, 'Did you meet any girls this weekend?'" Pittman said. "I'd say, 'I didn't meet any, but I sure do like to watch them.'"

After making that comment, one of Pittman's mates suggested he write a song about it. Coincidentally, about a month earlier, Pittman had written a melody without words. "When he said that, it was like a lightbulb went off in my head," Pittman related. The lyrics he concocted contained subject matter to which many a guy could relate.

"I was just a boy when I threw away my toys. I found a new pastime to dwell on," the first verse reads. "Whenever I detect members of the other sex, I play the game I do so well."

The single got lots of regional airplay along the Atlantic seaboard before ABC Records picked it up for national distribution. National sales topped 1 million by December 1968.

An album followed, but it was far from good, according to Pittman. "ABC wanted something quick and something fast, and we had to do the whole album in two days. It just wasn't a good product."

The next single, "Love Machine," failed to rise above number 76.

•••••••• ❖ ••••••••

"In The Year 2525 (Exordium & Terminus)" by Zager & Evans

Songwriter: Rick Evans
Peaked at number 1 on *Billboard* Hot 100
July 12, 1969
July 19, 1969
July 26, 1969
August 2, 1969
August 9, 1969
August 16, 1969

Zager & Evans

Denny Zager (February 14, 1944-?)
Born Dennis Zager in Wymore, Nebraska
Rick Evans (January 20, 1943-February 2018)
Born Richard S. Evans in Lincoln, Nebraska, and died in Santa Fe, New Mexico
Formed in 1968 in Lincoln, Nebraska

Rick Evans and Denny Zager

When legendary disc jockey Casey Kasem presented a special *"American Top 40 Book of Records"* radio show in the summer of 1980, he credited Zager & Evans with being "the biggest disappearing act" on the *Billboard* charts. And with good reason.

For a month and a half in 1969, Zager & Evans held the nation spellbound with their futuristic look at humanity in the song "In The Year 2525 (Exordium & Terminus)." Then, after the song dropped off the charts, the duo from Nebraska were practically not heard on the airwaves ever again.

Their next four singles, reaching into 1971, failed to enter the Hot 100.

Rick Evans wrote the song in 1964, but he and his partner Denny Zager did not record it until 1968. Thanks to airplay by radio stations in Omaha and Lincoln, "2525" became a regional hit. RCA Records then signed them to a contract and released the single with national distribution.

The scenario laid out in the song lyrics was a bit disturbing with lots of gloom and doom, but the public ate it up. For example, there is mind control achieved through daily consumption of a pill, machines performing each and every human task and reproduction done by picking embryos out of a test tube.

As millennia go by, the narrator muses whether "God is gonna shake His mighty head (and) either say I'm pleased where man has been, or tear it down, and start again."

The final verse brings this conclusion: "Now it's been ten thousand years, Man has cried a billion tears for what, he never knew, now man's reign is through. But through eternal night, the twinkling of starlight so very far away, maybe it's only yesterday."

The parenthetic part of the song title is Latin for "beginning & end."

Sales of the single eclipsed the 4 million mark, and "2525" topped the U.K. chart as well as the American.

Evans and Zager met while attending Nebraska Wesleyan University in Lincoln. According to author Fred Bronson, they became members of different bands for several years before dissatisfaction with their respective groups led them to form a duo in 1968.

In its lengthy stay at number 1, "2525" saw two major historic events: the Apollo 11 moon landing and the Woodstock Music & Art Festival.

•••••• ❖ ••••••

"Ride Captain Ride" by the Blues Image
Songwriters: Mike Pinera, Frank Konte
Peaked at number 4 on *Billboard* Hot 100
July 11, 1970

The Blues Image
Mike Pinera (September 29, 1948-?) vocals, guitar
Frank Konte (October 2, 1947-?) keyboards
Joe Lala (November 3, 1947-March 18, 2014) percussion, vocals
Manuel Bertematti (January 1946-?) drums
Malcolm Jones (DOB unknown-Feb. 22, 2020) – bass
Formed in 1966 in Tampa, Florida

The Blues Image

"Seventy-three men sailed up from the San Francisco Bay," is the opening line of "Ride Captain Ride." It's the only chartbuster created by the Blues Image.

60

You might have wondered over the years how that line was forged into the lyrics. It has nothing to do with the number of men on a ship.

Though he wasn't the keyboard player of the band, Mike Pinera owned a Fender Rhodes electric piano. He had crafted a 15-second intro for "Ride Captain Ride," but then he was stumped to begin the lyrics. He looked down at the keys in front of him, which numbered 73. A standard piano has 88 keys.

At that point, "The song wrote itself," Pinera was quoted by Bestclassicbands.com.

While some music pundits have speculated the lyrics have historical context, Pinera has shot down those theories. His response has been, "It's from my imagination."

Within the next three years, Donald Fagen would make the Fender Rhodes famous by using it extensively in Steely Dan recordings.

The Blues Image got its start in Tampa, Florida, and then began to perform regularly in the Miami area. It was there they began using blues and Latin rhythms. Eventually, they moved to California to try to improve their fortunes.

"Ride Captain Ride" slotted into the Blues Image's second album, and the single became a million-seller.

The chorus of the song reads: "Ride captain ride upon your mystery ship. Be amazed at the friends you have here on your trip. Ride captain ride upon your mystery ship, on your way to a world that others might have missed."

Before 1970 was over, the Blues Image began to crumble as members defected to other bands. A second single, "Gas Lamps And Clay," limped to a chart peak of number 81.

•••••••• ❖ ••••••••

"Mr. Big Stuff" by Jean Knight

Songwriters: Joe Broussard, Ralph Williams, Carrol Washington
Peaked at number 2 on *Billboard* Hot 100
August 14, 1971
August 21, 1971

Jean Knight

January 26, 1943–November 22, 2023
Born Jean Caliste on Jan. 26, 1943, in New Orleans, Louisiana, and died in Tampa, Florida

Jean Knight

"Mr. Big Stuff" was part funk and part women's anthem, sending Jean Knight to her only hit on the pop chart.

Recorded at the humble Malaco Studios in Jackson, Miss., it also was a number 1 hit for five weeks on the *Billboard* Soul Singles chart.

The melody is carried by a soulful horn section, much like the one that backed King Floyd on "Groove Me." Both songs were recorded at Malaco.

The narrator of the lyrics is telling a well-heeled suitor that, just because he wears fancy clothes and drives a nice, big car, he will not get her love.

"Now I know all the girls I've seen you with, I know you broke their hearts one after another now, bit by bit," she says. "You made 'em cry, many poor girls cry, when they tried to keep you happy, they just tried to keep you satisfied."

According to Concord.com, "Mr. Big Stuff" sold 2.7 million copies and became the biggest selling single in Stax Records history.

Biographer Steve Huey wrote disagreements between Knight and her producer and label ended her relationship with Stax.

"You Think You're Hot Stuff" was a disappointing follow-up at number 57 in 1971, and Knight's only other trip into the Hot 100 came with "My Toot Toot," a number 50 song in 1985.

••••••• ❖ •••••••

"I Can Help" by Billy Swan

Songwriter: Billy Swan

Peaked at number 1 on *Billboard* Hot 100

November 23, 1974

November 30, 1974

Billy Swan

Born William Lance Swan on May 12, 1942, in Cape Girardeau, Missouri

Billy Swan

It was a melody perfect for playing at a rolling skating rink, but it also proved to be perfect for playing on the car radio or the home stereo.

Billy Swan struck gold with "I Can Help," which isn't his only claim to fame but is the only hit single for which music fans remember him.

Swan wrote "Lover Please," which was a number 7 pop hit for Clyde McPhatter in 1962. At the time, Swan was in the band Mirt Mirly & the Rhythm Steppers in his hometown, Cape Girardeau, Missouri

A move across the Mississippi River into Tennessee enabled Swan to start writing songs for country artists such as Mel Tillis, Kris Kristofferson and Conway Twitty, according to editor Colin Larkin. In 1969 he produced Tony Joe White's hit, "Polk Salad Annie."

Biographer Steve Huey noted Swan moved to Nashville in 1972, whereupon he recorded his first album, "Rock On With Rhythm." In 1974 he wrote and recorded "I Can Help," using an RMI organ given to him as a wedding present by Kristofferson and his wife Rita Coolidge. He recorded the track in two takes.

Swan often took his young German shepherd, Bowser, to his recording sessions, and such was the case when he had the "I Can Help" session in Murfreesboro, Tenn. While Swan was playing a portable Farfisa keyboard, the dog began playfully tugging at his pant leg. Swan kept his focus, though, and finished the song without flaw. The applause at the end of the recording is from the musicians who were congratulating Swan for the feat.

The second verse states, "It's a fact that people get lonely – ain't nothing new. But a woman like you, baby, should never have the blues. Let me help. I've got two for me, let me help. It would sure do me good to do you good, let me help."

A million-seller, the single was number 1 pop and country in the United States and Canada. It topped 12 other charts around the world.

A follow-up single, "I'm Her Fool," peaked at number 53 on the pop chart but failed to show on the *Billboard* Country chart. "Everything's The Same (Ain't Nothing Changed)" topped out at number 91.

Without another hit to his recording credits, Swan continued his career as a songwriter and session musician.

•••••••• ❖ ••••••••

"Play That Funky Music" by Wild Cherry

Songwriter: Robert Parissi
Peaked at number 1 on *Billboard* Hot 100
September 18, 1976
September 25, 1976
October 2, 1976

Wild Cherry

Rob Parissi (December 29, 1950-?) lead vocals, guitar
Bryan Bassett (August 11, 1954-?) guitar
Mark Avsec (August 23, 1954-?) keyboards
Allen Wentz (bio unavailable) – bass
Ron Beitle (August 30, 1954-December 11, 2017) – drums
Formed in 1970 in Steubenville, Ohio

Wild Cherry

Wild Cherry was playing a gig at the 2001 Club on the north side of Pittsburgh, Pennsylvania, in the mid-1970s.

A table of African American patrons kept needling drummer Ron Beitle. "When are you going to play some funky music, white boy?" they persisted.

It was the catalyst Wild Cherry and it leader Rob Parissi needed to send the band on the path to a mega-hit record. Parissi wrote the phrase on a bar order pad and later set to work writing "Play That Funky Music." He wrote the first two verses in the club that night and the third in the car on the way home.

"We were a rock band, and disco music was coming in," Parissi told Harry Connick Jr. on his syndicated television show. "Rock clubs were closing down, and discos were opening up. And we were a hard-working band playing four, five, six nights a week."

Parissi borrowed the bass line and rhythm track from "Fire" by the Ohio Players and built "Funky Music" around it.

Talk about writing a hit song out of desperation. It was a case of coming up with something trendy or be out of work.

"'Play That Funky Music' is pretty autobiographical and quite literal," guitarist Bryan Bassett told Americansongwriter.com. "Club work was getting scarce if you didn't play dance music, so we decided to change.

"Someone actually did say that to us – play that funky music, white boy – insinuating that if we didn't, we probably wouldn't be working much longer."

Parissi told a Dutch TV station, "I took it around to every record label and got close but no deal. Everybody was worried about that white boy thing. Even my father (was concerned), when I played it for him for the first time. He took the needle off the record and said, 'Oh no, you can't do that. You have to take it out.'

"I said no, if you take that out it's gonna kill the record. That's the song."

It was the second incarnation of Wild Cherry, which got its start in 1970. They had a contract with Brown Bag Records, but their records failed to chart. They broke up in 1973, but Parissi reformed the band with new members in 1975.

In the aftermath of "Play That Funky Music," Wild Cherry went to number 43 with "Baby Don't You Know." Charting at number 61, "Hold On (With Strings) was the band's next-best appearance on the singles chart. Essentially, the band was finished by 1979.

•••••• ❖ ••••••

"Do You Wanna Make Love" by Peter McCann

Songwriter: Peter McCann

Peaked at number 5 on *Billboard* Hot 100

August 6, 1977

August 13, 1977

Peter McCann

Born Peter James McCann on March 6, 1948, in Bridgeport, Connecticut

Peter McCann

It was spring of 1977, and a friend asked me if I had yet heard a certain new song on the radio.

"It says do you want to make love, or do you just want to fool around," he said.

I was sure he was joking, until I heard the song play on the radio a couple of days later.

It's a rather funny lyric, considering many people equate making love with "fooling around."

Upon close examination, however, we see what Peter McCann, the songwriter and vocalist, means by his lyrics. The song, which he said was written for a woman to sing, has one lover asking another if she's serious about the relationship.

"You can take it seriously or take it somewhere else," is the ultimatum.

McCann's only appearance in the top 40 as a singer was a surprise. He had earned attention for writing a number 6 single for Jennifer Warnes, "Right Time Of The Night." Arista Records signed Warnes but not McCann.

20th Century Records took notice, though, and released McCann's recording with his version of "Right Time Of The Night" on the B-side.

The germ of an idea for the song grew out of a conversation McCann had in the bar of Los Angeles's Troubadour nightclub.

McCann's fellow conversant was "basically talking about the difference between one-night stands and being serious," McCann told interviewer Bart Herbison. "So, I wrote the song with those lines in it. A lot of people heard those two lines and thought it was a song was about gratuitous, meaningless one-night stands. But the song definitely was not about that."

With the record climbing the charts, McCann was not prepared to do a concert tour to support it. Instead, he did television appearances like *American Bandstand, Mike Douglas* and *The Merv Griffin Show.*

"We did everything that was on TV except the Carson show *(The Tonight Show starring Johnny Carson),*" McCann said in an interview. "We never worked that out. However, I had talked to a couple of artists who had taken money for album budget and then for tour support, and they basically had to have a gold album just to break even. And I was making money on the radio without leaving my house.

"So, I wasn't interested. And it's the reason why I'm in the one-hit wonder books. The record label realized this kid ain't going out there and do the standard opening act thing, build a following. He's not interested.

"I tried to convince them that we could do this through media, through television, because we were doing it that way. Everybody wanted to have me on their show, especially Merv Griffin. He thought I was a very good songwriter, and people were coming on the shows singing my songs, as well as me coming on and doing it."

Internationally, "Do You Wanna ..." sold over two million, and it hit number 1 in South Africa.

Without support from his labels, McCann's next five singles failed to chart.

•••••• ❖ ••••••

"Magnet And Steel" by Walter Egan

Songwriter: Walter Egan

Peaked at number 8 on *Billboard* Hot 100

August 26, 1978

Walter Egan

Born Walter Egan on July 12, 1948, in Queens, New York

Walter Egan

Picture this: a young singer/songwriter has a big crush on a young lady who also happens to be a singer/songwriter in an established rock band.

He writes a sizzling love ballad about his feelings for her. Then he gets her ex-boyfriend to co-produce the recording, while the object of his affection sings back-up on it. The single becomes the biggest hit – well, the only hit – of his career.

This fantasy came true for Walter Egan in 1978.

Stevie Nicks was the inspiration for "Magnet And Steel." She even dated Egan after she broke up with Lindsay Buckingham, but she and Egan were not an item for long.

"In 1976 I was living in Pomona, California, and I had a notion to write a song with the stroll beat, and so began the rough outline of what was tentatively called 'Don't Turn Away Now,'" Egan told Songfacts. "Now, this was also at the time of putting together my first album, 'Fundamental Roll,' and my two new friends and producers, Lindsey Buckingham and Stevie Nicks and I, were starting the recording process.

"On the night when Stevie did the background vocals for my song 'Tunnel O' Love,' my nascent amorous feelings toward her came into a sharper focus – I was smitten by the kitten, as they say.

"It was on my drive home at 3 a.m. from Van Nuys to Pomona that I happened to be behind a metal flake blue Continental with ground effects and a diamond window in back. I was inspired by the car's license plate: NOT SHY.

"By the time I pulled into my driveway, I had formulated the lyrics and come up with the magnet metaphor. From there the song was finished in 15 minutes. It was especially satisfying to have Stevie sing on 'Magnet,' since it was about her (and me)."

On Rockcellarmagazine.com, Egan admitted, "... no artist sets out to be a one-hit wonder, and the phrase itself implies a flash in the pan, someone who just got lucky through situation and circumstance.

"'Magnet and Steel' was on my second LP, and its run in 1978 was the culmination of 14 years of songwriting and eight years of trying to make it in the music business. I recognized that it was accomplishing things that none of my previous releases had done, and it was a heady feeling, like suddenly being admitted to a club that you had previously been denied.

"I was enjoying the moment way too much to even consider its long-term destiny. It was cool enough to just be able to turn on the radio and hear it at that time."

The second verse reads, "I can't hope that I'll hold you for long. You're a woman who's lost to your song. But the love that I feel is so strong, and it can't be wrong."

In a March 2022 interview with Lauri Reimer, Egan still basked in the glow of that once-upon-a-time fling with Nicks. "Most songwriters intend for their songs to be a hit. My intention in writing 'Magnet' was to express my infatuation for Stevie Nicks. I believe that the record was made that much more special when she sang on it with me."

Following "Magnet And Steel" proved to be a tough act for Egan, and the best he could do on the singles chart afterward was "Hot Summer Nights," which charted to number 55 in 1978.

"Key Largo" by Bertie Higgins
Songwriters: Bertie Higgins, Sonny Limbo
Peaked at number 8 on *Billboard* Hot 100
April 17, 1982
April 24, 1982

Bertie Higgins

Born Elbert Joseph Higgins on December 8, 1944, in Tarpon Springs, Florida

Bertie Higgins

The song invoked the title of a classic Hollywood movie. And its purpose was to win back a lost love.

In true Hollywood style, the plan worked for singer/songwriter Bertie Higgins with his hit "Key Largo."

The song's lyrics recall the romance Humphrey Bogart and Lauren Bacall had in the movie *Key Largo*, as well as in real life.

The book *Behind The Hits* quotes Higgins as saying, "I lived with a girl a long time in Florida. Her name was Beverly Seaberg. We used to watch old movies on the weekends and, to us, the Bogart and Bacall romance was a phenomenal one: because of their age difference – she was twenty, and he was forty-five – and because the world was clamoring constantly for them to make a relationship work in Hollywood.

"Bev left me, and I hurt for about two years. Finally I said, 'Well, I've got to reach her somehow.' And the only equipment I had to reach her with was a song. So, I wrote the song 'Key Largo.' It was a plea for her return. And she did. We became engaged."

A line in the second verse says, "Please say you will play it again. 'Cause I love you still, Baby, this can't be the end." Their marriage produced two children, but Bertie and Bev broke up in 1995.

"Just Another Day In Paradise" followed "Key Largo" up the charts, but it peaked at number 46. Higgins was left without another single that hit the pop chart.

• • • • • • • ❖ • • • • • • •

"Mickey" by Toni Basil

Songwriters: Michael Chapman, Nicky Chinn
Peaked at number 1 on *Billboard* Hot 100
December 11, 1982

Toni Basil

Born Antonia Christina Basilotta on September 22, 1943, in Philadelphia, Pennsylvania

Toni Basil

Her pedigree was that of a dancer, choreographer and actress, but Toni Basil struck gold in the music business, too, with her only hit, "Mickey."

The catchy song and its accompanying video evoked images of a cheerleading competition, with a chant-like vocal and varsity cheer uniforms.

The songwriters adapted "Mickey" from a 1979 song titled "Kitty" by the British band Racey. Basil inserted the chant "oh Mickey, you're so fine."

In hands-on fashion, Basil also directed, choreographed and produced the music video. The uniform she wore in the video was the same one she wore as a cheerleader at Las Vegas High School more than twenty years earlier. Other cheerleaders in the video were from Carson High School in Los Angeles, California.

According to Songfacts, Basil made the video before the MTV channel began broadcasting, making the United Kingdom the first market for it. TV stations in the U.K. already had music programming to some extent.

Some of the lyrics: "You've been around all night and that's a little long. You think you've got the right, but I think you've got it wrong. Why can't you say goodnight so you can take me home, Mickey?"

Basil has filed lawsuits against defendants, alleging unauthorized use of the recording in both advertising and television. Judges in the Ninth Circuit Court ruled in Basil's favor, largely due to her creative input. Greg Mathieson and Trevor Veitch were the producers.

Building on the success of "Mickey" was difficult for Basil, who went to number 77 with "Shoppin' From A To Z" and number 81 with "Over My Head." But she had her dance and acting chops on which to fall back.

Remarkable Remakes
Songs that have had more than one great life

Overview: A recording is the product of combined efforts by songwriters, musicians, producers, arrangers and studio personnel.

All of these people make money from their work, of course, but these audio gems are a gift to consumers who find great pleasure in listening to them. They enrich our lives.

Throughout the history of Rock & Roll, some recordings have been so special they became gifts that kept on giving. Different artists recorded them, sometimes twice, thrice or more.

In many cases, the remade versions of original hits became bigger than the first ones. These, and other high-charting songs, are remarkable remakes which caught "lightning in a bottle" more than once.

They're kind of like Christmas presents that have been regifted, with new packaging, wrapping and gift tags.

Two major artists in particular, Johnny Rivers and Linda Ronstadt, made careers out of recording songs that already had been hits for others.

A remake also is known as a cover version.

In this chapter, we give a nod to the music industry people who thought enough of these songs to give them new life.

To view the full lyrics of these songs, please log on to www.google.com, enter song titles & artist names and click Google Search.

To listen to these songs, please log on to www.youtube.com and enter song titles & artist names.

"Ain't That A Shame"

Songwriters: Antoine Domino, Dave Bartholomew

By Fats Domino
Peaked at number 10 on *Billboard* Most Played in Jukeboxes Chart
August 27, 1955

By Pat Boone
Peaked at number 1 on *Billboard* Most Played in Jukeboxes Chart
September 17, 1955
September 24, 1955

Fats Domino
February 26, 1928-October 24, 2017
Born Antoine Dominique Domino Jr. in New Orleans, Louisiana, and died in Harvey, Louisiana

Pat Boone Born
Patrick Charles Eugene Boone on June 1, 1934, in Jacksonville, Florida

Fats Domino

Pat Boone

It seems like the tape had just stopped rolling in Fats Domino's recording session for "Ain't That A Shame" when Pat Boone recorded a cover version of the song Domino created with his songwriting partner, Dave Bartholomew.

Domino's version went to market first, but Boone's was close behind, and the two shared the charts together for several weeks. Boone's version outperformed the original.

Both singles enjoyed their best success on the *Billboard* Most Played in Jukeboxes Chart, which the trade magazine published January 6, 1940, to July 20, 1940, and November 6, 1943, to June 17, 1957. It probably was the chart that best reflected what audiences liked. In 1955, the dawn of the Rock Era, there were two other *Billboard* charts – Best Sellers in Stores and Most Played by Jockeys Singles. Another chart, the *Billboard* Top 100, debuted November 12, 1955.

The Jukebox, Best Sellers, Most Played by Jockeys and Top 100 charts eventually were retired. *Billboard* introduced the Hot 100 on August 4, 1958, and it has been the industry standard for rating pop songs since.

On the Jockeys chart, the popularity of songs was measured by what radio disc jockeys put on their turntables. This was a subjective measurement, since most disc jockeys were white, and most radio stations had white owners and white programmers. Music consumers in the United States were predominantly white, and songs by black artists did not get the same promotion as those by whites. This was a product of the times, and things would change dramatically in a few years.

Lest you think Domino was robbed by another artist who had a better showing with his song, be advised this procedure is legal, and the Domino/Bartholomew team profited from Boone's success through songwriting royalties.

Domino's version originally was pressed on vinyl under the title "Ain't It A Shame." It is a song about a guy whose girlfriend broke his heart by breaking up with him.

"You made me cry when you said goodbye," the first verse says. "Ain't that a shame. My tears fell like rain. Ain't that a shame, you're the one to blame."

Boone found more success in 1956 when he covered two of Little Richard's songs – "Tutti Frutti" and "Long Tall Sally." His version of the former out-charted Little Richard's, number 12 to number 18. For the latter, Little Richard's version did slightly better.

Other artists have tried their hand at recording "Ain't That A Shame," including the 4 Seasons, John Lennon, Paul McCartney, Cheap Trick, Brownsville Station and Hank Williams Jr.

•••••• ❖ ••••••

"I'm Walkin'"
Songwriters: Antoine Domino, Dave Bartholomew

By Fats Domino
Peaked at number 5 on *Billboard* Top 100
April 13, 1957

By Ricky Nelson
Peaked at number 17 on *Billboard* Top 100
June 10, 1957

Ricky Nelson
May 8, 1940-December 31, 1985
Born Eric Hilliard Nelson in Teaneck, New Jersey, and died at De Kalb, Texas

Ricky Nelson

Ricky Nelson dipped into the Fats Domino bag of songs to help launch his recording career. In Nelson's first appearance on the charts, he scored a number 2 hit with "A Teenager's Romance." For his next single, he chose the Domino song "I'm Walkin." Although Nelson's cover did not match the popularity of Domino's, it was a solid hit, nonetheless. The record found favor in Australia, where it charted to number 10.

Songfacts posed the possibility of the lyrics being inspired by a comment from a person who saw Domino on foot after his car broke down. "Hey, look at Fats Domino, he's walking.," the observer supposedly said. When Domino reflected on the comment, he thought, *Yeah, I'm walking*, which gave him a tag line for the lyrical structure of the song.

The song is about a guy who is trying to get back together with his girlfriend. "I'm walking, yes indeed. I'm talking for you and me, and I'm hoping that you'll come back to me," the song begins. "I'm lonely as I can be, and I've waited for your company. And I'm hoping that you'll come back to me."

The subject matter is sad but hopeful. What makes the song succeed, though, is the quick, cheerful tempo. Domino's goal was to release "happy songs the people could remember," according to Songfacts.

With his youthful charm and handsome appearance, Nelson used his role on his family's television series, *The Adventures of Ozzie & Harriet*, to promote his songs. Domino had no such advantage in media exposure.

"Volaré"

Songwriters: Domenico Modugno, Francesco Migliacci, Mitchell Parish

By Domenico Modugno
Peaked at number 1 on *Billboard* Hot 100
August 18, 1958
September 1, 1958
September 8, 1958
September 15, 1958
September 22, 1958

By Bobby Rydell
Peaked at number 4 on *Billboard* Hot 100
September 5, 1960

Domenico Modugno
January 9, 1928-August 6, 1994
Born Domenico Modugno in Polignano a Mare, Italy, and died Lampedusa, Italy

Bobby Rydell
April 26, 1942-April 5, 2022
Born Robert Louis Ridarelli in Philadelphia, Pennsylvania, and died in Abington Township,
Montgomery County, Pennsylvania

Domenico Modugno

Bobby Rydell

Like Ricky Nelson, Bobby Rydell was just a teenager when he scored his biggest cover version. Rydell's feat had a peculiar nature – he took a foreign language song and remade it with English lyrics. Mitchell Parish reworked the lyrics and changed the meaning of the song in the process.

Italian crooner Domenico Modugno debuted the song with Italian lyrics that described a man who dreamed he painted his hands and face blue and took flight, as if he were kidnapped by the wind. It was the first foreign language single to top the American record charts during the Rock Era.

The Rydell version is a love song, although it does mention flight. "Let's fly way up to the clouds, away from the maddening crowds," it says. "No wonder my happy heart sings. Your love has given me wings."

The original title of the song is "Nel Blu Dipinto Di Blu (Volaré)," which translates to "In The Blue Sky Painted Blue (To Fly)." For more information on the Modugno version, please see my first book, *The Coffman Collection,* Chapter 9, "It's All Greek To Me."

Rydell, labeled a "teen idol" in the 1950s, went on to have a solid recording career. His biggest chart success was "Wild One," which peaked at number 2 earlier in 1960.

The British Invasion of 1964 knocked him off the American charts, but he remained a popular nostalgia act for many years. A liver and kidney transplant recipient, he was hospitalized when he died from complications of pneumonia at the age of seventy-nine.

.... ❖ ....

"If I Had A Hammer (The Hammer Song)"
Songwriters: Pete Seeger, Lee Hays

By Peter, Paul & Mary
Peaked at number 10 on *Billboard* Hot 100
October 13, 1962

By Trini Lopez
Peaked at number 3 on *Billboard* Hot 100
September 7, 1963
September 14, 1963
September 21, 1963

Peter, Paul & Mary

Peter Yarrow (May 31, 1938-?)
Paul Stookey (December 30, 1937-?)
Mary Travers (November 9, 1936-September 16, 2009)
Formed in 1961 in New York City, New York

Trini Lopez

May 15, 1937-August 11, 2020
Born Trinidad Lopez III in Dallas, Texas, and died in Palm Springs, California

Peter Yarrow, Mary Travers, Paul Stookey

Trini Lopez

It was a protest song written in 1949, and it made a statement.

After other artists recorded their interpretations of "If I Had A Hammer," Peter, Paul & Mary finally had a mainstream hit with it in 1962.

A year later, Trini Lopez gave the "Hammer Song" a light-hearted, upbeat treatment and out-charted PPM's version.

According to Wikiwand.com, Pete Seeger and Lee Hays, the song's co-writers, first performed "Hammer" on June 3, 1949, at a testimonial dinner for the leaders of Communist Party of the United States, who had been charged with advocating the overthrow of the U.S. government.

The song's message, Seeger wrote in his autobiography, was "we have got tools, and we are going to succeed. This is what a lot of spirituals say: we will overcome. I have a hammer."

Controversy surrounded "Hammer" because, as Seeger said, "in 1949 only 'commies' used words like peace and freedom."

The first version was recorded by the folk music quartet the Weavers, of which Seeger and Hays were members.

Other artists who eventually put their stamp on the song include Sam Cooke, Martha & the Vandellas, Leonard Nimoy, Johnny Cash and Bruce Springsteen.

Lopez's version succeeded because of its peppy, stripped-down production, which includes electric guitar licks and hand claps. Percussion is heavy on cymbals, and Lopez used scat vocals here and there.

It was recorded before an audience at PJ's nightclub in Hollywood, Calif., and light applause can be heard after the conclusion.

PPM's recording was lively but received backing only from an acoustic guitar. The trio's signature harmonies shine brightly on their first major hit.

"If I had a hammer, I'd hammer in the morning," the song begins. "I'd hammer in the evening, all over this land. I'd hammer out danger, I'd hammer out a warning, I'd hammer out love between my brothers and my sisters all over this land."

The lyrics then pose the same "what if?" for a bell and a song. The conclusion states, "It's the hammer of justice, it's the bell of freedom. It's the song about love between my brothers and my sisters all over this land."

Seeger, who died in 2014, told interviewer Paul Zollo in 1988, "The way I sing it now, what I often do is joke with an audience. I point out that you can sing it the way I wrote it or the way Peter, Paul & Mary rewrote it, or half a dozen other ways, and they all harmonize with each other.

"I say, this is a good moral for the world. As a matter of fact, I'm convinced that musicians have got a more important role to play in putting a world together than they're usually given credit for. Because musicians can teach the politicians not everybody has to sing the melody."

········ ❖ ········

"Twist And Shout"

Songwriters: Bert Russell, Phil Medley

By the Isley Brothers
Peaked at number 17 on *Billboard* Hot 100
August 11, 1962

By the Beatles
Peaked at number 2 on *Billboard* Hot 100
April 4, 1964
April 11, 1964
April 18, 1964
April 25, 1964

The Isley Brothers
Ronald Isley (May 21, 1941-?) lead vocals
O'Kelly Isley (December 25, 1937-March 31, 1986) backing vocals
Rudolph Isley (April 1, 1939-?) backing vocals
Began performing together in 1954 in Blue Ash, Ohio

The Beatles

John Lennon (October 9, 1940-December 8, 1980) lead vocals, rhythm guitar George Harrison
(February 25, 1943-November 29, 2001) lead guitar, backing vocals Paul McCartney (June 18,
1942-?) bass, backing vocals
Ringo Starr (July 7, 1940-?) drums
Formed in 1960 in Liverpool, England

O'Kelly, Ronald and Rudolph Isley

Ringo Starr, Paul McCartney,
John Lennon, George Harrison

Few people can say they heard the original recording of "Twist And Shout."

That recording was done by the African American band known as the Top Notes. Their
1961 effort was so lackluster, it didn't chart on the *Billboard* Hot 100.

Then along came the Isley Brothers the following year. Trying to cash in on the
continuing popularity of the Twist dance craze, they recorded a version produced by Bert
Berns (also known as Bert Russell), who was one of the song's writers. It was a crossover
hit that went into the top 20 of the Hot 100 and peaked at number 2 on the *Billboard* Hot
Rhythm & Blues Singles.

The song had yet to reach its potential, though. The Beatles recorded it on February 11,
1963, and held it for a year before releasing it in the United States. That was a wise decision.

In the early months of 1964, every song released by the Beatles was catching fire on
the charts. "Twist And Shout" settled in for a four-week stay at number 2 on the pop chart
and was one of the five Beatles' singles that consumed the top five of the Hot 100 on April
4, 1964. "Can't Buy Me Love" kept "Twist And Shout" from being number 1.

The Beatles' version, produced by George Martin, had a slightly slower tempo than that
of the Isleys but otherwise was similar. It was not released as a single in the United Kingdom
in 1964, but in America it was released on Tollie, an affiliate label of Vee Jay Records.

78

One take was all John Lennon needed to sing his lead vocal. His passionate effort nearly shredded his vocal cords, and a second take was scrapped because Lennon had nothing left in his voice. Allmusic.com calls it "the most famous single take in rock history." It was the final take in a twelve-hour recording session, according to engineer Norman Smith. The Beatles recorded 10 songs that day.

Author Ian MacDonald quoted Lennon as saying, "You can hear that I'm just a frantic guy doing his best."

"Twist And Shout" by the Beatles finally made its debut on the U.K. Singles Chart in November 2010. It was one of several songs by the Fab Four charting in the aftermath of their availability in digital form on Apple's iTunes. It reached a peak of number 48.

After the song was included in the movie Ferris Bueller's Day Off, it charted again on the *Billboard* Hot 100, reaching number 23 on September 27, 1986.

• • • • • • ❖ • • • • • •

"Over And Over"
Songwriter: Robert Byrd

By Bobby Day
Peaked at number 41 on *Billboard* Hot 100
August 25, 1958

By the Dave Clark Five
Peaked at number 1 on *Billboard* Hot 100
December 25, 1965

Bobby Day
July 1, 1930-July 27, 1990
Born Robert James Byrd in Ft. Worth, Texas, and died in Los Angeles, California

The Dave Clark Five
Dave Clark (December 15, 1939-?) drums
Mike Smith (December 6, 1943-February 28, 2008) lead vocals, keyboards
Lenny Davidson (May 30, 1944-?) guitar
Rick Huxley (August 5, 1940-February 11, 2013) bass
Denis Payton (August 11, 1943-December 17, 2006) saxophone
Formed in 1958 in Tottenham, London, England

Bobby Day

Mike Smith, Lenny Davidson, Denis Payton,
Rick Huxley, Dave Clark

The man who wrote "Over And Over" gave the song its first life. It was issued as a B-side opposite the number 2 smash "Rock-In Robin."

In the summer of 1958, Bobby Day saw his B-side chase the A-side up the charts. "Over And Over" crested at number 41, not a bad showing for the flip side of a major hit.

Seven years later, the Dave Clark Five, one of the major bands of the British Invasion, saw something in the song they liked. They used their drum-heavy style to convert "Over And Over" into their only number 1 single in America. Oddly, the U.K. Chart had it peaking at number 45. Dave Clark himself was the producer, and he altered a few of the original lyrics.

The lyrics describe a guy going to a dance, an occurrence which was commonplace in the 1950s and '60s. He has low expectations of having a good time until he sees a certain girl.

"Won't you come over and talk to me, and be my girl?" he enquires.

But the young lady already has a boyfriend, and she aims to be true to him. "She said she was sorry, but I was a little bit late," the third verse tells us. "She would wait and wait and wait and wait for her steady date."

At that point, the DC-Five version ends. But there is yet another verse in Day's original recording. "Now, my poor heart was broken, all of my life where had she been? But I'll try over and over and over and over again." The Dave Clark Five from London never attained the same level of popularity as the Beatles, although they nearly matched the Liverpool Lads hit for hit over a span of about two years. Ed Sullivan welcomed the quintet onto his CBS-TV Sunday night show 12 times.

"We'd never been to anywhere like that," Clark told Songfacts. "We came to Kennedy Airport (in the borough of Queens), and there were 30,000 people there – they had to fly us out on a helicopter to get us into (Manhattan). That's how we hit America. It was amazing."

•••••• ❖ ••••••

"Handy Man"

Songwriters: Otis Blackwell, Jimmy Jones

By Jimmy Jones
Peaked at number 2 on *Billboard* Hot 100
February 29, 1960

By Del Shannon
Peaked at number 22 on *Billboard* Hot 100 August 22, 1964

By James Taylor
Peaked at number 4 on *Billboard* Hot 100
September 10, 1977
September 17, 1977

Jimmy Jones
June 2, 1930-August 2, 2012
Born James Jones in Birmingham, Alabama, and died in Aberdeen, North Carolina

Del Shannon
December 30, 1934-February 8, 1990
Born Charles Weedon Westover in Coopersville, Michigan, and died in Santa Clarita, California

James Taylor
Born James Vernon Taylor on March 12, 1948, in Boston, Massachusetts

Jimmy Jones

Del Shannon

James Taylor

TV host Dick Clark called it "one of the swingingest records of the day," and Jimmy Jones' rendition of "Handy Man" became one of the biggest records of 1960.

The recording featured a lot of whistling, and it swooped up the *Billboard* Hot 100 until only "Theme From A Summer Place," the top single of the year, sat above it. On *Billboard*'s year-end list, "Handy Man" was rated number 8.

The up-tempo, cheerful melody had lyrics about a guy offering to repair the damaged feelings of girls who've had bad romances. "If your broken hearts need repair, I'm the man to see," he crows. "I whisper sweet things, you tell all your friends, they'll come running to me."

This handy man, who is "not the kind who uses pencil or rule," is open around the clock. "Here is the main thing I want to say – I'm busy 24 hours a day. I fix broken hearts, I know I truly can."

Del Shannon covered "Handy Man" four years later and upped the tempo a notch. He kept the "come-a, come-a, come-a, come-on" phrasing used in Jones' version but replaced the whistling with his signature Musitron sound. The Musitron is an electric organ that was a forerunner of the synthesizer.

With the 1964 record charts rife with singles by British artists, Shannon's version still attained a respectful showing of number 22 on the Hot 100.

In 1977, James Taylor made "Handy Man" the lead single from his successful album *JT*. The single and the album both peaked at number 4 on their respective *Billboard* charts.

With Taylor on acoustic guitar, his version slowed to a sleep-inducing crawl. Whereas the Jones version clocked in a 1 minute 58 seconds and the Shannon version at 2:11, Taylor took 3:17 to get through the song.

Background harmonies are prevalent, provided by Leah Kunkel and Taylor's overdubbed voice.

The Taylor version hit number 1 on the *Billboard* Adult Contemporary and the Canadian pop charts.

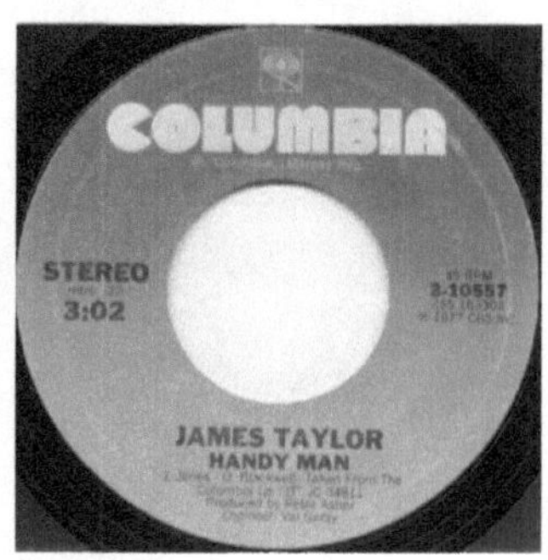

••••••• ❖ •••••••

"See See Rider"
Songwriters: Ma Rainey, Lena Arant

By Chuck Willis
Peaked at number 12 on *Billboard* Top 100
July 15, 1957

By LaVern Baker
Peaked at number 34 on *Billboard* Hot 100
January 19, 1963

By Eric Burdon & the Animals
Peaked at number 10 on *Billboard* Hot 100
October 22, 1966
October 29, 1966

Chuck Willis
January 31, 1926-April 10, 1958
Born Harold Willis in Atlanta, Georgia, and died in Chicago, Illinois

LaVern Baker
November 11, 1929-March 10, 1997
Born Delores LaVern Evans in Chicago, Illinois, and died in Queens, New York

Eric Burdon & the Animals
Eric Burdon (May 11, 1941-?) lead vocals
Alan Price (April 19, 1942-?) organ
Hilton Valentine (May 21, 1943-January 29, 2021) guitar
Bryan "Chas" Chandler (December 18, 1938-July 17, 1996) bass
John Steel (February 4, 1941-?) drums
Formed in 1962 in Newcastle upon Tyne, England

Chuck Willis

LaVern Baker

John Steel, Alan Price, Eric Burdon,
Chas Chandler, Hilton Valentine

Like the Rolling Stones, the Animals were a British band that loved American blues music. In "See See Rider," they found a song that fit right in with the kind of material that defined their repertoire.

The Animals were the third act to score a big hit with the song in the Rock Era.

The tune goes back to 1924, when vaudeville star Gertrude "Ma" Rainey first recorded it. The lyrics paint a picture of a person, who could be female or male, who has an unfaithful lover. Back in the day, this type of cheat was known as an "easy rider," and word play resulted in the similarly sounding "See See Rider."

Chuck Willis's version in the 1950s was true to the song's blues pedigree with a slow tempo. It is embellished with xylophone on the intro and a lot of saxophone. In the next decade, LaVern Baker sped up the tempo and kept in the sax.

Eric Burdon & the Animals seemed to find the right formula for Rock & Roll audiences, and they had the biggest chart success. They kept the tempo fast and replaced the sax with a driving organ riff from Alan Price.

Each artist tweaked the lyrics to put their personal stamp on "See See Rider." Baker's version, for example, has her going out to buy a shotgun "as long as I am tall," which she says she will use on her cheating man. This threat does not appear in the Willis or Animals version.

A consensus of the bridge goes something like this: "See See Rider, I love you, yes I do. And there isn't one thing darlin' I would not do for you. You know I want you, See See, I need you by my side. See See Rider, keep me satisfied."

Dozens of artists have covered the song over the years. Elvis Presley was not one of them, but he used the song in many of his concert performances. Most famously, Presley sang it in his *Aloha From Hawaii* television special, which was broadcast via satellite January 14, 1973.

.... ❖ ....

"Barbara Ann"
Songwriter: Fred Fassert

By the Regents
Peaked at number 13 on *Billboard* Hot 100
June 12, 1961
June 19, 1961

By the Beach Boys
Peaked at number 2 on *Billboard* Hot 100
January 29, 1966
February 5, 1966

The Regents
Guy Villari (August 11, 1942-September 21, 2017) lead vocalist
Sal Cuomo (1939-2013) first tenor
Chuck Fassert (bio unavailable) second tenor
Tony Gravagna (bio unavailable) bass
Ron Hunerberg (1941-2017) drums
Formed in 1958 in the Bronx, New York

The Beach Boys
Brian Wilson (June 20, 1942-?) bass, lead vocals with guest Dean Torrence
Carl Wilson (December 21, 1946-February 6, 1998) guitar, backing vocals
Dennis Wilson (December 4, 1944-December 28, 1983) drums
Mike Love (March 15, 1941-?) backing vocals
Al Jardine (September 3, 1942-?) guitar, backing vocals
Formed in 1961 in Hawthorne, California

The Regents: Guy Villari, Tony Gravagna, Chuck Fassert,
Sal Cuomo, Ron Hunerberg

The Beach Boys: Dennis Wilson, Brian Wilson,
Mike Love, Al Jardine, Carl Wilson

As good a song as it was in its day, "Barbara-Ann" by the Regents would have gone into the history books as a forgotten doo-wop song if it hadn't been for the Beach Boys.

The Beach Boys recorded the song for their 1965 album *Beach Boys' Party!* And the track sounds as if a party is going on in the recording studio, with off-the-cuff comments and adlibs audible on the single. Other songs on the album had chatter from friends and family dubbed in later to convey the party effect.

Guy Villari did a falsetto lead vocal on the original. Brian Wilson and in-studio guest Dean Torrence of Jan & Dean used some of that technique on the Beach Boys' version.

Songwriter Fred Fassert, brother of Regent Chuck Fassert, used the name of their sister, Barbara Ann Fassert, in the title.

The Regents recorded the original in 1958, during the heyday of the Doo-wop Era. It was released three years later when the band was under contract to Gee Records.

The Beach Boys were coming off their album titled *Summer Days (And Summer Nights!!)* when they went to work on the "Party" album in September 1965. With "California Girls" highlighting a new sophistication of the band, they had a mind to stick with serious music. Capitol Records requested an album for the Christmas shopping season, so they did the "Party" songs before going to work on their highly acclaimed "Pet Sounds" album.

Music professor Daniel Harrison of Yale University commented, "Party was an exercise in minimalistic production. The performances seem unrehearsed, the instrumental support is minimal (acoustical guitar, bongo drums, tambourine), and fooling around (laughing, affected singing, background conversation) pervades every track."

Al Coury, vice president of Capitol Records, rushed "Barbara Ann" to market without telling the Beach Boys. In just its fifth week on the *Billboard* Hot 100, it was in its first week at number 2.

The Beach Boys' version hit number 1 in Austria, Norway and Switzerland.

•••••••• ❖ ••••••••

"Dedicated To The One I Love"
Songwriters: Lowman Pauling, Ralph Bass

By The Shirelles
Peaked at number 3 on *Billboard* Hot 100
March 27, 1961
April 10, 1961

By The Mamas & the Papas
Peaked at number 2 on *Billboard* Hot 100
March 25, 1967
April 1, 1967
April 8, 1967

The Shirelles
Shirley Owens (June 10, 1941-?)
Beverly Lee (Aug. 3, 1941-?)
Addie "Micki" Harris (January 22, 1940-June 10, 1982)
Doris Coley (August 2, 1941-February 4, 2000)
Formed as the Poquellos in 1957 in Passaic, New Jersey

The Mamas & the Papas
Michelle Phillips (June 4, 1944-?)
John Phillips (August 30, 1935-March 18, 2001)
Denny Doherty (November 29, 1940-January 19, 2007)
Cass Eliot (September 19, 1941-July 29, 1974)
Formed in 1965 in Los Angeles, California

Shirelles: Micki Harris, Shirley Owens,
Doris Coley, Beverly Lee

Mamas/Papas: Denny Doherty,
John Philips, Michelle Philips, Cass Eliot

Thanks to the minimal exposure the "5" Royales gave to "Dedicated To The One I Love," the song became highly successful for two other vocal groups.

On February 13, 1961, the original version of the song hit a peak of number 81 on the *Billboard* Hot 100. Ironically, that was a week after the Shirelles ended a two-week stay at number 1 with "Will You Love Me Tomorrow."

The Shirelles made the song their next single and rode it up to number 3. Oddly, the girl group from New Jersey had released the song in 1959 with disappointing results (number 83). Apparently the quartet's newly acquired fame inspired record buyers to give their version another try.

Doris Coley sang the lead vocal for the Shirelles, instead of group leader Shirley Owens.

Fast forward to 1967. The red-hot Mamas & the Papas chose "Dedicated" as their sixth single and nearly made it their second number 1. Michelle Phillips sang lead vocals for the first time on an M&P single.

Only "Happy Together" by the Turtles kept "Dedicated" from topping the Hot 100.

One of the factors that made the song a success for the Mamas & the Papas was their stunning four-part harmony. But Michelle Phillips played a key role with her silky solo vocal on the first verse. Lou Adler filled his customary role as producer.

"Each night before you go to bed, my baby, whisper a little prayer for me, my baby," the romantic lyrics say. "And tell all the stars above this is dedicated to the one I love."

•••••• ❖ ••••••

"Respect"
Songwriter: Otis Redding

By Otis Redding
Peaked at number 35 on *Billboard* Hot 100
November 6, 1965

By Aretha Franklin
Peaked at number 1 on *Billboard* Hot 100
June 3, 1967
June 10, 1967

Otis Redding
September 9, 1941-December 10, 1967
Born Otis Ray Redding Jr. in Dawson, Georgia, and died near Madison, Wisconsin

Aretha Franklin
March 25, 1942-August 16, 2018
Born Aretha Louise Franklin in Memphis, Tennessee, and died in Detroit, Michigan

Otis Redding

Aretha Franklin

When Aretha Franklin covered "Respect," which originally was recorded by the man who wrote it, she made Otis Redding's song her own.

Many music fans may not even have heard Redding's version, since mainstream pop radio stations did not give it much exposure.

Redding wrote the song from a man's perspective but Franklin, with help from producer Jerry Wexler, turned the tone of the song into a strong woman's statement.

In the original version, Redding sings, "You can do me wrong, honey, if you want to. But only do me wrong, honey, while I'm gone. All I'm asking is give it, give it when I get home."

Franklin's rendition declares, "I ain't gonna do you wrong while you're gone. Ain't gonna do you wrong 'cause I don't wanna. All I'm asking is for a little respect when you come home."

Franklin recorded the song during a week of sessions in New York City after she had switched labels to Atlantic from Columbia. "We just did it by the seat of our trousers," recording engineer Tom Dowd told *The Record Producers*. "She'd sit down at the piano, play a song … we were doing Aretha in gospel/blues tradition, unlike the elegant production things she had been doing at Columbia."

Aretha's sisters, Carolyn and Erma Franklin, sang backing vocals on the track. "Aretha said that she liked that song, and she started running it in, although her sister Carolyn was instrumental in the tempo aspect of it, the way they did it with the r-e-s-p-e-c-t lines," Dowd said.

Toward the end of the song, the Franklin sisters sang a rapid-fire "sock it to me, sock it to me, sock it to me, sock it to me" line. Aretha explained in a 1999 interview with radio station WHYY, "Some of the girls were saying that to the fellas, like 'sock it to me' in this way or 'sock it to me' in that way. It's not sexual. It was nonsexual, just a cliché line."

Another difference in lyrics sees Redding singing, "Hey, little girl, you're so sweeter than honey. And I wanna give you all of my money. But all I want you to do is give it, give it, give it when I come home."

Franklin's version is, "Ooh, your kisses, sweeter than honey. And guess what? So is my money. All I want you to do for me is give it to me when you get home."

With the exception of his posthumous number 1 single, "Dock Of The Bay," Redding's songs were peaking in the 20s and 30s of the pop chart in 1965-67. But "Respect" threw Franklin's career into overdrive. She reached the top 40 of the *Billboard* Hot 100 twenty-nine more times in the 1960s and 1970s.

On the *Billboard* Hot Rhythm & Blues Singles chart, Redding's "Respect" peaked at number 4, and Franklin's hit number 1.

A film chronicling the first three decades of Franklin's life, Respect, was released in 2021. Jennifer Hudson played the role of Aretha.

Franklin died at the age of seventy-six of a malignant pancreatic neuroendocrine tumor.

• • • • • • • ❖ • • • • • • •

"I Heard It Through The Grapevine"
Songwriters: Norman Whitfield, Barrett Strong

By Gladys Knight & the Pips
Peaked at number 2 on *Billboard* Hot 100
December 16, 1967
December 23, 1967
December 30, 1967

By Marvin Gaye
Peaked at number 1 on *Billboard* Hot 100
December 14, 1968
December 21, 1968
December 28, 1968
January 4, 1969
January 11, 1969
January 18, 1969
January 25, 1969

Gladys Knight & the Pips
Gladys Knight (May 28, 1944-?) lead vocals
Merald "Bubba" Knight (September 4, 1942-?) backing vocals
William Guest (July 2, 1941-December 24, 2015) backing vocals
Edward Patten (August 27, 1939-February 25, 2005) backing vocals
Formed in 1952 in Atlanta, Georgia

Marvin Gaye
April 2, 1939-April 1, 1984
Born Marvin Pentz Gay Jr. in Washington, DC, and died in Los Angeles, California

The Pips: (clockwise) William Guest,
Edward Patten, Bubba Knight,
Gladys Knight

Marvin Gaye

90

If music fans thought the Gladys Knight & the Pips version of "I Heard It Through The Grapevine" was a big hit, they had to wait only a year to find out Marvin Gaye could make it even bigger.

Neither version was the first, though. That distinction goes to Smokey Robinson & the Miracles. But Motown Records released their recording only as an album track. The Isley Brothers recorded a rendition that was never released.

For about twelve years, Gaye's version remained the biggest *Billboard* number 1 single on any of the Motown labels.

Knight's version tells the story of a woman who finds out second-hand her man is cheating and is about to dump her. The pace is quick and bouncy and is great for dancing.

Gaye's is a slower, sexier version, told from the viewpoint of a man who has a cheating lover.

According to author David Ritz, producer Norman Whitfield was influenced by the sound of Aretha Franklin's "Respect" and was determined to "out-funk" that song with Knight & the Pips on "Grapevine." The quartet worked on their vocal arrangement for several weeks before entering Studio A at Motown.

Whitefield and Barrett Strong wrote the lyrics for a man to sing, so Knight's version got altered lyrics.

In the fall of 1968, Gaye's "Grapevine" was tucked into his latest album, and the Motown executives selected "Your Unchanging Love" to be his next single.

At Chicago radio station WVON, however, disc jockey E. Rodney Jones was playing Gaye's "Grapevine" on a regular basis. The positive reception caused Motown head Berry Gordy to change his mind and issue Gaye's version as a single.

Whitfield also produced the Gaye version. He had Gaye sing the song in a note higher than Gaye normally sang, which projected a feeling of angst.

As quoted by NME.com, Gaye said, "I simply took direction, as I felt the direction he was expounding was a proper one. Had I done it myself, I would not have sung it at all like that but, you see, there are many benefits in just singing other peoples' material and taking directions.

"The job of interpreting is quite an important one because, when people are not able to express what is in their souls if there is an artist who can, then I think that is very valuable."

Both Knight's and Gaye's versions reached number 1 on the *Billboard* R&B Chart.

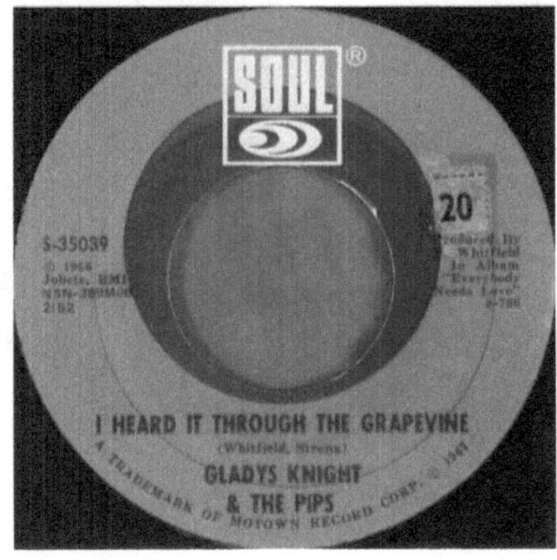

•••••• ❖ ••••••

"I'm Gonna Make You Love Me"
Songwriters: Kenny Gamble, Jerry Ross, Leon Huff

By Madeline Bell
Peaked at number 26 on *Billboard* Hot 100
March 23, 1968

By Diana Ross & the Supremes and the Temptations
Peaked at number 2 on *Billboard* Hot 100
January 11, 1969
January 18, 1969

Diana Ross & the Supremes
Diana Ross (March 26, 1944-?) lead vocals
Mary Wilson (March 6, 1944-February 8, 2021) backing vocals
Cindy Birdsong (December 15, 1939-?) backing vocals
Formed in 1959 as the Primettes in Detroit, Michigan

The Temptations
Eddie Kendricks (December 17, 1939-October 5, 1992) lead vocals
Otis Williams (October 30, 1941-?) backing vocals
Dennis Edwards (February 3, 1943-February 1, 2018) backing vocals
Paul Williams (July 2, 1939-August 17, 1973) backing vocals
Melvin Franklin (October 12, 1942-February 23, 1995) backing vocals
Formed in 1957 as the Primes in Detroit, Michigan

Madeline Bell

(front) Supremes: Mary Wilson, Diana Ross,
Cindy Birdsong
(rear) Temptations: Paul Williams, Melvin Franklin,
Eddie Kendricks, Otis Williams, Dennis Edwards

"I'm Gonna Make You Love Me" had humble beginnings but, by the time its third recorded version hit the stores, its fate was anything but humble.

Going back to 1966, Dee Dee Warwick gave it a shot, with her version reaching a lowly number 88 on the *Billboard* Hot 100.

In 1968, Madeline Bell had a legitimate hit with it after Dusty Springfield passed on it. She was working in England when her record made a strong move up the American charts, and she had to rush back home to promote it.

Then Motown Records brought out its big guns to give it a unique treatment later in '68.

The two biggest groups in the Motown stable joined forces to record the song together, with Eddie Kendricks (first verse) and Diana Ross (second verse) doing the lead vocals.

The Supremes were coming off their eleventh number 1 single, "Love Child," and the Temptations recently had a number 6 hit with "Cloud Nine." Together their version nearly topped the chart. An album of duets by the two groups spawned the single, which Frank Wilson and Nickolas Ashford produced.

On the *Billboard* R&B Chart, "I'm Gonna Make You Love Me" crested at number 2 for the Motown consortium.

· · · · · · ❖ · · · · · ·

"Ain't No Mountain High Enough"
Songwriters: Nickolas Ashford, Valerie Simpson
By Marvin Gaye and Tammi Terrell
Peaked at number 19 on *Billboard* Hot 100
July 15, 1967
July 22, 1967
By Diana Ross
Peaked at number 1 on *Billboard* Hot 100
September 19, 1970
September 26, 1970
October 3, 1970

Marvin Gaye and Tammi Terrell
Marvin Gaye (April 2, 1939-April 1, 1984)
Tammi Terrell (April 29, 1945-March 16, 1970)

Diana Ross
Born Diane Ernestine Earle Ross on March 26, 1944, in Detroit, Michigan

Tammi Terrell and Marvin Gaye

Diana Ross

Diana Ross was on a hot streak.

After she had her last number 1 hit with the Supremes on December 27, 1969, "Someday We'll Be Together," she left the popular Motown trio to start a solo career. It took her less than ten months to have her first solo *Billboard* number 1.

To achieve that distinction, she dipped into the Motown archives for a song Marvin Gaye and Tammi Terrell recorded in 1967, "Ain't No Mountain High Enough."

Harvey Fuqua and Johnny Bristol produced the Gaye/Terrell version, but the songwriters themselves, Nickolas Ashford and Valerie Simpson, produced Ross's recording. They had Ross do a spoken word version, with Simpson providing backing vocals.

"We thought Diana had such an interesting speaking voice," Simpson told author Fred Bronson. "We thought it was very sexy and wanted to incorporate that into the production."

While the Gaye/Terrell duet was upbeat, the Ross effort was slow and sensuous. It clocked in at six minutes eighteen seconds and built to a crescendo, with the chorus being held back until well into the song.

Motown president Berry Gordy was not happy with the arrangement of Ross's recording. "We presented it to him, and he wanted to change the whole thing around," Simpson said. "and start with the chorus and forget all the slow build and drama – just get to the point. We had to fight him on that because he really wanted to change it."

At first, radio station programmers were doing their own edits of the lengthy single. Eventually, Motown issued a single that reduced the playing time to 3:32.

Ashford, who is originally from South Carolina, got the idea for the song shortly after he moved to New York City. Determined to become successful in the competitive environment of the Big Apple, one day the phrase "ain't no mountain high enough" popped into his head. He and Simpson finished the song in short order. The songwriting pair married in 1974.

The acceptance of the Gaye/Terrell version opened the door for more Motown duets. Gaye recorded six more singles with Terrell and, in the 1970s, sang two duets with Ross. In 1980, Ross teamed with Lionel Richie on "Endless Love," which became Motown's biggest single.

•••••• ❖ ••••••

"Gypsy Woman"
Songwriter: Curtis Mayfield

By The Impressions
Peaked at number 20 on *Billboard* Hot 100
December 4, 1961
December 11, 1961

By Brian Hyland
Peaked at number 3 on *Billboard* Hot 100
December 5, 1970
December 12, 1970

The Impressions
Curtis Mayfield (June 3, 1942-December 26, 1999)
Richard Brooks (May 13, 1940-?)
Arthur Brooks (1933-November 22, 2015)
Sam Gooden (September 2, 1939-?)
Fred Cash (October 8, 1940-?)
Formed in 1958 in Chattanooga, Tennessee

Brian Hyland
Born Brian Hyland on November 12, 1943, in Queens, New York

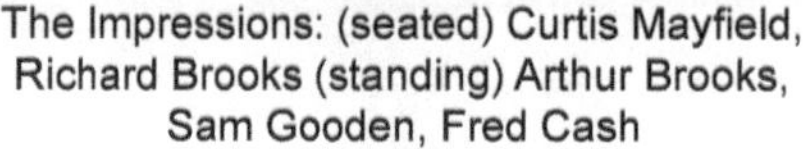

The Impressions: (seated) Curtis Mayfield,
Richard Brooks (standing) Arthur Brooks,
Sam Gooden, Fred Cash

Brian Hyland

The two versions of "Gypsy Woman" are as different as night and day. Yet, both are great recordings.

The Impressions' original version, written by the group's lead singer Curtis Mayfield, has a tinge of rhythm & blues. The production is minimal, with a bit of percussion from castanets and tambourine. The members' five voices fill out the sound adequately.

The story of the song is delivered by a narrator who is traveling with a gypsy caravan. When the travelers stop for the night, he watches enchantedly as one of the women dances around the campfire.

He observes "a lovely woman in motion, with hair as dark as night. Her eyes were like that of a cat in the dark, that hypnotized me with love."

In the second verse, his passion rises. "She danced around and round to a guitar melody. From the fire her face was all aglow, how she enchanted me. Oh, how I'd like to hold her near and kiss and forever whisper in her ear, 'I love you, gypsy woman.'"

The song is notable for being the first single released by the Impressions after Jerry Butler left them to go solo.

Brian Hyland, who broke onto the pop music scene at the age of 16, singing about a girl in a skimpy bikini, was an unlikely performer to cover "Gypsy Woman." But, by 1970, he was a decade older and more mature. Fortunately for him, his voice was still lithe and could hit the high notes of the song.

"Gypsy Woman" was Hyland's biggest hit since "Sealed With A Kiss" in 1962.

The producer of Hyland's version was none other than Del Shannon, who had put his singing career on the back burner. He infused the instrumentation with an electrified keyboard and a prominent drumbeat. There is even a little gypsy fiddle to enhance the mood.

The Impressions, who formed in Chattanooga, Tenn., but migrated to Chicago, Illinois, had a fine career on the R&B charts. The local pop chart in Chicago, compiled by radio station WLS, had "Gypsy Woman" peaking at number 11.

•••••• ❖ ••••••

"I Hear You Knocking"
Songwriter: Dave Bartholomew

By Gale Storm
Peaked at number 2 on *Billboard* Juke Box chart
December 10, 1955
December 17, 1955
December 24, 1955

By Fats Domino
Peaked at number 67 on *Billboard* Hot 100
December 4, 1961

By Dave Edmunds
Peaked at number 4 on *Billboard* Hot 100
February 13, 1971
February 20, 1971

Gale Storm
April 5, 1922-June 27, 2009
Born Josephine Owaissa Cottle in Bloomington, Texas, and died in Danville, California

Dave Edmunds
Born David William Edmunds on April 15, 1944, in Cardiff, Wales

Gale Storm

Dave Edmunds

When Dave Edmunds revived "I Hear You Knocking" in 1970, he gave a unique treatment to the song that was first recorded 15 years earlier.

Smiley Lewis recorded an R&B version of the song in 1955, which was not a top 40 hit. Later that year, actress/singer Gale Storm took a shot at it and made it a big hit.

Fats Domino's 1961 rendition debuted at number 67 on the *Billboard* Hot 100 but got no higher. It seemed unthinkable for the song to have another life.

Across the Atlantic in Wales, Dave Edmunds was looking for songs to put on his first album. His original plan was to record "Let's Work Together," written by Wilbert Harrison.

"When I first came to America in 1969, I heard ('Let's Work Together') on the car radio, and I thought, *Oh, this is great. When I get back home I'm going to do a cover of this,*" Edmunds told writer Carl Wiser. "By the time I got home, Canned Heat had done a cover of it. "Then an album of Smiley Lewis was released on United Artists in Britain, and they played 'I Hear You Knocking' on the radio in Britain while I was driving along. I thought, *Hang on, the two songs have an identical format. You could use the same backing track for both songs. It's just a simple 12-bar thing.* So I thought, *I'll do that.*

"Smiley Lewis's version was in 6/8 time, so I brought it into 4/4 time to make it a bit more modern for the time. I played around with it and tried several different versions, but it was sounding too ordinary. I just had drums, piano, and acoustic guitar and electric guitar going all the way through, and it didn't jump out at all.

"I put it on the shelf, then I went back to it after a few weeks. I stripped it right down and came up with what it is now."

Edmunds gave "I Hear You Knocking" a rock music treatment and made his slide guitar work the recording's signature.

During the instrumental middle part, Edmunds calls out the names of some of rock music's pioneers and influencers – Fats Domino, Smiley Lewis, Chuck Berry, Huey Smith and Bob Dylan.

The recordings by Storm and Domino, on the other hand, were piano-oriented pop versions. Storm's was stripped down, employing guitar licks instead of percussion to keep time. She had backing vocals from male singers. Domino had a saxophone dominating the instrumentation.

The Edmunds version was released in Great Britain ahead of its American release, and it spent six weeks at number 1 on the U.K. Chart.

The song is about a former lover who wants to reunite with the narrator. "You went away and left me a long time ago," the lyrics begin. "Now you're knocking on my door. I hear you knocking, but you can't come in. I hear you knocking, go back where you been."

Storm forged a successful film and television acting career in the 1950s, in addition to recording six top 40 hits.

Edmunds had been hitting the U.K. Chart since 1968. His only other major hit in America was "Slipping Away" in 1983.

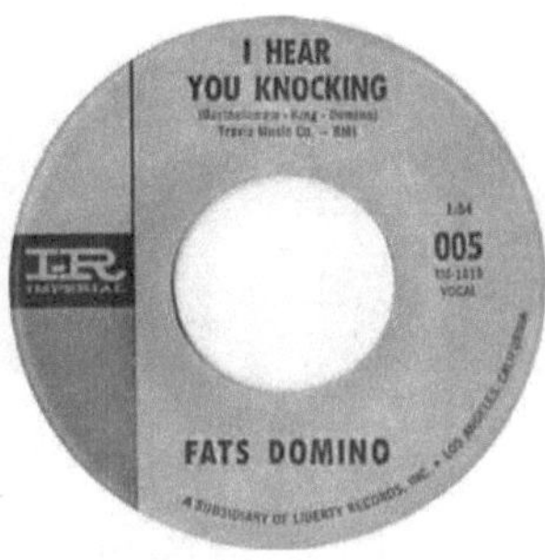

• • • • • • • ❖ • • • • • • •

"Go Away Little Girl"
Songwriters: Gerry Goffin, Carole King

By Steve Lawrence
Peaked at number 1 on *Billboard* Hot 100
Janaury 12, 1963
Janaury 19, 1963

By Donny Osmond
Peaked at number 1 on *Billboard* Hot 100
September 11, 1971
September 18, 1971
September 25, 1971

Steve Lawrence
Born Sidney Liebowitz on July 8, 1935, in Brooklyn, New York

Donny Osmond
Born Donald Clark Osmond on December 9, 1957, in Ogden, Utah

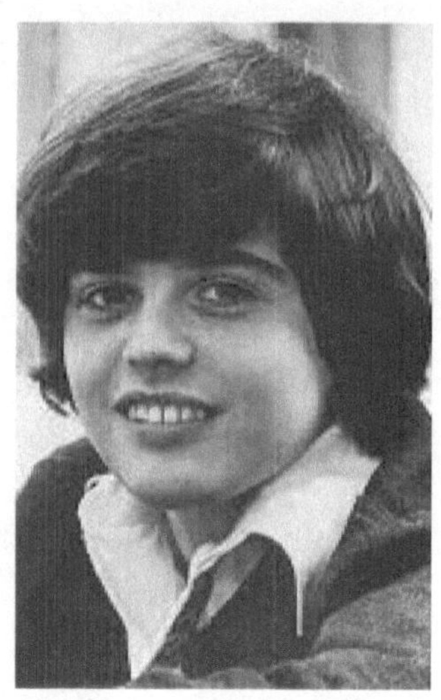

Steve Lawrence   Donny Osmond

"Go Away Little Girl" was the first song of the Rock Era since 1957 to hit number 1 by both its original artist and a cover artist.

That feat was first accomplished when Sonny James put "Young Love" on the *Billboard* charts in January 1957 and topped the Disc Jockey and Country & Western charts. A version by Tab Hunter entered the *Billboard* charts two weeks later and soon topped the Best Sellers, Disc Jockey, Juke Box and Top 100 charts.

Hunter's rendition of "Young Love" earned a *Billboard* ranking of number 4 for the year 1957 and, according to notes in *Wikipedia*, influenced the Warner Bros. Studio, where Hunter was a contract actor, to enter the music recording industry.

Steve Lawrence recorded the first version of "Go Away Little Girl," taking it to the top of the *Billboard* Hot 100 in early 1963. The song's narrator is a man who is in a committed relationship but finds himself fending off the romantic advances of a woman much younger than himself.

"I know that your lips are sweet, but our lips must never meet," he tells her. "I belong to someone else, and I must be true."

When Donny Osmond recorded the song, he was just thirteen and his voice had not yet changed. Therefore, his version had him singing, "… I'm dating somebody else, and I must be true."

It was a meteoric rise to the top for Osmond, who sang lead vocals on "One Bad Apple," a debut hit for him and his brothers that stayed at number 1 for five weeks earlier in 1971. The Osmonds barely had time to issue a second single, "Double Lovin," before Donny became a solo star.

Donny's version of "Go Away" was flying out of record stores the same time its cowriter, Carole King, was having mega-success as a solo performer. Her "It's Too Late" was a number 1 single just two months before Donny Osmond topped the Hot 100, and she had "So Far Away" on the way up the charts in the fall of '71. King's mailbox must have had some whopper royalty checks filling it that year.

Bobby Vee was the first to record the song, in March 1962. His version was not released as a single.

••••••• ❖ •••••••

"Rockin' Robin"

Songwriter: Jimmie Thomas

By Bobby Day
Peaked at number 2 on *Billboard* Hot 100
October 13, 1958
October 20, 1958

By Michael Jackson
Peaked at number 2 on *Billboard* Hot 100
April 22, 1972
April 29, 1972

Michael Jackson
August 29, 1958-June 25, 2009
Born Michael Joseph Jackson in Gary, Indiana, and died in Los Angeles, California

Michael Jackson

A profile of "Over And Over" appears earlier in this chapter. It's A-side also became a remarkable remake.

"Rock-In Robin" by Bobby Day nearly made it to number 1, and the same song (spelled "Rockin' Robin") had similar success when Michael Jackson covered it in 1972. It was the second hit single by Jackson as a solo artist after he and his brothers took the music world by storm in 1970 as the Jackson 5.

The two versions have the same basic arrangement, but a contrast appears in the voices of the two singers. Day had a rather deep voice, while the fourteen-year-old Jackson sang in a high voice.

Day's version hit number 1 on the *Billboard* Rhythm & Blues Records chart. Fourteen years later, that chart was known as the Best Selling Soul Singles chart, and Jackson's rendition peaked at number 2 there.

The lyrics talk about a spunky bird who "rocks in the treetops all day long, hopping and bopping and singing his song." Jackson's voice lent itself very well to this narrative, since it was chirpy and squeaky.

"A pretty little raven at the bird bandstand taught him how to do the bop, it was grand," the bridge relates. "They started going steady and, bless my soul, he out-bopped the buzzard and the oriole."

Not surprisingly, "Rockin' Robin" was featured in an episode of television's *The Muppet Show* in 1980, when the show's band, the Electric Mayhem, performed the song in a tree.

Jackson died at his home in Los Angeles from acute propofol poisoning. He took the drug nightly, under a doctor's supervision, to treat pain resulting from burns he suffered in the 1980s.

"Rockin' Pneumonia and the Boogie Woogie Flu"
Songwriters: Huey Smith, Johnny Vincent

By Huey Smith & the Clowns
Peaked at number 52 on *Billboard* Top 100
1957

By Johnny Rivers
Peaked at number 6 on *Billboard* Hot 100
Janaury 20, 1973

Huey "Piano" Smith
Janaury 26, 1934-February 13, 2023
Born Huey Pierce Smith in New Orleans, Louisiana., and died in Baton Rouge, Louisiana

Johnny Rivers
Born John Henry Ramistella on November 7, 1942, in New York City, New York

Huey Smith

Johnny Rivers

Although he was born in New York City, Johnny Rivers moved with family to Baton Rouge, Louisiana, at an early age. There he received exposure to the Louisiana music style.

That influence was never more evident than when he recorded "Rockin' Pneumonia and the Boogie Woogie Flu" in 1972. His version of the 1950s song eclipsed the popularity of the Huey "Piano" Smith original.

Rivers' remake features an upgraded vocal while it keeps a piano accompaniment, played by Larry Knechtel in the style of Smith. The feel is faithful to the '50s boogie woogie. The Rivers rendition has handclaps and backing vocals.

There is a great piano solo on the instrumental middle part, and Rivers added a great rock guitar solo on the outro.

While Rivers' career had been in decline for several years, "Rockin' Pneumonia" gave it a shot in the arm and became a million seller by the end of January 1973.

The lyrics are about an imaginary affliction brought about by boogie woogie music. This prevents the narrator from approaching a woman in a nightclub. "Rocking pneumonia" is a play on words with "walking pneumonia." The Asian flu was prevalent in the United States around the time the song was written.

"I wanna jump, but I'm afraid I'll fall," the first verse begins. "I wanna holler, but the joint's too small. Young man rhythm's got a hold of me, too, I got the rocking pneumonia and the boogie woogie flu."

A native Louisianan, Smith pioneered the boogie woogie sound and became an early influencer in the Rock Era. The Rhythm and Blues Foundation honored him with a Pioneer Award in 2000.

••••••• ❖ •••••••

"Hooked On A Feeling"

Songwriter: Mark James

By B.J. Thomas
Peaked at number 5 on *Billboard* Hot 100
January 11, 1969
January 18, 1969

By Blue Swede
Peaked at number 1 on *Billboard* Hot 100
April 6, 1974

B.J. Thomas
August 7, 1942-May 29, 2021
Born Billy Joe Thomas in Hugo, Oklahoma, and died in Arlington, Texas

Blue Swede
Björn Skifs (April 20, 1947-?) lead vocals
Anders Berglund (July 21, 1948-?) piano
Bosse Liljedahl (bio unavailable) bass
Hinke Ekestubbe (April 14, 1945-?) saxophone
Tommy Berglund (bio unavailable) trumpet
Michael Areklew (1950-?) guitar
Jan Guldbäck (bio unavailable) drums
Formed in 1973 in Stockholm, Sweden

B.J. Thomas

Blue Swede

All I remember is a feeling of total revulsion smote me, like a punch in the face. That's the way I felt the first time I heard Blue Swede's cover version of "Hooked On A Feeling."

How could anyone take a beautiful love song that was sung so well by B.J. Thomas and turn it into a series of ooga chakas? I wondered. The arrangement of the new version was so different from the original, it didn't seem like the same piece of music.

The record-buying public saw the remake quite differently, though, and the second coming of "Hooked On A Feeling" became the first release by a Swedish band to hit number 1 in the U.S.

Texan Thomas recorded his version in 1968 in Memphis, Tenn., with a rich vocal taking the song into the pop top five. It was one of the first recordings to feature an electric sitar.

Blue Swede, whose Swedish name translates into "Blue Denim," used an arrangement similar to that of British singer/songwriter/producer Jonathan King in 1971. King said in an interview that he was not inspired by any other recording. "I just wanted different instruments to make a reggae rhythm and decided on male voices," he said.

According to Wikilivre.org, the Jamaican reggae band the Twinkle Brothers inspired Blue Swede's arrangement.

King admitted to the *Toronto Star* that the *ooga chaka* chant sounded like "six guys grunting like gorillas."

Mark James, who wrote "Hooked On A Feeling," told author Roben Jones he had thoughts of his romantic feelings for his childhood sweetheart when he wrote the song. James married that girl, and they were still together well into the 21st century.

"This is a fun record, and it's well made," James said of the Blue Swede effort in an interview with Spin.com. "It's a hit."

Blue Swede made another significant change to the song by altering some lyrics to get around a possible reference to drug usage. Instead of "I got it bad for you, babe, but I don't need a cure. I'll just stay addicted if I can endure," they sang "I got a bug from you, girl, but I don't need no cure. I'll just stay a victim if I can for sure."

One more remake by Blue Swede, "Never My Love," got the band back into the *Billboard* top 10. Then they broke up after lead singer Björn Skifs started a solo career.

"The Loco-Motion"

Songwriters: Gerry Goffin, Carole King

By Little Eva
Peaked at number 1 on *Billboard* Hot 100
August 25, 1962

By Grand Funk
Peaked at number 1 on *Billboard* Hot 100
May 4, 1974
May 11, 1974

By Kylie Minogue
Peaked at number 3 on *Billboard* Hot 100
November 12, 1988
November 19, 1988

Little Eva
June 29, 1943-April 10, 2003
Born Eva Narcissus Boyd in Belhaven, North Carolina, and died in Kinston, North
Carolina

Grand Funk
Don Brewer (September 3, 1948-) drums, backing vocals
Mark Farner (September 29, 1948-) guitar, lead vocals
Mel Schacher (April 8, 1951-) bass, backing vocals
Craig Frost (April 20, 1948-) keyboards, backing vocals
Formed in 1968 in Flint, Michigan

Kylie Minogue
Born Kylie Ann Minogue on May 28, 1968, in Melbourne, Victoria, Australia

Little Eva

Grand Funk

Kylie Minogue

Few songs have enjoyed the long life and success of "The Loco-Motion," which was
a force on the charts for three different acts in three different decades.

It started out as a vehicle for New York City songwriters Carole King and Gerry Goffin
to record their babysitter, Eva Boyd. They couldn't have imagined in 1962 how a hard rock
band would give it another life in the 1970s.

For more information on the Little Eva original, see my second book, Radio Stations & Record Stores, Chapter 9, "Dance Fever." *Billboard* ranked the Little Eva original as the number 7 single of '62.

Singer/songwriter Todd Rundgren produced the cover version by Grand Funk. He gave it a treatment that reflected the passage of 12 years' time.

Drummer Don Brewer told Songfacts, "The idea of 'Loco-Motion' came when we were working on the 'Shinin' On' album in the studio with Todd. We basically finished the album – 'Shinin' On' was going to be the first single, and we were thinking about what we were going to do for another song.

"Mark (Farner) came in one day and off the top of his head was singing, 'Everybody's doing a brand new dance now,' just for fun. And we all went, 'Yeah, Grand Funk doing the Loco-Motion.' It was a tongue-in-cheek kind of thing, and we said, 'Let's try it, let's do it.'

"So, we sent off to New York, got the lyrics, and Todd had the idea of doing the song kind of like the Beach Boys' 'Barbara Ann,' where it sounded like a big party going on, except Todd could really crank up everything with the hand claps and all that stuff. "It just had this huge sound to it. It sounded like a big party."

Rundgren worked with the band on its previous album, "We're An American Band," which yielded a number 1 single by the same name.

Regarding Grand Funk recording cover songs, Brewer commented, "It was always a matter of taking a song and making it be ours. To do that, we as a band had to feel it. So, when somebody came up with the idea of doing a cover song, it was like the whole band could feel, 'Oh yeah, this feels great.' "We were really kind of a jam band in the studio, we would endlessly jam on stuff."

As a four-member group, Grand Funk adorned their version of "The Loco-Motion' with layered vocal harmonies.

Goffin remarked to *Rolling Stone Magazine*, "It's like a nice gift. It is kind of weird hearing it done in a different way, but you can still hear how it appeals to the kids."

The Michigan rockers began their career as Grand Funk Railroad (a word play on the automobile-transporting Grand Trunk Railroad). The musicians had to alter their name after they split with manager Terry Knight, who claimed he owned the name.

Under the title "Locomotion," Kylie Minogue released the song in July 1987 as her first single. It received a warm reception in her native Australia, and it earned her a record deal with PWL in London, England.

In 1988, it became Minogue's second release in America as a re-recorded and retitled single. It became her biggest hit on the *Billboard* charts, and it also gained top five status on the U.K. and Canadian charts.

•••••• ✦ ••••••

"Breaking Up Is Hard To Do"
Songwriters: Neil Sedaka, Howard Greenfield

By Neil Sedaka (1962)
Peaked at number 1 on *Billboard* Hot 100
August 11, 1962
August 18, 1962

By Neil Sedaka (1975)
Peaked at number 8 on *Billboard* Hot 100
February 21, 1976

Neil Sedaka
Born Neil Sedaka on March 13, 1939, in Brooklyn, New York

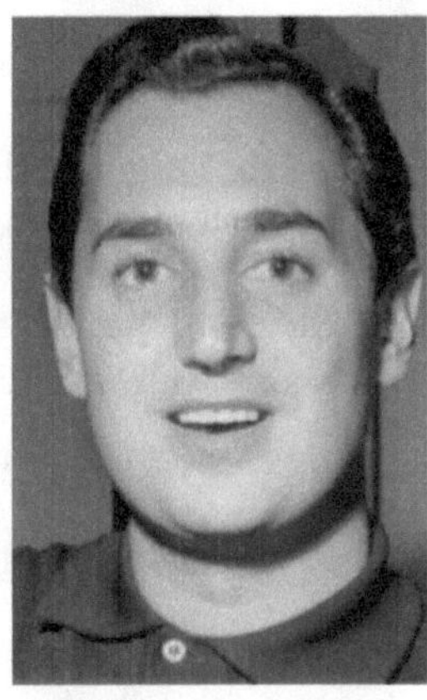

Neil Sedaka (1962)   Neil Sedaka (1976)

As part of his phenomenal, triumphant return to the American record charts in the mid-1970s, Neil Sedaka accomplished an improbable feat when he reworked and re-recorded his own 1962 number 1 song. He took "Breaking Up Is Hard To Do" into the top 10 of the *Billboard* Hot 100 in 1976.

As collateral damage of the British Invasion, Sedaka disappeared from the top 40 after Dec. 28, 1963. Sedaka's reaction from the stage of the Royal Albert Hall during a show was: "The Beatles – not good!"

For several years he wrote songs that became hits for other artists, but his own recordings failed to find favor in his home country. So, he went to Australia and England, where his music was welcomed and where he forged an alliance with emerging star Elton John. When he learned Sedaka did not have a record deal, John suggested he sign with his label, Rocket Records.

No quitter, Sedaka returned to the United States. His album "Sedaka's Back" was released in 1974 along with the single "Laughter In The Rain."

"So, the basic plan," John said in Story of a Pop Special, "was as simple as finding out what he wanted to have on his album – which turned out to be a compilation from his British albums. It had been like Elvis coming up and giving us the chance to release his records. We couldn't believe our luck."

"Laughter In The Rain" became a number 1 smash in early 1975, and Sedaka began to put together another album. As a nod to the hard times he endured over the previous decade, he titled it *"The Hungry Years."*

In addition to the number 1 single "Bad Blood," featuring backing vocals by Elton John, one of the tracks on the new LP was the recrafted version of "Breaking Up Is Hard To Do."

The recording begins with the intro of the original, followed by Sedaka singing, "You tell me that you're leaving, I can't believe it's true. Girl, there's just no living without you." Then Sedaka goes into the original lyrics with a pace substantially slower than the original.

Sedaka had slowed the song to the tempo of a torch ballad for Lenny Welch in 1970, and he gave the same treatment to his own remake. It sounded like it could be delivered by a lounge act at a local Holiday Inn, but it won over a new generation of Sedaka fans and topped the *Billboard* Adult Contemporary chart.

The new version spent fourteen weeks on the *Billboard* Hot 100.

Missing from the remake are the trademark "comma down dooby doo down down" phrasing and the overdubbed lead vocal, a recording technique Sedaka used extensively in the 1960s. The remake has no backing vocals.

According to Songfacts, "It Will Stand" by the Showmen, a moderate hit in early 1962, inspired Sedaka to compose "Breaking Up Is Hard To Do."

In the song's lyrics, Sedaka notes, "If you go, then I'll be blue." Also, "think of all that we've been through. Don't say that this is the end. Instead of breaking up I wish that we were making up again."

Sedaka enjoyed his comeback success through the rest of the 1970s. As of this writing, he hosted a satellite radio program on the '50s channel of Sirius/XM, "In The Key Of Neil."

· · · · · · · ❖ · · · · · · ·

"Blue Bayou"

Songwriters: Roy Orbison, Joe Melson
By Roy Orbison
Peaked at number 29 on *Billboard* Hot 100
October 19, 1963

By Linda Ronstadt
Peaked at number 3 on *Billboard* Hot 100
December 17, 1977
December 24, 1977
December 31, 1977
January 7, 1978

Roy Orbison
April 23, 1936-December 6, 1988
Born Roy Kelton Orbison in Vernon, Texas, and died in Hendersonville, Tennessee

Linda Ronstadt
Born Linda Maria Ronstadt on July 15, 1946, in Tucson, Arizona

Roy Orbison   Linda Ronstadt

Roy Orbison cowrote and sang the original "Blue Bayou" and did a fine job on it. But 14 years after his recording became a modest hit, Linda Ronstadt came along with her cover and made listeners forget Orbison ever sang it.

Ronstadt's interpretation of the song was so popular, it got in the way of her follow-up hit, "It's So Easy." Both songs were in the top five of the *Billboard* Hot 100 at the same time for four weeks.

While the Orbison original roamed the charts in the fall of 1963 as the B-side to "Mean Woman Blues," he had recorded it in November 1961. Both it and "Mean Woman Blues" ascended to number 3 on the U.K. chart.

With Don Henley of the Eagles singing backing vocals, Linda Ronstadt's version became her first million-selling single. It peaked at number 2 on the *Billboard* Country Singles chart and number 3 on the Easy Listening chart.

Her amazing voice went from soft and silky on the verses to strong and powerful on the chorus.

The song begins, "I feel so bad, I got a worried mind. I'm so lonesome all the time since I left my baby behind on Blue Bayou. Saving nickels, saving dimes, working till the sun don't shine. Looking forward to happier times on Blue Bayou."

As Ronstadt walked a fence that bordered country music and rock in the 1970s, she made fans on both sides. "Blue Bayou" became a great example of her appeal to multiple audiences. Peter Asher, who worked with Ronstadt for years, produced it.

"J.D. (Southern) and Glenn (Frey) simultaneously suggested (the song) to me, sorta like Twiddle Dee and Twiddle Dum," Ronstadt told Circus Magazine. "We sat up all night talking like mice at incredible speeds, playing and singing half the song we knew, all of us singing in different keys. I've got a tape of it, and it's the fastest tape I've ever heard. It sounds like R2D2."

The Ronstadt single eventually was certified platinum, with sales of over two million.

The song is so identified with Ronstadt that former baseball commentator Dave Campbell referred to a blazing fastball as a "Linda Ronstadt pitch," saying it "blew by you."

Orbison, who died of a heart attack at 52, once spoke with *NME Magazine* about the themes in his music. "Take a song like 'Blue Bayou,' for instance," he said. "That's simply a song about being on the road. And that is really a happy song. "It probably sounds very strange to you for me to say that. The fellow's bound and determined to get back to where you sleep all day, and the catfish play, and the sailing boats and the girls and all that stuff. It's a beautiful thought. Now, granted, it is a sad song, a lonely song, but it's a loneliness that precedes happiness. And I'm not sitting here trying to tell you that I don't sing lonely songs or anything like that."

Ironically, the two versions were placed on albums with similar names. Orbison's album was titled "In Dreams," and Ronstadt's was "Simple Dreams."

• • • • • • • ❖ • • • • • • •

"Venus"
Songwriter: Robbie van Leeuwen

By the Shocking Blue
Peaked at number 1 on *Billboard* Hot 100
February 7, 1970

By Bananarama
Peaked at number 1 on *Billboard* Hot 100
September 6, 1986

The Shocking Blue
Mariska Veres (October 1, 1947-December 2, 2006) lead vocals
Robbie van Leeuwen (October 29, 1944-?) guitar
Klaasje van der Wal (February 1, 1949-February 12, 2018) bass
Cor van der Beek (June 9, 1949-April 2, 1998) drums
Formed in 1967 in The Hague, Netherlands

Bananarama
Sara Dallin (December 17, 1961-?)
Keren Woodward (April 2, 1961-?)
Siobhan Fahey (September 10, 1958-?)
Formed in 1980 in London, England

The Shocking Blue

Bananarama: Siobhan Fahey,
Sara Dallin, Keren Woodward

The Shocking Blue became the first Dutch act to have a number 1 hit on the *Billboard* Hot 100 when they rode "Venus" to the top. The leader of the band, Robbie van Leeuwen, wrote the song, which is not the same "Venus" popularized by Frankie Avalon in 1959.

Another foreign act, the girl group Bananarama, also scored a number 1 smash with the song more than 16 years later.

The Shocking Blue original did not even hit number 1 in the band's home country, where it stalled at number 3 in the summer of 1969, according to author Fred Bronson. It did top charts in Belgium, Italy, France, Spain and Germany.

"Venus" came to the United States after producer Jerry Ross (see "I'm Gonna Make You Love Me" earlier in this chapter) bought the rights to it and two other songs from the Netherlands. He released it on his Colossus label.

Vocal trio Bananarama had rehearsed "Venus" ever since their formation in 1980. "When we first got together … and were rehearsing in a basement, we were trying out various old songs," Siobhan Fahey said in a radio interview. "That was one of the songs we used to sing, and it always sounded great. But we wouldn't record it for years because we wanted to do our own songs … so that people would take us seriously.

"But then we stopped worrying about whether people took us seriously … we just thought it's a great song, let's do it. And it proved to be a good idea."

The trio had to wait until 1984 to have their first hit in America, which was "Cruel Summer," a song that got a boost from inclusion in the film *The Karate Kid.*

The British production team of Stock, Aitken, Waterman gave the song an arrangement similar to the original, but they boosted the pace with an up-tempo electronic dance beat. The song topped charts in Australia, Finland, New Zealand, Switzerland and South Africa.

"We changed Bananarama," producer Pete Waterman told Record Mirror in 1986. "They were a bit dowdy and a bit of a joke. Now, they're so sexual, it's unbelievable. They've grown up into the '80s very well. I love working with them. Bananarama are my Supremes.

It is hard to say just how the three young women picked their name, since Fahey had two differing explanations in separate interviews. In one, she told Jon Young, "We just wanted a silly name that expressed enjoyment and light-heartedness. Our first single was sung in Swahili, so we thought of something tropical – bananas – and added 'rama' because it sounded silly.

Fahey said in another interview the name was an adaptation of the Roxy Music song "Pyjamarama."

•••••• ❖ ••••••

"I Think We're Alone Now"
Songwriter: Ritchie Cordell

By Tommy James & the Shondells
Peaked at number 4 on *Billboard* Hot 100
April 22, 1967

By Tiffany
Peaked at number 1 on *Billboard* Hot 100
November 7, 1987 November 14, 1987

Tommy James & the Shondells
Tommy James (April 29, 1947-?) lead vocals
Eddie Gray (February 27, 1948-?) guitar, backing vocals
Mike Vale (July 17, 1949-?) bass, backing vocals
Ron Rosman (February 28, 1945-?) keyboards
Pete Lucia (February 2, 1947-January 6, 1997) drums
Formed as the Echoes in 1959 in Niles, Michigan

Tiffany
Born Tiffany Renee Darwish on October 2, 1971, in Norwalk, California

Tommy James (center) & the Shondells   Tiffany

Twenty years can make a lot of difference in the music industry.

The same song recorded by a popular five-man rock band that became a hit in 1967 was remade by a fifteen-year-old girl in 1987, and the cover version actually out-performed the original on the charts.

Tommy James & the Shondells, on the way to a stellar chart career with three top 40 hits under their belt, recorded "I Think We're Alone Now" on December 24, 1966, and watched it glide up and down the *Billboard* Hot 100 for seventeen weeks. It crested on its 11th week on the chart.

The song's lyrics caused a bit of a firestorm. The term "culture war" didn't exist in 1967, but one broke out as the song gained favor with a teen audience. The lyrics are about a young guy and girl who want to be alone together to enjoy each other's company and express their love for one another. The teens are cautioned by "they" (presumably their parents) to "behave" and "watch how you play."

The letters-to-the-editor page of the Chicago Daily News turned into a battleground for several weeks, as adults criticized the song for promoting teen sex. Teens defended the song for its beautiful portrayal of normal, innocent adolescent affection.

Commentary flew back and forth for a month or two before the newspaper pulled the plug on the subject. Teenaged respondents in favor of the song's lyrics far outnumbered the adults who were against them.

The Shondells' version was number 1 for five weeks on the Chicago WLS radio station chart, the *Silver Dollar Survey.*

With the recording of "I Think We're Alone Now," James claims in his autobiography, "I put on a nasally, almost juvenile-sounding lead vocal, and without realizing it, we invented bubblegum music."

According to notes in *Wikipedia,* only James and guitarist Eddie Gray played on the track. Studio musicians who filled out the lineup were Artie Butler on electric keyboard, Al Gorgoni on guitar, Joe Macho on bass, Paul Griffin on piano and Bobby Gregg on drums. The other Shondells provided backing vocals.

Four years after the hubbub died down, Tiffany Darwish was born in California. Her talent for singing drew attention by the time she was nine.

"When I was fifteen, someone told a producer, George Tobin, about this 'girl with a great voice,'" Tiffany told *The Guardian* in 2019. "George helped me get a record deal, and things started to roll pretty quickly.

"'I Think We're Alone Now' had been a hit for Tommy James & the Shondells in the '60s. I didn't know about the song, and it didn't sound so modern. When I came back the next day, they'd remade it as a dance track. I didn't want to record it, but I took the song home, and my girlfriends were dancing around the room. My producer said, 'Trust me on this.'"

Tiffany said she completed the recording session in Tobin's studio in four takes. "I don't think I realized that the song was about the prohibition of teenage sex, but we got away with it. The lyrics are about going behind a bush and kissing and whatever.

"The song took off when I sang it live. Because I was too young for clubs, we did a tour of shopping malls and shot some of it for the video. At first, I could go and have pizza afterwards, but soon there were so many people that I could barely even get into the mall.

"Having a number 1 hit (at 16) was a wild ride. I met Michael Jackson. Girls copied my earrings and my crimped hair. I love the song now and never tire of singing it."

Tiffany had a record deal with MCA, which she said never intended to promote the single. But, according to author Fred Bronson, program director Lou Simon at KCPX in Salt Lake City, Utah, saw great potential in her recording. Two of his disc jockeys began playing it on the air, and the audience response was positive. Simon kept nagging MCA executives for "four or five weeks" until the label gave the single widespread distribution and promotion.

James was agog at the resurrection of his songs. "Twenty years later, I watched in disbelief as Tiffany's version … and Billy Idol's version of 'Mony Mony' – another of our songs – flew up the charts together like they were holding hands," he told *The Guardian.* "Neither of them knew about the other before they were released.

"Tiffany came up to me at a convention to apologize for covering us. I said, 'Are you nuts? I should be thanking you.' She did a great job, and she's a real sweet girl."

••••••• ❖ •••••••

"I Will Always Love You"
Songwriter: Dolly Parton

By Dolly Parton
Peaked at number 53 on *Billboard* Hot 100
September 25, 1982

By Whitney Houston
Peaked at number 1 on *Billboard* Hot 100
November 28, 1992
December 5, 1992
December 12, 1992
December 19, 1992
December 26, 1992
January 2, 1993
January 9, 1993
January 16, 1993
January 23, 1993
January 30, 1993
February 6, 1993
February 13, 1993
February 20, 1993
February 27, 1993

Dolly Parton
Born Dolly Rebecca Parton on January 19, 1946, in Pittman Center, Tennessee

Whitney Houston
August 9, 1963- February 11, 2012
Born Whitney Elizabeth Houston in Newark, New Jersey, and died in Beverly Hills, California

Dolly Parton

Whitney Houston

Possibly the most remarkable remake in pop music history? Yes!

Whitney Houston threw all her talent and soul into recording "I Will Always Love You" in 1992, and the cover version sat at number 1 on the *Billboard* Hot 100 for a stay that touched four different months.

It would be unfair to say that the Dolly Parton original version was a flop. It may have peaked at number 53 on the pop chart, but it hit number 1 on the *Billboard* Hot Country Songs chart – twice.

Parton's first fling with the song came in 1974, shortly after she wrote it. By then, the talented Tennessean had issued 13 albums.

She wrote the lyrics as a farewell to her former mentor and performing partner, Porter Wagoner. Parton chose to end her seven-year relationship with him and continue her career as a solo act. The lyrics easily can be construed to apply to a romantic break-up situation, as well.

The single earned a second chart run in 1982 following the release of the movie *The Best Little Whorehouse In Texas,* in which she played a starring role. That version of the song was a re-recording of the original. Parton's cash register started ringing with royalties again when Houston covered it. It was the most phenomenal recording to come along in years, going to number 1 in only its third week on the Hot 100. It showcased the song's full potential. Houston's version also came from a movie soundtrack – *The Bodyguard,* in which she also played the role of a singing star. Besides the Hot 100, the single also topped the Hot Adult Contemporary Tracks and Hot R&B Singles charts.

According to a history blurb on Kool.cbslocal.com, Parton almost lost a large chunk of royalties for "I Will Always Love You." After Parton's version gained country music fame, Elvis Presley – perhaps the most famous singer of all time – expressed interest in recording it. There was a catch, though.

Col. Tom Parker, Presley's manager, informed Parton it was standard procedure in that situation for the songwriter to sign over half the publishing rights to songs Elvis recorded. Tearfully, Parton refused.

"I said, 'I'm really sorry,' and I cried all night. I mean, it was like the worst thing," Parton said in an interview with CMT. "You know, it's like, Oh, my God… Elvis Presley. And other people were saying, 'You're nuts. It's Elvis Presley.'

"I said, 'I can't do that. Something in my heart says, don't do that.' And I just didn't do it. He would have killed it. "Then when Whitney (Houston's version) came out, I made enough money to buy Graceland."

Maureen Crowe, music supervisor for *The Bodyguard,* was tasked with finding a song that would be playing in the background of a scene in a Western bar. That same song was to be sung to Kevin Costner's character after he saves the life of Houston's character. She located "I Will Always Love You" on Linda Ronstadt's 1975 album *Prisoner In Disguise.* Producer David Foster had Houston and her band fly to Miami, Florida, to record the song.

"She loved it," Crowe told author Fred Bronson. "It was a typical film thing where we did it with three cameras rolling at one time so she could do it live. She did only five takes, and the fourth was the magic take.

"Kevin and I just jumped, and David came out of the truck, and we all went up on stage and said, 'That was definitely it.'"

Costner had requested an a cappella opening for the song, but Foster fought him on the point, calling it "a really stupid idea." Fortunately, Costner's request was honored, at first just for the film version, and Foster gladly ate his words when the single opened the same way.

Houston's death at age forty-eight was ruled by the Los Angeles County Coroner's Office to be caused by drowning (in a bathtub) and "the effects of atherosclerotic heart disease and cocaine use."

DOLLY PARTON
Producer: Bob Ferguson
RCA
STEREO
APB0-0234
APB0-0234A
Victor
Owepar Pub.
Inc., BMI
2:53
I WILL ALWAYS LOVE YOU
(from the "Jolene" album)
(Dolly Parton)

ARISTA
WHITNEY
HOUSTON
SIDE A
STEREO
45 RPM
Carlin Music
Corp.
74321
120 657
74321 120 657 A1
℗ 1992
The copyright in this
sound recording is
owned by Arista
Records Inc.
© 1992 Arista
Records Inc.
I WILL ALWAYS LOVE YOU
(Dolly Parton)
Produced and Arranged by David Foster
Executive Producers Clive Davis and
Whitney Houston

Bye-bye, So Long, Farewell
Songs of separation

Overview: It's tough being away from someone you care about. Especially when that someone is the object of your deep affection.

In the early years of the Rock Era, songwriters began to pick up on this heart-rending emotion. The songs they cranked out over the years did a good job of conveying the yearning, loneliness and despair boyfriends felt for their absent girlfriends, and vice versa. It's a theme that has appeared in charted songs every couple of years.

The singers of these songs also did a fine job of delivering the feeling of someone who is away from a loved one. It takes talent to deliver emotion through the voice, and that talent has made it into recording studios across the United States, Canada and England throughout the history of Rock & Roll.

The songs profiled in this chapter talk about separation and the various factors that caused loved ones to be parted. Some are similar to one another, either mournful or hopeful, while others are distinctly unique.

To view the full lyrics of these songs, please log on to www.google.com, enter song titles & artist names and click Google Search.

To listen to these songs, please log on to www.youtube.com and enter song titles & artist names.

"Beyond The Sea" by Bobby Darin
Songwriters: Charles Trenet, Jack Lawrence
Peaked at number 6 on *Billboard* Hot 100
February 29, 1960

Bobby Darin

May 14, 1936-December 20, 1973
Born Walden Robert Cassotto in New York City, New York, and died in Los Angeles, California

Bobby Darin

When Frenchman Charles Trenet composed "La Mer" in the mid-1940s, he could not have known it would become a major pop hit in 1960.

After Jack Lawrence rewrote the lyrics to make it an English language love song, Bobby Darin recorded it as "Beyond The Sea" late in 1959. The theme depicts a transoceanic love affair, with the narrator missing his girlfriend.

Harry James & His Orchestra made the first recording of "Beyond The Sea" in 1947.

Apparently, the narrator is a sailor. "Somewhere beyond the sea, somewhere waiting for me, my lover stands on golden sands and watches the ships that go sailing," the song begins. "Somewhere beyond the sea she's there watching for me. If I could fly like birds on high then straight to her arms I'd go sailing."

The narrator states that, when he is reunited with his lover, "We'll kiss just as before. Happy we'll be beyond the sea, and never again I'll go sailing."

It's touching to think a man would give up his vocation to be with his soul mate full time.

Darin's style has been described as a cross between two legendary singers – Elvis Presley and Frank Sinatra. On this song, he definitely sounds like Sinatra.

A motion picture about Darin's life was released in 2004. Starring Kevin Spacey, it was titled *Beyond The Sea*.

The Carnival Cruise Line has used the song in a television advertising campaign.

"Beyond The Sea" was used in films such as *Goodfellas* and *A Quiet Place Part II*.

Many people don't know what a prolific songwriter Darin was. He wrote or co-wrote over 40 songs that charted on the *Billboard* Hot 100 for himself and other artists. Some examples are "18 Yellow Roses," "Dream Lover," "If A Man Answers" and "You're The Reason I'm Living."

He adapted his stage name from the first name of actor Darren McGavin, who played the television role of detective Mike Hammer in 1958-59. Darin told the *Saturday Evening Post,* "My legal name will remain Cassotto. Cassotto was my mother's name, and it will be my children's name." Darin never knew his father, and his mother never revealed his identity.

Darin was plagued by poor health throughout his life. During his childhood, rheumatic fever weakened his heart. He had two artificial heart valves implanted in 1971, but he died in Cedars of Lebanon Hospital in Los Angeles at age thirty-seven after undergoing his final heart surgery.

•••••• ❖ ••••••

"Please Mr. Postman" by the Marvelettes

Songwriters: Brian Holland, Georgia Dobbins, William Garrett, Robert Bateman, Freddie Gorman
Peaked at number 1 on *Billboard* Hot 100
December 11, 1961

The Marvelettes

Gladys Horton (May 30, 1945-January 26, 2011)
Katherine Anderson (January 16, 1944-?)
Georgeanna Tillman (February 6, 1944-January 6, 1980)
Wanda Young (August 9, 1943-December 15, 2021)
Juanita Cowart (January 8, 1944-?)
Formed in 1960 in Inkster, Michigan

The Marvelettes: Wanda Young, Georgeanna Tillman, Gladys Horton, Juanita Cowart, Katherine Anderson

"Please Mr. Postman" by the Marvelettes always will be known as the first number 1 record for the Motown family of labels, and it put a unique spin on the separation theme.

The narrator pleads with her mailman to deliver correspondence from boyfriend, "just a card or just a letter, saying he's returning home to me."

It was a different world back then, with the postal service doing the heavy lifting in providing communication across America. Long distance telephone rates were so high in 1961 that most middle class families, like the one in which I grew up, made such phone calls sparingly. There was no email, social media or Zoom calls.

Therefore, the scenario of a lovesick teen girl waiting by her mailbox for a note from an absent boyfriend was not a stretch. The beau, very possibly, could be deployed at a far-flung military base.

The lonely girl sends the postman on a bit of a guilt trip by saying, "So many days you passed me by, you saw the tears standing in my eye. You wouldn't stop to make me feel better by leaving me a card or a letter."

As a parting request, she pleads, "Please check and see just one more time for me" and "deliver the letter, the sooner the better."

One of the song's creators was a member of the Marvelettes, but she wasn't in the group when they recorded "Please Mr. Postman."

Georgia Dobbins asked a songwriter friend, William Garrett, if he had a song she and the Marvelettes could record after they impressed Motown executives in an audition. Garrett gave her a blues song titled "Please Mr. Postman." Dobbins took it home and totally rewrote the lyrics overnight.

Then Dobbins taught Gladys Horton how to sing it because Dobbins had to drop out of the Marvelettes so she could tend to her ailing mother.

The genesis of the song took place before Motown had its own in-house songwriters, which eventually became Brian Holland, Lamont Dozier and Eddie Holland.

The Marvelettes were the second girl group, after the Shirelles, to top the *Billboard* Hot 100. For more information about the Marvelettes, see my first book, *The Coffman Collection*, in the "Motown" chapter.

In the next couple of years, girl groups steadily gained popularity, with ensembles such as the Crystals, the Ronettes, the Angels, Martha & the Vandellas, the Shangri-Las, the Cookies, the Dixie Cups and the Supremes finding success on both the R&B and pop charts.

••••••• ❖ •••••••

"Sealed With A Kiss" by Brian Hyland

Songwriters: Peter Udell, Gary Geld
Peaked at number 3 on *Billboard* Hot 100
July 28, 1962
August 4, 1962

Brian Hyland

Born Brian Hyland on November 12, 1943, in Queens, New York

Brian Hyland

"It's gonna be a cold, lonely summer," is the lament in "Sealed With A Kiss."

The second huge hit for Brian Hyland has him pining over a girlfriend he won't be seeing for the duration of a summer. Hyland stormed onto the charts in 1960 as a sixteen-year-old, hitting number 1 on the *Billboard* Hot 100 with "Itsy Bitsy Teenie Weenie Yellow Polka Dot Bikini." He had seven other songs on the pop chart before he returned to the top five.

He makes a promise to his girlfriend with these words: "Though we gotta say goodbye for the summer, Darling, I promise you this. I'll send you all my love every day in a letter, sealed with a kiss."

In the bridge, he says, "I'll see you in the sunlight. I'll hear your voice everywhere. I'll run to tenderly hold you, but Darling you won't be there."

If you're a teenager in love, possibly for the first time, you know how the weeks of a lonely summer can seem endless.

Late in the song we hear, "Oh, let us make a pledge to meet in September and seal it with a kiss."

Songwriters Gary Geld and Peter Udell wrote this and several other of Hyland's recordings. The duo wrote over 100 songs together, according to Songfacts. Geld played piano on "Sealed With A Kiss."

Blackie Shackner played the mournful harmonica part.

Quoted in *1000 UK #1 Hits,* Hyland said, "'Sealed With A Kiss was recorded about a year before I did it by The Four Voices, who had a sound like The Brothers Four. It dragged and didn't have any life in it, so it wasn't a hit. I told them we should do it. Gary Geld was a classically trained musician, and he had been inspired to write it from a finger exercise for the piano."

• • • • • • • • ❖ • • • • • • • •

"It Might As Well Rain Until September" by Carole King

Songwriters: Gerry Goffin, Carole King
Peaked at number 22 on *Billboard* Hot 100
October 6, 1962
October 13, 1962

Carole King

Born Carol Joan Klein on February 9, 1942, in Manhattan, New York

Carole King

Ah, this is another case of the summertime blues, teen love style.

The lyrics of "It Might As well Rain Until September" don't mention vacation or school break, but I think we can assume that's what Carole King had in mind when she and her then-husband Gerry Goffin wrote it. Goffin wrote the lyrics and King composed the melody.

"The weather here has been as nice as it can be," King sings, "although it doesn't really matter much to me. For all of the fun I'll have while you're so far away, it might as well rain until September."

It sounds like her boyfriend has taken a lengthy trip between school semesters.

In the bridge, she relates, "My friends look forward to their picnics on the beach. Yes, everybody loves the summertime. But you know, Darling, while your arms are out of reach, a summer isn't any friend of mine."

The timing of the record's release was a bit odd. Given the title and subject matter of the song, it logically should have been released in May or June. But it entered the *Billboard* Hot 100 on August 25, 1962, and it peaked in October, with summer in the rearview mirror.

King spent most of her early career writing songs other artists recorded. One of the most famous is "Take Good Care Of My Baby," the only number 1 hit in Bobby Vee's stellar career. But she also entered the recording studio as a singer starting in 1958, when she was just sixteen.

As of 1962, "It Might As Well Rain Until September" was her biggest hit. King wouldn't have another until she recorded the "Tapestry" album in 1971.

She married at age seventeen in 1959. With two young children at home, King had no interest in going on a concert tour to promote her song in 1962. But she did leave her New York home to go to Philadelphia for an appearance on the TV show *American Bandstand*.

Shortly after the release of "September," a teen panel on the *American Bandstand* Rate-A-Record segment judged the song. The ratings parameters had the panel give each record a score between 35 and 98. "September" had an average score of 42. Public acceptance was much higher, to King's relief.

Goffin and King wrote "September" for Vee, but his label declined to issue it as a single. His version appeared only on the album "The Night Has A Thousand Eyes."

King recorded her demo of the song on acetate and, hence, there never was a master tape of the recording. Don Kirshner, owner of Dimension Records, liked her take on "September" so well, he decided to release it. The single had its best showing on the U.K. chart, where it peaked at number 3.

••••••• ❖ •••••••

"500 Miles Away From Home" by Bobby Bare
Songwriters: Bobby Bare, Charlie Williams, Hedy West
Peaked at number 10 on *Billboard* Hot 100
November 16, 1963

Bobby Bare

Born Robert Joseph Bare on April 7, 1935, in Ironton, Ohio

Bobby Bare

He's cold, tired and broke but, most importantly, he is away from his family.

That's the scenario in "500 Miles Away From Home," a mournful song that gave a country flavor to the separation theme.

Apparently a young man has left his hometown to seek his fortune, but things have not worked out the way he would have liked, which is a familiar story. After his mother sent him a letter asking him to return, he quickly decided to do just that.

"Teardrops fell on mama's note when I read the things she wrote," the lyrics begin. "She said we miss you son, we love you, come on home. Well, I didn't have to pack – I had it all right on my back. Now I'm 500 miles away from home."

The second verse is spoken rather than sung. "I know this is the same road I took the day I left home, but it sure looks different now. Well, I guess I look different too because time changes everything. I wonder what they'll say when they see their boy looking this way. Oh, I wonder what they'll say when I get home."

The journey back to his loved ones will be long and slow. Without the funds to buy a ride on a bus, train or plane, the narrator is forced to hitchhike. He'll be doing that on an empty stomach, to boot.

The single peaked at number 5 on the *Billboard* Hot Country Songs chart and number 4 on the *Billboard* Adult Contemporary chart.

••••••• ❖ •••••••

"Big Man In Town" by the 4 Seasons featuring the "Sound" of Frankie Valli
Songwriter: Bob Gaudio
Peaked at number 20 on *Billboard* Hot 100
December 5, 1964
December 12, 1964

The 4 Seasons

Frankie Valli (May 3, 1934-?) lead vocals
Bob Gaudio (November 17, 1942-?) keyboards, backing vocals
Tommy DeVito (June 19, 1928-September 21, 2020) guitar, backing vocals
Nick Massi (September 19, 1927-December 24, 2000) bass
Formed in 1956 in Newark, New Jersey, as the Four Lovers

The 4 Seasons: Nick Massi (top), Bob Gaudio, Frankie Valli, Tommy DeVito

"Big Man In Town" is packed with angst. In this song by the 4 Seasons, we have a narrator who is a poor, downtrodden man. He is speaking to his girlfriend, who is far away. Ostensibly, it is a long distance telephone conversation.

"Each day as I grow older, the nights are getting colder," he laments. "Someday the sun will shine on me. "Money, I don't have any. I'm down to my last penny. But, Darling, don't cry over me."

In boxing parlance, the guy may be down, but he's not out.

"I'll be a big man in town, honest Honey … just you wait and see, you'll be proud of me."

In the next verse, he imparts how others may think of him as a rover. That's all behind him now. He tells his girl eventually her parents will think better of him. And they can be married.

"I went away a small man, but I'll come home a tall man. Then, what a pretty bride you'll be."

He has a plan, and he seems determined to carry it through and make a success of himself.

Bob Gaudio, the keyboardist of the band, wrote this song and several others for the 4 Seasons. They had a history not unlike the protagonist of "Big Man In Town." Coming out of New Jersey, they had their ups and downs before starting an incredible run of hits in 1962.

127

One of their last failures came in 1961, when they auditioned for a job as a lounge act in Union, N.J., at the Four Seasons Bowl. At the time, the band was known as the Four Lovers.

"We figured we'll come out of this with something," Gaudio told Songfacts, "so we took the name of the bowling alley."

"Big Man In Town" was the third single issued by the 4 Seasons in 1964 that carried a theme of poverty. "Dawn Go Away" and "Rag Doll" were the other two. This was a contrast to the lyrical stylings of artists like the Beach Boys and Jan & Dean.

Frankie Valli said to Songfacts, "Our songs were more about real people and the real world they lived in – a world which wasn't always that pretty."

•••••• ❖ ••••••

"Save Your Heart For Me" by Gary Lewis & the Playboys
Songwriters: Peter Udell, Gary Geld
Peaked at number 2 on *Billboard* Hot 100
August 21, 1965

Gary Lewis & the Playboys

Gary Lewis (July 31, 1945-?) lead vocals, drums
David Costell (March 15, 1944-?) lead guitar
David Walker (May 12, 1943-?) rhythm guitar
Allan Ramsay (July 27, 1943-November 27, 1985) bass
John West (July 31, 1939-?) keyboards
Formed in 1964 in Los Angeles, California

The Playboys: David Costell, David Walker, Gary Lewis, John West, Allan Ramsey

The narrator of "Save Your Heart For Me" is nervous. His girlfriend is about to leave town for her summer vacation, and he begs her not to find a replacement for him while she is gone.

This was the third big hit in a row for Gary Lewis & the Playboys, who were helping to stage a comeback for American bands a year after the British Invasion took over the music scene. The Playboys hit number 1 with their first release, "This Diamond Ring," and peaked at number 2 with the second, "Count Me In." Their next two singles would also wind up in the top four of the pop chart.

The fearful narrator tells his girl, "Have yourself a summer fling or two, but remember I'm in love with you and save your heart for me."

In the bridge, he says, "When you're all alone, far away from home, someone's gonna flirt with you. I won't think it's wrong if you play along – just don't fall for someone new."

Everything will be back to normal after the summer is over, if she follows his advice. "When the autumn winds begin to blow and the summertime is long ago, you'll be in my arms again I know. So, save your heart for me."

Songwriters Peter Udell and Gary Geld, mentioned earlier in this chapter under "Sealed With A Kiss," wrote the song for Brian Hyland. It appeared as the B-side of Hyland's single "I'm Afraid To Go Home." Producer Snuff Garrett slowed the tempo for the Playboys' version.

Asked if he could personally relate to the lyrics, Lewis told Songfacts, "I was never hurt by a girl going away for the summer and liking some other guy ... that stuff never happened. But I guess it does happen to people who take their kids on family vacations to different parts of the country, and they probably find boyfriends there or girlfriends. And then come home and they'll never see that person again. I can relate to that stuff, but it's not personal experience."

The Playboys played on the song, but some of the instrumentation was contributed by session musicians who later became known as the Wrecking Crew.

One specific part required a call to Los Angeles' American Federation of Musicians Local 47 because they needed a whistler who could proficiently do whistling parts on the intro and the break. Lewis, Garrett and session keyboardist Leon Russell all tried and did miserably.

"He came in and did it," Lewis said to Songfacts. "Just an old guy, very strait-laced. (His attitude was) this is my job, and I'm going to do it."

Lewis, whose birth name is Gary Harold Lee Levitch, is a son of the late Jerry Lewis, famed comedian, actor, singer and filmmaker. When he and the Playboys auditioned to land a gig at Disneyland, they did not divulge their celebrity connection. They were hired on the spot in 1964 and soon were playing to a full house of enthusiastic fans. Their recording career began in '65, and they had 10 hits in the top 25 of the *Billboard* Hot 100 in their first two years. The U.S. Army drafted Lewis in January 1967, which greatly curtailed the band's future success.

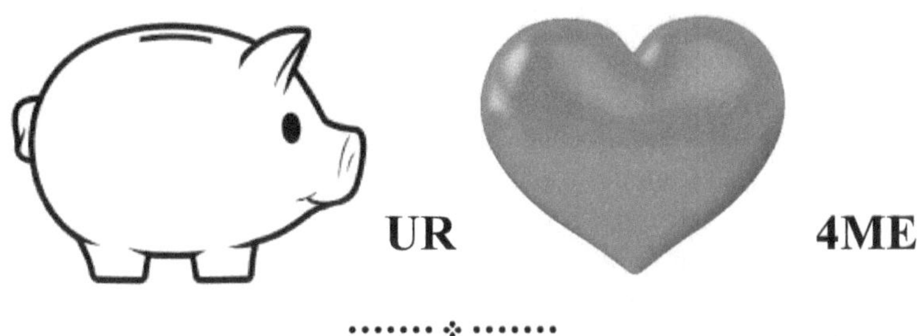

•••••• ❖ ••••••

129

"See You In September" by the Happenings
Songwriters: Sherman Edwards, Sid Wayne
Peaked at number 3 on *Billboard* Hot 100
August 27, 1966
September 3, 1966

The Happenings

Dave Libert (January 20, 1943-) bass
Bob Miranda (bio unavailable) lead
Tom Giuliano (bio unavailable) tenor
Ralph DiVito (bio unavailable) baritone
Formed in 1961 in Paterson, New Jersey

The Happenings

The Tempos from Pittsburgh, Pa., were the first to record this song of separation. They rode it up the *Billboard* Hot 100 to a respectable number 23 in 1959.

As many great songs do, "See You In September" found its way to other singers looking to capitalize on its quality. The Quotations, Shelley Fabares, Bobby Rydell, the Chiffons and Mike Clifford gave it forgettable treatments.

Then along came the Happenings, who enabled the song to reach its potential as a catchy tune that carried a relatable message. While the Tempos' version had a slow, calypso beat, the Happenings sped it up.

Members of the vocal group the Tokens, who owned B.T. Puppy Records, produced the recording. Herb Bernstein was the arranger and conductor.

"(It was) a great song and kind of a bad record," the Happenings' Bob Miranda remarked to Classicbands.com, evaluating the Tempos' version. "We always looked for that. If you want to revise something and put your own sound to it, I think you should look for a great song that was not a great record."

"See You In September" is another message from a young guy to his girlfriend as she prepares to board a train for a summer trip. "I'll be alone each and every night," he tells her. "While you're away don't forget to write."

He continues, "Here we are, saying goodbye at the station. Summer vacation is taking you away. Have a good time, but remember – there is danger in the summer moon above. Will I see you in September, or lose you to a summer love?"

Lyricist Sid Wayne met with composer Sherman Edwards one Friday in June 1959 in New York City's Brill Building at about 11 a.m. After Edwards asked Wayne what he would like to write that day, Wayne replied, "I'd like to write a song called 'See You In September.'

"We talked it back and forth, and I think I may have contributed part of the opening music. But with Sherman it didn't matter because he could throw me back half the lyric – that's how he worked. I think probably by 2:00 in the afternoon we got the song finished. It needed to be written. It was like boiling inside of us," Wayne said in an interview.

But the songwriting pair was not done. They took the lyrics and reworked them to appeal to a teen audience, finishing by 4:30 p.m.

After the Happenings' version was released, the song found early success in Boston, Massachusetts, where it was in the top 10 of the local chart by June. It was in the top five of the national chart by mid-August. Sales eventually passed a million.

••••••• ❖ •••••••

"Last Train To Clarksville" by the Monkees

Songwriters: Tommy Boyce, Bobby Hart
Peaked at number 1 on *Billboard* Hot 100
November 5, 1966

The Monkees

Davy Jones (December 30, 1945-February 29, 2012) vocals, percussion
Peter Tork (Febraury 13, 1942-February 21, 2019) bass
Michael Nesmith (December 30, 1942-December10, 2021) guitar
Micky Dolenz (March 8, 1945-?) vocals, drums

Formed in 1966 in Los Angeles, California

The Monkees: (top) Peter Tork, Micky Dolenz
(bottom) Davy Jones, Michael Nesmith

What a recipe Screen Gems used to concoct "Last Train To Clarksville." It went something like this:

- The studio placed an advertisement in *The Hollywood Reporter* and *Daily Variety,* entertainment publications, asking for young men to audition for parts in a television show. The theme of the show would combine slapstick comedy with pop music. The show would be about a struggling rock band that tries to find success.
- With an emphasis on good looks and acting ability, Englishman Davy Jones and Americans Peter Tork, Michael Nesmith and Micky Dolenz (a former child actor) were selected to play parts of rock band members on the NBC-TV series *The Monkees,* which debuted in September 1966. The ad had been answered by 437 actors, according to a report.
- Professional songwriters Tommy Boyce and Bobby Hart, who had worked out of the Brill Building in New York City, were hired to write and produce songs for the band, which were released on the Colgems label.
- Professional musicians were hired to play instruments behind vocals by members of the Monkees.
- The records and the television show, both aimed at a teen audience, fed off each other, creating massive sales and ratings.
- The first single release by the band was a song about a young man being separated from his girlfriend by the fact he was going off to serve in the military. The Vietnam War was raging at the time. The storyline of the song has him talking to her on the telephone, asking her to rendezvous with him in Clarksville for one last meeting before he is inducted.

"Take the last train to Clarksville, and I'll meet you at the station," he instructs. "You can be here by 4:30 'cause I've made your reservation."

Nowhere in the lyrics is there mention of the military or war. "We couldn't be too direct (about the war) with the Monkees," Hart said to Songfacts. "We couldn't really make a protest song out of it – we kind of snuck it in."

Hart chose the city name of Clarksville because he had memories of passing through Clarkdale, Ariz., on the way to scenic Sedona. "We were throwing out names, and when we got to Clarkdale, we thought Clarksville sounded even better," he said.

In the break, Dolenz sings a series of "doo doo doo doo doos." Hart had written words for that part of the song but Dolenz, who was exhausted in the recording studio after spending many hours filming on the TV stage, wasn't able to learn them late at night. So Hart had him do a fill with phonetic sounds.

A sobering thought appears in the lyrics. The narrator says, "We'll have one more night together till the morning brings my train and I must go, oh, no, no, no. And I don't know if I'm ever coming home."

Hart's inspiration for the title came from listening to the Beatles' "Paperback Writer." Hart mistakenly thought he heard "last train" in that song's lyrics.

The Monkees won two Emmy Awards in 1967, and it lasted two seasons before it was cancelled.

Members of the band eventually gained proficiency playing musical instruments and attempted to record by themselves. That didn't work out well, and they were off the charts after 1968.

••••••• ❖ •••••••

132

"Darling Be Home Soon" by the Lovin' Spoonful

Songwriter: John Sebastian
Peaked at number 15 on *Billboard* Hot 100
March 18, 1967

The Lovin' Spoonful

John Sebastian (March 17, 1944-?) lead vocals
Steve Boone (September 23, 1943-?) bass
Zal Yanovsky (December 19, 1944-December 13, 2002) guitar
Joe Butler (September 16, 1941-?) drums
Formed in 1964 in New York City, New York

The Lovin' Spoonful: Zal Yanovsky, John Sebastian, Steve Boone, Joe Butler

The lyrics to "Darling Be Home Soon" have a dual application.

On the one hand, the song is a monologue by a guy whose girlfriend is about to travel. On the other hand, it has a traveling musician reading a spoken letter to his faraway lover.

The song, commissioned by director Francis Ford Coppola for the 1967 film You're A Big Boy Now, was written by lead singer John Sebastian and recorded by his band the Lovin' Spoonful. It was the first song they recorded backed by a full orchestra on the instrumental middle part.

The Lovin' Spoonful played on the recording, with the exception of drummer Joe Butler. Session musician Billy LaVorgna played drums, according to author Marc Myers.

"Come and talk of all the things we did today here," the first verse says. "and laugh about our funny little ways while we have a few minutes to breathe. Then I know that it's time you must leave."

The refrain has the narrator imploring, "But darling be home soon. I couldn't bear to wait an extra minute if you dawdled. It's not just these few hours but I've been waiting since I toddled, for the great relief of having you to talk to."

Revealing the power of the lyrics, a woman left this comment about the song online: "My husband was in (an intensive care unit) for 26 days, unable to hear or speak. One thing for me during this horrific ordeal was I wanted so desperately just 'to talk' with him." The song imparts a similar sentiment.

As quoted by Songfacts, Sebastian said, "From the singer's perspective, the verses are pleas for a partner to spend a few minutes talking before leaving. What made the song interesting is that you never knew if the other person was actually there listening or was already gone."

Sebastian composed the entire soundtrack for the movie.

The New York City tunesmith went to the 1969 Woodstock Festival to be a spectator, but he was pressed into service as a performer. A heavy rainfall had flooded the stage, and a crew needed time to sweep away water so that Santana's amps could be positioned. Concert organizer Michael Lang asked Sebastian to play a few songs to keep the audience entertained during the delay.

Sebastian sang five songs, and "Darling Be Home Soon" was the fourth. "The audience didn't identify the song with the movie, since most probably hadn't seen it," Sebastian told Songfacts. "Instead, they sort of quieted down and took it in as a love song. My job wasn't to incite but to mellow everyone out until the stage was swept.

"When I finished, the applause from so many people was loud and wide and knocked the wind out of me. The feeling was delicious."

•••••• ❖ ••••••

"The Letter" by The Box Tops
Songwriter: Wayne Carson
Peaked at number 1 on *Billboard* Hot 100
September 23, 1967
September 30, 1967
October 7, 1967
October 14, 1967

The Box Tops

Alex Chilton (December 28, 1950-March 17, 2010) lead vocals
John Evans (June 18, 1948-?) keyboards, backing vocals
Gary Talley (August 17, 1947-?) guitar
Bill Cunningham (January 23, 1950-?) bass
Danny Smythe (August 25, 1948-July 6, 2016) drums
Formed in 1967 in Memphis, Tennessee

The Box Tops: Bill Cunningham, Danny Smythe, Alex Chilton, Gary Talley, John Evans

It all started out with a missive.

This guy has a girlfriend who is in a distant city. She wrote him a letter to tell him how much she misses him, and now he's revved up to see her – urgently.

The boyfriend tells a ticket agent in the opening verse of "The Letter," "Give me a ticket for an aeroplane, ain't got time to take a fast train. Lonely days are gone, I'm going home. My baby just wrote me a letter."

Money is no object. He just wants to see his girl as soon as possible.

"Well, she wrote me a letter, said she couldn't live without me no more," the lyrics continue. "Listen mister, can't you see I got to get back to my baby once more?"

The record was a radio programmer's dream, playing to just one minute fifty-eight seconds. And radio stations across the U.S. played it many times a day. The end result was over a million in sales, and *Billboard* ranked it as the number 2 single of 1967.

In 1968, the Beatles had a number 1 hit with "Hey Jude," which ran a lengthy 7:11. Singles would never be shorter than two minutes thereafter.

It was a mountain of success for Memphis band the Box Tops, who experienced mega success with their first release. They had a number 2 smash the next year with "Cry Like A Baby," but they never visited the top 10 after that.

Songwriter Wayne Carson credited his father, "a songwriter of sorts," for laying the groundwork for "The Letter."

"He would come with ideas and pass them on to me," Carson told author Fred Bronson. "Give me a ticket for an aeroplane was all he had. I took that one line and wrote the rest of the words and the melody."

Carson won a Grammy Award in 1983 for writing the Willie Nelson hit "Always On My Mind."

Producer Dan Penn inserted the sound of a jet airplane taking off in the outro of the recording. He got the sound from a special effects record he had checked out from the local Memphis library.

"That was a big part of the record," Penn told author Holly George. "When I finished it up, I played it for Chips (Moman, owner of American Sound Studio), and he said, 'That's a pretty good little Rock & Roll record, but you've got to take that airplane off it.' I said, 'If the record's going out, it's going out with the airplane on it.'

"He said, 'Okay, it's your record.'"

········ ❖ ········

"By The Time I Get To Phoenix" by Glen Campbell
Songwriter: Jimmy Webb
Peaked at number 26 on *Billboard* Hot 100
December 16, 1967

Glen Campbell

April 22, 1936-August 8, 2017
Born Glen Travis Campbell in Delight, Arkansas, and died in Nashville, Tennessee

Glen Campbell

He has had it with his girlfriend, and he hotfooted it out of Los Angeles in the dead of night. His drive will take him all the way to Oklahoma, which is the home state of Jimmy Webb, who wrote "By The Time I Get To Phoenix."

The fed-up boyfriend predicts his girl will be rising by the time he passes through Phoenix. "She'll find the note I left hanging on her door," he muses. "She'll laugh when she reads the part that says I'm leaving, because I've left that girl so many times before."

In the second verse, he foresees himself in Albuquerque when she is working. "She'll probably stop at lunch and give me a call," a call that won't be answered.

The third verse has him entering Oklahoma about the time she goes to bed. "She'll turn softly and call my name out low," he says. "And she'll cry just to think I'd really leave her, though time and time I tried to tell her so. She just didn't know I would really go."

If you're thinking that's a lot of miles to drive in one day, you're right. It was especially true in 1965, when Webb wrote the song. Interstate 10, now a major artery connecting Los Angeles and Phoenix, wasn't completed until 1991.

But, fear not. Webb did not intend the song's storyline to be literal. "A guy approached me one night after a concert," Webb told author Terry Gross, "and he showed me how it was impossible for me to drive from LA to Phoenix, and then how far it was to Albuquerque. In short, he told me, 'This song is impossible.'

"And so it is. It's a kind of fantasy about something I wish I would have done, and it sort of takes place in a twilight zone of reality."

Webb's relationship with his own girlfriend, Suzy Horton, inspired him to write it.

Johnny Rivers was the first to record "By The Time ..." and he chose not to release it as a single – a decision he later would regret.

Frank Sinatra, as quoted by author Jonathan Takiff, called it "the greatest torch song ever written."

According to Songfacts, Campbell was driving on the streets of LA one day when he heard Rivers' version on the car radio. He thought, "I could cut that record and make a hit out of it." It became Campbell's first top 40 success in a solo career that stretched decades. Heretofore, he had been working as a session musician and a concert tour fill-in for the Beach Boys.

Campbell used another Webb song, "Wichita Lineman," to craft a number 3 hit in 1968. He died at the age of eighty-one from complications of Alzheimer's disease.

•••••••• ❖ ••••••••

"You Better Sit Down Kids" by Cher
Songwriter: Sonny Bono
Peaked at number 9 on *Billboard* Hot 100
December 23, 1967

Cher

Born Cherilyn Sarkisian on May 20, 1946, in El Centro, California

Cher

There haven't been many songs in the Rock Era about marital breakup and the shattering of a family, but this was one.

For Cher's second visit to the top 10 as a solo artist, her then-husband Sonny Bono wrote her a song delivered from a man's point of view. That's right – Cher sang the part of a man!

The lyrics are addressed to the man's children on the eve of his departure from the home. Ostensibly, their mother will have custody of them, but he has a few parting words to say.

"You better sit down, kids. I'll tell you why, kids. You might not understand, kids, but give it a try, kids," the dad begins. "Now, how should I put this – I've got something to say. Your mother is staying, but I'm going away."

The divorce will be hard on all of them. "I know you don't want this, neither do we," he says. "But sometimes things happen that we can't foresee.

"Now try to be calm, kids, and don't look so sad. Just 'cause I'm leaving, I'll still be your dad. Just remember I love you, though I'm not here. Just call if you need me, and I'll always be near."

The soon-to-be-absent father reminds the children to get to school on time and say their prayers at bedtime. Their mother is going to need their help more than ever, and they need to knock off their petty squabbles because Dad won't be there to break them up.

The emotion of the situation gets to him at the very end. He says, "My eyes are just red, kids. I'm too big to cry."

Unlike today, divorce was fairly uncommon in 1967, and songs about it were even rarer. Because of the novelty of its subject, "You Better Sit Down Kids" received a lot of attention from the news media.

•••••••• ❖ ••••••••

"Will You Be Staying After Sunday" by the Peppermint Rainbow

Songwriters: Al Kasha, Joel Hirschhorn
Peaked at number 32 on *Billboard* Hot 100
May 3, 1969
May 10, 1969

The Peppermint Rainbow

Bonnie Lamdin – lead vocals
Patty Lamdin – backing vocals
Doug Lewis – guitar
Skip Harris – bass
Anton Corey – drums, percussion
Formed as the New York Times in 1967 in Baltimore, Maryland

Peppermint Rainbow: Bonnie Lamdin, Skip Harris, Anton Corey,
Doug Lewis, Patty Lamdin

They had a nice, fun thing going on. He would come to visit her from another town on Friday. They'd have an enjoyable weekend together, and then he'd go back home.

She is not satisfied anymore. She wants him all seven days of the week, and she begs him, "Don't let lonely Monday come again!"

That's the separation situation in "Will You Be Staying After Sunday" by the Peppermint Rainbow.

The girlfriend tells her guy, "Your lips are warm on Friday night. The next two days you hold me tight. But when it's done, you always run, and I'm alone."

She has to level with him, so she admits, "I'll keep waiting for that one day you'll be mine. I'd give the world to keep you here – why do you need to disappear? And when I press, you do your best to stall for time."

Do you think he has another girlfriend back in the town where he lives? Hmmm...

The girl tries to soften her stance in the bridge, where she says, "I wouldn't try to own your soul, you can be free. I only want you here each night loving me."

It's not exactly an ultimatum, but she ends her appeal by saying, "We gotta let this feeling grow or let it end."

Still known as the New York Times, the band got their big break courtesy of Cass Elliot. "We were in D.C. one night," lead singer Bonnie Lamdin told the *Baltimore Post-Examiner,* "playing at a place across the street from where Cass Elliot was performing … Cass came over and joined us onstage for a medley of Mamas & Papas songs. After we were done, she said, 'I'm going to get you a contract.'

"Twenty-four hours later, we were contacted by Decca Records. A few days later, we did a gig in New York, and within a week or two we got signed. We also got a new agent, who said the New York Times wasn't gonna work. So, she came up with the name Peppermint Rainbow because bubblegum music was so big at the time (1968).

"We were just at the right place at the right time. It was totally accidental that Cass came in and then got us connected with the folks in New York."

Bonnie Lamdin and her sister Patty got recruited into the band because it needed a feminine touch. "We ran across a group of guys (in 1967) who had their own band," Bonnie told the *Post-Examiner.* "They said they needed a female voice or two, so we formed a group that our first manager named the New York Times. I'm not sure why he chose that name, since we were from Baltimore."

She said the end of the Peppermint Rainbow came when "we had a difficult situation where we found out our manager wasn't paying us our entire share, so we became disillusioned. Then I got married, and that was the final nail in the coffin."

After she exited the music industry, Bonnie Lamdin earned two degrees from Georgia State University. Ultimately, she became the chief executive officer of a healthcare system in Baltimore. She has sat on the boards of eight corporations.

Patty Lamdin became a magistrate in the Baltimore juvenile court system.

•••••• ❖ ••••••

"Band Of Gold" by Freda Payne

Songwriters: Edythe Wayne, Ron Dunbar
Peaked at number 3 on *Billboard* Hot 100
July 25, 1970

Freda Payne

Born Freda Charcilia Payne on September 19, 1942, in Detroit, Michigan

Freda Payne

A dysfunctional relationship is revealed in "Band Of Gold." It's a relationship that blossomed into marriage and then quickly disintegrated, with a wedge being driven between the partners.

This is not the song of the same title recorded by Don Cherry in 1955.

In the words sung by Freda Payne, she clings to one symbol – her wedding ring. It is basically all she has since her man is gone. She sings the lyrics to him.

"Now that you're gone, all that's left is a band of gold," she laments, "all that's left of the dreams I hold is a band of gold – and the memories of what love could be if you were still here with me."

In the second verse, the narrator mentions her man "took me from the shelter of my mother I had never known, or loved any other."

Subsequently, we find out the couple slept in separate rooms on their wedding night. Was the couple too young when they married? Is the man impotent – or gay?

The story spun by the lyrics is certainly open to interpretation. Most of us listeners heard only the 45 rpm version of the song, which runs two minutes fifty-three seconds. There was an earlier recorded version which had lyrics removed from the final edited version.

Payne balked at recording the song, saying the lyrics made no sense.

Payne told interviewer Dave Simpson that co-writer Ron Dunbar ordered, "You don't have to like it – just sing it. I dubbed that tune 25, maybe 30 times just to get enough parts of it that we could edit to get the song."

The other writers, identified on the disc as Edythe Wayne, actually were former Motown staffers Lamont Dozier, Eddie Holland and Brian Holland. They had left Motown in 1968 because of a dispute over royalties and profit sharing. They were legally still contracted to Motown's publishing company and could not use their own names on songs they wrote. A lawsuit over the issue was settled in 1977.

In deleted words we find the woman spurned her new husband on their wedding night, and she felt remorse later. She speaks of " the dream of what love could be if you were still here with me."

Dunbar also told Simpson, "… it was too long, so we had to cut a section out of the tune, so the section we cut out of the song really brought the whole song (story) together."

One deleted section went like this: "Each night, I lie awake, and I tell myself the vows we made gave you the right to have a love each night."

In an interview with Songfacts, Dozier commented, "The story was, the girl found out this guy was not all there. He had his own feelings about giving his all. He wanted to love this girl, he married the girl, but he couldn't perform on his wedding night because he had other issues.

"It was about this guy that was basically gay, and he couldn't perform. He loved her, but he couldn't do what he was supposed to do as a groom, as her new husband."

That was a lot of baggage to put into a pop song in 1970. Perhaps the omission of some lyrics made it more appealing to listeners, who snatched up 1 million-plus copies. The record turned out to be Payne's biggest single.

Renowned Detroit session musician Dennis Coffey played the signature electric sitar. Ray Parker Jr., who eventually would have a stellar solo career with "Ghostbusters" and other hits, played lead guitar.

•••••••• ❖ ••••••••

"Julie, Do Ya Love Me" by Bobby Sherman

Songwriter: Tom Bahler
Peaked at number 5 on *Billboard* Hot 100
September 19, 1970
September 26, 1970
October 3, 1970

Bobby Sherman

Born Robert Cabot Sherman on July 22, 1943, in Santa Monica, California

Bobby Sherman

The summertime separation blues have a stranglehold on the narrator of "Julie, Do Ya Love Me." Sung by Bobby Sherman, the song reveals heartbreak of being apart from his girlfriend for a few weeks.

141

How bad is the guy hurting? Check out the first verse: "Being alone at night makes me sad, girl. Yeah, it brings me down all right. Tossing and turning and freezing and burning, and crying all through the night."

Speaking directly to his girlfriend in the chorus, he asks, "Julie, Julie, Julie do ya love me? Julie … do ya care? Julie … are ya thinking of me? Julie … will you still be there?"

He has tons of insecurity about his relationship with her, which he is not shy about verbalizing. After spending time with her, he was sure she was his steady girl. "But leaving you, baby, is driving me crazy. It's got me wondering all the time."

In the final verse we find out the guy is the one who is leaving for the summer. He vows to her, "But baby, remember, I'll be back September. But till then I'll write you every day."

With a strong chart performance, the song obviously struck a chord with a lot of love sick teens.

Sherman began recording in 1962, but this work went unnoticed for years. In the fall of 1968, however, he landed a regular role in the weekly ABC-TV series *Here Come The Brides*. This gave him the exposure and popularity to get his records played, and "Little Woman" charted to number 3 on the pop chart in 1969, providing him with a million seller.

After *Brides* ended after two seasons, Sherman found work as a guest star on several television drama and variety shows.

Upon retiring from show business, Sherman became an emergency medical technician. He volunteered with the Los Angeles Police Dept., giving first aid and CPR classes, and other training.

••••••• ❖ •••••••

"It Don't Matter To Me" by Bread

Songwriter: David Gates
Peaked at number 10 on *Billboard* Hot 100
November 14, 1970

Bread

David Gates (December 11, 1940-?) lead vocals, acoustic guitar, electric guitar, bass
Jimmy Griffin (August 10, 1943-January 11, 2005) guitar, keyboards
Robb Royer (December 6, 1942-?) guitar
Mike Botts (December 8, 1944-December 9, 2005) drums
Formed in 1968 in Los Angeles, California

Bread: David Gates, Robb Royer, Jimmy Griffin, Mike Botts

What a nice guy. His girlfriend has left him, but he graciously tells her she can have all the time and space she needs to figure out what she wants to do next.

That's a synopsis of "It Don't Matter To Me," the second in a long run of single hits for Bread.

"It don't matter to me if you really feel that you need some time to be free," the abandoned lover says, "time to go out searching for yourself."

In the second verse, he really sounds generous with his wishes for the girl. "And it don't matter to me if you take up with someone who's better than me, because your happiness is all I want for you to find … your peace of mind."

With his "I don't care" attitude, it kind of sounds like he has a new girlfriend already.

But he declares in the bridge, "Lot of people have an ego hang-up because they want to be the only one. How many came before really doesn't matter, just as long as you're the last. Everybody's moving on and try to find out what's been missing in the past."

In the final verse, he leaves the proverbial door open for a reconciliation. "And it don't matter to me if your searching brings you back together with me. Because there'll always be an empty room waiting for you, an open heart waiting for you."

He sounds like the nicest guy any girl ever broke up with.

David Gates wrote the song before the formation of the band Bread. It was included on their first album in 1969, but Gates reworked the song for its release as a single in the fall of 1970.

"I wrote that song a year or so before joining Bread, mostly for my personal pleasure," Gates told Songfacts. "I thought it would be good for the group. It has this unusual bridge that takes off and does some crazy things musically."

We don't get to know whether the guy and his former girlfriend get back together, but it would have made for an interesting sequel in a subsequent song.

•••••• ❖ ••••••

"Ain't No Sunshine" by Bill Withers

Songwriter: Bill Withers
Peaked at number 3 on *Billboard* Hot 100
September 18, 1971
September 25, 1971

Bill Withers

July 4, 1938-March 30, 2020
Born William Harrison Withers Jr. in Slab Fork, West Virginia, and died in Los Angeles, California

Bill Withers

This was Bill Withers, in his first chart success, telling us about the pain of being separated from the woman he loved. The song came from the heart.

His world is enveloped in darkness in the absence of his love. "Ain't no sunshine when she's gone," he says. "It's not warm when she's away. Ain't no sunshine when she's gone, and she's always gone too long anytime she goes away." It's clear this woman is the light of his life.

The elusive lady has slipped away to parts unknown, and her return is anything but certain. "Wonder this time where she's gone," he laments. "Wonder if she's gone to stay. Ain't no sunshine when she's gone, and this house just ain't no home anytime she goes away."

Following the lead of the Zombies, Withers goes into a repeat of the phrase "I know" – twenty-six times. It's the song's signature feature. In their 1964-65 hit "Tell Her No," the Zombies sang the word "no" 63 times.

"I know … hey I ought to leave the young thing alone, but ain't no sunshine when she's gone."

The recording has the Memphis sound all over it, although it was recorded in Los Angeles. Booker T. Jones produced it, Donald "Duck" Dunn played bass and Al Jackson Jr. played drums. Stephen Stills added guitar work.

Withers told Songfacts: "I wasn't going to do that (repetition), then Booker T. said, 'No, leave it like that.' I was going to write something there, but there was a general consensus in the studio. It was an interesting thing because I've got all these guys that were already established, and I was working in the (airplane) factory at the time.

"Graham Nash was sitting right in front of me, just offering his support. Stephen Stills was playing and there was Booker T. and Al Jackson and Donald Dunn – all of the MGs except Steve Cropper. They were all these people with all this experience and all these reputations, and I was this factory worker just sort of puttering around. So, when their general feeling was, 'Leave it like that,' I left it like that."

Withers' inspiration was not a personal romance but rather a 1962 movie he had watched. *Days Of Wine And Roses* was a story of a married couple who were out-of-control alcoholics.

"They were both alcoholics who were alternately weak and strong," Withers told interviewer Carl Wiser. "It's like going back for seconds on rat poison. Sometimes you miss things that weren't particularly good for you. It's just something that crossed my mind from watching that movie, and probably something else that happened in my life that I'm not aware of."

"So Far Away" by Carole King
Songwriter: Carole King
Peaked at number 14 on *Billboard* Hot 100
October 9, 1971
October 16, 1971

Instructions on the sheet music of "So Far Away," dictating the song's tempo, say "very slow." As in heart-wrenchingly slow.

The song is the product of a world class singer/songwriter (Carole King) meeting a legendary producer (Lou Adler). It truly is a work of art.

Most of the accompaniment is King's piano, which she plays with great skill and feeling. Along the way we hear James Taylor on acoustic guitar, Charlie Larkey on bass, a minimal amount of drumming by Russ Kunkel and soulful flute by Curtis Amy on the outro. There are no backing vocals.

The whole production solidly delivers the loneliness, pain and sadness King concocted in her composition and lyricism. The song is one of the gems on King's break-out solo album, "Tapestry."

"So far away – doesn't anybody stay in one place anymore?" she asks. "It would be so fine to see your face at my door. It doesn't help to know you're just time away.

"Long ago I reached for you, and there you stood. Holding you again could only do me good. How I wish I could, but you're so far away."

It is plain to see the man she is missing, either real or fictional, is extremely important to her. I was separated from a woman I loved when "So Far Away" was on the radio, and I knew firsthand exactly the emotion the song was trying to convey.

But what about the thought in the first line, the one about staying in one place? King seems to be making a statement about the human condition, with many people moving or traveling away from the places and people they started out with. The year was 1971, and she may have had her finger on the pulse of society when she wrote the line.

"'So Far Away' is my favorite song on 'Tapestry,'" Adler said in an interview with *Rock's Backpages*. "I use the phrase a lot – 'doesn't anybody stay in one place anymore?'

"It's the road, it's the people traveling. It just seems to me an anthem of that particular time, and so well written and one of the earlier songs she wrote for this album."

While the record peaked at only number 14, it should be remembered "Tapestry" was racking up sales of over fourteen million in the United States. By the time "So Far Away" was released as a single, a great many listeners already had the song at home on their copy of the album.

"Tapestry," by the way, spent fifteen consecutive weeks at number 1 on the *Billboard* 200, and it produced four Grammy Award wins.

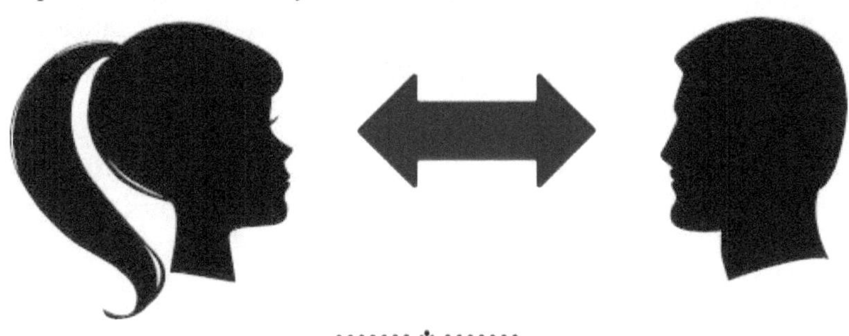

• • • • • • • ❖ • • • • • • •

"Last Song" by Edward Bear
Songwriter: Larry Evoy
Peaked at number 3 on *Billboard* Hot 100
March 3, 1973
March 10, 1973

Edward Bear

Larry Evoy – drums
Paul Weldon – keyboards
Roger Ellis – guitar
Formed in 1966 in Toronto, Ontario, Canada

Edward Bear: Paul Weldon, Larry Evoy, Roger Ellis

He has been a patient man, but his patience is about to run out.

Ever since the protagonist of "Last Song" saw his girlfriend run out on him, he has maintained hope she will return. Every night he leaves on a light at his home, "hoping you'd come by and know that I was home and still awake."

With the passage of two years, he still has the light on at night, but he tells her through the song, "This is hard for me to say, but this is all that I can take."

He declares this is the last song he'll ever write for her and the last time he will tell her how much he cares for her. "You'll come looking for the light, and it won't be there. But I love you, oh yes I do."

Indeed, there comes a time for all jilted lovers to move on.

In the second verse the man tells the woman, "All the times that I spent waiting, wondering where you are, always knew the time would come when I would start to wonder why. Now the time is here, I don't know where you are. So I'll write you one more song, but it's the last time that I'll try."

The keyboard-driven song climbed to number 1 on the *Billboard* Adult Contemporary chart. "Last Song" spent 18 weeks on the *Billboard* Hot 100.

Edward Bear took their name from a character in the A.A. Milne series of children's books featuring Winnie-The-Pooh.

While "Last Song" was still on the pop chart, Edward Bear released a sequel song, "Close Your Eyes." As in the original, the sequel did not have a happy ending.

In "Close Your Eyes," the man dreams his girlfriend returns. Then, she actually does return. She seems to have changed and wants to go back to school. "But you know it didn't take too long till she lost her way," the lyrics say, "and all the reason in the world could see she couldn't stay."

The sequel didn't have quite the same panache as "Last Song," and it peaked at number 37 on the Hot 100.

Larry Evoy, who wrote both songs, revealed in an interview posted on CSHF.ca the subject matter came from personal experience.

"At the time I wrote 'Last Song,' I was living ... in Toronto. I tried to translate what I was hearing in my head onto the piano as much as I could," Evoy said. "The song meant exactly what it said, you know, the girl is gone and that I'm sort of over it now. I don't know how many songs were about her – six at least. 'Close Your Eyes' was also about her.

"That one girl (inspired the song). It was written over a period of time, and it was literal. I would actually go to sleep with my light on, hoping she'd think I was still awake and would drop by, and she did. There is also the analogy of one's own light and not just the physical one in the lyric. I did have a fan come to me at some point and tell me exactly how much it would cost to leave that light on for two years!"

"Last Song" hit number 1 on the Canadian chart and sold over 1 million copies.

••••••• ❖ •••••••

"Come Monday" by Jimmy Buffett

Songwriter: Jimmy Buffett
Peaked at number 30 on *Billboard* Hot 100
July 13, 1974
July 20, 1974

Jimmy Buffett

December 25, 1946-September 1, 2023
Born James William Buffett in Pascagoula, Mississippi., and died in Sag Harbor, New York

Jimmy Buffett

Jimmy Buffett's introduction to the record charts, "Come Monday," drew inspiration from the way he missed his girlfriend, Jane Slagsvol, while he was on a concert tour.

Buffett wrote the song in 1973, and Slagsvol became his second wife four years later. They had met in Key West, Fla., when she was on spring break from the University of South Carolina.

A native of Mississippi who lived in Alabama and Tennessee before the recording was released, Buffett found himself writing about places in the western United States because his tour stops took him there.

First he mentions "heading up to San Francisco for a Labor Day weekend show." Later he invokes memories of "westbound trains" and "that night in Montana."

The chorus reads, "Come Monday, it'll be all right. Come Monday, I'll be holding you tight. I spent four lonely days in a brown L.A. haze, and I just want you back by my side."

The term "brown L.A. haze" may refer to more than smog, since Buffett was part of a star-studded party scene in Los Angeles for a while. According to Cheatsheet.com., Buffett used to hang out with over-indulgent rockers like Jim Morrison, John Bonham and the Rolling Stones.

Buffett's first marriage was brief, lasting from 1969 to 1971. But he truly loved Jane. In the second verse he states, "… now you're off on vacation, something you tried to explain. And, darlin' since I love you so, that's the reason I just let you go."

And later: "I hope you're enjoying the scenery, I know that it's pretty up there. We can go hiking on Tuesday, with you I'd walk anywhere. California has worn me quite thin, I just can't wait to see you again."

Producer Don Gant incorporated orchestral strings into the recording, a feature that wasn't used in Buffett's songs after he perfected the "Caribbean Rock & Roll" genre which ultimately made him famous.

After six years of marriage, Jane had had enough of Jimmy's partying ways and left him for half a dozen years.

When they met to finalize their divorce, a funny thing happened – they reconciled. They stayed together until his death. Buffett died of skin cancer lymphoma after a lengthy illness.

•••••• ❖ ••••••

"I'm Sorry" by John Denver
Songwriter: John Denver
Peaked at number 1 on *Billboard* Hot 100
September 27, 1975

John Denver

December 31, 1943-October 12, 1997
Born Henry John Deutschendorf Jr. in Roswell, New Mexico, and died near Pacific Grove, California

John Denver

"I'm Sorry" deals with one of the most painful separations – one caused by marital break-up.

John Denver, who would be divorced twice, wrote the song in 1975. But he wouldn't go through his first divorce until 1982. "I'm Sorry" shows us Denver had the ability to see into his own future.

Tremendous strain was put on Denver's marriage to Annie Martell. They wed at a young age in 1967 and then struggled to cope with John's sudden leap to superstardom in the entertainment industry in '71. His show business commitments took him away from home much of the time.

In the lyrics, we find the narrator apologizing for the downturn of the union in several ways. He's not divorced yet, but he's taking ownership of most of the causes.

"I'm sorry for the way things are in China," he says. "I'm sorry things ain't what they used to be. But more than anything else, I'm sorry for myself, because you're not here with me."

It's Denver's way of saying, for all the time he spent away from home cultivating his career, he might as well have been in China.

"I'm sorry for all the lies I told you," he continues. "I'm sorry for the things I didn't say. But more than anything else I'm sorry for myself. I can't believe you went away."

With divorce still seven years away, one might think Denver had time to save the marriage. But "I'm Sorry" sounds like the damage is done and his wife won't be coming back.

"I'm sorry if I took some things for granted. I'm sorry for the chains I put on you. But more than anything else, I'm sorry for myself for living without you."

•••••• ❖ ••••••

"Babe" by Styx

Songwriter: Dennis DeYoung
Peaked at number 1 on *Billboard* Hot 100
December 8, 1979
December 15, 1979

Styx

Dennis DeYoung (February 18, 1947-?) lead vocals, keyboards
Tommy Shaw (September 11, 1953-?) guitar
James Young (November 14, 1949-?) guitar
Chuck Panozzo (September 20, 1948-?) bass
John Panozzo (September 20, 1948-July 16, 1996) drums
Formed in 1972 in Chicago, Illinois

Styx: Tommy Shaw, John Panozzo, Dennis DeYoung,
James Young, Chuck Panozzo

What a gift!

Styx keyboardist Dennis DeYoung wrote "Babe" to flesh out his feelings about being away from his wife Suzanne while out on tour with the band. Then he presented it to her on her birthday as a personal message.

DeYoung recorded a demo of the song, with him on Fender Rhodes electric piano, Chuck Panozzo on bass and John Panozzo on drums. Then he handed it over to his wife of fifteen years. After A&M Records released it as a single off the album *Cornerstone,* it quickly became Styx's biggest hit.

"Being on the road for six years puts a strain on a relationship," DeYoung told author Fred Bronson. "I wanted to tell her how much I missed her when I was gone."

In a career of guitar-based, hard-rocking songs, Styx formed a template for power ballads other bands would follow in the 1980s.

The sound of "Babe" even prompted Casey Kasem to call Styx a "keyboard oriented band" when he played the song on his weekly *American Top 40* syndicated radio program.

Suzanne was a little leery of taking the song public as a single. "I wasn't sure I wanted to share our feelings with the world," she told Bronson.

It took some convincing for DeYoung to persuade his bandmates to record "Babe." They tried playing new takes of the song but, in the end, none of them stood up to the demo. With just a Tommy Shaw guitar solo added on the instrumental middle part, they kept it the way it was originally. DeYoung's voice was overdubbed to create backing vocals.

"Babe, I'm leaving, I must be on my way. The time is drawing near," the lyrics begin. "My train is going, I see it in your eyes – the love, the need, your tears."

Then comes reassurance. "But I'll be lonely without you, and I'll need your love to see me through. So please believe me, my heart is in your hands, and I'll be missing you."

DeYoung commented to Bronson, "Change is a scary thing for everyone. According to some people, you're either a Rock & Roll band, or you're not. And anybody who plays ballads was looked down upon by the radio establishment."

The single went to number 1 in Canada and South Africa and number 6 in the U.K. It was certified as a million seller.

Suzanne and Dennis DeYoung as newlyweds

•••••• ❖ ••••••

"Everytime You Go Away" by Paul Young

Songwriter: Daryl Hall
Peaked at number 1 on *Billboard* Hot 100
July 27, 1985

Paul Young

Born Paul Antony Young on January 17, 1956, in Luton, Bedfordshire, England

Paul Young

When Daryl Hall and John Oates recorded "Everytime You Go Away" in 1980 for their album "Voices," it became the most powerful ballad they would ever sing.

They produced the song in a slow-paced gospel-tinged format, allowing Hall's lead vocal to ooze with feeling. It was not one of the four songs on *Voices* released as singles, leaving it as a secret known only to fans who bought the album.

Along came Englishman Paul Young in 1985, adding the song to his list of remakes in a career that heretofore had not made much of an impact in the United States.

With the help of Laurie Latham's production, "Everytime ..." was speeded up and given a pop sound. Young showed the quality of the craftsmanship Hall put into it by taking it to number 1 on the *Billboard* Hot 100. Young's version comes in at 4:15, one minute nine seconds shorter than Hall & Oates' version.

The narrator of the song agonizes about his feelings when his girlfriend goes out with another man. "Hey, if we can solve any problem, then why do we lose so many tears?" he moans. "Oh, so you go again when the leading man appears."

His pain is summarized in the chorus: "Every time you go away, you take a piece of me with you."

In the second verse, he seems to be giving her total freedom. "Go on and go free, yeah, maybe you're too close to see," he says. "I can feel your body move, doesn't mean that much to me. I can't go on saying the same thing, because can't you see we got everything?"

John Turnbull turned in fine work on Spanish guitar, giving Young's recording an individual flair.

The first word of the song title isn't a word at all. It should be two words, but Hall wrote it as one.

In evaluating the job Young did with his song, Hall said in an interview with *Music Connection,* "I never thought of it any other way than the way it was till Paul Young did it. I was just doing a kind of gospel/soul song – that was all I had in mind for it. I was really surprised to hear the production they did because it kept the elements but commercialized it – made it sound like a pop record."

Young, who had covered songs by the Four Preps, Marvin Gaye and Jack Lee, followed "Everytime …" with a remake of the Chi-Lites' "Oh Girl." He took it to number 8 on the pop chart.

•••••• ❖ ••••••

"Tears In Heaven" by Eric Clapton
Songwriters: Eric Clapton, Will Jennings
Peaked at number 2 on *Billboard* Hot 100
March 28, 1992
April 4, 1992
April 11, 1992
April 18, 1992

Eric Clapton

Born Eric Patrick Clapton on March 30, 1945, in Ripley, Surrey, England

Eric Clapton

On March 20, 1991, Eric Clapton became separated from his son, Conor. They never will be reunited on Earth.

The four-year-old boy died from a fall out of the window of a fifty-third-floor apartment in New York City, where he and his mother, Lory Del Santo, were living with her friend..

After a period of mourning, Clapton wrote "Tears In Heaven" with Will Jennings to deal with his grief. At the same time, Clapton was writing music for the soundtrack of the film *Rush*.

In an interview with Sue Lawley, Jennings commented, "(Clapton) said to me, 'I want to write a song about my boy.' Eric had the first verse of the song written, which, to me, is all the song, but he wanted me to write the rest of the verse lines and the release (time can bring you down, time can bend your knees...), even though I told him that it was so personal he should write everything himself.

"He told me that he had admired the work I did with Steve Winwood and, finally, there was nothing else but to do as he requested, despite the sensitivity of the subject. This is a song so personal and so sad that it is unique in my experience of writing songs."

In the 1992 interview with Lawley, Clapton said, "It was in the back of my head, but it didn't really have a reason for being until I was scoring this movie ... then it sort of had a reason to be. And it is a little ambiguous because it could be taken to be about Conor, but it also is meant to be part of the film."

The lyrics begin, "Would you know my name if I saw you in heaven? Would it be the same if I saw you in heaven? I must be strong and carry on, because I know I don't belong here in heaven."

Later in the song, the lyrics say, "Beyond the door there's peace I'm sure, and I know there'll be no more tears in heaven."

It was a masterful, heart-wrenching ballad that became Clapton's biggest selling hit in America. It was kept out of the number 1 position on the *Billboard* Hot 100 by Vanessa Williams' "Save The Best For Last." But it went to number 1 in nine countries, as well as the *Billboard* Adult Contemporary chart.

"I almost subconsciously used music for myself as a healing agent and, lo and behold, it worked," Clapton told interviewer Daphne Barak. "I have got a great deal of happiness and a great deal of healing from music."

Conor Clapton

Take My Advice
Songs that contain a bit of counseling

Overview: It's a well-known adage that free advice is worth exactly what you pay for it. But what about advice you do pay for? How much is that worth?

Over the decades that comprise the Rock Era, many of us have paid anywhere from 65 cents to $1.25 for a 45 rpm record.

For that price, you can hear vocalists singing and musicians playing instruments. And you also might get some advice, thanks to songwriters who put it into their lyrics.

While advice to the lovelorn probably is the most common advice inserted into rock recordings, there are other forms of it, as well.

In this chapter, we will examine a sampling of the advice dispensed in songs that reached the upper echelon of the record charts. It will be up to you to determine whether you got your money's worth.

To view the full lyrics of these songs, please log on to www.google.com, enter song titles & artist names and click Google Search.

To listen to these songs, please log on to www.youtube.com and enter song titles & artist names.

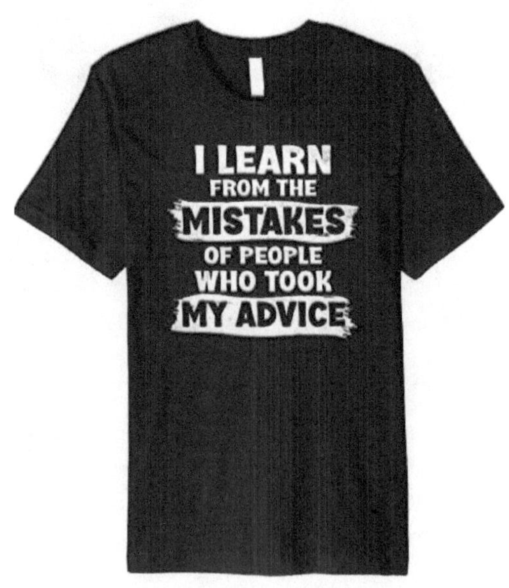

"Hit The Road Jack" by Ray Charles & His Orchestra with the Raelettes
Songwriter: Percy Mayfield
Peaked at number 1 on *Billboard* Hot 100
October 9, 1961
October 16, 1961

Ray Charles

September 23, 1930-June 10, 2004
Born Ray Charles Robinson in Albany, Georgia, and died in Beverly Hills, California

Ray Charles

In his second number 1 single on the pop charts, Ray Charles didn't give the advice – he received it.

Charles sang "Georgia On My Mind" to the top of the *Billboard* Hot 100 in 1960. Several charted hits later, he was back on top, singing a song about a deadbeat guy who is getting the boot from his girlfriend.

The rhythm & blues veteran's backing singers, the Raelettes, played a major part in the song. They consisted of Margie Hendricks, Patricia Lyles, Darlene McCrea and Gwendolyn Berry. Hendricks sang the part of the girlfriend, who advises the narrator to "hit the road."

The narrator laments, "Woman, oh woman, don't treat me so mean. You're the meanest old woman that I've ever seen. I guess if you say so, I'll have to pack my things and go."

His woman tells him in the chorus to "hit the road, Jack, and don't come back no more."

The guy objects, saying he'll be back on his feet eventually. But the girl retorts, "Don't care if you do because it's understood you ain't got no money, you just ain't no good."

It was a cute call-and-response format devised by producer Sid Feller. The song won a Grammy Award for best rhythm & blues recording.

Charles had been a jazz singer early in his career. He began to record pop songs in 1959, which increased his fan base manyfold.

Hendricks and Charles had an affair which produced a son born in 1959, Charles Wayne Hendricks. Ray was married to Della Beatrice Howard at the time.

•••••••• ❖ ••••••••

"Runaround Sue" by Dion

Songwriters: Ernie Maresca, Dion DiMucci
Peaked at number 1 on *Billboard* Hot 100
October 23, 1961
October 30, 1961

Dion

Born Dion Francis DiMucci on July 18, 1939, in the Bronx, New York

Dion

The advice given in this song is simple: stay away from Sue.

Why should men take Dion's advice in his biggest hit, "Runaround Sue?" Because she is an unfaithful girlfriend.

"Yeah, I should have known from the very start this girl would leave me with a broken heart," the song's narrator laments. "Listen people what I'm telling you: keep away from Runaround Sue."

What she did to the narrator is take his love and then "ran around with every single guy in town."

He was deeply in love with Sue, and he cautions his peers, "So if you don't wanna cry like I do, I'd keep away from a Runaround Sue."

In the end, Dion couldn't heed his own advice. In 1963, he married a woman named Sue – Susan Butterfield. She wasn't the cheating, heart-breaking type, though, and to this day they are still married.

Dion explained the making of the song to interviewer Marc Myers. "(At a friend's birthday party) we had a portable phonograph, but we soon turned it off and began making up our own songs. I got everyone to lay down a beat on boxes and bottles and to clap hands rhythmically in time. I then came up with background vocal harmony parts and had everyone sing them over and over.

"It went like hape-hape bum da hey di hey di hape-hape. With this going on, I made up a melody and lyrics. When I left the party that night, I couldn't let go of that riff and melody.

"The next morning, I called my friend Ernie Maresca, who was writing songs then. After Ernie heard where I was going with the song, we went to work on the melody and lyrics."

So, was Sue a real person? "It really was about a girl (from his neighborhood) who was kind of loose," Dion was quoted on Genius.com. "The word Sue just fit for the song – you couldn't use Roberta or Alice or whatever. I'm not going to mention who it's really about but, between you and me, the girl called in to an interview show I was on … she had married a rabbi, had six kids and sounded wonderful. And I thought how good it was to hear from her, you know.

"Chalk it up to being young and foolish, like a lot of young people are, but she turned out wonderful."

•••••• ❖ ••••••

"Little Town Flirt" by Del Shannon
Songwriters: Del Shannon, Maron McKenzie
Peaked at number 12 on *Billboard* Hot 100
February 23, 1963

Del Shannon

December 30, 1934-February 8, 1990
Born Charles Weedon Westover in Coopersville, Michigan, and died in Santa Clarita, California

Del Shannon

Del Shannon's "Little Town Flirt" is like a public service announcement.

With the lyrics, he warns all the guys in town about a pretty girl who is tempting to date but is a heartbreaker. She's quite an engaging coquette, but when boys fall in love with her she quickly moves on to another conquest.

"Here she comes, that little town flirt," the song begins. "You're falling for her, and you're gonna get hurt. Yeah, I know it's so hard to resist the temptation of her tender red lips. But you can get hurt, fooling around with that little town flirt."

In the second verse, we hear, "Here she comes with that look in her eye. She plays around with every guy that goes by. I know she's gonna treat you wrong, so your heart just better be strong."

Advice comes in the outro. "You better run and hide now, boy. You better pass her by now … you better run away now."

An amusing line appears in the bridge: "But you think you've got a paper heart when she starts to tear it apart. That's when she'll let you go."

Shannon was one of rock music's pioneers of the falsetto singing style. After he had his first chart hits in 1961, singers such as Frankie Valli and Lou Christie successfully used the high-pitched technique.

As "Little Town Flirt" entered the Hot 100, *Billboard* had this to say about Shannon: "The lad's back with another solid sounding side. His voice is smartly double-tracked, and the vocal is handled brightly against an effective girls' chorus."

Shannon's early recordings were unique, in that they featured a Musitron, a keyboard instrument that was a forerunner of the synthesizer.

After the British Invasion came to America, Shannon's career took a hit, and his final top 10 single was "Keep Searchin' (We'll Follow The Sun)" in 1965. Though he kept recording albums through 1981, he never recaptured the magic he generated in 1961-65.

Shannon's life ended at age fifty-five when he shot himself with a rifle in his home.

•••••••• ❖ ••••••••

"Walk Like A Man" by the 4 Seasons
Songwriters: Bob Crewe, Bob Gaudio
Peaked at number 1 on *Billboard* Hot 100
March 2, 1963
March 9, 1963
March 16, 1963

The 4 Seasons

Frankie Valli (May 3, 1934-?) lead vocals
Bob Gaudio (November 17, 1942-?) keyboards, backing vocals
Tommy DeVito (June 19, 1928-September 21, 2020) guitar, backing vocals
Nick Massi (September 19, 1927-December 24, 2000) bass vocals, bass guitar
Formed in 1956 in Newark, New Jersey

The 4 Seasons: Bob Gaudio, Nick Massi, Frankie Valli, Tommy DeVito

Here's a squabble between two young lovers, being aired in the form of a pop song. This time it's the boy's father who is offering advice to his son.

As the lyrics of "Walk Like A Man" are written, the boy is talking to his girlfriend. "Oh, how you tried to cut me down to size, telling dirty lies to my friends," he tells her. "But my own father said, 'Give her up, don't bother. The world isn't coming to an end.'"

Then comes the chorus: "He said, 'Walk like a man, talk like a man. Walk like a man, my son. No woman's worth crawling on the earth, so walk like a man, my son.'"

In modern parlance, Dad is telling his Junior to "man up."

The final chorus is altered to indicate a break-up is imminent. "I'm gonna walk like a man, fast as I can," he crows. "Walk like a man from you. I'll tell the world, 'Forget about it, girl.' And walk like a man from you."

"Walk Like A Man" was written by 4 Seasons' keyboard player Bob Gaudio and the band's producer, Bob Crewe. They formed a successful songwriting team throughout the early years of the 4 Seasons' stardom.

The arrangement of the song by Charles Calello features a contrast between the deep voice of Nick Massi and the falsetto of Frankie Valli.

The song needed only six weeks to move up the *Billboard* Hot 100 to the top spot.

Recording sessions for "Walk" were held in a tiny studio in the building that housed the Abbey Victoria Hotel on Fifty-Street in New York City. A room above the studio caught fire during a session one day, but Crewe didn't want recording to be interrupted and blocked the door. He was trying to attain perfection with one more take of the song.

Firemen eventually had to use their axes to break through the door to rescue Crewe and the musicians, according to author Joe Sasfy.

•••••••• ❖ ••••••••

"If You Wanna Be Happy" by Jimmy Soul
Songwriters: Carmella Guida, Joseph Royster, Frank Guida
Peaked at number 1 on *Billboard* Hot 100
May 18, 1963
May 25, 1963

Jimmy Soul

August 24, 1942-June 25, 1988
Born James Louis McCleese in Harlem, New York, and died in Spring Valley, New York

Jimmy Soul

A bit of homespun wisdom lies in the humorous lyrics of "If You Wanna Be Happy."

Simply (and delicately) put, the advice is for men to marry unattractive women if they want happy lives.

It was the second and final appearance of Jimmy Soul on the *Billboard* Hot 100. In 1962 he had a number 22 hit with "Twistin' Matilda." Gary U.S. Bonds had turned down that song and "If You Wanna Be Happy." Frank Guida produced both Bonds and Soul, so he fed the rejected songs to Soul.

"If you want to be happy for the rest of your life, never make a pretty woman your wife," the lyrics caution. "So, from my personal point of view, get an ugly girl to marry you."

And why is this sound advice? "A pretty woman makes her husband look small, and very often causes his downfall. As soon as he marries her and then she starts to do the things that will break his heart. But if you make an ugly woman your wife, you'll be happy for the rest of your life.

"An ugly woman cooks meals on time, she'll always give you peace of mind."

Toward the end of the song, we have the narrator meeting a friend. He tells the narrator he saw the narrator's wife recently, and she looked ugly. The narrator retorts, "She's ugly, but she sure can cook."

The songwriters adapted "If You Wanna Be Happy" from a calypso song, "Ugly Woman" written by Rafael de Leon, which Frank Guida heard in Trinidad.

The recording virtually flew under the radar of feminist groups and didn't really catch any flack for its insulting rhetoric. The National Organization for Women wasn't formed until 1966 and now is the largest advocate for women's rights and causes.

"If You Wanna Be Happy," a million seller, was used in the motion pictures *Clean And Sober* (1988), *Chances Are* (1989), *Mermaids* (1990) and *My Best Friend's Wedding* (1997).

•••••••• ❖ ••••••••

"Be Careful Of Stones That You Throw" by Dion

Songwriter: Bonnie Dodd
Peaked at number 31 on B*illboard* Hot 100
August 3, 1963

Sometimes the best advice in song is the kind we don't expect.

In "Be Careful Of Stones That You Throw," we find advice we can actually live by, each and every day.

Dion did a fine cover version of the song first released in 1952 by Hank Williams, recording under the pseudonym of Luke the Drifter. Bonnie Dodd, Williams' steel guitar player, wrote it.

The song exposes the prejudice and hypocrisy that pervades our daily lives and the gossip that spreads it.

The chorus is sung at the beginning, middle and end of the song. It goes like this: "Oh, a tongue can accuse and carry bad news. Gossip is cheap and it's low. So, unless you've made no mistakes in your life, just be careful of stones that you throw."

The title and tag phrase refer to Bible verse John 8:7, in which Jesus seeks forgiveness for a woman who had been an adulterer. He said to the Pharisees who wanted to punish her with stoning, "He that is without sin among you, let him first cast a stone at her."

The first and last verses are spoken rather than sung. The narrator relates how a neighbor passed by his garden one day and stopped to gossip. She had nasty things to say about a certain woman of the town, whom she said "should be run from our midst" because of her drinking and gossiping.

Suddenly a car comes careening down the street, and the sound of squealing brakes is heard. The gossiping woman's daughter had been saved by an unknown brave person, who was hit and killed by removing the girl from harm's way.

The person who saved the girl is the very woman who had been the target of the gossiper's harsh judgement just seconds earlier.

Toward the end of the 1960s, Dion began to express his faith in more of his recordings.

•••••••• ❖ ••••••••

160

"Don't Let The Sun Catch You Crying" by Gerry & the Pacemakers
Songwriter: Gerry Marsden
Peaked at number 4 on *Billboard* Hot 100
July 4, 1964
July 11, 1964

Gerry & the Pacemakers

Gerry Marsden (September 24, 1942-January 3, 2021) lead vocals, guitar
Freddie Marsden (November 23, 1940-December 9, 2006) drums
Les Chadwick (May 11, 1943-December 26, 2019) bass
Les Maguire (December 27, 1941-?) piano
Formed in 1956 in Liverpool, Merseyside, England

The Pacemakers: Les Chadwick, Gerry Marsden, Freddie Marsden, Les Maguire

Gerry Marsden took on the role of advice columnist when he wrote this ballad.

His lyrics advise heartbroken lovers to do their weeping in the nighttime. "The morning will bring joy for every girl and boy," Marsden predicts.

Gerry & the Pacemakers were not the first to release the song in their native England. Briton Louise Cordet, who was 19 at the time, released a version of it in February 1964. It failed to chart, so the Pacemakers recorded Marsden's song. It became their first hit in America.

"The nighttime shadows disappear," the second verse says, "and with them go all your tears."

The final verse declares, "It may be hard to discover that you've been left for another. But don't forget that love's a game, and it can always come again. So, don't let the sun catch you crying."

Gerry & the Pacemakers were the second band signed by manager Brian Epstein – the Beatles being the first. The early part of their career loosely paralleled that of the Beatles, as they played many of the venues in Liverpool, England, and Hamburg, Germany, as did the Fab Four. Beatles' producer George Martin even performed his magic on "Don't Let The Sun Catch You Crying."

However, as the Beatles' career got stronger, the Pacemakers' seemed to wane. They'd had three number 1 singles in England in 1963, but they were off the American charts by 1967.

The band started out as Gerry Marsden & the Mars Bars. After Mars, Inc., filed a complaint about the band carrying the name of its chocolate bar, the group altered its moniker.

Canadian John Hopps invented the first cardiac pacemaker in 1950. The first successful human pacemaker implantation in the United States was performed in 1960.

•••••• ❖ ••••••

"Don't Throw Your Love Away" by the Searchers
Songwriters: Billy Jackson, Jimmy Wisner
Peaked at number 16 on *Billboard* Hot 100
July 11, 1964

The Searchers

Mike Pender (March 3, 1941-?) lead vocals, guitar
Chris Curtis (August 26, 1941-February 28, 2005) drums
Tony Jackson (July 16, 1938-August 18, 2003) bass
John McNally (August 30, 1941-?) guitar
Formed in 1957 in Liverpool, England

The Searchers: John McNally, Mike Pender, Tony Jackson, Chris Curtis

One of the early groups of the British Invasion had some sage words about being selective with your affections.

The Searchers, with a lineup that had evolved since 1957, tied for being the second band from Liverpool, England, to enter the *Billboard* Hot 100 when they and the Swinging Blue Jeans had songs debut on the chart the same week, March 7, 1964. The Beatles, of course, were the first.

162

Their second American hit, "Don't Throw Your Love Away," nearly matched the success of their first, "Needles And Pins," which peaked at number 13 on the Hot 100.

"Don't throw your love away … for you might need it someday," the Searchers advise. "Don't throw your dreams away … keep them another day, for you might need them someday."

The problem, the lyrics point out, is love often is given away too easily.

"Lovers of today just throw their dreams away and play at love," the bridge states. "They give their love away to anyone who'll say, 'I love you.'"

In conclusion, the song urges, "Go out and have your fun, you better have your fun with anyone. But don't throw your love away."

It's actually pretty good advice, but I wonder how many teenaged listeners really took it to heart as they were dancing their cares away in the mid-1960s.

The Orlons of Philadelphia, Pa., were the first to record the song, which was a B-side single in 1963.

The Searchers took their name from the 1956 movie of the same name, starring John Wayne.

"In 1957 John (McNally) and I went to see the film The Searchers," lead singer/guitarist Mike Pender is quoted in Wikipedia. "I was an ardent Western fan, and so I dragged John along with me to see it. I take the credit for choosing the name the Searchers and for co-founding the band in its original form."

The Searchers blitzed the American charts in 1964 with five top singles. Their biggest success was a remake of the Clovers' "Love Potion Number Nine," which crested at number 3. Two minor hits in 1965 were all the Searchers could muster, and they never were able to crack the American top 50 again.

••••••• ❖ •••••••

"Wishin' And Hopin'" by Dusty Springfield
Songwriters: Burt Bacharach, Hal David
Peaked at number 6 on *Billboard* Hot 100
August 1, 1964
August 8, 1964
August 15, 1964

Dusty Springfield

April 16, 1939-March 2, 1999
Born Mary Isobel Bernadette O'Brien in London, England, and died in Henley-on-Thames

Dusty Springfield

Dusty Springfield was doing a little girl talk in the summer of 1964, but a lot of guys listened in. It was her biggest hit until 1966.

The twenty-five-year-old songstress, who was the first female to conquer America during the British Invasion, had some advice for romance-minded females.

"So, if you're looking to find love you can share, all you gotta do is hold him and kiss him and love him and show him that you care," Springfield says in the lyrics of "Wishin' And Hopin'"

The song was the second U.S. hit for Springfield, but it was withheld from the U.K. market because she already had a song on the charts there.

More sage words contained in the song: "Show him that you care just for him. Do the things he likes to do. Wear your hair just for him, 'cause you won't get him thinkin' and a-praying, wishin' and a-hopin'.

Plannin' and dreamin' his kisses will start – that won't get you into his heart. So, if you're thinking how great true love is, all you gotta do is hold him and kiss him and squeeze him and love him. Yeah, just do it and after you do, you will be his."

The message in the music could be excused as an attitude of the times. A few years later, with women's liberation gaining prominence, listeners may have found the topic to be insulting to women, who should be evaluated more by their intellect and personality than their hairstyles or the way they kiss.

According to Songfacts, Springfield said she never saw the song in those terms and was amazed anyone would think that way.

Dionne Warwick recorded the song in 1962, and it became the B-side of her 1963 release "This Empty Place."

Burt Bacharach, who composed the melody of "Wishin' And Hopin'," said to *Record Collector Magazine,* "I remember talking Dusty into putting the record out. Dusty was always very insecure – about what to release, about her voice. What a great singer. Powerful. She was a great girl. Wishin' And Hopin' was great, and it was a big hit."

Springfield died at age 59 from breast cancer. At her induction into the Rock & Roll Hall of Fame, Elton John commented, "I'm biased, but I just think she was the greatest white singer there ever has been ... every song she sang, she claimed as her own."

•••••••• ❖ ••••••••

"Treat Her Right" by Roy Head & the Traits
Songwriter: Roy Head
Peaked at number 2 on *Billboard* Hot 100
October 16, 1965
October 23, 1965

Roy Head

January 9, 1941-September 21, 2020
Born Roy Kent Head in Three Rivers, Texas, and died in Porter, Texas

Roy Head

164

With all of the female bashing going on in pop music, it was time for someone to deliver advice on a way to treat women differently.

That someone turned out to be Roy Head, and "Treat Her Right" was his biggest hit.

The Traits from San Marcos, Texas, a band that played rockabilly, rhythm & blues and rock, backed Head on the record. A brass section of studio musicians added some punch.

"I wanna tell you a story every man ought to know," the lyrics begin. "If you want a little loving, you gotta start real slow. She's gonna love you tonight if you just treat her right."

The next bit of advice might sound a bit like womanizing. "Oh, squeeze her real gentle, gotta make her feel good. Gotta tell her that you love her, like you know you should. If you don't treat her right, she won't love you tonight."

The narrator claims "if you practice my method as hard as you can, you're gonna get a reputation as a lovin' man. And you'll be glad every night that you treated her right."

"Treat Her Right" received an enthusiastic reception from the listening public. It climbed to number 2 on the *Billboard* R&B Chart and, over the next 30 years, it was covered by as many as 20 major artists.

Estimates say worldwide sales of the single have reached four million. The song has appeared in such movies as *The Commitments* (1991) and *Once Upon A Time In Hollywood* (2019).

······· ❖ ·······

"Try A Little Tenderness" by Otis Redding
Songwriters: Jimmy Campbell, Reg Connelly, Henry Woods
Peaked at number 25 on *Billboard* Hot 100
January 28, 1967

Otis Redding

September 9, 1941-December 10, 1967
Born Otis Ray Redding Jr. in Dawson, Georgia, and died near Madison, Wisconsin

Otis Redding

The "King of Soul" put a soulful spin on an old standard, which advises men how to effectively treat their women.

Otis Redding relented to the nagging of label executives at Stax Records and recorded the song in 1966, thirty-four years after the first version was recorded by the Ray Noble Orchestra with vocals by Val Rosing. Redding did not want to record it, according to Songfacts, and it took a lot of persuasion to change his mind.

Here are some examples of the advice built into the lyrics:

"Oh, she may be weary … but when she gets weary, try a little tenderness.

"You know she's waiting … for things that she'll never possess. But while she's waiting without them, try a little tenderness.

"Squeeze her, don't tease her, never leave her."

"Try A Little Tenderness" was recorded by a number of major artists over several decades, including Frank Sinatra, Bing Crosby, Sam Cooke and Aretha Franklin. It's durable popularity identifies it as a song that has stood the test of time.

In 1968, after Redding's death, Three Dog Night recorded a version of the song that was a tribute to Redding's style. He began the song slowly and built to a crescendo.

•••••• ❖ ••••••

"Let's Live For Today" by the Grass Roots
Songwriters: David Shapiro, Giulio Rapetti, Michael Julien
Peaked at number 8 on *Billboard* Hot 100
July 1, 1967
July 8, 1967

The Grass Roots

Rob Grill (November 30, 1943-July 11, 2011) lead vocals, bass
Warren Entner (July 8, 1944-?) guitar, backing vocals
Creed Bratton (February 8, 1943-?) guitar, backing vocals
Rick Coonce (August 1, 1946-February 25, 2011) drums
Formed in 1966 in Los Angeles, California

The Grass Roots: (front) Warren Entner, Creed Bratton (rear) Rob Grill, Rick Coonce

In what evolved into a rallying cry for American troops serving in the Vietnam War, "Let's Live For Today" roamed the record charts during the Summer of Love in 1967 as a piece of advice for lovers.

"When I think of all the worries people seem to find," the song begins, "and how they're in a hurry to complicate their minds by chasing after money and dreams that can't come true, I'm glad that we are different – we've better things to do. May others plan their future, I'm busy loving you."

The chorus states, "Sha la la la la la, live for today, and don't worry about tomorrow."

It was a call for boys and girls and men and women in love to ditch the conflicts of the day and turn to one another for sustenance.

The Hippies listening to the song also found words of comfort – "we'll take the most of living, have pleasure while we can."

But across the Pacific Ocean, the men fighting in the jungles of Vietnam were coming back to America in body bags by the hundreds. They never knew if they would live to see another day.

Writing for Allmusic.com, Bruce Eder wrote, "… where the single really struck a resonant chord was among men serving in Vietnam. The song's serious emotional content seemed to overlay perfectly with the sense of uncertainty afflicting most of those in combat. Parts of the lyric could have echoed sentiments in any number of letters home, words said on last dates and thoughts directed to deeply missed wives and girlfriends. Not surprisingly, Vietnam veterans almost universally profess a deep and abiding love of the song."

For whatever reason the record was purchased, sales surpassed the two-million mark.

"Let's Live For Today" originally was written in 1966 with Italian lyrics and an Italian title. The song's publisher in England, Dick James Music, assigned staffer Michael Julien to write new words.

The Grass Roots, a folk/rock concept band created by Los Angeles producers P.F. Sloan and Steve Barri, went through two incarnations before they persuaded an L.A. group called the 13th Floor to change their name and become the new Grass Roots. That lineup performed "Let's Live For Today" and many of the band's subsequent hits.

••••••• ❖ •••••••

"Don't Sleep In The Subway" by Petula Clark

Songwriters: Tony Hatch, Jackie Trent
Peaked at number 5 on *Billboard* Hot 100
July 8, 1967
July 15, 1967

Petula Clark

Born Petula Sally Olwen Clark on November 15, 1932, in Ewell, Surrey, England

Petula Clark

167

If it seems "Don't Sleep In The Subway" lacks clarity and continuity, there's a reason.

The melody is an amalgamation of three unfinished songs written by Tony Hatch, Petula Clark's producer. And some of the verbiage in the lyrics is a British idiom.

A "subway" is a pedestrian underpass to the English.

The words are spoken from the female partner to her lover as they are quarreling. The woman advises the man to stay with her and work things out rather than storm out and end up standing in the rain or sleeping outdoors.

She urges him to remove his coat, close the door and settle their differences there and then. Over-reacting won't solve anything.

"You wander around on your own little cloud when you don't see the why or the wherefore," she begins. "You walk out on me when we both disagree, because to reason is not what you care for."

In the chorus, she says, "Don't sleep in the subway, darling. Don't stand in the pouring rain. The night is long, forget your foolish pride. Nothing's wrong, now you're beside me again."

Later she states, "Goodbye means nothing when it's all for show. So, why pretend you've somewhere else to go?"

Clark has said she considers this song to be one of her two favorite songs of the many she has recorded. "I Couldn't Live Without Your Love," another song written by Hatch and his wife Jackie Trent, is the other.

Apparently, Clark never bothered to analyze the meaning of "Don't Sleep In The Subway." She told Songfacts in 2013, "It's a bit of a mystery to me, the song. But it's got to be one of my favorites, though I'm not quite sure what it's about. It doesn't matter."

Clark, who was the most prolific female recording star of the British Invasion, started a long, illustrious show business career during World War II when her songs were broadcast on the BBC. Later, she did acting in motion pictures and was dubbed "Britain's Shirley Temple."

She began appearing on television in 1946, at the age of thirteen, and began recording songs in 1949. Her career fell on hard times in the early 1960s but, with Hatch's help, it was reborn in late 1964 when she entered the realm of pop music with the number 1 hit "Downtown."

Clark was a novelty on the pop charts, releasing her first song in America at the age of thirty-two and then successfully competing with the likes of the Beatles, the Rolling Stones, the Animals and Herman's Hermits.

"Hey Jude" by the Beatles

Songwriters: John Lennon, Paul McCartney
Peaked at number 1 on *Billboard* Hot 100
September 28, 1968
October 5, 1968
October 12, 1968
October 19, 1968
October 26, 1968
November 2, 1968
November 9, 1968
November 16, 1968
November 23, 1968

The Beatles

Paul McCartney (June 18, 1942-?) lead vocals, bass, handclaps
John Lennon (October 9, 1940-December 8, 1980) backing vocals, acoustic guitar, handclaps
George Harrison (February 25, 1943-November 29, 2001) backing vocals, electric guitar, handclaps
Ringo Starr (July 7, 1940) backing vocals, drums, tambourine, handclaps
Formed in 1960 in Liverpool, England

The Beatles: George Harrison, Paul McCartney, John Lennon, Ringo Starr

Paul McCartney was like an uncle to John Lennon's first son, Julian. After John ended his marriage with Julian's mother, Cynthia, Paul drove out one day to visit Cynthia and Julian at the family's home in Weybridge, Surrey, England.

In the car, McCartney put together part of a song. According to Paul, it started with "Hey, Jules," a shortened form of Julian. Later, he thought a better name was Jude.

It was a form of consolation for the kid, who was five years old at the time.

In comforting Julian, McCartney offered some advice: "Don't make it bad. Take a sad song and make it better. Any time you feel the pain, refrain. Don't carry the world upon your shoulders."

Lennon helped McCartney finish the song on July 26, 1968, according to author Fred Bronson.

There are metaphors throughout the lyrics which make the target of the advice ambiguous. One school of thought has the advice targeted at Lennon, who had recently begun a romance with Yoko Ono. Another says it was about McCartney, consoling himself after breaking up with long-time girlfriend Jane Asher.

More advice in the lyrics: "For well you know that it's a fool who plays it cool by making his world a little colder. And don't you know that it's just you, hey Jude, you'll do. The movement you need is on your shoulder."

Cynthia Lennon remarked to writer John Kehe, "I was touched by his obvious concern for our welfare. On the journey down, he composed 'Hey Jude' in the car. I will never forget Paul's gesture of care and concern in coming to see us."

While McCartney desired a hundred-piece orchestra to play behind his vocals, producer George Martin could come up with only 40 musicians on short notice. Recording concluded on August 1, 1968. "Hey Jude" became the first single released on the Beatles' new label, Apple Records.

The final take was revolutionary. The track timed out at seven minutes eleven seconds, which set a record for a number 1 single. The final four minutes consists of an assembled group of vocalists singing, "Na na na na na na na, na na na na, hey Jude." During that span, McCartney added some improvised phrases.

"Hey Jude" entered the *Billboard* Hot 100 at number 10, and two weeks later it started a nine-week run at number 1. That makes it the Beatles' most successful hit in America.

Worldwide sales of the single have exceeded the eight-million mark.

•••••••• ❖ ••••••••

"Only The Strong Survive" by Jerry Butler

Songwriters: Kenny Gamble, Leon Huff, Jerry Butler
Peaked at number 4 on *Billboard* Hot 100
April 19, 1969

Jerry Butler

December 8, 1939-February 20, 2025
Born Jerry Butler Jr. in Sunflower, Mississippi and died in Chicago, Illinois

Jerry Butler

"I remember my first love affair. Somehow or another, the whole darn thing went wrong. But my mama had some great advice, so I thought I'd put it in the words of this song."

Those spoken words begin one of the great advice songs of the 1960s.

The fictitious mama delivered these words, among others: "… there's gonna be a whole lot of trouble in your life, so listen to me, get up off your knees, 'cause only the strong survive. "You gotta be strong, you better hold on."

Jerry Butler sang and cowrote the song. The former lead singer of the Impressions, whose family moved to Chicago, Illinois, from Mississippi when he was 3, was recording for Mercury Records in 1968. He was joined by Philadelphia producers Leon Huff and Kenny Gamble to make the album *The Ice Man Cometh* in late '68.

"Only The Strong Survive" was destined to be just another track on the album until a radio disc jockey from Texas started playing it on the air. After the song rose to number 4 on the pop chart and number 1 on the R&B chart, it became Butler's biggest hit.

More advice from Mama: "There's a whole lot of girls looking for a good man like you, but you'll never meet 'em if you give up now and say your life is through … you've gotta be a man, you've gotta take a stand."

As a solo artist, Butler was on the pop chart from 1960 to 1977. His songs kept hitting the R&B chart until 1983. Philadelphia DJ Georgie Woods gave him the name "Ice Man" while doing a show at a Philadelphia theater because of Butler's cool singing style.

He began a second career as a politician in 1985 when he began serving as a Cook County (Ill.) commissioner. He retired from public service in 2018.

•••••••• ❖ ••••••••

"It's Your Thing" by the Isley Brothers

Songwriters: Ronald Isley, O'Kelly Isley, Rudolph Isley
Peaked at number 2 on *Billboard* Hot 100
May 3, 1969

The Isley Brothers

Ronald Isley (May 21, 1941-?)
O'Kelly Isley (December. 25, 1937-March 31, 1986)
Rudolph Isley (April 1, 1939-?)
Began performing together in 1954 in Blue Ash, Ohio

The Isley Brothers: O'Kelly, Ronald, Rudolph

If it feels good, do it.

That hedonistic catchphrase has been a song title. And it is an oversimplification of the meaning of "It's Your Thing."

The narrator of the lyrics is advising a girl to go where her heart leads her and date whomever she wants. He will be there for her if she wants him – maybe.

"It's your thing, do what you want to do," he says. "I can't tell you who to sock it to. "If you want me to love you, maybe I will. Believe me, woman, it ain't no big deal."

It sounds as if he seriously wanted to date her exclusively at one time. After she decided to play the field, he doesn't care as much anymore. Likely, he has had his feelings crushed and doesn't want that pain again.

"I'm not trying to run your life, I know you wanna do what's right," he frankly states. "Give your love now to whoever you choose. How can you lose, with the stuff you use?"

The song began to form in Ronald Isley's head one day when he was driving his daughter Tawana to school. So that he wouldn't lose his train of thought, he kept humming the melody while he rushed to his mother's house, where he wrote down the lyrics. O'Kelly and Rudolph helped him finish the song.

"It's Your Thing" received a funky treatment with horns and piano, and 16-year-old brother Ernie played bass in his first recording session.

In the 1970s, brothers Vernon and Marvin joined Ernie and vocalists Ronald, O'Kelly and Rudolph to turn the family act into a full band.

For the Isleys, the success of "It's Your Thing" was sweet. Atlantic Records dropped them in 1965, and they signed with Motown. However, they felt they were getting far less promotion than other Motown vocal groups, such as the Temptations, Miracles and Four Tops. So they cut ties with Motown in 1968 and went back to recording on their dormant label, T-Neck Records.

Berry Gordy, head of Motown, claimed the Isley's still were under contract to him when they recorded "It's Your Thing." He sued and, according to Songfacts, the case stayed in the courts for eighteen years before a federal judge decided the Isleys had recorded the song after their Motown contract had been terminated.

The song hit number 1 on the *Billboard R&B Chart*, and it won a Grammy Award for best R&B vocal performance by a duo or group.

•••••••• ❖ ••••••••

"Clean Up Your Own Back Yard" by Elvis Presley
Songwriters: Billy Strange, Mac Davis
Peaked at number 35 on *Billboard* Hot 100
August 9, 1969
August 16, 1969

Elvis Presley

January 8, 1935-August 16, 1977
Born Elvis Aron Presley in Tupelo, Mississippi, and died in Memphis, Tennessee

Elvis Presley

Here's a familiar phrase. According to author and motivational speaker Larry Winget, "clean up your own backyard" means, "Change by example. Just be the way you want others to be, and hope they pay attention."

The songwriting team of Mac Davis and Billy Strange posed this axiom, which Elvis Presley sang in the 1969 movie *The Trouble With Girls (and How to Get into It)*.

The lyrics examine three examples of people who need to do some "cleaning up:"
- A "back porch preacher" who rails about morals, yet is lying in his bed with a hangover on Sunday mornings.
- A "drug store cowboy" who stands on a sidewalk and advises people how to act and what to do, acting like he is better than them. At night he sneaks out and cheats on his wife.
- An "armchair quarterback" who meddles in other peoples' lives, yet won't admit he has ever been wrong about anything.

Advice from the song: "Don't hand me none of your lines. You tend to your business, I'll tend to mine."

The Trouble With Girls is set in a small town in Iowa in 1927. That makes the term "armchair quarterback" an anachronism, since it was coined in the 1960s, when televised football games began to proliferate. The term identifies a person who second-guesses decisions after someone else made them.

Production of the film began before the airing of Presley's comeback NBC television special on December 3, 1968. *Singer Presents … Elvis* was used to revive a lifeless recording career. The Svengali-like manager Col. Tom Parker wasn't letting Elvis do anything but soundtrack albums from his movies until this act of revolt. The special was taped at NBC Studios the previous June.

The soundtrack of the movie failed to generate excitement among fans. The movie itself did poorly in cinemas but seemed to be popular at drive-in theaters.

•••••• ❖ ••••••

"Arizona" by Mark Lindsay
Songwriter: Kenny Young
Peaked at number 10 on *Billboard* Hot 100
February 14, 1970

Mark Lindsay

Born Mark Allen Lindsay on March 9, 1942, in Eugene, Oregon

Mark Lindsay

The narrator's girlfriend is a hippie, and he believes it is time for her to grow up and change her ways.

"Arizona" was written in the heyday of the Hippie Movement, in which young Americans were rejecting traditional values, starting with the war in Vietnam. Mark Lindsay, who was still employed as the lead singer of Paul Revere & the Raiders, recorded the song in 1969 to begin a solo career.

The narrator dishes out advice left and right to this starry-eyed girl: "… take off your rainbow shades… have another look at the world… cut off your Indian braids … take off your hobo shoes."

He also tells "Arizona" to "strip off your pride, you're acting like a teeny-bopper runaway child. And scrape off the paint from the face of a little town saint."

In an effort to get the girl to adopt his ideals, he tells her, "Hey, won't you go my way?"

But, in the last verse, he appears to give in to her, since he doesn't want to lose her.

"Follow me up to San Francisco," he says, "I will be guide your way. I'll be the Count of Monte Cristo, you'll be the Countess May. You can believe in Robin Hood and brotherhood and rolling the ball in the hay, and I will be reading you an Aesop's fable, anything to make you stay."

The success of the single made it clear Lindsay could step outside the band he had fronted since 1961 to be a solo star. He was back in the top 25 later in 1970 with "Silver Bird."

•••••• ❖ ••••••

174

"Walk A Mile In My Shoes" by Joe South & the Believers
Songwriter: Joe South
Peaked at number 12 on *Billboard* Hot 100
February 14, 1970
February 21. 1970
February 28, 1970

Joe South

February 28, 1940-September 5, 2012
Born Joseph Alfred Souter in Atlanta, Georgia, and died in Buford, Georgia

Joe South

It's an old message that Joe South poignantly brought to the realm of pop music: take my advice, and don't judge me if you haven't experienced what I've had to go through.

In other words, "Walk A Mile In My Shoes" before criticizing me.

It was a way of trying to bring people together, and just a few weeks later Ray Stevens released a song with a similar message, "Everything Is Beautiful."

"If I could be you, if you could be me for just one hour, if we could find a way to get inside each other's mind," the lyrics begin. "If you could see you through my eyes instead of your ego, I believe you'd be surprised to see that you've been blind."

The chorus advises, "… before you abuse, criticize and accuse, walk a mile in my shoes."

More advice comes in the way of cautioning us not to ostracize another person just because he doesn't think or wear his hair the same as we do.

Hearkening back to a song profiled earlier in this chapter, the lyrics say, "So unless you've lived a life of total perfection, you better be careful of every stone that you should throw. And yet we spend the day throwing stones at one another …"

The lyrics also broach the subject of race. "There are people on reservations and out in the ghettos. And brother, there but for the grace of God go you and I."

The dawn of the 1970s was a time of racial strife, war protest and generational divide. "Walk A Mile In My Shoes" was kind of a one-stop shop for visiting all of those issues.

The Believers, who sang back-up on the track, consisted of Tommy South, Joe's brother, and his sister-in-law Barbara South. Joe South also served as producer.

The *Billboard* Easy Listening chart, which later became the Adult Contemporary chart, had the song peaking at number 3.

South went through a dark period in his life in which he used recreational drugs heavily. "I didn't see myself doing (drugs) for the kicks. I did it more or less to keep going, and to tap into inspiration. I equated the chemicals with the inspiration."

His 1968 song "Games People Play" won two Grammy Awards. "The Grammy is a little like a crown," South told the Los Angeles Times. "After you win it, you feel like you have to defend it. In a sense, I froze. I found it hard to go back in to the recording studio because I was afraid the next song wouldn't be perfect."

He died of a heart attack in his home at the age of seventy-two, according to BBC.com.

•••••••• ❖ ••••••••

"Treat Her Like A Lady" by the Cornelius Brothers & Sister Rose

Songwriter: Eddie Cornelius
Peaked at number 3 on *Billboard* Hot 100
July 3, 1971
July 10, 1971

The Cornelius Brothers & Sister Rose

Eddie Cornelius (June 19, 1943-?)
Carter Cornelius (October 5, 1948-November 7, 1991)
Rose Cornelius (1948-?)
Formed in 1970 in Dania Beach, Florida

From top: Eddie, Carter and Rose Cornelius

Webster's New Universal Unabridged Dictionary defines *lady* as: a woman of good breeding or some social position; the correlative to *gentleman*.

This is how a man should treat a woman, according to Eddie Cornelius, who wrote "Treat Her Like A Lady" and was the lead singer of the Cornelius Brothers and Sister Rose.

This sentiment echoes the message in "Treat Her Right."

"All my friends had to ask me something they didn't understand," the advice begins. "How I get all the women in the palm of my hand. "I told them, treat her like a lady, do the best you can do. You gotta treat her like a lady, she'll give in to you."

Perhaps that last phrase should be worded "she'll respect you."

The bridge has more advice. "Oh, you've got to love her, tease her, but most of all you've got to please her. You've got to hold her and want her and make her feel you'll always need her."

Another nugget of wisdom: "You know a woman is sentimental and so easy to upset. So, make her feel that she's for real, and she'll give you happiness."

The narrator of the lyrics has a sly motive, it turns out. "If you fail to do this, don't blame her if she looks my way. 'Cause I'm gonna treat her like a lady, so affectionately."

A song about treating women in a warm way received a great reception. "Treat Her Like A Lady" became a million seller and paved the way for the Cornelius Brothers & Sister Rose to hit number 2 in 1972 with another million seller, "Too Late To Turn Back Now." In '72 the trio welcomed another sister, Billie Jo, into the vocal group.

•••••••• ❖ ••••••••

"Follow Your Daughter Home" by the Guess Who

Songwriters: Burton Cummings, Donnie McDougall, Garry Peterson, Bill Wallace, Kurt Winter

Peaked at number 61 on *Billboard* Hot 100

March 10, 1973

March 17, 1973

The Guess Who

Burton Cummings (December 31, 1947-?) vocals, keyboards

Garry Peterson (May 26, 1945-?) drums, backing vocals

Kurt Winter (April 2, 1946-December 14, 1997) lead guitar, backing vocals

Bill Wallace (May 18, 1949-?) bass

Donnie McDougall (November 5, 1948-?) rhythm guitar

Formed in 1962 in Winnipeg, Manitoba, Canada

The Guess Who: (standing) Bill Wallace, Garry Peterson
(seated) Donnie McDougall, Kurt Winter, Burton Cummings

Concerned dads, or parental stalkers?

Fans who listened to their radios in 1973 pondered this choice when the Guess Who advised them to "Follow Your Daughter Home."

Sure, the concern is there. Parents should always know where their teenaged girls are going, what they're doing and who they are running around with.

But the lyrics may be going too far when they say, "Is she still a virgin … tie her up!"

A lively calypso beat drives the melody, and a flute plays a prominent part.

"Keep her out of trouble, staying out late in the mall with the bad men," says the first verse. "Keep her out of mischief. What are the boys like she's running and dancing with?"

We also hear the advice, "… ask her a lot of questions about the boys she's sleeping with."

The message may have been a turn-off for fans of the Guess Who. While the song reached number 20 on the Canadian chart, it didn't get within shouting distance of the top 40 of the *Billboard* Hot 100.

Yet, it stands as one of the more unique pieces of advice issued in the history of rock & roll.

········ ❖ ········

"You Can't Always Get What You Want" by the Rolling Stones

Songwriters: Mick Jagger, Keith Richards
Peaked at number 42 on *Billboard* Hot 100
June 9, 1973

The Rolling Stones

Mick Jagger (July 26, 1943-?) vocals
Keith Richards (December 18, 1943-?) electric and acoustic guitars
Bill Wyman (October 24, 1936-?) bass
Charlie Watts (June 2, 1941-August 24, 2021)
Brian Jones (February 28, 1942-July 3, 1969)
Formed in 1962 in London, England

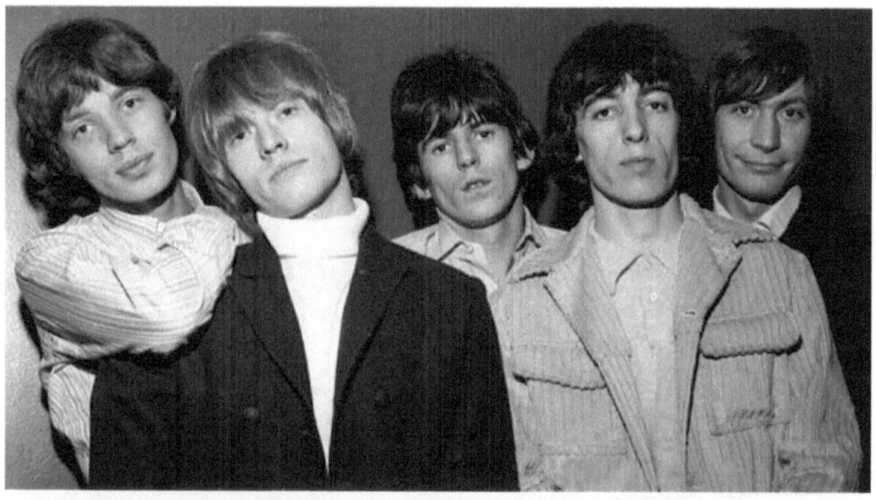

The Rolling Stones: Mick Jagger, Brian Jones, Keith Richards, Bill Wyman, Charlie Watts

Words of advice, yes. And words to live by, as well.

The Rolling Stones' "You Can't Always Get What You Want" got its first release in the summer of 1969 as the B-side of "Honky Tonk Women." Four years later, it got pressed onto 45 rpm records again as an A-side.

By that time, the song title and the phrase "but if you try sometime, you'll find you get what you need" had found their way into the lexicon of pop culture.

The five-minute single, having been shortened by 2½ minutes from the *Let It Bleed* album version, features French horn played by Al Kooper. The intro sung by the youths in the London Bach Choir was omitted from the single.

Lyrical content deals with three topics: love, politics and drugs. In the chorus following each verse, we are reminded that we can't have what we desire all the time, but our needs are met.

In the book *According To The Rolling Stones,* Mick Jagger is quoted as saying, "'You Can't Always Get What You Want' was something I just played on the acoustic guitar – one of those bedroom songs. It proved to be quite difficult to record because Charlie (Watts) couldn't play the groove, and so Jimmy Miller had to play the drums. (Miller was the band's record producer from 1968 to '73.)

"I'd also had this idea of having a choir, probably a gospel choir, on the track, but there wasn't one around at that point. (Choral arranger) Jack Nitzsche, or somebody, said that we could get the London Bach Choir and we said, 'That will be a laugh.'"

British pop star and former Jagger girlfriend Marianne Faithfull told author Max Bell, "I know they used me as a muse for those tough drug songs. I knew I was being used, but it was for a worthy cause." Faithfull famously lost her career after she suffered drug addiction, which permanently damaged her voice.

Guitarist Brian Jones, who died the day before the single's release in '69, was still a member of the Rolling Stones when the track was recorded but did not play on it.

In 2004, *Rolling Stone Magazine* rated "You Can't Always Get What You Want" as number 100 on its list of 500 Greatest Songs of All Time.

•••••• ❖ ••••••

"Rikki Don't Lose That Number" by Steely Dan

Songwriter: Donald Fagen, Walter Becker
Peaked at number 4 on *Billboard* Hot 100
August 3, 1974

Steely Dan

Donald Fagen (January 10, 1948-?) vocals
Walter Becker (February 20, 1950-September 3, 2017) bass, backing vocals
Jeff Baxter (December 13, 1948-?) lead guitar
Studio musicians:
Dean Parks – acoustic guitar
Michael Omartian – piano
Jim Gordon – drums
Victor Feldman – flapamba, percussion
Formed in 1971 in Hicksville, New York

Steely Dan: Walter Becker and Donald Fagen

Maybe this has happened to you. At a party, you meet someone for whom you have a strong attraction. Despite long odds of you and this person ever having a relationship, you give him/her your telephone number in hopes of getting a call. Perhaps you reinforce the exchange with the advice, "Don't lose this number."

That is basically what happened to Donald Fagen when he was a student at Bard College in the late 1960s. The person he met at a party one night was Bard student Rikki Ducornet, who not only was married to one of Fagen's professors, but was also pregnant at the time.

Fagen turned a real life experience into a song, something he became very good at.

"We hear you're leaving, that's okay," the first verse begins. "I thought our little wild time had just begun. I guess you kind of scared yourself, you turn and run. But if you have a change of heart, Rikki don't lose that number."

The narrator adds, "You might use if you feel better when you get home."

Later, he tells Rikki, "You tell yourself you're not my kind, but you don't even know your mind. And you could have a change of heart …"

After leaving Bard, Ducornet became a writer, poet and artist. In an interview with Steven Moore, she said, "Philosophically, it's an interesting song. I mean, I think his 'number' is a cipher for the self.

"Maybe Fagen intuited that, at the time we met, I was indeed losing my number."

Steely Dan recorded "Rikki Don't Lose That Number" at a time when Fagen and Walter Becker were beginning to transition the band from a set, five-man lineup into a duo that would employ some of the top studio musicians in the world on a song-by-song basis. They stopped touring in 1974 to concentrate on creating masterpieces in the recording studio.

On practically every track they recorded, Steely Dan used elements of jazz. "We're basically all jazz fans, and most of the records we listen to are jazz," Fagen said in 1975, according to Faroutmagazine.co.uk.

"We're pretty cold at the moment. We've more or less abandoned hope of being one of the big, important Rock & Roll groups, simply because our music is somehow a little too cheesy at times and turns off the rock intelligentsia for the most part, and at other times it's too bizarre to be appreciated by anybody."

Steely Dan graduated from being a band with a cult following into a worldwide phenomenon with the release of their album "Aja" in 1977. The album spawned three hit singles, peaked at number 3 on the *Billboard* 200 and sold over two million units in the United States alone.

•••••• ❖ ••••••

"Fooling Yourself (The Angry Young Man)" by Styx

Songwriter: Tommy Shaw
Peaked at number 29 on *Billboard* Hot 100
April 22, 1978

Styx

Tommy Shaw (September 11, 1953-?) lead vocals, acoustic guitar
James Young (November 14, 1949-?) electric guitar, backing vocals
Dennis DeYoung (February 18, 1947-?) keyboards, backing vocals
Chuck Panozzo (September 20, 1948-?) bass
John Panozzo (September 20, 1948-July 16, 1996) drums
Formed in 1972 in Chicago, Illinois

Styx: Dennis DeYoung (seated), Chuck Panozzo, James Young,
Tommy Shaw, John Panozzo

A big dose of personal advice comes in this progressive rock song, which has a lengthy intro of one minute twenty-two seconds.

The recipient of the advice was not just any person.

Tommy Shaw wrote and sang lead vocals on "Fooling Yourself (The Angry Young Man)," and his advice was aimed at Styx bandmate Dennis DeYoung.

"You see the world through your cynical eyes – you're a troubled young man, I can tell," the lyrics begin. "You've got it all in the palm of your hand, but your hand's wet with sweat, and your head needs a rest. And you're fooling yourself if you don't believe it … why must you be such an angry young man, when your future looks quite bright to me?"

The answer to the cynicism? "Get up, get back on your feet. You're the one they can't beat, and you know it. Come on, let's see what you've got. Just take your best shot, and don't blow it."

Shaw told Songfacts, "In a way, that song was from me to Dennis. The seeds of discontent had started to take over on the road. The rest of us were all really happy at the time, but Dennis wasn't getting quite the same joy.

"I was trying to tell him there was all this great stuff going on and to enjoy it more. It was frustrating to see someone so talented and loved, but not getting more out of the experience. Whether or not he understood, I don't know. It was fairly subtle."

In a twist of irony, in later years Shaw saw himself in the lyrics, since he, too, had a cynical streak.

As the instrumental middle part of the recording is about to begin, with DeYoung playing a synthesizer solo, a muffled voice can be heard. It is Shaw beckoning DeYoung by his nickname, "Come on, Doctor."

Styx performed a small routine during their live performances at the point in which the various band members would be introduced by name. DeYoung would be held for last, and Shaw would enquire of the audience, "Has anyone seen the Doctor?" DeYoung then would enter the stage wearing a lab coat and stethoscope and prescribe "more rock & roll."

"Fooling Yourself," with a lackluster showing on the pop chart, nonetheless helped its album "The Grand Illusion" become a number 6 entry on the *Billboard* 200 and a 3 million seller in the U.S.

•••••••• ❖ ••••••••

"Take The Long Way Home" by Supertramp
Songwriters: Roger Hodgson, Rick Davies
Peaked at number 10 on *Billboard* Hot 100
December 15, 1979
December 22, 1979
December 29, 1979

Supertramp

Roger Hodgson (March 21, 1950-?) lead vocals, piano, electric guitar
Rick Davies (July 22, 1944-?) harmonica, synthesizers, Hammond organ
Dougie Thomson (March 24, 1951-?) bass
Bob Siebenberg (October 31, 1949-?) drums, tambourine
John Helliwell (February 15, 1945-?) synthesizer, clarinet
Formed in 1969 in London, England

Supertramp: Dougie Thomson, Bob Siebenberg, John Helliwell, Roger Hodgson, Rick Davies

So, your marriage has lost its spark? Your wife is treating you like dirt? Maybe you should grab a little me-time and "Take The Long Way Home" to keep your distance from the situation.

That's the advice from Supertramp in a hit song that was part of a monster album from 1979, "Breakfast In America."

"There are times that you feel you're part of the scenery," the lyrics say. "All the greenery is coming down, boy. And then your wife seems to think you're part of the furniture. Oh, it's peculiar, she used to be so nice."

Primary songwriter Roger Hodgson provided some insight on the song's message. "I'm talking about not wanting to go home to the wife. Take the long way home to the wife because she treats you like part of the furniture, but there's a deeper level to the song, too.

"I really believe we all want to find our home, find that place in us where we feel at home, and to me, home is in the heart and that is really when we are in touch with our heart and we're living our life from our heart. Then we do feel like we found our home.

"It was another angle on the question that ran deep inside me, which is 'where's my home? Where's peace?' It felt like I was taking a long way to find it."

It's a bummer when you think you're doing well in life, but your spouse throws put-downs at you.

"When you're up on the stage, it's so unbelievable," a later verse says. "Oh, unforgettable, how they adore you. But then your wife seems to think you're losing your sanity. Oh, calamity, is there no way out? Does it feel that your life's become a catastrophe? Oh, it has to be for you to grow, boy.

"So when the day comes to settle down, who's to blame if you're not around? You took the long way home."

According to Songfacts, when Hodgson held a press conference upon the release of *Breakfast In America,* he addressed "Take The Long Way Home" individually. He explained, "This song is about a guy who thinks he's really cool ('so you think you're a Romeo, playing a part in a picture show'), but it seems that he's the only one who thinks that. This implies that our hero avoids getting home because, when he's on the road, he has a few more moments of being alone with his dreams, and in his dreams he's a superstar."

"Take The Long Way Home" was the last of four singles released from *Breakfast In America.* The album spent six weeks at number 1 on the *Billboard* 200, and it sold more than four million units in the United States and over three million in France.

•••••• ❖ ••••••

"Don't Fall In Love With A Dreamer" by Kenny Rogers with Kim Carnes

Songwriters: Kim Carnes, David Ellingson
Peaked at number 4 on *Billboard* Hot 100
May 24, 1980
May 31, 1980
June 7, 1980

Kenny Rogers

August 21, 1938-March 20, 2020
Born Kenneth Ray Rogers in Houston, Texas, and died in Sandy Springs, Georgia

Kim Carnes

Born Kim Carnes on July 20, 1945, in Los Angeles, California

Kim Carnes and Kenny Rogers

Advice for women looking for romance: don't fall in love with a dreamer.

Kenny Rogers delivered these sage words during a torrid streak: he put seventeen songs on the top 40 of the *Billboard* Hot 100 between 1977 and 1983.

Pop singer Kim Carnes and her husband David Ellingson wrote "Don't Fall In Love With A Dreamer" as part of Rogers' concept album, "Gideon." The modern cowboy theme centers around fictional character Gideon Tanner.

As the male narrator of the duet, Rogers imparts, "… it'd be so easy to tell you I'd stay, like I've done so many times."

Carnes counters, "I was so sure this would be the night you'd close the door and want to stay with me."

It's all about the man warning the woman that, despite their mutual attraction, he is no good for her. Falling in love with him would be a mistake.

The two spend a night together, but it's going to be a one-night stand.

"Now it's morning and the phone rings, and you say you've got to get your things together. You just gotta leave before you change your mind," Carnes sings.

Rogers' reply: "And if you knew what I was thinking, girl, I'd turn around if you'd just ask me one more time."

The situation is distilled in the chorus. "Don't fall in love with a dreamer, 'cause he'll always take you in. Just when you think you've really changed him, he'll leave you again. Don't fall in love with a dreamer, 'cause he'll break you every time."

As they concocted the lyrics, Carnes and Ellingson painted Gideon Tanner as a ladies' man and a rogue, according to Countrythangdaily.com.

The ballad scored highly on several charts. The *Billboard* Adult Contemporary Chart showed it peaking at number 2, and it crested at number 3 on the Hot Country Songs Chart. In Canada it hit number 1 on the country and adult contemporary charts.

•••••••• ❖ ••••••••

"Don't Let Him Go" by REO Speedwagon
Songwriter: Kevin Cronin
Peaked at number 24 on *Billboard* Hot 100
August 1, 1981
August 8, 1981

REO Speedwagon

Gary Richrath (October 18, 1949-September 13, 2015) lead guitar
Kevin Cronin (October 6, 1951-?) vocals, rhythm guitar
Alan Gratzer (November 9, 1948-?) drums
Bruce Hall (May 3, 1953-?) bass
Neal Doughty (July 29, 1946-?) synthesizer
Formed in 1966 in Champaign, Illinois

REO Speedwagon: Neil Doughty, Bruce Hall, Gary Richrath, Kevin Cronin, Alan Gratzer

If a guy is a little on the wild side – maybe not exactly what a girl wants in a boyfriend – have patience and give him time to straighten out. Don't drop him just yet.

That's the advice REO Speedwagon issued in "Don't Let Him Go," a single from one of the most successful albums of the 1980s, "High Infidelity."

"He's the kind of lover that the ladies dream about … he's got plenty of cash, he's got plenty of friends," the lyrics point out. "He drives women wild, then he drives off in a Mercedes-Benz.

"He's got a long wick with a flame at both ends. He's hot, but don't let him go. Just give him a chance to grow. Take it easy, take it slow, and don't let him go."

Sure, this guy has some downside. But that doesn't make him worth dumping.

"He makes you so angry, he makes you so sore. The wait may be worth it, but how can you wait anymore when you're wondering what you're waiting for? "Baby, I don't know, but don't let him go."

In an interview with Matt Wardlaw, songwriter Kevin Cronin said the song is based on the experiences of all the members of REO Speedwagon and basically is a plea to all their girlfriends to have patience with them. Cronin admitted the melody is based on a "slightly modified Bo Diddley beat."

Several of the songs on "High Infidelity" were inspired by stormy relationships the band members had with women. The album was number 1 on the *Billboard* 200 for fifteen weeks, non-consecutively, making it the top album of 1981. It generated over 10 million units sold in the United States.

•••••• ❖ ••••••

"Don't Talk To Strangers" by Rick Springfield

Songwriter: Rick Springfield
Peaked at number 2 on *Billboar*d Hot 100
May 22, 1982
May 29, 1982
June 5, 1982
June 12, 1982

Rick Springfield

Born Richard Lewis Springthorpe on August 23, 1949, in Guildford, New South Wales, Australia

Rick Springfield

Advice mothers often give to their young children: don't talk to strangers.

Rick Springfield took this gem and applied it to a boyfriend giving advice to his girlfriend. He is hopeful of keeping another suitor from swiping his girl.

"When you were just a young girl and still in school, how come you never learned the golden rule?" he asks his girlfriend. "Don't talk to strange men, don't be a fool. I'm hearing stories, I don't think that's cool. Why don't you tell me someone is loving you?"

Why is the girl at risk? "You know he'll only use you up."

Here's a clever line of lyrics: "Love hurts when only one's in love. Did you fall at first sight, or did you need a shove?"

In explaining how the song came to be, *Variety* printed this Springfield quote: "It was (written) to my girlfriend (Barbara Porter), who is my wife now, because I was being a bad boy on the road, and I was nervous that she was doing the same thing. I never had marriage on the radar until I met Barbara. She's the reason I'm still alive.

186

"Back then, I was scared that she was (messing) around because I was doing the same thing. Strangely enough, I had originally titled 'Jessie's Girl' 'Don't Talk To Strangers,' and then I came up with a better title."

Springfield married Porter, a native of Wisconsin, in October 1984 at his family's church in Australia. They have two sons.

"Don't Talk To Strangers" was the first track released as a single from the album *Success Hasn't Spoiled Me Yet.* The album reached number 2 on the *Billboard* 200 and was a million seller in the U.S.

Soft sell
How mellow rock dominated the first half of the 1970s

Overview: A few notable things were happening in rock music as 1970 started a new decade. The Beatles had disbanded, the drug-fueled Psychedelic Era was ending and a different kind of rock swooped in to fill the void. It was soft rock.

While some of the 1960s artists like B.J. Thomas and Neil Diamond stayed around to push the mellow music movement, a raft of new artists used light rock to get their careers going.

Ironically, the Beatles played a significant role in the light rock surge, even though they had not recorded since the summer of 1969. A cover version of their 1965 number 1 single "Ticket To Ride" became the break-out hit for the Carpenters. Although it was released in November 1969, it peaked at number 54 on the *Billboard* Hot 100 in May 1970. The tempo was slowed to make it a sad ballad.

In 1970, the Beatles released two singles from the Get Back sessions of 1969, which became number 1 hits in America: "Let It Be" and "The Long And Winding Road." Both were keyboard dominant and played at a slow pace.

The 1970s also gave rise to the FM radio format, which had existed for years but finally got utilized by rock radio outlets. This enabled niche stations to satisfy fans of both hard rock and mellow rock.

Hard rock groups like Led Zeppelin, Grand Funk Railroad and Black Sabbath sustained their popularity in the '70s, but soft rock was king for a solid five years.

At the midpoint of the decade, soft rock was buried under the avalanche of the powerful disco music fad.

To view the full lyrics of these songs, please log on to www.google.com, enter song titles & artist names and click Google Search.

To listen to these songs, please log on to www.youtube.com and enter song titles & artist names.

"Raindrops Keep Fallin' On My Head" by B.J. Thomas
Songwriters: Burt Bacharach, Hal David
Peaked at number 1 on *Billboard* Hot 100
January 3, 1970
January 10, 1970
January 17, 1970
January 24, 1970

B.J. Thomas

August 7, 1942-May 29, 2021
Born Billy Joe Thomas in Hugo, Oklahoma, and died in Arlington, Texas

B.J. Thomas

It was a marriage made in Rock & Roll heaven – a hit movie like *Butch Cassidy and the Sundance Kid* paired with a theme written by Burt Bacharach and Hal David and sung by golden-throated B.J. Thomas.

Working with a budget of $6 million, the 1969 film grossed over $102 million in North America. The single blew away the competition, becoming the first number 1 song of the 1970s while selling over two million copies in its first four months.

Bacharach and David offered the song to Ray Stevens, who turned it down, according to Musicaloud.com. There are rumors that Bob Dylan also rejected the song.

Bacharach got the idea for the song as he viewed the Paul Newman-Katharine Ross bicycle scene in the movie. Dionne Warwick, who had worked closely with Bacharach and David for years, recommended Thomas to them.

"It was a very unique and different sounding song," Thomas said in a 2011 interview. The intro, for example, is played on ukulele. "Bacharach and David never had any qualms about trying to do anything different or push the envelope, so to speak.

"So nowadays, it sounds pretty tame, but back then, radio resisted it to some degree. But, when the movie came out, it hit hugely and sold about 200,000 to 300,000 records a day for about three years."

Thomas was a bit intimidated by Bacharach, who produced the record.

"I asked Mr. Bacharach if I could do my thing on the song," Thomas told *The Tennessean* shortly before he died of cancer. "He said, 'B.J., after you do the song precisely how I've written it, if you have room to do something, you can do it.'

"So, it really didn't happen until the 'me-e-e-e-e' at the end."

On that final word, Thomas stretched the single syllable into a trademark five-syllable ending.

189

    "They were doing an art film, and the score was very different" Thomas said. "The only instruments used on the film were on 'Raindrops.' The entire film's score was done vocally. They were making an artistic statement, but to us it was a great Western, not necessarily an art film. That was (actor Robert Redford's) reason for objecting to having this song in the movie. "Thank goodness he got over that and admitted later that he felt he was wrong about that, and that the song fit perfectly."

    Thomas kept ringing up light rock songs on the pop charts for the next three years with songs like "I Just Can't Help Believing," "Most Of All," No Love At All" and "Mighty Clouds Of Joy."

Courtesy of 20th Century Fox

•••••• ❖ ••••••

"Mama Told Me (Not To Come)" by Three Dog Night

Songwriter: Randy Newman
Peaked at number 1 on *Billboard* Hot 100
July 11, 1970
July 18, 1970

Three Dog Night

Cory Wells (February 5, 1941-October 20, 2015) vocals
Chuck Negron (June 8, 1942-?) vocals
Danny Hutton (September 10, 1942-?) vocals
Joe Schermie (February 12, 1946-March 26, 2002) bass
Jimmy Greenspoon (February 7, 1948-March 11, 2015) keyboards
Michael Allsup (March 8, 1947-?) guitar
Floyd Sneed (November 22, 1942-?) drums
Formed as Redwood in 1967 in Los Angeles, California

Three Dog Night: (back) Joe Schermie, Floyd Sneed, Michael Allsup, Jimmy Greenspoon; (front) Danny Hutton, Cory Wells, Chuck Negron

Admittedly, Three Dog Night had some raucous moments in some of their early singles, on such recordings as "Try A Little Tenderness," "One" and "Celebrate."

By the time they released "Mama Told Me (Not To Come)," they had settled into a mellow mood that would take them well into the 1970s.

The song is about a trepidatious guy who goes to a party that has elements his mother told him to avoid. There's alcoholic beverages and drugs. After he looks for his girlfriend, he finds she has passed out on the floor. Loud music permeates the scene.

"Don't turn on the lights, because I don't want to see," he begs. The drug culture was beginning to wane when the single hit the stores, but the song had been written four years earlier by Randy Newman, who was little known at the time. Eric Burdon and the Animals put it on their 1967 album *Eric Is Here*.

Going to outside songwriters for their hits was nothing new for Three Dog Night. They recorded songs by Harry Nilsson, Hoyt Axton, Danny More and Paul Williams, to name a few.

Cory Wells, one of three lead singers in the band, convinced TDN to record "Mama," and he sang lead. After the single became the first of the band's three number 1 hits, Newman called Wells to tell him, "I just want to thank you for putting my kids through college."

Newman wrote and recorded his own hit single in 1977 with the sarcastic "Short People." He also wrote and sang "It's A Jungle Out There," the theme song to the hit USA Network television show *Monk* in 2003.

Three Dog Night found more success with light rock hits "Out In The Country," "Liar," "An Old Fashioned Love Song," "Never Been To Spain" and "Black & White."

Ironically, Wells was the first of the TDN singers to die, as he succumbed to multiple myeloma at the age of seventy-four. He was the only one of the three who didn't have a drug or alcohol problem.

••••••• ❖ •••••••

"(They Long To Be) Close To You" by the Carpenters
Songwriters: Burt Bacharach, Hal David
Peaked at number 1 on *Billboard* Hot 100
July 25, 1970
August 1, 1970
August 8, 1970
August 15, 1970

The Carpenters

Richard Carpenter (October 15, 1946-?)
Born Richard Lynn Carpenter in New Haven, Connecticut
Karen Carpenter (March 2, 1950-February 4, 1983)
Born Karen Anne Carpenter in New Haven, Connecticut, and died in Downey, California
First performed as a duo in 1969

Richard and Karen Carpenter

A song written by Burt Bacharach and Hal David in 1963 became the Carpenters' first number 1 smash and did as much as any other song to cement the trend toward mellow rock in 1970.

"(They Long To Be) Close To You" turned up when Richard Carpenter was searching for songs to put into a medley for a charity fundraiser. Bacharach had wanted Herb Alpert to record it, but Alpert wasn't comfortable singing a line like "… they sprinkled moon dust in your hair of gold."

Alpert was the co-founder of A&M Records, which signed the Carpenters. A career trumpet player, he had a number 1 hit as a singer with "This Guy's In Love With You" in 1968.

Carpenter's arrangement, along with his sister Karen's velvety vocal, helped propel "Close To You" to a prolonged stay at number 1 on the *Billboard* Hot 100, as well as the Adult Contemporary chart. It took the single only three months to attain million-selling status.

Richard Chamberlain, Dionne Warwick and Dusty Springfield recorded early, unheralded versions of the song.

On the Carpenters' version, Alpert was supposed to play the flugelhorn solo on the instrumental middle part. But he was unavailable during the recording sessions, so Chuck Findley played it. Richard Carpenter played acoustic piano, Wurlitzer electric piano and harpsichord.

The original take had Karen playing the drums. Producer Jack Daugherty thought the sound was a little "light," according to Songfacts. So session drummer Hal Blaine took over in a subsequent session.

The syrupy love song contains the verse: "Why do birds suddenly appear every time you are near? Just like me, they long to be close to you."

Alpert was so elated with the success of the recording, he sent the Carpenters a handwritten note dated July 22, 1970, proclaiming, "We're number 1." Fifty years later, Richard still had the framed missive on a wall in his home.

The Carpenters' success lasted virtually a decade. Follow-up soft rock hits included "We've Only Just Begun," "For All We Know," "Rainy Days And Mondays," Superstar" and "Hurting Each Other."

Karen Carpenter died of complications of anorexia nervosa at the age of thirty-two.

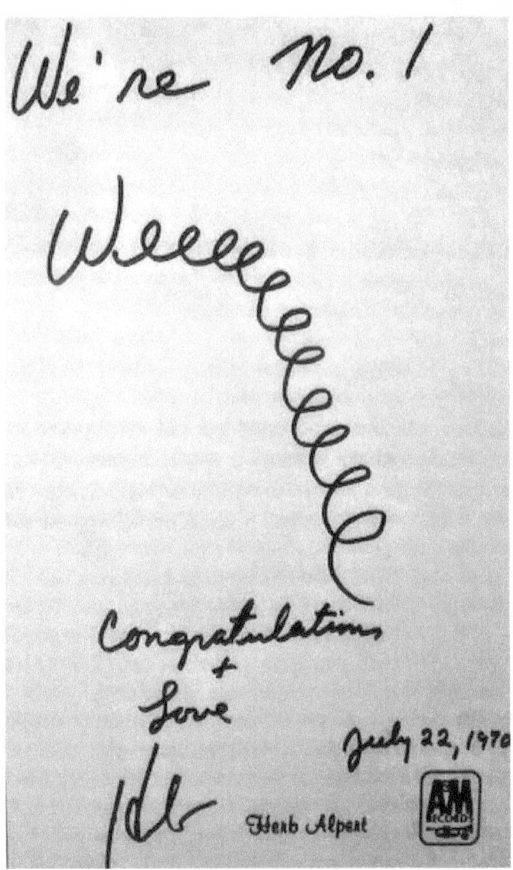

Herb Alpert's note to the Carpenters

•••••• ❖ ••••••

"Make It With You" by Bread

Songwriter: David Gates
Peaked at number 1 on *Billboard* Hot 100
August 22, 1970

Bread

David Gates (December 11, 1940-?) lead vocals, acoustic guitar, electric guitar, bass
Jimmy Griffin (August 10, 1943-January 11, 2005) guitar, keyboards
Robb Royer (December 6, 1942-?) guitar
Mike Botts (December 8, 1944-December 9, 2005) drums
Formed in 1968 in Los Angeles, California

Bread: Robb Royer, David Gates, Mike Botts, Jimmy Griffin

After the first album recorded by Bread was a failure, the band members decided to record one more before they would consider dissolving the group.

It was a great decision. Among the tracks recorded for their sophomore effort "On The Waters" was "Make It With You," which sent Bread on their way to a four-year run of soft rock hits.

David Gates, who had written songs for other artists, wrote "Make It With You" and produced the recording. It was the first time he had heard his own voice on the radio, and it was a thrill for him.

To keep their momentum going, Bread reworked a song from their eponymous first album, "It Don't Matter To Me." The result was a top 10 hit.

According to author Greg Metzer, Gates described the selection of the band's name thusly: "A bread truck came along right at the time we were trying to think of a name. We had been saying, 'How about bush, telephone pole? Ah, bread truck, bread.'

"It began with a B, like the Beatles and the Bee Gees. Bread also had a kind of universal appeal. It could be taken a number of ways. Of course, for the entire first year, people called us the Breads."

While a couple of their subsequent releases were up-tempo rock numbers, Bread's forte was romantic ballads. A few examples: "If, " "Baby I'm-A Want You," "Everything I Own" and "Diary."

•••••• ❖ ••••••

194

"Candida" by Dawn

Songwriters: Toni Wine, Irwin Levine
Peaked at number 3 on *Billboard* Hot 100
October 3, 1970
October 10, 1970

Dawn

Tony Orlando [born Michael Anthony Orlando Cassavitis] (April 3, 1944-?)
Telma Hopkins (October 28, 1948-?)
Joyce Vincent (December 14, 1946-?)
Formed in 1970 in New York City

Dawn: Telma Hopkins, Tony Orlando, Joyce Vincent

A few music fans, such as myself, thought they were getting a great song by a new artist when "Candida" by Dawn started getting play on radio stations in the summer of 1970.

We didn't know at the time the lead singer was Tony Orlando, who had hits with "Halfway To Paradise" and "Bless You" in 1961. That was a little before I became deeply immersed in pop/rock music.

Fast forward to 1970. Producers Dave Appell and Hank Medress sought to record "Candida" for Bell Records. The artist selected to record it was Frankie Paris, according to author Marti Smiley Childs. Paris's effort met with dissatisfaction, and the producers looked for another singer.

They put a heavy Latin feel on "Candida" because of the New York City areas in which they grew up, and Medress thought "an ethnic feel" would be appropriate. He turned to his friend, Orlando, because Tony's heritage was Puerto Rican and Greek. At the time, Orlando was managing Columbia Records' publishing division.

Orlando was reluctant to sing it, for fear of jeopardizing his job at a rival record label. Medress assured him that his name would not be used, since the song would be released under a ghost name. Not believing the song had hit potential, Orlando agreed. Toni Wine, the song's cowriter, and Jay Siegel of the Tokens sang backing vocals, according to Childs.

Bell released the single under the moniker Dawn in July of '70, and it caught on like wildfire with mainstream radio stations. On Sept. 28, WLS radio rated it the number 1 song in Chicago.

"Tony not only is a great singer, but he has great ears," Wine told Songfacts. "He really does. As a person that could marry a song to an artist. And that was what he did. So, he had a very successful career as a music publisher/rep, but he still had that great voice that he wasn't singing."

Orlando filled out an album of songs with the help of Wine, Robin Grean, Ellie Greenwich, Leslie Miller and Linda November. A second release, "Knock Three Times," became a national number 1 song, and Bell executives were desperate to have a real band promote the music.

Orlando invited career back-up singers Telma Hopkins and Joyce Vincent to join him as Dawn, and they quickly came on board. Eventually, they became known as Tony Orlando & Dawn.

According to Wine, the name Dawn was used because it was the name of Bell executive Steve Wax's daughter.

The act churned out hits like "Summer Sand," "Tie A Yellow Ribbon Round The Ole Oak Tree" and "Say, Has Anybody Seen My Sweet Gypsy Rose."

From 1974 to 1977, they had their own variety show on CBS-TV.

•••••••• ❖ ••••••••

"Cracklin' Rosie" by Neil Diamond

Songwriter: Neil Diamond
Peaked at number 1 on *Billboard* Hot 100
October 10, 1970

Neil Diamond

Born Neil Leslie Diamond on January 24, 1941, in Brooklyn, New York

Neil Diamond

For his first number 1 single, songwriter/singer Neil Diamond turned to the lore of the indigenous people of northern Canada.

Supposedly, Diamond got the idea from a reporter during an interview in Toronto, Ontario.

He was told of a small town where the men badly outnumbered the women. On Saturday nights, men would go out to find a date. But after all the women were taken, the others resorted to buying the inexpensive wine called crackling rosé. That would be their "woman" for the weekend. Hence, the song title was a play on the wine's name.

This was Diamond's second song about wine. In 1967 he wrote and recorded "Red Red Wine." After Diamond had left Bang Records, the label continued to release some of his recordings as singles, and that one peaked at number 62 on the *Billboard* Hot 100 in 1968. Bang also placed the track on Diamond's first greatest hits album.

The opening lines of "Cracklin' Rosie:"

"Aw, Cracklin' Rosie, get on board. We're gonna ride till there ain't no more to go, taking it slow. And Lord, don't you know, we'll have me a time with a poor man's lady."

Later we hear, "Girl, if it lasts for an hour, well that's all right 'cause we got all night to set the world right."

The record's best chart performance was in New Zealand, where it stayed at number 1 for five weeks.

The Good Wine Co. of Auckland, New Zealand, sells a crackling rosé (named for its crisp flavor and reddish color) from the Westbrook winery, described as "juicy, summery and slightly spritzy." It is a blend of three varietals – pinot noir, malbec and cabernet franc.

The now-defunct Andres Wines of British Columbia produced a crackling rosé that was popular among small-town native Canadians.

Over the next two years Diamond cranked out more mellow recordings like "I Am … I Said," "Stones," "Song Sung Blue," "Play Me" and "Walk On Water."

•••••••• ❖ ••••••••

"One Less Bell To Answer" by the 5th Dimension
Songwriters: Burt Bacharach, Hal David
Peaked at number 2 on *Billboard* Hot 100
December 26, 1970
January 2, 1971

The 5th Dimension

Marilyn McCoo (September 30, 1943-?)
Billy Davis Jr. (June 26, 1938-?)
Ron Townson (January 29, 1933-August 2, 2001)
Florence LaRue (February 4, 1942-?)
Lamonte McLemore (September 17, 1939-?)
Formed as the Versatiles in 1965 in Los Angeles, California

5th Dimension: Florence LaRue, Ron Townson, Billy Davis Jr.,
Lamonte McLemore, Marilyn McCoo

Marilyn McCoo established herself as the mainstay on lead vocals of the 5th Dimension in 1969 when she belted out "Wedding Bell Blues," a number 1 single.

A year later, the vocal group utilized her talents as a torch singer. Her passionate effort on "One Less Bell To Answer" produced a number 2 hit on the *Billboard* Hot 100 and a number 1 entry on the *Billboard* Adult Contemporary Chart.

The song was another success for the songwriting team of Bacharach & David. According to notes in Wikipedia, they wrote the song in 1967 for Keely Smith, who never recorded it. Bones Howe, the 5th Dimension's producer, rediscovered the song late in 1969.

The mournful song is about a woman who has lost her man. She laments, "One less man to pick up after. I should be happy, but all I do is cry.

"I don't know how in the world to stop thinking of him 'cause I still love him so. I end each day the way I start out, crying my heart out."

Hal David told The Independent in 2008 how he came up with some of the song's lyrics. "I paid attention to what people said. One time I was at a dinner party when it was announced someone wasn't turning up, and the hostess said, 'That's one less bell to answer.'

"I went home and wrote 'One Less Bell To Answer.' One less spells the answer. One less egg to fry."

Shortly after the single was released, the 5th Dimension made a guest appearance on the ABC-TV series It Takes A Thief, and they performed the song during the episode.

The 5th Dimension followed up the song with mellow hits such as "Love's Lines, Angles And Rhymes," "Never My Love," "(Last Night) I Didn't Get To Sleep At All" and "If I Could Reach You."

•••••••• ❖ ••••••••

"Your Song" by Elton John

Songwriters: Elton John, Bernie Taupin
Peaked at number 8 on *Billboard* Hot 100
January 23, 1971
January 30, 1971
February 6, 1971
February 13, 1971

Elton John

Born Reginald Kenneth Dwight on March 25, 1947, in Pinner, Middlesex, England

Elton John

This love ballad launched the international superstardom of Elton John, who was unknown outside of England at the time.

John recorded "Your Song" in January 1970, but Uni Records did not release it until October of that year.

Three Dog Night, with whom John was touring, actually released their version first, as an album track on "It Ain't Easy." They declined to issue their recording as a single so that John could take his shot at a chart breakthrough with it.

Bernie Taupin, who would stay in a lengthy songwriting partnership with John, wrote the lyrics. As would become customary, John composed the melody.

Taupin and John met after a record company passed along some of Taupin's lyrics to John, according to Songfacts. Ultimately, they both moved into the home of John's parents and began crafting songs together.

According to a blog, Taupin said, "I scribbled the ("Your Song") lyric down on a lined notepad at the kitchen table of Elton's mother's apartment in the London suburb of Northwood Hills, breakfast time sometime in 1969. That's it. Plain and simple."

The accompaniment features John's trademark acoustic piano, as well as acoustic guitar, orchestral strings, a double bass and harp.

The lyrics portray the protagonist as a man of modest means who is professing his love to his sweetheart. "I don't have much money but, boy, if I did, I'd buy a big house where we both could live … "And you can tell everybody this is your song. It might be quite simple but, now that it's done, I hope you don't mind that I put down in words how wonderful life is when you're in the world."

In a 1989 interview with *Music Connection,* Taupin remarked, "It's like the perennial ballad … which has got to be one of the most naïve and childish lyrics in the entire repertoire of music, but I think the reason it still stands up is because it was real at the time. That was exactly what I was feeling. I was 17 years old, and it was coming from someone whose outlook on love or experience with love was totally new and naïve."

One rock music fan whose life was greatly impacted by "Your Song" is Juan Navarro of Glendale, Ariz. He recalls it being one of Elton John's first "great romantic hits."

Navarro commented, "I was excited to hear the lyrics and the melody, a romantic song that was a total success in the United States." He was thrilled to buy John's first greatest hits album, which contained "Your Song," and listening to the songs on that album cemented his undying love for the British star.

On the heels of "Your Song," John released mellow hits such as "Friends," "Levon," "Rocket Man," "Honky Cat," "Daniel" and "Don't Let The Sun Go Down On Me."

•••••••• ❖ ••••••••

"If You Could Read My Mind" by Gordon Lightfoot
Songwriter: Gordon Lightfoot
Peaked at number 5 on *Billboard* Hot 100
February 20, 1971
February 27, 1971
March 6, 1971

Gordon Lightfoot

November 17, 1938-May 1, 2023
Born Gordon Meredith Lightfoot Jr. in Orillia Ontario, Canada, and died in Toronto, Ontario

Gordon Lightfoot

A dark, brooding ballad about a broken marriage vaulted Canadian Gordon Lightfoot into the limelight of the American music scene early in 1971.

In a 2010 interview with The Canadian Press, Lightfoot revealed the words of "If You Could Read My Mind" came to him as he sat in his Toronto home, which was empty and up for sale due to his pending divorce.

"I was, of course, going through some emotional trauma leading up to a separation, so that … manifested itself in that particular song on that particular afternoon," Lightfoot said. "I'll never forget that afternoon."

The empty house was one Lightfoot had sought to use for lyrical inspiration, he explained. "I would go in there with a chair and a table. I have a Quebec table here that fits in the trunk of my car that I take with me. (I have) just the chair and the table and the pad and the manuscript."

Lightfoot was divorced twice and, at the time of his death, was on his third marriage.

The second verse of "If You Could Read …" says "If I could read your mind, love, what a tale your thoughts could tell. Just like a paperback novel, the kind the drugstore sells. When you reach the part where the heartaches come, the hero would be me. "But heroes often fail, and you won't read that book again because the ending's just too hard to take."

The acoustic treatment of the recording allows a listener to hear and savor the words. An acoustic twelve-string guitar is augmented only by symphonic strings. There is no percussion. Lenny Waronker and Joe Wissert produced it. Wissert would produce some Boz Scaggs albums in later years.

Bob Dylan has said, "I can't think of any Gordon Lightfoot song I don't like. Every time I hear a song of his, it's like I wish it would last forever. Lightfoot became a mentor for a long time. I think he probably still is to this day."

Lightfoot died of natural causes in a Toronto hospital at the age of eighty-four.

His other songs in the early '70s also were light fare: "Beautiful," "Sundown," "Carefree Highway" and "Rainy Day People."

•••••••• ❖ ••••••••

"I Don't Know How To Love Him" by Helen Reddy

Songwriters: Andrew Lloyd Webber, Tim Rice
Peaked at number 13 on *Billboard* Hot 100
June 5, 1971
June 12, 1971
June 19, 1971

Helen Reddy

October 25, 1941-September 29, 2020
Born Helen Maxine Reddy in Melbourne, Australia, and died in Los Angeles, California

Helen Reddy

It took Helen Reddy about twenty-six years to become an overnight sensation with this song from the rock opera *Jesus Christ Superstar.*

Reddy had begun her career at the age of four as a vaudevillian singer and dancer in her native Australia. By the time she was twenty-five, she won a talent competition on a local television show and was awarded a trip to New York City and a recording audition.

The audition didn't produce a contract, but she made attempts to break into the business in Chicago and Los Angeles. She recorded "I Believe In Music" in 1970 on Capitol Records, and the B-side, "I Don't Know How To Love Him," broke through on the American and Canadian charts.

Yvonne Elliman, who sang the song in the role of Mary Magdalene in the stage production of Jesus Christ Superstar, also had a version on the charts the same time as Reddy's. The Elliman version peaked at number 28.

Both versions preceded the premier of the Broadway production, building interest in the show. Andrew Lloyd Webber and Tim Rice began writing music for the rock opera in 1969. The album was released in 1970.

"Ironically, the whole thing was not what we'd aimed for, because we were still really trying to write for the theatre, and this album was a kind of demonstration record," Rice told Songfacts.

Elliman reprised her role in the 1973 film Jesus Christ Superstar, and she won a Golden Globe Award for her efforts.

The song's first verse reads, "I don't know how to love him, what to do, how to move him. I've been changed, yes, really changed. In these past few days when I've seen myself, I seem like someone else."

Reddy released her signature song, "I Am Woman," in 1972 and remained a strong contributor of mellow hits with songs such as "Peaceful," "Delta Dawn," "Leave Me Alone (Ruby Red Dress)," "You And Me Against The World" and "Angie Baby."

Before she died at the age of seventy-eight, Reddy suffered from Addison's disease and dementia. Publicly, no cause for her death was given.

•••••• ❖ ••••••

"It's Too Late" by Carole King
Songwriters: Carole King, Toni Stern
Peaked at number 1 on *Billboard* Hot 100
June 19, 1971
June 26, 1971
July 3, 1971
July 10, 1971
July 17, 1971

Carole King

Born Carol Joan Klein on February 9, 1942, in Manhattan, New York

Carole King

After Carole King released "It's Too Late" and the blockbuster album "Tapestry," I had one rhetorical question: Carole, why did you wait so long?

She had a modestly successful single in 1962, "It Might As Well Rain Until September." Then she concentrated on her other specialty, songwriting, for nine years.

"It's Too Late" shook me to my core. I cannot believe how much I loved, and still love, that song and the spell it puts me under.

The song has just a few elements: King's amazing vocals and acoustic piano; electric guitar (Danny Kortchmar); soprano saxophone (Curtis Amy); bass (Charlie Larkey); electric piano (Ralph Schuckett), and drums (Joel O'Brien). The way producer Lou Adler put them together is pure magic.

Toni Stern wrote the lyrics, while King composed the melody. According to author Sheila Weller, Stern said she penned the lyrics in one day, following her breakup with James Taylor.

Stern often would write lyrics on a notepad and then hand it to King. "She would take that pad, put it on the piano stand, and within an hour, hour and a half at the most, she would have the melody," Stern told Americansongwriter.com.

Author Fred Bronson revealed King said in a 1970 interview, "I didn't want people to interpret what I wrote. I think I have a block against that. People can point to a phrase in lyrics." That explained her reluctance to record her own songs.

King also commented, "I want to make LPs. I don't want to be a star."

Make LPs, she did. But she failed on the star part. Her albums and songs were so successful over the next five years that she became an international star. "It's Too Late," a double A-side hit with the rocker "I Feel The Earth Move," won a Grammy Award for Record of the Year and sold over a million units. Tapestry was a Billboard 200 number 1 album for fifteen weeks.

The songs on Tapestry were a series of tales woven from a female perspective, but men found them appealing, as well. In the lyrics of "It's Too Late," it's the woman who is breaking off the relationship with her man. There is a heap of sorrow and regret in King's voice.

King's own marriage to Gerry Goffin, her songwriting partner for many years, hit the rocks in 1968. Then she moved from New York City to southern California, where she met Stern.

"I'm sure there was a California quality in me that appealed to Carole," Stern told Songfacts. "She was moving from a familial, middle class lifestyle to Laurel Canyon, where she started to let her hair down, literally and figuratively. We worked off our contrasts."

The break-up is finalized in the song's last verse: "There'll be good times again for me and you, but we just can't stay together, don't you feel it too? Still, I'm glad for what we had and how I once loved you."

King used her momentum from "It's Too Late" to stay on the charts with mellow songs like "So Far Away," "Sweet Seasons," "Been To Canaan," "Believe In Humanity" and "Jazzman."

•••••••• ❖ ••••••••

"That's The Way I've Always Heard It Should Be" by Carly Simon

Songwriters: Jacob Brackman, Carly Simon
Peaked at number 10 on *Billboard* Hot 100
July 10, 1971
July 17, 1971

Carly Simon

Born Carly Elisabeth Simon on June 25, 1945, in The Bronx, New York

Carly Simon

When Carly Simon blew onto the record charts with her first hit single, it was a breath of fresh air for the music industry.

"That's The Way I've Always Heard It Should Be" laid bare the failures of family relationships in a powerful, sophisticated way. The piano-dominated production includes strings, as well as heavy drum riffs at the end of each verse.

Simon once told a concert audience it is "a weird song about marriage."

Surprisingly, it was Simon who composed the melody, while her collaborator Jacob Brackman wrote the lyrics. The lyrical observations come from a woman's point of view.

According to Songfacts, Simon met Brackman in 1967 at a summer camp, where they both were counselors. She credits him with being a substantial influence on her development as a songwriter.

"When I first wrote it," Simon told The Independent in 2010, "I thought it was an unusual thing for people to break up, and now all my friends are divorced."

The second verse reads, "My friends from college, they're all married now. They have their houses and their lawns. They have their silent noons, tearful nights, angry dawns. Their children hate them for the things they're not, they hate themselves for what they are. And yet they drink, they laugh – close the wound, hide the scar."

Simon had her own failed marriages, which bound her to singer/songwriter James Taylor from 1972 to 1983, and writer James Hart from 1987 to 2007.

Her father was Richard Simon, co-founder of the Simon and Schuster publishing company. She has said her parents expected a boy when she was born and even had the name Carl picked out. They kept the name for their third daughter and just added a "y" to the end.

Having sung as a duo with her sister Lucy, Carly first approached Columbia Records in an effort to get a solo contract. Legendary Columbia president Clive Davis turned her down, but Elektra signed her.

Simon developed a stuttering problem at the age of six. "I had a stammer," she told Brainandlife.org. "And the only time it went away was when I sang. One day, my mother said to me, 'Don't speak it, sing it.' And that's what I did."

She later became a spokesperson for stuttering awareness.

Simon's popularity increased through the early '70s with soft rock songs like "Anticipation," "You're So Vain," "The Right Thing To Do" and "Haven't Got Time For The Pain."

•••••• ❖ ••••••

"You've Got A Friend" by James Taylor

Songwriter: Carole King
Peaked at number 1 on *Billboard* Hot 100
July 31, 1971

James Taylor

Born James Vernon Taylor on March 12, 1948, in Boston, Massachussets

James Taylor

Lurking within Carole King's fourteen-time platinum album *Tapestry,* the gem "You've Got A Friend" sent James Taylor to the top of the singles chart for the only time in his illustrious career.

King wrote the song, but Ode Records did not release her version as a single.

"The song was as close to pure inspiration as I've ever experienced. "The song wrote itself. It was one of those moments when I sat down at the piano and it wrote itself from some place other than me," King told *Mojo Magazine.*

It was a case of one friend helping another, since the King-Taylor friendship goes way back. Guitarist Danny Kortchmar introduced them, and King served as opening act on Taylor's concert tour in the spring of 1971.

King's version came with her accompaniment on piano, while Taylor's was acoustic guitar oriented. But the result was the same: both won a Grammy Award, with King getting the trophy for writing Song of the Year and Taylor winning one for Best Pop Male Vocal Performance.

According to Taylor, King told him the inspiration for the song came from James himself. His 1970 hit "Fire And Rain" contains the line "I've seen lonely times when I could not find a friend."

Taylor and King went on a four-month, fifty-seven-show concert tour together in 2010 to celebrate the 40th anniversary of their first performance together at the Troubadour Club in West Hollywood, Calif. Gross ticket sales were over $1 million in all but ten cities, even though some venues were quite small.

"When you're down and troubled and you need some loving care," the song begins, "and nothing is going right, close your eyes and think of me, and soon I will be there to brighten up even your darkest night."

To this day, "You've Got A Friend" evokes feelings of unconditional, friendly love, which restores faith that people are on Earth to help one another through challenging times.

Taylor followed up with other mellow hits like "Long Ago And Far Away," "Don't Let Me Be Lonely Tonight," "Mockingbird" (with his wife Carly Simon) and "How Sweet It Is (To Be Loved By You)."

•••••••• ❖ ••••••••

"How Can You Mend A Broken Heart" by the Bee Gees

Songwriters: Barry Gibb, Robin Gibb
Peaked at number 1 on *Billboard* Hot 100
August 7, 1971
August 14, 1971
August 21, 1971
August 28, 1971

The Bee Gees

Barry Gibb (September 1, 1946-?)
Robin Gibb (December 22, 1949-May 20, 2012)
Maurice Gibb (December 22, 1949-January 12, 2003)
First performed in 1956 in Chorlton, Manchester, England

The Bee Gees: Barry, Robin and Maurice Gibb

What a difference a break makes – a break from performing together, in the case of the Brothers Gibb.

They had been performing together as musicians since the mid-1950s, but a feud among them came to a head in 1969. According to Smoothradio.com, Robin Gibb believed the band's manager, Robert Stigwood, was trying to push older brother Barry to be the front man. Robin wanted lead vocals to be his alone. So, he quit and set out on a solo career.

What followed was a bit of chaos, as Gibb sister Lesley briefly joined the band, as did Colin Petersen. Then Barry and Maurice recorded the album *Cucumber Castle* by themselves.

That album sold poorly, and Maurice and Barry went off to record their own solo albums, which were never released.

By then, Robin had his own album on the market, *Robin's Reign.* And it struggled to find buyers.

206

In mid-1970, Robin extended a proverbial olive branch by calling Barry and suggesting a Bee Gees reformation. Said Maurice, "We just discussed it and re-formed. We want to apologize publicly to Robin for the things that have been said."

Robin commented to *Time Magazine,* "If we hadn't been related, we would probably never have gotten back together."

Barry told a New Zealand publication in 2017, "I remember lots of intense arguments, not speaking to each other for weeks and then coming back together again.

"It doesn't stop you being brothers. We broke up in 1969, and yet my brothers came to my wedding in 1970 and we started talking again – and suddenly we were back in the studio."

The reunion sparked new creativity in the trio's writing. "Lonely Days" became a number 3 smash on the *Billboard Hot 100,* and "How Can You Mend A Broken Heart" was the Bee Gees' first number 1 single in America.

These songs did not have the same musical formula as the ones that made the Bee Gees the toast of the Disco Era in the late 1970s. Quiet ballads were their mainstay in the first half of the decade.

"How Can You Mend" is sung from the point of view of a man who is suffering from a broken heart. He asks several rhetorical questions in the chorus:

"How can you mend a broken heart? How can you stop the rain from falling down? How can you stop the sun from shining? What makes the world go round? How can you mend a broken man? How can a loser ever win? Please help me mend my broken heart and let me live again."

The next few Bee Gees releases were "My World," "Run To Me" and "Alive."

•••••••• ❖ ••••••••

"If Not For You" by Olivia Newton-John
Songwriter: Bob Dylan
Peaked at number 25 on *Billboard* Hot 100
September 4, 1971

Olivia Newton-John

September 26, 1948-August 8, 2022
Born Olivia Newton-John in Cambridge, England, and died at her home in Santa Ynez Valley, California

Olivia Newton-John

Olivia Newton-John recorded her first single in 1966 – "Till You Say You'll Be Mine." It didn't chart in any market.

Five years later she was ready to launch an international career, and she picked an easy-going song to get it started. "If Not For You" charted in five English-speaking countries.

The song already had a pedigree. Bob Dylan wrote it and included it on his 1970 album *New Morning*. He wrote the lyrics in honor of his first wife, Sara. The Dylans' marriage ended in divorce in June 1977.

George Harrison placed it on his 1970 debut solo album, "All Things Must Pass." Newton-John's version adopted Harrison's arrangement.

On the *Billboard* Easy Listening chart, her rendition spent three weeks at number 1.

"I wasn't keen on that song at all," Newton-John is quoted in 1,000 UK number 1 Hits. "But I'm so glad John (Farrar) chose it because it's not one that I would have picked. I didn't think I sang it well, so when it was a hit, you know I had to really say it was my management, and Bruce Welch and John Farrar who produced it, that were really the ones that thought it was a good record for me.

"Because in those days I loved singing those big, dramatic ballads – talk about being sentimental!"

Songs ONJ recorded later in the 1970s and early 1980s overshadowed her work in the early '70s. But she took her place in shaping the soft side of the decade with other hits like "Let Me Be There," "If You Love Me (Let Me Know)," "I Honestly Love You" and "Have You Never Been Mellow."

The songstress/actress died of cancer a month and a half before her seventy-fouth birthday.

•••••• ❖ ••••••

"A Horse With No Name" by America

Songwriter: Dewey Bunnell
Peaked at number 1 on *Billboard* Hot 100
March 25, 1972
April 1, 1972
April 8, 1972

America

Dewey Bunnell (January 19, 1952-?) lead vocal, acoustic guitar
Gerry Beckley (September 12, 1952-?) 12-string guitar, backing vocals
Dan Peek (November 1, 1950-July 24, 2011) bass, backing vocals
Formed in 1970 in London, England

America: (front) Dan Peek (rear) Gerry Beckley, Dewey Bunnell

Two years after the Beatles broke up and went on to their respective solo careers, another musical "invasion" came from England.

Late winter 1972 brought to the United States of America the acoustic sounds of a trio of young men who called themselves America.

Dan Peek, Dewey Bunnell and Gerry Beckley had been living in Britain for several years but laid a legitimate claim to their moniker. They were sons of Americans who were stationed at an Air Force base in London, and an Americana jukebox in a local pub inspired their name.

The three produced some of the purest acoustic rock ever recorded, and their sound fit in perfectly with the mellow music of the early 1970s.

When their music first hit the American airwaves Peek was twenty-one, Bunnell was twenty, and Beckley was nineteen. They had met at London's Central High School and previously belonged to a five-man band called the Daze.

Their attention-grabbing debut single, "A Horse With No Name," was more of an accident than a stroke of marketing genius by the band's label, Warner Bros. Peek recounted in an interview, "The album was released with 'I Need You' planned as the first single. However, Warner's, always cautious, declined to issue a single for the album. Their decision was for us to cut four new tunes to go for a stronger initial release."

America reentered the studio to record one more song. Bunnell, who was inspired by homesickness for California, wrote it. He had lived briefly at Vandenberg Air Force Base near Santa Maria. The riddle-laden lyrics of "A Horse With No Name" caught the attention and imagination of the record buying public, lifting it to million-selling status.

After "Horse" shot up the American record charts, Peek, Bunnell and Beckley quickly moved back to the States, where they joined a tour as the opening act for the Everly Brothers.

The song beat some stiff opposition from a few radio stations around the U.S., who believed the lyrics carried references to drugs. "Horse" is a slang term for heroin.

"The song was born out of pure boredom," Bunnell told Americansongwriter.com in 2020. "I had just graduated high school in London, and my family moved up to Yorkshire, where my mother was from. I wanted to stay in London, so I moved into the home of a friend and his family.

"I wrote the song alone in this guy's bedroom that I shared. I wrote it all in one fell swoop. I wrote it in a couple of hours.

"I didn't question the song. I felt like it suddenly appeared, like waking up in a dream. It was a dream of being on a horse and realizing that I don't even know the name of this horse. And there was serious heat. I remember getting sunburned severely as a kid on a beach – it wasn't in the desert. But I guess, in my mind's eye, I was thinking I'm on this horse, I'm going somewhere, who knows where? I don't know the name of the horse."

Beckley, speaking with Songfacts in 2016, said, "I'm always asked, 'What's your favorite song?' And I usually default to 'Horse' because the song itself represents the start of the journey.

"You know, 'On the first part of the journey.' It actually says it in the song. But that's what it's been – it's been an unbelievable journey."

The song's chorus reads: "I've been through the desert on a horse with no name, it felt good to be out of the rain. In the desert you can remember your name 'cause there ain't no one for to give you no pain."

As of this writing, America still was performing shows as a duo. Peek left the group in 1977. He died of uremic pericarditis at the age of sixty at his home in Farmington, Missouri.

America stayed on the path of soft rock for several years with songs like "I Need You," "Ventura Highway," "Tin Man" and "Lonely People."

••••••• ❖ •••••••

"The First Time Ever I Saw Your Face" by Roberta Flack

Songwriter: Ewan MacColl

Peaked at number 1 on *Billboard* Hot 100

April 15, 1972

April 22, 1972

April 29, 1972

May 6, 1972

May 13, 1972

May 20, 1972

Roberta Flack

Born Roberta Cleopatra Flack on February 10, 1937, in Black Mountain, North Carolina

Roberta Flack

Movie fans who saw the 1971 release of *Play Misty For Me*, starring Clint Eastwood, got a sneak preview of "The First Time Ever I Saw Your Face" by Roberta Flack before the single took the charts by storm the next year.

But it was neither a new song nor the first time Flack sang it.

English singer/songwriter Ewan MacColl wrote the song in 1957. Over the next few years, it was recorded by his lover, Peggy Seeger, and several folk singers, such as the Kingston Trio, Peter, Paul & Mary, the Brothers Four and Gordon Lightfoot. "The First Time" came to Flack's attention when she was in high school in Washington, D.C., and she included it in her set list when she was a nightclub singer in 1968.

After Eastwood, who also directed *Play Misty,* heard her version on the radio, he telephoned Flack at her home in Alexandria, Va. According to author Rick de Yampert, Flack related that Eastwood said, "I'd like to use your song in this movie ... about a disc jockey (with) a lot of music in it. I'd use it in the only part of the movie where there's absolute love."

Flack's response: "I said okay."

Eastwood: "Anything else?"

Flack: "I want to do it over again. It's too slow."

Eastwood: "No, it's not."

They settled on a payment of $2,000 to Flack.

Joel Dorn, who produced the recording, suggested Flack sing it with a slightly faster tempo. She resisted and stood her ground, even in the face of risking the popularity of the single. Flack was right, of course, as the disc became *Billboard's* number 1 single of 1972. The record hit number 1 in Canada and Australia and number 14 in the U.K. It won two Grammy Awards the next year.

Justine Picardie, MacColl's daughter-in-law, commented to author Michael Brocken, "He hated all of (the cover versions). He had a special section in his record collection for them, entitled The Chamber of Horrors. He said that the Elvis (Presley) version was like Romeo at the bottom of the Post Office Tower (a London landmark) singing up to Juliet. And the other versions, he thought, were travesties: bludgeoning, histrionic and lacking in grace."

The first verse of "The First Time" reads: "The first time ever I saw your face, I thought the sun rose in your eyes. And the moon and the stars were the gifts you gave to the dark and the endless skies, my love."

Flack followed her biggest-ever hit with other mellow offerings, such as "Where Is The Love," "Killing Me Softly With His Song," "Jesse" and "Feel Like Makin' Love."

••••••• ❖ •••••••

"Doctor My Eyes" by Jackson Browne

Songwriter: Jackson Browne
Peaked at number 8 on *Billboard* Hot 100
May 6, 1972

Jackson Browne

Born Clyde Jackson Browne on October 9, 1948, in Heidelberg, Germany

Jackson Browne

Jackson Browne, born in Europe to an American father serving in the U.S. Army, was largely unknown outside of Los Angeles until "Doctor My Eyes" gave him name recognition all across the United States.

Browne, whose family moved to California when he was three, spent time on both the West and East coasts in the 1960s as a member of the Nitty Gritty Dirt Band and the Velvet Underground and as a solo artist.

In 1971 he signed with David Geffen and Elliot Roberts' new label, Asylum Records, and his eponymous first album spawned the single "Doctor My Eyes."

The lyrics of the song question whether it is better to gloss over harsh reality by looking on the bright side of life. The narrator of the lyrics has realized he must accept his fate.

"I have wandered through this world as each moment has unfurled. I've been waiting to awaken from these dreams," the second verse says. "People go just where they will, I never noticed them until I got this feeling that it's later than it seems."

The song was a product of Browne's personal vision crisis.

"I did, in fact, have something happen to my eyes," Browne told Rolling Stone. "They became red, I could barely see – I didn't know what it was. They gave me some drops (and told me) to keep (my) eyes shut for a few days.

"By the time I wrote this, I could see again. But it was a metaphor for having seen too much, a loss of innocence."

211

Graham Nash and David Crosby sang harmony vocals on the recording.

Browne became branded as primarily an album-oriented artist. But some of his early mellow singles were "Rock Me On The Water," "Take It Easy," "Redneck Friend," "Walking Slow" and "Fountain Of Sorrow."

•••••• ❖ ••••••

"Alone Again (Naturally)" by Gilbert O'Sullivan

Songwriter: Gilbert O'Sullivan
Peaked at number 1 on *Billboard* Hot 100
July 29, 1972
August 5, 1972
August 12, 1972
August 19, 1972
September 2, 1972
September 9, 1972

Gilbert O'Sullivan

Born Raymond Edward O'Sullivan on December 1, 1946, in Waterford, Ireland

Gilbert O'Sullivan

A sweet-but-melancholy tune brought Gilbert O'Sullivan to the fore of the American soft rock movement, about two years after he'd had his first hit record in England.

The lyrics are sad, but the melody turned out to be irresistible. The single spent six weeks atop the Billboard Hot 100 and sold over three million copies.

In the first verse, we find the narrator has been stood up at the altar on his wedding day and then contemplating suicide. The second verse finds him mulling God's existence after "reality came around and, without so much as a mere touch, broke me into little pieces. For if He really does exist, why did He desert me in my hour of need?"

The third verse has him reliving the sorrow of his father's death. Then his sixty-five-year-old mother dies of a broken heart.

"Everyone wants to know if it's an autobiographical song," O'Sullivan was quoted by Superseventies.com, "based on my father's early death (when Gilbert was eleven). Well, the fact of the matter is, I didn't know my father very well, and he wasn't a good father anyway. He didn't treat my mother very well."

O'Sullivan has protected the song's legacy over the years. "Because it means so much to some people, I will not allow it to be used for karaoke or commercials," he said to the authors of 1000 UK #1 Hits.

Indeed, listeners who were suffering or going through ordeals in their lives found it easy to embrace the lyrics.

The rousing success of "Alone Again" earned O'Sullivan three Grammy nominations in 1973. In Ireland he was voted Top International Singer of 1972. The Songwriters Guild of Great Britain named him Songwriter of the Year.

But United Press International bestowed a dubious award upon O'Sullivan, calling him "the worst potential influence on the direction of pop music since Tiny Tim." UPI offered "Alone Again" its Schlock Rock Trophy of 1972.

Before O'Sullivan exited the recording industry at the end of the 1970s, he put several other mellow hits on the charts: "Clair," "Out Of The Question," "Get Down" and "Ooh Baby."

•••••••• ❖ ••••••••

"Saturday In The Park" by Chicago

Songwriter: Robert Lamm
Peaked at number 3 on *Billboard* Hot 100
September 23, 1972
September 30, 1972

Chicago

Robert Lamm (October 13, 1944-?) lead vocals, piano
Peter Cetera (September 13, 1944-?) bass, backing vocals
Terry Kath (January 31, 1946-January 23, 1978) guitar
Danny Seraphine (August 28, 1948-?) drums
James Pankow (August 20, 1947-?) trombone
Walt Parazaider (March 14, 1945-?) alto saxophone
Lee Loughnane (October 21, 1946-?) trumpet
Formed in 1967 in Chicago, Illinois

Robert Lamm

When Chicago first hit the charts in 1970, their hits were loud. A guitar wailed, horns blared and vocals soared.

By 1972, though, the Windy City band had songs that began to blend in with the trend of mellow rock. "Saturday In The Park" was the first such hit.

"Saturday in the park, I think it was the fourth of July," the lyrics begin. Fittingly, Columbia Records released the single on July 13, 1972. In just over two months, it became Chicago's biggest hit to date.

213

Keyboard player Robert Lamm, who wrote "Saturday" and sang lead, told *Billboard,* "It was written as I was looking at footage from a film I shot in Central Park, over a couple of years, back in the early '70s. I shot this film and, somewhere down the line, I edited it into some kind of a narrative. And, as I watched the film, I jotted down some ideas based on what I was seeing and had experienced.

"And it was really kind of that peace and love thing that happened in Central Park and in many parks all over the world, perhaps on a Saturday, where people just relax and enjoy each other's presence, and the activities we observe and the feelings we get from feeling a part of a day like that."

The first verse mentions a man selling ice cream, singing Italian songs. That line is followed by an Italian phrase, "Eh Cumpari, ci vo sunari," which doesn't have a literal translation, although "could you play for us" has been suggested.

In his interview with *Billboard,* Lamm added, "My songs are very much autobiographical, and inspired and informed by living in the world."

In the wake of "Saturday In The Park," Chicago released light rock tunes like "Feelin' Stronger Every Day," "Just You 'N' Me," "(I've Been) Searchin' So Long," "Call On Me" and "Wishing You Were Here."

•••••••• ❖ ••••••••

"Summer Breeze" by Seals & Crofts
Songwriters: James Seals, Dash Crofts
Peaked at number 6 on *Billboard* Hot 100
November 25, 1972
December 2, 1972

Seals & Crofts

Jim Seals (October 17, 1942-June 6, 2022)
Born James Eugene Seals in Sidney, Texas, and died in Nashville, Tennessee
Dash Crofts (August 14, 1940-?)
Born Darrell George Crofts in Cisco, Texas
Formed in 1969 in Los Angeles, California

Jim Seals and Dash Crofts

"Summer Breeze" brought a refreshing earful of vocal harmony and lyrical images in the autumn of 1972.

Texans Dash Crofts and Jim Seals had gone to Los Angeles in the 1950s, where they joined the Champs after that group had a number 1 instrumental it with "Tequila" in 1958. In 1963 they joined Glen Campbell in the GCs before joining the Dawnbreakers.

After the Dawnbreakers broke up, they settled on performing as a duo, which turned out to be the best idea of their career. Their second album for Warner Brothers Records produced "Summer Breeze," which would expose their talents to an entire nation.

Seals & Crofts' formula for success was a sound that was largely acoustic, and their voices blended beautifully on song after song.

The lyrics of "Summer Breeze" evoke happiness, contentment and satisfaction with life. For example: "See the smile waiting in the kitchen, food cooking and the plates for two. Feel the arms reach out to hold me in the evening when the day is through."

Lyricist Jim Seals told Rare.us, "It's a very simple song about a man coming home from work and hearing the dog barking and things like that. And, to a lot of people, the song's about looking for security.

"Our meaning goes further than that, for prison can be the prison of self, and a person can become insecure and paranoid if he doesn't have a direction in his personal life."

Seals described his goal with Crofts: "We operate on a different level. We try to create images, impressions and trains of thought in the minds of our listeners."

Ensuing hits for the duo were "Hummingbird," "Diamond Girl," "We May Never Pass This Way (Again)" and "I'll Play For You."

•••••••• ❖ ••••••••

"I'd Love You To Want Me" by Lobo
Songwriter: Lobo
Peaked at number 2 on *Billboard* Hot 100
November 18, 1972
November 25, 1972

Lobo

Born Roland Kent LaVoie on July 31, 1943, in Tallahassee, Florida

Lobo

After Lobo had a top five hit with "Me And You And A Dog Named Boo" in the spring of 1971, he struggled to repeat that success. Several releases fell short of the top 40.

A year and a half later, however, he scored his biggest American hit with "I'd Love You To Want Me." The singer/songwriter's high school art teacher provided inspiration for the lyrics.

In an interview with *loBURN Magazine,* Lobo revealed, "I wanted to write the big ballad. There was a conscious effort to do that. The premise behind that was what I imagined in school.

"I had a pretty art teacher. I was a high school senior, and the teacher was twenty-two. She looked at me and I looked at her, and there was a connection.

"That line, 'The obligation that you made for the title that they gave,' was about that. It was the love you couldn't have, you know?"

The lyrics imply a desire on the part of the teacher. "Something in my soul just died," they say. "I see the want in your blue eyes."

Lobo consistently recorded songs in almost the truest acoustic form. Six-string guitar and piano were staples in his arrangements.

"I'd Love You To Want Me" was a number 1 song in seven countries, and it was one of four number 1 hits Lobo had on the *Billboard* Adult Contemporary chart.

Subsequently, Lobo released mellow hits like "Don't Ask Me To Be Your Friend," "It Sure Took A Long, Long Time," "How Can I Tell Her," "Rings" and "Don't Tell Me Good Night."

•••••• ❖ ••••••

"Peaceful Easy Feeling" by the Eagles
Songwriter: Jack Tempchin
Peaked at number 22 on *Billboard* Hot 100
March 10, 1973

The Eagles

Glenn Frey (November 6, 1948-January 18, 2016) lead vocals, acoustic guitar
Don Henley (July 22, 1947-?) drums, backing vocals
Randy Meisner (March 8, 1946-July 26, 2023) bass, backing vocals
Bernie Leadon (July 19, 1947-?) electric guitar, backing vocals
Formed in 1971 in Los Angeles, California

The Eagles: Bernie Leadon, Glenn Frey, Don Henley, Randy Meisner

The Eagles began their singles chart career with the fast-paced "Take It Easy" and the hard-pounding "Witchy Woman."

For the third release, Asylum Records opted for the gentle "Peaceful Easy Feeling." It comfortably fit with the sounds of the day.

The opening line is, "I like the way your sparkling earrings lay against your skin so brown." Songwriter Jack Tempchin was visiting Old Town San Diego Historic State Park one day when he spotted a girl wearing "turquoise earrings against her dark skin." He incorporated the sight into the song lyrics, which he completed in the parking lot behind a fast food restaurant in San Diego.

"I never spoke with her, but I put her in the first line of the song." Tempchin told Nodepression.com. "I guess I was trying to distill the beauty of every girl I saw into words on paper and then into a song."

Tempchin was living with a group of other aspiring musicians when he got the idea for "Peaceful Easy Feeling."

"We'd sit in front of the picture window (of our house) and watch the beautiful girls on the bus stop bench and fall in love with them until their bus came," Tempchin said. "We talked in those days about how love never seems to show up until you stop looking for it. But, as young guys, we were unable to stop looking for love even for one day."

Subsequently, Tempchin migrated to Los Angeles, where he rubbed elbows with up-and-coming musicians like Jackson Browne, J.D. Souther and Glenn Frey. Frey heard "Peaceful Easy Feeling" and asked if he could develop it for his new band, the Eagles, which had formed only eight days earlier. The song, with Frey singing lead vocals, wound up on the Eagles' debut album.

Tempchin also contributed "Already Gone" to the Eagles' catalog, and he wrote or cowrote several songs Frey recorded during his solo career. When I saw Frey in concert in November 1992, Tempchin was the opening act.

The song's second verse reads, "I found out a long time ago what a woman can do to your soul. Oh, but she can't take you any way you don't already know how to go."

Englishman Glynn Johns produced the Eagles' first two albums. "I was a little confused," he said in an interview. "Glenn Frey wanted to be in a Rock & Roll band, and Bernie Leadon was into acoustic and country music."

Although he rejected the Eagles' initial request to be their producer, Johns heard Frey, Leadon and Randy Meisner sing a song a capella in three-part harmony and was so impressed that he changed his mind."

Leadon commented, "I really think that part of the reason the Eagles succeeded the way they did was because the country – and young people – needed to feel things were okay."

Drummer Don Henley said, "I always wanted the band to be a hybrid to encompass blue grass and country and rock & roll."

The Eagles kept their peaceful, easy sounds going through the first half of the 1970s with "Tequila Sunrise," "Desperado" and "The Best Of My Love."

•••••• ❖ ••••••

"Time In A Bottle" by Jim Croce

Songwriter: Jim Croce
Peaked at number 1 on *Billboard* Hot 100
December 29, 1973
January 5, 1974

Jim Croce

January 10, 1943-September 20, 1973
Born James Joseph Croce in South Philadelphia, Pennsylvania, and died at Natchitoches, Louisiana

Jim Croce

In a career cut short by his unexpected death, Jim Croce saved some of his best releases for last. "I Got A Name" was one such song.

"Time In A Bottle" was released as a single after his death and became one of four posthumous number 1 songs on the *Billboard* Hot 100.

The other three are "Dock Of The Bay," by Otis Redding in 1968, "Me And Bobby McGee" by Janis Joplin in 1971 and "(Just Like) Starting Over" by John Lennon in 1980-81.

"Time In A Bottle" was recorded in 1972 and landed on Croce's album *You Don't Mess Around With Jim.* He wrote the lyrics after his wife Ingrid told him she was pregnant in 1970. The couple had been married five years, and Ingrid had visited a fertility specialist.

"If I could save time in a bottle, the first thing that I'd like to do," the song begins, "is to save every day till eternity passes away, just to spend them with you."

The sentimentality struck a chord with thousands of listeners, sending the single to the top of the *Billboard* Hot 100 and the *Billboard* Easy Listening charts.

Croce's record producer, Terry Cashman, told Songfacts, " Jim and Maury (Muehleisen) got together, and all of a sudden Jim started writing these great songs, and Maury came up with these really wonderful guitar parts – the two guitars were like an orchestra."

Muehleisen died with Croce in a plane crash on Sept. 20, 1973.

"Time In A Bottle" features a harpsichord, which producer Tommy West enhanced in an unusual fashion.

"The night before we were going to mix, I was watching a horror movie on TV, and something must have lodged in my brain because, when I walked into the studio the next day, I saw this harpsichord sitting in a corner and got an idea," West told Mixonline.com. "A jingle company had used it on a session, and in walked a couple of guys from SIR (Studio Instruments Rental) to haul it away.

"I asked them to take a lunch break and told (engineer) Bruce (Tergersen) to put a couple of mics on it. He was whining that it was out of tune, but I asked him to let me try something.

"I added two tracks of harpsichord, told the movers they could remove it, walked into Jerry's office and asked if I could borrow the electric bass that was sitting on his couch. I played that on just the second verse and the outro, and that was that. Radio compression worked in our favor on that record. It made the harpsichord blend with the two guitars in an unusual way. But we thought this record would only be an album cut."

The catalyst for making "Time" into a single was the song's appearance on the soundtrack of the television film *She Lives,* starring Desi Arnaz Jr. and Season Hubley, airing on ABC-TV on Sept. 12, 1973. After watching the emotional movie, thousands of listeners telephoned ABC affiliates to ask where they could purchase the recording.

Between 1972 and '74 Croce's mellow rock contributions included "You Don't Mess Around With Jim," "Operator (That's Not The Way It Feels)," "One Less Set Of Footsteps," I Got A Name," "I'll Have To Say I Love You In A Song" and "Workin' At The Car Wash Blues."

•••••• ❖ ••••••

"Annie's Song" by John Denver

Songwriter: John Denver
Peaked at number 1 on *Billboard* Hot 100
July 27, 1974
August 3, 1974

John Denver

December 31, 1943-October 12, 1997
Born Henry John Deutchendorf Jr. in Roswell, New Mexico, and died near Pacific Grove, California

John Denver

John Denver personified the soft side of the early 1970s, and that earned him the anchor leg of this chapter.

Denver's music consistently was acoustic with stripped-down production, and his lyrics were always understandable.

Such was the case with "Annie's Song," his second straight number 1 hit on the *Billboard* Hot 100. It was beautiful in its simplicity. And it also was a real ear-grabber, going to number 1 on the U.K. Chart and becoming his only hit in Britain.

Denver wrote the lyrics in a flash of inspiration while he was riding a chairlift up to the Ajax trail on Aspen Mountain near his home in Colorado. The exhilaration of skiing a tough run on a steep mountain and seeing the beauty of mountains, trees and snow brought the words into his head, relating it all to how he felt about his wife, Anne Martell.

The marriage of John and Anne was rocky. It lasted from 1967 to 1982, and the couple suffered some difficult stretches after John's career soared suddenly in 1971. They had separated, and John fled to Switzerland for six days to let things cool off. By 1974, they were back together, and the troubadour found a way to express the joy he found in their marriage.

The strain on the Denvers' marriage surfaced in John's 1972 song "Goodbye Again." In the lyrics, he wrote, "You think if I were always here, our love would be the same? Why do we always fight when I have to go?"

Songfacts quoted Denver in 1974, "Suddenly, I'm hypersensitive to how beautiful everything is. All of these things filled up my senses and, when I said this to myself, unbidden images came one after the other. All of the pictures merged, and I was left with Annie. That song was the embodiment of the love I felt at that time."

While the song title bears Annie's name, she is mentioned nowhere in the lyrics.

"You fill up my senses like a night in a forest, like the mountains in springtime, like a walk in the rain," the song begins. It took Denver all of ten minutes to complete the lyrics.

Recalling the day Denver wrote the song, Annie commented, "It was written after John and I had gone through a pretty intense time together, and things were pretty good for us. He left to go skiing … and the song just came to him. He skied down and came home and wrote it down.

"Initially, it was a love song, and it was given to me through him and, yet, for him it became a bit like a prayer."

To wit, a few weeks after the single had its chart run, my sister Renie told me the words could be interpreted as a conversation with God. I think she was right.

Within the next year, Denver had seven pop hits on the *Billboard* top 40, two of which were number 1s. He made several guest appearances on television shows and, starting in 1976, did charitable work through his Windstar Foundation.

His contributions to the mellow first half of the '70s included "Take Me Home, Country Roads," Rocky Mountain High," "Sunshine On My Shoulders," "Back Home Again" and "Sweet Surrender."

Annie and John Denver on their wedding day, September 6, 1967

The Disco Years 1974-79
The world danced up a storm in the late '70s

Overview: I guess you could say the world was just in a mood to dance in the second half of the 1970s.

And dance we did, until an entire subculture was established. We danced nightly at discotheques, and the disco sound densely permeated the pop music of the day. If a song had a good dance beat, it had a great chance at success.

Then there was the disco clothing. It was colorful and flashy. And hairdos were big, with the Afro gaining widespread popularity. The leisure suit, featuring button-down shirts with open, oversized collars, was a product of the era. Bell bottom pants, which became the rage in the late 1960s, were still popular.

Can you imagine a pair of platform shoes with hollow acrylic heels containing a few ounces of water and a live goldfish? They existed during the Disco Era, and a person wearing them definitely would own the dance floor!

Dancers may have been wearing mood rings or fondling pet rocks, two fads that emerged in 1975.

In the mixing rooms at recording studios, longer versions of pop songs were cranked out to keep the dancing going for more than just three or four minutes.

The capital of the disco world was New York City, which boasted not only the famous discotheque Studio 54 in Manhattan among its hundreds of discos but also the Empire Rollerdrome in Brooklyn, where patrons could dance on roller skates. In the 1970s management even renamed it "Empire Roller Disco."

Dances that were either invented during the disco surge or became popular then included the Hustle, the Bump, the Funky Chicken, the Disco Finger, the Bus Stop, the Lawnmower and the Electric Slide.

The final two years of disco frenzy were fueled by the 1977 movie *Saturday Night Fever,* which was based on a *New York Magazine* article by Nik Cohn. John Badham directed it, and John Travolta played the lead role of an everyday young man who showed off his dancing skills at a local club on weekends. Robert Stigwood produced the film, and the soundtrack was anchored by several mega-hits performed and/or written by the Bee Gees, whom Stigwood produced for his record label. There is much more about the Bee Gees in this chapter.

The film exposed dancing and discotheques as cultural phenomena, which likely played out in real life in many cities worldwide.

"Studio 54 was more than a discotheque," Matt Tyrnauer told CBS News in 2018. "It was more than a night club. It was a cultural phenomenon." Tyrnauer produced a film about the club's history.

Studio 54 was Mecca for disco lovers, but the trendy club was rife with debauchery. Lines outside the club were filled with would-be patrons, most of whom were not admitted past the velvet ropes. But well-known celebrities were welcomed through the door without ever having to wait.

In the Studio 54 restrooms, the beautiful people ingested recreational drugs. And sexual activity was open and unchecked.

The fate of Studio 54, located at 254 W. fifty-fourth St. in Manhattan, mirrored that of the disco craze. Owners Ian Schrager and Steve Rubell welcomed 4,000 guests on opening night, April 26, 1977, during the height of discomania. But later they were convicted of tax evasion, and each was sentenced to 3½ years in prison in January 1980. The demise of the Disco Era came around that time. Studio 54 closed in 1981.

The sentences of Rubella and Schrager later were reduced to thirteen months.

Disco music suffered a gut punch on July 12, 1979. With the heavy saturation of disco music on the radio and legions of fans craving a return of old time Rock & Roll, the Chicago White Sox chose that date to hold a Disco Demolition Night at Comiskey Park as part of the backlash.

The promotion was held on the outfield grass between games of a doubleheader between the White Sox and the Detroit Tigers. A crate filled with disco records was detonated, and many zealous spectators then rushed onto the field. A sponsoring Chicago radio station had reduced ticket prices to 98 cents for patrons who brought a disco record for destruction. That swept over fifty thousand through the turnstiles.

After a delay to clear the rioters from a damaged field, the second game was postponed and later forfeited by the Sox. But the message was clear: disco had to go. An era of good times passed, but not before an avalanche of great dance music had passed through our ears, along with a tsunami of great dancing.

To view the full lyrics of these songs, please log on to www.google.com, enter song titles & artist names and click Google Search.

To listen to these songs, please log on to www.youtube.com and enter song titles & artist names.

••••••• ❖ •••••••

"Rock The Boat" by the Hues Corporation

Songwriter: Wally Holmes
Peaked at number 1 on *Billboard* Hot 100
July 6, 1974

The Hues Corporation

Fleming Williams (December 26, 1943-February 15, 1998)
Bernard St. Clair Lee (April 24, 1944-March 8, 2011)
H. Ann Kelley (April 24, 1947-?)
Formed in 1969 in Santa Monica, California

The Hues Corporation: Fleming Williams, H. Ann Kelley, Bernard St. Clair Lee

Whether "Rock The Boat" is truly a disco song is debatable. But there is no doubt the song set the table for the disco movement that was on the way.

It was a struggle for the song to become the chart topper that it was. It was the third single released from the Hues Corporation's album "Freedom for the Stallion."

"It was not even considered for (single) release," songwriter Wally Holmes told author Fred Bronson. Holmes founded the Hues Corporation, initially wanting to name the group the Children of Howard Hughes. Legal obstacles scuttled that idea.

"It was just an afterthought," Holmes said. "It was put (on the album) like it had absolutely no chance of happening."

Holmes wanted to have Ann Kelley sing lead, but others talked him out of it. Female lead singers, it seems, were not in vogue for vocal groups at the time. Fleming Williams got the nod, then he left the group.

A small lounge in the Circus Circus Hotel in Las Vegas proved to be the place where the Hues Corporation began to get noticed. But, after they recorded "Rock The Boat," the single appeared headed for doom.

Then dance clubs in New York City started spinning it frequently and getting positive feedback from their clientele.

"There was this mad, incredible rush to find the record," Holmes said. "Disc jockeys were jumping on it and sending copies to disc jockeys they knew in other places." The end result was over 2 million in sales.

Band member Bernard St. Clair Lee told Classicbands.com, "It was a song that you could do anything on. You could cuddle or you could get crazy if you wanted to. It was a love song without being a love song. But it was a disco hit, and it happened because of the discos."

A dance eventually evolved from "Rock The Boat." Performed mainly at parties and receptions, the dance involved people sitting on the floor in a line, facing the same direction and pretending to row a boat.

The lyrics promote a nautical theme. For example, the narrator claims, "Ever since our voyage of love began, your touch has thrilled me like the rush of the wind. And your arms have held me safe from a rolling sea. There's always been a quiet place to harbor you and me."

Revelers do the Rock the Boat dance

•••••••• ❖ ••••••••

"Rock Your Baby" by George McCrae
Songwriters: Harry Wayne Casey, Richard Finch
Peaked at number 1 on *Billboard* Hot 100
July 13, 1974
July 20, 1974

George McCrae

Born George Warren McCrae Jr. on October 19, 1944, in West Palm Beach, Florida

George McCrae

From "Rock The Boat" to "Rock Your Baby," the disco movement was quickly gaining momentum.

On a second consecutive number 1 disco record, two musicians behind the scenes would have their own time in the limelight a year later. And the guy who sang the vocal got the job by happenstance.

Harry Casey and Richard Finch, a couple of recording studio geeks, created "Rock Your Baby" during their hours of making demos in a Hialeah, Fla., studio. They were the backbone of K.C. & the Sunshine Band, which released its third single, "Sound Your Funky Horn," in the spring of 1974. That single did not chart on the *Billboard* Hot 100, but it reached number 21 on the *Billboard* R&B chart. There will be more about K.C. & the Sunshine Band later in this chapter.

Casey told Jon Marlowe, "We had always done demos for other people. But one night we went into the studio to cut a whole, finished track, but the vocals (were) way too high for me to sing. Now, we already had a record released at the time, so we decided to give the song to somebody else."

That somebody happened to be George McCrae, who walked into the studio the next day. He finished the vocals over Casey and Finch's instrumental track in just two takes. T.K. Records released the single in June 1974, and it topped the *Billboard* Hot 100 the next month. Worldwide sales zoomed past the eleven-million mark.

McCrae had been a down-on-his-luck singer who left the recording industry to study criminal justice and assist the singing career of his wife Gwen, according to author Fred Bronson.

"The important thing at the time was that I had the responsibility of rearing a family, and it just wasn't happening for me in the music business," McCrae said. "It wasn't an easy decision. After two years, I finally decided that I had to give it one more try, so I went to Steve Alaimo (head of T.K.'s artists and repertoire) and asked him if he had any material I could record."

Finch talked about the genesis of "Rock Your Baby" to Songfacts. "(Timmy Thomas's) organ was left up in the studio, and 'Rock Your Baby' became born unto this crazy drum machine that was inside of this Lowry organ that he had left there. I used to use that as a tempo map, and I would play along with the drum machine.

"In the beginning, it would hide my errors, but it would also teach me to be a better drummer because I was paying attention to it that closely. Then we would build on that. We had a one-inch 8-track (tape) machine, and I had a cheap Japanese bass. We were just recording and recording and recording. And one night, this one track came out like better than anything else.

"It was like God was in the building or something – we had been blessed. It was like the hunger and desire was so incredibly overwhelming that some magical moment happened in there. We knew we had to build on that track."

Talk about making a hit on a budget! The studio work took about forty-five minutes. Casey and Finch used scrap tape, and they paid Jerome Smith $15 to play guitar. They played the tape for Alaimo, and he told them not to change anything. The electric keyboard is the same Casey would use over and over to drive hits by the Sunshine Band.

The lyrics are simple love song material that concentrate on the rhyming lines. For example: "There's nothing to it, just say you want to do it. Open up your heart, and let the loving start."

Rolling Stone Magazine named "Rock Your Baby" its top song of 1974. An album by the same name peaked at number 38 on the *Billboard* 200. At the next Grammy Awards, McCrae had a nomination for Best Male R&B Vocalist.

McCrae never came close to repeating the success he had with "Rock Your Baby." After he and Gwen divorced in 1976, he moved to Canada, and later he relocated to the Netherlands.

•••••••• ❖ ••••••••

"Kung Fu Fighting" by Carl Douglas

Songwriter: Carl Douglas
Peaked at number 1 on *Billboard* Hot 100
December 7, 1974
December 14, 1974

Carl Douglas

Born Carlton George Douglas on May 10, 1942, in Kingston, Jamaica

Carl Douglas

Carl Douglas, who was born in Jamaica but has lived most of his life in England, is another artist whose disco record benefitted from play in dance clubs.

"Kung Fu Fighting" was tabbed the B-side of a single titled "I Want To Give You My Everything." But fate turned the tables on the disc issued by Pye Records, which was recorded in two takes with only ten minutes of studio time.

Pye originally had the recording, and it's a good thing label executive Robin Blanchflower wanted to hear both sides of the 45 rpm record. A song that wasn't taken seriously by the writer or producer (Biddu) suddenly was promoted to A-side status.

The fact that Bruce Lee films like Fist Of Fury and Enter The Dragon were highly popular aided the acceptance of "Kung Fu Fighting." Judo and karate had been popular forms of martial arts for years, but kung fu was even bigger. Actor David Carradine and his series Kung Fu had been on ABC-TV since the fall of 1972.

The record was going nowhere the first five weeks after its release, but exposure in discotheques finally lit the fuse and rocketed it to number 1 on worldwide charts. That's when 20th Century Records stepped in to aid with distribution in the United States.

Besides topping the U.S. pop chart, "Kung Fu Fighting" went to number 1 in Canada, Australia, Belgium, Austria, France, Ireland, Netherlands, South Africa, New Zealand and the U.K. In America, it also topped the Hot R&B chart. Sales exceeded a million in the U.S. alone.

The lyrics include: "They were funky China men from funky Chinatown. They were chopping them up, and they were chopping them down. It's an ancient Chinese art, and everybody knew their part. From a feint into a slip, and kicking from the hip."

Songfacts reported Douglas got the idea for the lyrics from watching two youths in London practicing some kung fu moves.

Following his smash hit proved to be difficult for Douglas, whose next release, "Dance The Kung Fu," peaked at number 48 on the *Billboard* Hot 100.

Biddu, originally from India, told author Fred Bronson, "If I had a theory why the record was a hit, I'd have more hits. You never know why a record is a hit.

"It had street appeal, I think. It was a bit of a novelty, but … it was a hit all over the world. Maybe it was just a good pop record without us knowing about it."

········ ❖ ········

"Never Can Say Goodbye" by Gloria Gaynor
Songwriter: Clifton Davis
Peaked at number 9 on *Billboard* Hot 100
January 25, 1975

Gloria Gaynor

Born Gloria Fowles on September 7, 1943, in Newark, New Jersey

Gloria Gaynor

"Never Can Say Goodbye" by then-unknown Gloria Gaynor proved to be a kind of barometer for the direction of the disco movement. From the record's acceptance, all indications were that disco was here to stay for quite a while.

She dusted off a song that had been a number 2 smash by the Jackson 5 in 1971, which the producers revived with a quicker tempo for dancing. One of the three producers, Meco Monardo, would have a number 1 instrumental disco hit himself in 1977, "Star Wars Theme/Cantina Band."

Isaac Hayes also had a number 22 hit with the song in 1971.

The songwriter was Clifton Davis, an actor who was starring in the ABC-TV sitcom *That's My Mama* when Gaynor's single broke into the top 10.

Gaynor sang "Never Can Say Goodbye" to number 2 on the U.K. chart and number 3 in Canada, Spain, Australia and Ireland. Her version has the distinction of being the first number 1 record on *Billboard's* Dance/Disco Chart in January 1975.

The lyrics portray a protagonist who is in a hurtful relationship. When it comes to breaking it off, however, the star-crossed lover just can't do it.

"Even though the pain and heartache seem to follow me wherever I go, though I try and try to hide my feelings, they always seem to show," the narrator says. "Then you try to say you're leaving me, and I always have to say no. Tell me why is it so that I never can say goodbye?"

The song was featured on an album by the same name and was part of a nineteen-minute disco suite. This presentation of extended mixing broke ground for other disco releases yet to come. The album contained some tracks on which Gaynor was a contributing writer.

•••••• ❖ ••••••

"Doctor's Orders" by Carol Douglas

Songwriters: Roger Cook, Geoff Stephens, Roger Greenaway
Peaked at number 11 on *Billboard* Hot 100
February 8, 1975

Carol Douglas

Born Carolyn Strickland on April 7, 1948, in Brooklyn, New York

Carol Douglas

A remade version of a British song put Carol Douglas (no relation to Carl Douglas) in the disco fray at the dawn of 1975.

"Doctor's Orders" had been a single recorded in 1973 by Sunny, a former member of the English pop group Brotherhood Of Man. Likewise, the songwriters were English.

Douglas, who was unknown at the time, successfully auditioned for Midland International Records to record that specific song. Douglas, who married her childhood sweetheart Ken Douglas, used his last name as her stage name.

According to New York journalist Deardra Shuler, Douglas said she was told at the audition she "sounded great, but too black." To change that, "producers wanted to capture my more melodic pop/commercial tones, which undeniably made me sound white on the radio."

Meco Monardo produced Douglas in the studio. "I felt the minute I heard the music that it was going to be something, and after hearing my voice on the track it was even more amazing," Douglas remarked. "(It) did throw me off when they played me the (Sunny) version. So I had to approach (singing the song) in my own way."

228

Monardo's production involved using a full orchestra, including strings. The 45 rpm version played at just under three minutes, but the album version was a dance hall pleasing five minutes.

Because of contractual complications, the production credit was assigned to Midland International vice-president Ed O'Loughlin, according to Disco-disco.com.

Test pressings of "Doctor's Orders" in late 1974 received a positive response in New York City discos. After the single's release in November, 100,000 units sold in the first week. It peaked at number 2 on the new *Billboard* Disco Chart. It charted in several other countries, including Canada, where it hit number 1.

Douglas's version begins with her making a telephone call to her boyfriend. She tells him she went to see a doctor because, ever since her beau has been gone, she's had a "pain deep down inside." The doc said there's really nothing wrong with her, and she's just missing her man. She implores the boyfriend to "come home as soon as you can."

The rest of the song is filled with medical metaphors and the like. "You're away, but please don't treat me like a stranger. Doctor's orders say one kiss from you and I am out of danger," Douglas sings.

Once "Doctor's Orders" faded from the charts, Douglas's star never shone quite as brightly. However, her name was placed on the marquee of the disco featured in the movie Saturday Night Fever when it was filmed in 1977.

●●●●●●● ❖ ●●●●●●●

"Get Dancin'" by Disco Tex & the Sex-O-Lettes

Songwriters: Bob Crewe, Kenny Nolan
Peaked at number 10 on *Billboard* Hot 100
February 8, 1975

Disco Tex & the Sex-O-Lettes

Sir Monti Rock III [born Joseph Montanez Jr.] (May 29, 1942-?)
Cindy Bullens (March 21, 1950-?)
Bob Crewe (November 12, 1930-September 11, 2014)
Kenny Nolan (September 30, 1949-?)
Formed in 1974 in The Bronx, New York

Sir Monti Rock III

I've always thought of "Get Dancin'" as a four-minute party for my ears. It is fun, entertaining and infectious. And very danceable.

I'm sure that's what the creators of the song intended. Veteran songsmiths Bob Crewe and Kenny Nolan penned it, and Crewe produced the recording.

Almost unbelievably, as "Get Dancin'" crested on the *Billboard* Hot 100, Crewe and Nolan as cowriters would have two number 1 songs on the chart within the next two months. Those songs were "My Eyes Adored You" by Frankie Valli and "Lady Marmalade" by Labelle.

Crewe and Nolan also were vocalists in the Sex-O-Lettes. Joseph Montanez Jr., under the stage name Sir Monti Rock III, supplied the lead vocal, and Cindy Bullens was the fourth singer.

Rock III didn't sing as much as he spoke the vocals throughout the song. For example: "America needs you, we need you to go dance. We need to get together and boogie-woogie, woogie-boogie. Radar love is here, the star of stars."

At the end of the 45 rpm edit, Rock III sounds exhausted as he says, "I am tired. My chiffon is wet, my chiffon is wet, my wig is wet." With a little imagination, a listener can visualize Rock dancing throughout the fast-paced song. The album version of "Get Dancin'" exceeds seven minutes.

One of the verses references the Hues Corporation's 1974 hit when it says, "Guaranteed to rock the boat, machine gun rap and locomote. Get dancin'!"

The whole presentation is pure, schlocky theater, but it's all meant as good fun. The record-buying, disco-dancing public bought it, and the single hit number 1 on the *Billboard* Disco Chart.

Disco Tex & the Sex-O-Lettes had one more disco top 40 hit, "I Wanna Dance Wit' Choo (Doo Dat Dance)" before they moved over to make way for a crush of talented disco music makers.

········ ❖ ········

"Shame, Shame, Shame" by Shirley (and Company)
Songwriter: Sylvia Robinson
Peaked at number 12 on *Billboard* Hot 100
March 29, 1975

Shirley and Company

Shirley Goodman (June 19, 1936-July 5, 2005) vocals
Jason Alvarez (December 28, 1951-?) vocals
Seldon Powell (November 15, 1928-January 25, 1997) saxophone
Bernadette Randle (1947-2016) keyboards
Clarence Oliver (1954-?) drums
Jonathan Williams (1953-?) bass
Walter Morris (1949-March 24, 2011) guitar
Formed in 1974 in Englewood, New Jersey

Shirley Goodman and Jason Alvarez

Shirley Goodman, a voice from the 1950s, came out of recording retirement to dip her toe in the disco waters.

Teaming with Leonard Lee in the duo Shirley & Lee, Goodman had her first chart hit in 1952, "I'm Gone." She and Lee are best remembered for their 1956 smash "Let The Good Times Roll," which reached number 2 on the *Billboard* R&B Chart.

At the age of thirty-eight, Goodman let loose on a fast-paced dance record, "Shame, Shame, Shame." She shared the vocals with twenty-three-year-old Cuban immigrant Jason Alvarez. It nearly reached the top 10 on the pop chart and spent one week at number 1 on the R&B Chart.

Sylvia Robinson was the mastermind behind the popular single. That's the same songstress who sang in the duo Mickey & Sylvia in the 1950s and had a solo hit with "Pillow Talk" in 1973. She wrote and produced "Shame, Shame, Shame," and the recording was issued on Vibration Records, a division of All Platinum, which she founded in 1967 with her husband Joe Robinson.

The lyrics proclaim the narrator's intention to head for a discotheque and "dance … till the break of day." The tag line is, "Shame on you if you can't dance too."

Robinson's lyrics reference some songs that graced the record charts in previous years. "Got my sunroof down, got my diamond in the back" comes from "Be Thankful For What You Got" by William DeVaughn in 1974.

"Remember, one monkey don't stop no show" is the line from a similarly named 1971 song by Honey Cone. "If you really think you're fast, try to catch me if you can" is a loose reference to the Dave Clark Five's "Catch Us If You Can" from 1965.

"Don't stop the motion if you get the notion" refers to a line in 1974's "Rock The Boat" by the Hues Corporation.

"Shame" spent four weeks atop the *Billboard* Disco/Dance Chart. It was a number 1 hit in three European countries.

Robinson originally intended the song for Donnie Elbert, according to Songfacts. After he rejected it, New Orleans native Goodman got the nod.

A follow-up for the Company, "Cry Cry Cry," fell flat. Goodman was back in retirement by 1976.

• • • • • • • ❖ • • • • • • •

"Get Down, Get Down (Get On The Floor)" by Joe Simon

Songwriters: Raeford Gerald, Joe Simon
Peaked at number 8 on *Billboard* Hot 100
June 21, 1975
June 28, 1975

Joe Simon

September 7, 1936-December 13, 2021
Born Josiah Simon in Simmesport, Louisiana, and died at his home in Buffalo Grove, Illinois

Joe Simon

Joe Simon shifted gears in his rhythm & blues career to briefly become a disco hitmaker.

He released his first single in 1960 and hit the *Billboard* Hot 100 in 1966 for the first time with "A Teenager's Prayer."

"The Chokin' Kind" (number 13 in 1969), "Drowning In The Sea Of Love" (number 11 in 1971) and "Power Of Love" (number 11 in 1972) were his biggest hits on the pop chart until he danced his way into the top 10 with "Get Down, Get Down (Get On The Floor)."

The beat and the lyrics leave no doubt that this song was created specifically for the Disco Era. It also became Simon's third number 1 hit on the *Billboard* R&B Chart.

"Grab your partner and dance to the beat," the lyrics encourage. "Let the music control your feet. Get on the floor and let the good time roll."

The lyrics also mention "kung fu bumpin'," but I could not find any record of a dance by that name.

It was to be Simon's final time in the pop music spotlight. His follow-up song, "Music In My Bones," topped out at a dismal number 92, and he was unable to chart in the *Hot 100* again.

232

But that was not a defeat for the man who did a stint as a disco singer at age thirty-five. Simon became a Christian preacher in the late 1970s and recorded faith-based music, as well.

A native of Louisiana who moved to the Oakland, California, area in his youth, Simon was quoted in a 2016 documentary: "I went from the cotton field to the chicken coop to a superstar of rhythm and blues. You can't tell me I ain't gonna be nothin'."

Yet another of Simon's accomplishments was writing the theme song for the 1973 film *Cleopatra Jones*.

•••••• ❖ ••••••

"Bad Luck Part 1" by Harold Melvin & the Blue Notes

Songwriters: Victor Carstarphen, Gene McFadden, John Whitehead
Peaked at number 15 on *Billboard* Hot 100
June 14, 1975
June 21, 1975

Harold Melvin & the Blue Notes

Harold Melvin (June 25, 1939-March 24, 1997)
Teddy Pendergrass (March 26, 1950-January 13, 2010)
Jerry Cummings (August 23, 1951-?)
Bernard Wilson (July 12, 1946-December 26, 2010)
Lawrence Brown (November 5, 1946-April 6, 2008)
Formed in 1954 in Philadelphia, Pennsylvania

The Blue Notes: Jerry Cummings, Lawrence Brown, Harold Melvin, Teddy Pendergrass, Bernard Wilson

Eleven weeks at number 1 on the *Billboard* Disco Chart says a lot about the popularity of "Bad Luck Part 1."

When the two sides of the single are combined, "Bad Luck Parts 1 and 2" play to about 6 minutes 40 seconds, which made it a favorite at many discotheques around the world.

Production wizards Kenny Gamble and Leon Huff, who owned the Philadelphia International record label, put their golden touch on the song. Their studio musicians, known as MFSB, had a number 1 instrumental about a year earlier and played behind the vocals of Harold Melvin & the Blue Notes.

Drummer Earl Young, according to a documentary written by John A. Jackson, played his hi-hat so loudly that it could not be quieted in the final mix. As a result, disco music henceforth featured prominent hi-hat instrumentation.

The song opens with: "Look down-hearted and confused because lately you've been startin' to lose. Losin' out on everything you might try to do – bad luck's there, it's got a hold on you."

This was one of several songs from 1975 that coincidentally featured the word "bad" in the title. There also was "Bad Time" by Grand Funk, "Bad Blood" by Neil Sedaka, "Good Lovin' Gone Bad" by Bad Company and "Bad Sneakers" by Steely Dan. The irony was 1975 was such a great year for music.

••••••• ❖ •••••••

"Get Down Tonight" by K.C. & the Sunshine Band

Songwriters: Harry Wayne Casey, Richard Finch
Peaked at number 1 on *Billboard* Hot 100
August 30, 1975

K.C. & the Sunshine Band

Harry Wayne Casey (January 31, 1951-?) vocals, keyboards
Rick Finch (January 23, 1954-?) bass
Jerome Smith (June 18, 1953-July 28, 2000) guitar
Robert Johnson (March 21, 1953-July 20, 2000) drums
Fermin Coytisolo (Dec. 31, 1951-?) congas
Ronnie Smith, Denvil Liptrot, James Weaver, Charles Williams – horn section
Formed in 1973 in Hialeah, Florida

Mainstays of the Sunshine Band: Rick Finch, Robert Johnson,
Harry Wayne Casey, Jerome Smith

From working at a record store to doing odd jobs at a record warehouse without pay to the top of the disco music world. In a nutshell, that was the rags-to-riches ascent Harry Wayne Casey's career took.

During his rapid rise in Hialeah, Florida, Casey studied the sound of various music genres and gained an understanding of how they were received by music listeners and dance fans. By the time he met Rick Finch, a co-worker in a recording studio, he'd gotten experience as a record producer.

They put together a band, but their first two singles didn't sell well. Then Casey and Finch wrote "Get Down Tonight," which contained the recipe for a disco smash. Their jobs in the record store and recording studio gave them knowledge of what the public was buying.

"I couldn't believe it was such an incredible sound," Casey told author Fred Bronson. "I remember they must have played it back a hundred times, and I couldn't believe it – it had that strange, mystical feeling, a feeling I had never felt before."

With Casey on keyboards and Finch on bass, the two white musicians surrounded themselves with band members of color. But they remained true to their own style without taking on vocal inflections of black artists.

"A lot of times I will have an idea of a song," Casey told Songfacts, "and during recording I'll just sing whatever comes into my mind and then go back, and if I don't like that, will change it to another complete title. I do it a little bit differently now. I start with titles most of the time and already have the idea of what the title is going to be. But for that particular song … it was different.

"My working title was 'What You Want Is What You'll Get,' and that's what I used during the recording. Then I came back and decided to change it to 'Get Down Tonight.' I just thought, *What are the things I like to do?' I love to dance, and so do other people. Do a little dance, make a little love, get down tonight.*

"It was just a story about life, about the things that one likes to do." After seeing a recording engineer slow down a tape machine, Finch got the idea to use the technique on the intro of "Get Down Tonight." It features a guitar solo run at double speed in front of a guitar riff at normal speed in the background.

"That really keeps the buzz, that really keeps the excitement going all the way through without being too artificial sounding," Finch related to Songfacts.

K.C. & the Sunshine Band, which used female backing vocalists Beverly Champion and Margaret Reynolds, stayed on top of the charts with their sound for about five years. Their other number 1 hits on the *Billboard* Hot 100 were "That's The Way (I like It)," "(Shake, Shake, Shake) Shake Your Booty," "I'm Your Boogie Man" and "Please Don't Go." "Keep It Comin' Love" spent three weeks at number 2.

.... ❖ ....

"Love Hangover" by Diana Ross

Songwriters: Pam Sawyer, Marilyn McLeod
Peaked at number 1 on *Billboard* Hot 100
May 29, 1976
June 5, 1976

Diana Ross

Born Diane Ernestine Earle Ross on March 26, 1944 in Detroit, Michigan

Diana Ross

The First Lady of Motown Records, Diana Ross, transformed herself from a soulful balladeer into a disco diva with this smash.

It was the first Motown release in the disco genre, and it became Ross's second number 1 single in the span of five months.

The album "Diana Ross" spawned the single "Love Hangover," but it wasn't the first release from the album. Since Motown was reluctant to put out disco music, the label made "Theme From Mahogany" and "I Thought It Took A Little Time (But Today I Fell In Love)" the first two singles.

Ross herself was hesitant to record a disco song, so producer Hal Davis made special arrangements for the session. He began the session at about 9 p.m. and poured a vodka drink (her favorite) to get her in a relaxed mood. He also set up some red lights in the studio, as well as a strobe.

After she removed her shoes, author Fred Bronson wrote, she was relaxed and began the song with the first few lines in a slow tempo. When the tempo picked up, the lights went on and the atmosphere was like a discotheque. Ross kicked her vocals into high gear and even did some ad-libbing.

Ross told biographer Randy Taraborrelli, "It was a spontaneous thing that we captured on record. And, if I had to go back in and do it again, I couldn't have. The music was me, and I was the music. Things came out of my mouth that I didn't even expect."

"Love Hangover" was residing only on the album when the 5th Dimension recorded a version and released it as a single. This prompted Motown to put Ross's version on a single, which entered the Hot 100 the same week as the 5th Dimension's. The quintet's single topped out at number 80.

The lyrics portray a woman who is still feeling the effects of lovemaking. She doesn't want the feeling to end.

"If there's a cure for this, I don't want it," the lyrics say. "If there's a remedy, I'll run from it. Think about it all the time, never let it out of my mind 'cause I love you. I've got the sweetest hangover I don't wanna get over."

Besides topping the U.S. pop chart, the song was number 1 on the R&B chart and number 1 on the Disco chart.

•••••••• ❖ ••••••••

"More, More, More (Pt. 1)" by the Andrea True Connection

Songwriter: Gregg Diamond
Peaked at number 4 on *Billboard* Hot 100
July 17, 1976

Andrea True

July 26, 1943-November 7, 2011
Born Andrea Marie Truden in Nashville, Tennessee, and died in Kingston, New York

Andrea True

How crazy was the Disco Era? A porno movie actress had one of the biggest disco hits of 1976!

Andrea True, a daughter of immigrants from Slovenia, had appeared in pornographic films in Scandinavia and the United States in the 1960s. By 1975, she added the job of director to her résumé.

In 1973 she was an extra in the films *The Way We Were and 40 Carats*. But her path to recording a hit song was quirky.

While still in her prime as a porn star, True contracted with a Jamaican real estate outfit to appear in their television commercial. She went to Jamaica to do the filming. But she couldn't take her earnings out of the country because the Jamaican government, directed by prime minister Michael Manley, banned money transfers in response to U.S. sanctions. Manley, it seems, was a supporter of Cuban dictator Fidel Castro.

For True, the choices were to forfeit her money or spend it in Jamaica. She decided to invest the cash in recording a demo of "More, More, More." She had been working on the song with writer Gregg Diamond, who also became the arranger and producer of the Andrea True Connection.

237

According to *The Rialto Report* podcast, True said, "I'd rather be a waitress or a typist than make another adult film. Don't think of me as a porn star any more, think of me as a recording star. I just want to record and perform." So recording star became the next item on her résumé, although she remained active in the film industry until 1979.

"My producer, Gregg Diamond, flew down to Jamaica with the instrumental tracks, and we put the vocals on in a studio there," True told the *Los Angeles Times*. "We used local horn men. That was a problem because they had never played American music before.

"We were going to make it with a lot of lyrics, but then it occurred to us that 'Fly Robin Fly' and 'Love To Love You Baby' had only a few lyrics."

Federal Records originally owned the recording and released it in Jamaica, but Buddah bought a version mixed by engineer Tom Moulton and distributed it in the U.S. only to disco clubs. After acceptance proved to be widespread, Buddah put the disc in record stores. It went to number 1 on the Disco chart and number 1 on the Canadian chart.

In the lyrics of "More, More, More," we hear, "But if you want to know how I really feel, just get the cameras rolling, get the action going." That sounds like a nod to her involvement in the film industry. The B-side of the single featured more dance music with "More, More, More – Pt. II."

Sexual innuendo is there, but sexual activity is not described explicitly.

Almost a year later, Buddah released another True dance song, "New York, You Got Me Dancing." That one peaked at number 27, and the end of True's singing career was near.

The Canadian band Len sampled the percussion track of "More..." in their 1999 song "Steal My Sunshine."

•••••••• ❖ ••••••••

"You Should Be Dancing" by the Bee Gees

Songwriters: Barry Gibb, Robin Gibb, Maurice Gibb
Peaked at number 1 on *Billboard* Hot 100
September 4, 1976

The Bee Gees

Maurice Gibb (December 22, 1949-January 12, 2003)
Robin Gibb (December 22, 1949-May 20, 2012)
Barry Gibb (September 1, 1946-?)
First performed together in 1956 in Chorlton, Manchester, England

The Bee Gees: Robin, Barry and Maurice Gibb

After ending a four-year recording slump in 1975 with the hit album *Main Course,* the Bee Gees were determined to remain relevant on the pop music scene.

There was one problem, however, as they set about putting together their next album, *Children Of The World.* Due to the politics of the recording industry, they had to part with their producer, Arif Mardin.

At Criteria Studios in Miami, Florida, they solved that problem when they began working with Albhy Galuten and Karl Richardson, who shared production credits with the three Bee Gee brothers. With Barry Gibb's newly perfected falsetto vocal technique, the trio was on its way to creating another fine album and three potent singles.

The first single gave not-so-subtle notice the Bee Gees were jumping into the disco action with "You Should Be Dancing." Public acceptance was swift, as the song zoomed to number 1 on the pop chart and spent seven weeks atop the Disco chart.

The song tells of the influence the narrator's girlfriend has over his dancing habits. "My baby moves at midnight," the lyrics say, "goes right on till the dawn. My woman takes me higher, my woman keeps me warm.

"What you doin' on your bed on your back? You should be dancing, yeah."

During sessions at Criteria, Stephen Stills was there with the Stills-Young Band to record their own album. Stills and Joe Lala contributed percussion to "You Should Be Dancing," and George Perry played bass.

Robert Stigwood, owner of RSO Records, which issued the song, also produced the 1977 film *Saturday Night Fever.* "You Should Be Dancing" was featured in that movie.

•••••• ✧ ••••••

"A Fifth Of Beethoven" by Walter Murphy & the Big Apple Band
Songwriter: Walter Murphy
Peaked at number 1 on *Billboard* Hot 100
October 9, 1976

Walter Murphy

Born Walter Anthony Murphy Jr. on December 19, 1952, in New York City, New York

Walter Murphy

In the early months of the Disco Era, there were several instrumental recordings that did well on the pop chart. Some examples are: "Express" by B.T. Express; "Dynomite" by Tony Camillo's Bazuka; "Do It Any Way You Wanna" by People's Choice; and "Fly, Robin, Fly" by Silver Connection. All of those songs had limited lyrics and vocals.

The first instrumental disco record without any vocals to hit number 1 on the *Billboard* Hot 100 was "A Fifth Of Beethoven" by Walter Murphy & the Big Apple Band.

The Big Apple Band did not exist. Murphy played virtually every instrument on the record, but executives at Private Stock Records thought the disc would have a better chance at success if it were credited to a group. They soon found out there already was a Big Apple Band, and later pressings of the single credited it to The Walter Murphy Band and then just Walter Murphy.

Oh, by the way, that original Big Apple Band changed its name to Chic and became a major hitmaker during the last years of the Disco Era. There will be more on Chic later in this chapter.

Murphy was inspired by earlier hit records that had used melodies written by Johann Sebastian Bach – "A Lover's Concerto" by the Toys (1965) and "Joy" by Apollo 100 (1972). His demo tape of reworked classical compositions, however, failed to impress the record companies of New York City.

His version of "Symphony number 5 in C Minor" by Ludwig van Beethoven, written between 1804 and 1808, drew interest from Larry Uttal, owner of Private Stock. He gave Murphy the green light to develop a full treatment of the classic in disco mode. Thomas Valentino produced it.

After "A Fifth Of Beethoven" entered the Hot 100 at number 80, it took nineteen weeks for it to reach number 1.

It sold two million copies and hit number 1 in Canada, number 6 in Norway, number 7 in New Zealand and number 8 in Switzerland. It also earned inclusion on the soundtrack of the movie *Saturday Night Fever.*

Murphy used his formula again with "Flight 76," which was a disco adaptation of "Flight Of The Bumble Bee" by Nikolai Rimsky-Korsakov. It peaked at number 44, indicating that Murphy's experiment with classical and disco music had run its course.

•••••••• ❖ ••••••••

"Don't Leave Me This Way" by Thelma Houston
Songwriters: Kenny Gamble, Leon Huff, Cary Gilbert
Peaked at number 1 on *Billboard* Hot 100
April 23, 1977

Thelma Houston

Born Thelma Jackson on May 7, 1946, in Leland, Mississippi

Thelma Houston

240

A remake of an album track by Harold Melvin & the Blue Notes gave Motown Records its second number 1 disco smash.

Producer Hal Davis (see "Love Hangover" earlier in this chapter) had heard the Blue Notes' version of "Don't Leave Me This Way" at a party, and he put Thelma Houston in a studio to record it in 1976. It was released on Motown's Tamla label.

Houston was a hard-luck singer who had bounced from label to label. She had a number 74 single with "Save The Country" in 1970 but soon found herself without a record deal. In 1971, Houston finally signed with Motown, where she was assigned to its MoWest subsidiary.

A divorcee raising two teenagers, she sang at rhythm & blues clubs, polished her style and waited for a break.

"Don't Leave Me This Way," a product of the songwriting geniuses at Philadelphia International Records, is a plea by the narrator for her lover to ditch his plans to dump her. "Don't leave me this way. I can't survive, I can't stay alive without your love," the first verse says. "Oh baby, don't leave me this way. No, I can't exist, I'll surely miss your tender kiss. Don't leave me this way." The lyrics are gender neutral.

The instrumentation includes heavy hi-hat percussion, electric keyboard and thumping bass.

Chart-wise, the single achieved a trifecta. Besides going to number 1 on the pop chart, it also topped the R&B chart and the Disco chart.

"These have been some tough years, full of disappointment," Houston told the *Los Angeles Times* in 1977. "You release a record and you say, 'This is it.' But it's not. You release another one and go through the same thing. It's awful to have to rely on a hit record to get your career going, but that's the way it is."

Though Houston eventually became one of the most prominent one-hit wonders in pop music history, she remained philosophical. "The material was never right or something else wasn't right," she said to the *L.A. Times*. "I can't put my finger on what the problem has been. I don't want to blame anybody. I only know that I've been trying as hard as I can."

"Don't Leave Me This Way" earned Houston a Grammy Award for best R&B vocal performance for a female vocalist. Later in 1977 it was included in the movie soundtrack of *Looking For Mr. Goodbar.*

•••••••• ❖ ••••••••

"Stayin' Alive" by the Bee Gees
Songwriters: Barry Gibb, Robin Gibb, Maurice Gibb
Peaked at number 1 on *Billboard* Hot 100
February 4, 1978
February 11, 1978
February 18, 1978
February 25, 1978

After disco music experienced a slow year in 1977, it picked back up in a big way the following year. The Bee Gees played a huge part in the resurgence.

Their label owner, Robert Stigwood, asked them to write songs for the movie he was about to produce, *Saturday Night Fever.* "How Deep Is Your Love," a ballad, became the first single released from the film's soundtrack. Before it hit number 1 on the *Billboard* Hot 100, RSO Records released "Stayin' Alive." It chased its predecessor up the chart and became one of the anthems of the disco era.

A fast-paced dance song, "Stayin' Alive" originally had the title "Saturday Night, Saturday Night." The Bee Gees changed the title, to Stigwood's displeasure. The three brothers were stationed in France at the Chateau D'Herouville recording studio while they wrote songs and recorded demos.

The Bee Gees had received only the barest plot sketch of the movie, but they were on the mark with the title and lyrics they chose. Anyone who has seen *Saturday Night Fever* will never forget the song playing over the opening credits, with Tony Manero (played by John Travolta) strutting down a Brooklyn sidewalk with a gallon can of paint in his hand.

"Well, you can tell by the way I use my walk I'm a woman's man, no time to talk," the opening lines declare. "Music loud and women warm, I've been kicked around since I was born."

Later we hear, "Life going nowhere, somebody help me."

While the film centers on Manero's exploits at a local dance club on Saturday nights, it also exposes the strife, struggle and frustrations of a young man stuck in a dead-end job while still living at home with his parents, grandmother and younger sister. He badly wants to win a dance competition. Then, after he and his partner are declared the winners, he gives the trophy to a couple he thought deserved it more. Late in the movie, one of his friends dies by falling off New York City's Verrazano Narrows Bridge.

Instrumentally, "Stayin' Alive" skillfully combines electric guitar with symphonic strings and a dance beat that never quits.

Beatles' producer George Martin, quoted by writer Andrew Hughes, commented, "The great thing about 'Stayin' Alive' is that it had a great guitar hook to start with, which set up the theme, that pulsating beat. It's no coincidence, by the way, that the disco beat of 120 beats per minute coincides with the beat of your heart when you're excited. This was a key thing which underlined the whole tune, and when the vocals came in, the vocals were so designed that they pushed that beat further."

In a review of the single, *Billboard* praised it as one of the Bee Gees' best songs and "an almost irresistible dance tune."

Showing the power of the Bee Gees' influence over disco music, the Hot 100 charts of February 25 and March 4, 1978, had three of their records in the top 10 – "Stayin' Alive," "Night Fever" and "How Deep Is Your Love." Additionally, a song sung by their younger brother Andy and co-written by Barry and Andy Gibb, was in the top 10 – "(Love Is) Thicker Than Water." The pop music world had not seen dominance of that scope by one group since the Beatles in 1964.

Barry Gibb had a hand in writing these four songs that were *Billboard* Hot 100 consecutive number 1 songs:

- "Stayin' Alive" by the Bee Gees
- "(Love Is) Thicker Than Water" by Andy Gibb
- "Night Fever" by the Bee Gees
- "If I Can't Have You" by Yvonne Elliman

That makes **Barry Gibb** the **only songwriter in the history** of the *Billboard* pop chart to have four number 1 singles in a row.

"Stayin' Alive" hit number 1 in eight countries and sold over 3.9 million copies in the United States alone.

While "Stayin' Alive" was climbing the charts, the Bee Gees were in California filming the movie *Sgt. Pepper's Lonely Hearts Club Band.* One afternoon, on a day off from shooting, the Gibb brothers wrote "Too Much Heaven" and "Tragedy," which they converted into number 1 singles in 1979. According to Songfacts, they wrote "Shadow Dancing" the same evening. Younger brother Andy Gibb recorded it and watched it become a number 1 single for seven weeks in the summer of 1978.

•••••••• ❖ ••••••••

"Dance, Dance, Dance (Yowsah, Yowsah, Yowsah)" by Chic
Songwriters: Kenny Lehman, Bernard Edwards, Nile Rodgers
Peaked at number 6 on *Billboard* Hot 100
February 25, 1978
March 4, 1978

Chic

Nile Rodgers (September 19, 1952-?) guitar
Bernard Edwards (October 31, 1952-April 18, 1996) bass
Norma Jean Wright (July 15, 1956-?) lead vocals
Tony Thompson (November 15, 1954-November 12, 2003) drums
Formed 1976 in New York City, New York

Chic: Bernard Edwards, Norma Jean Wright, Nile Rodgers, Tony Thompson

Are you serious? The word "dance" is heard over 100 times in this song? It must be a disco record!

"Dance, Dance, Dance (Yowsah, Yowsah, Yowsah)" didn't try to fool anyone. It was made for dancing, and the leaders of Chic made dance clubs of New York City the target audience for it.

Getting the song to market for a national or international audience was not easy for Nile Rodgers and Bernard Edwards, though. According to Songfacts, the band made a demo and shopped it to many record companies. No one wanted to take it.

Finally, Buddah Records took a chance on it and released it to discotheques as a 12-inch single. After the song's popularity grew in those venues, Atlantic Records signed Chic to a contract and released the 7-inch single nationally.

Drummer Tony Thompson told *The Independent,* "We actually started as a rock band. At the time, no one would hear of three black brothers playing Rock & Roll. So Bernard and Nile came up with the whole disco thing.

"I didn't even know what disco was. We pressed 'Dance, Dance, Dance' ourselves, as we didn't have a record deal. We took it to a club, the DJ played it and people just freaked. From there, we signed to Atlantic."

Raymond Jones, who later became a member of the band, was a keyboard player on Chic's eponymous 1977 debut album. Luther Vandross, who became a prominent solo performer in the 1980s, contributed backing vocals. Luci Martin did not sing on "Dance, Dance, Dance" but joined the band a few months later as a second vocalist. Pursuing a solo career, Norma Jean Wright dropped out of Chic in mid-1978 and was replaced by Alfa Anderson.

"Yowsah, yowsah, yowsah" is a historic term used by African Americans as a way of saying "yes." Radio personality/violinist Ben Bernie popularized it in the 1920s.

"Dance, Dance, Dance" went to number 1 on the *Billboard* Dance Club Songs chart, which had replaced the Disco Chart. It peaked at number 6 on the R&B chart.

Some of the lyrics: "We're just dancing to the beat, feel the heat, I'm moving my feet. Headed towards the floor, gonna get down, get down some more. Rumba and tango, Latin hustle, too. Yowsah, yowsah, yowsah, I wanna boogie with you."

•••••• ❖ ••••••

"Night Fever" by the Bee Gees
Songwriters: Barry Gibb, Robin Gibb, Maurice Gibb
Peaked at number 1 on *Billboard* Hot 100
March 18, 1978
March 25, 1978
April 1, 1978
April 8, 1978
April 15, 1978
April 22, 1978
April 29, 1978
May 6, 1978

The Bee Gees turned in the best chart performance of any disco record of the 1970s with "Night Fever," their third single from the blockbuster movie *Saturday Night Fever.*

With eight weeks at number 1 and a *Billboard* year-end rank of number 2, the success of the song mirrored the popularity of the movie, which garnered five Grammy Awards and grossed $237.1 million worldwide.

The song had a bit of a tempestuous beginning, though. The Bee Gees had written and titled it before the film had a title. According to author Fred Bronson, the Bee Gees suggested *Night Fever* for the film's title, but producer Robert Stigwood rejected it as sounding too pornographic.

Stigwood was leaning toward the title *Saturday Night,* which the Gibb brothers didn't like. They struck a compromise with *Saturday Night Fever.* RSO Records held the single for the third release from the soundtrack, and its chart performance eclipsed both "How Deep Is Your Love" and "Stayin' Alive."

The book *The Ultimate Biography of the Bee Gees* quotes record producer Albhy Galuten as saying, "For 'Night Fever' the group had the hook-line and rhythm ... and parts of the verses. They usually pat their legs to set up a song's rhythm when they first sing it. They had the emotion, same as on the record. We put down battery (drums) first, so the feel was locked in. The electric piano part was put on before the bass, then the heavy guitar parts. We had the sound, but we needed something there to shake it, so we used the thunder sound."

Inspiration for the song came from an unexpected source from 1960. Welsh keyboardist Blue Weaver told Songfacts, "'Night Fever' started off because Barry walked in one morning when I was trying to work out something. I always wanted to do a disco version of 'Theme from *A Summer Place*' by the Percy Faith Orchestra. I was playing that, and Barry said, 'What was that?' And I said, 'Theme from A Summer Place.' And Barry said, 'No, it wasn't.' It was new. Barry heard the idea – I was playing it on a string synthesizer and sang the riff over it."

Four years before his death, Robin Gibb told Observer Music Monthly in 2008, "Until the film came out, disco meant something very different in the U.K. to the U.S. We were writing what we considered to be blue-eyed soul. We never set out to make ourselves the kings of disco, although plenty of other people tried to jump on the bandwagon after the success of the film.

"When we went to the premiere at (Grauman's Chinese Theatre in Hollywood), it was obvious the film and the songs really gelled, but none of us had any idea how huge it would become."

A sample of lyrics from "Night Fever:"

"Listen to the ground, there is movement all around. There is something going down, and I can feel it. On the waves of the air there is dancing out there. It's something we can't share, we can't steal it.

"That sweet city woman, she moved through the light, controlling my mind and my soul. When you reach out for me, yeah, and the feeling is right, then I get night fever."

"Night Fever" hit number 1 in six countries and sold over 2.5 million copies in the United States. It peaked at number 3 on the *Billboard* Dance Club Songs chart.

•••••• ❖ ••••••

"Disco Inferno" by the Trammps
Songwriters: Leroy Green, Ron "Have Mercy" Kersey
Peaked at number 11 on *Billboard* Hot 100
May 27, 1978
June 3, 1978

The Trammps

Jimmy Ellis (November 15, 1937-March 8, 2012)
Earl Young (June 2, 1940-?)
Stanley Wade (died Jan. 12, 2021)
Harold "Doc" Wade (January 1943-?)
Robert Upchurch (bio unavailable)
Formed in 1972 in Philadelphia, Pennsylvania

The Trammps: (seated) Robert Upchurch, Harold Wade, Jimmy Ellis
(standing) Stanley Wade, Earl Young

They didn't exactly set the world on fire when they first released "Disco Inferno" in 1976. The Trammps had to settle for a number 53 showing on the *Billboard* Hot 100 on April 16, 1977.

The record spent six weeks at number 1 on the *Billboard* Dance Club Songs chart around that time, but it was having a hard time getting played by radio station programmers.

Later that year, Robert Stigwood & Co. came calling to request the song for inclusion on the *Saturday Night Fever* movie soundtrack. That quickly changed the fate of "Disco Inferno."

The next thing they knew, their trademark single had climbed to number 11 on the Hot 100, and the Trammps shared a Grammy Award for album of the year with other contributors.

Having evolved from the Volcanos and the Moods in Philadelphia, Pennsylvania, the Trammps had their first brushes with pop chart success with "Hold Back The Night" (number 35 in 1975) and "That's Where The Happy People Go" (number 27 in 1976).

"Disco Inferno" was inspired by the 1974 film The Towering Inferno, starring Steve McQueen, Paul Newman and Faye Dunaway. A scene in the movie depicts a dance club atop a 138-story skyscraper, which is being ravaged by an out-of-control fire. According to Songfacts, the scene was filmed at the 2001 Odyssey, where the Trammps often would perform in Brooklyn, New York.

Song lyrics include: "To my surprise, one hundred stories high, people getting loose, getting down on the roof. Folks are screaming, out of control. It was so entertaining when the boogie started to explode. I heard somebody say 'Burn, baby, burn, disco inferno. Burn the mother down."

If "burn, baby burn" sounds familiar, perhaps it is because the phrase was used by rioters in Los Angeles during the 1965 Watts Uprising.

How did the Trammps get their name? In their early days, they would stand on street corners to rehearse their songs, as many kids were wont to do. Nearby shop owners would say to them, "All you guys will ever be is tramps."

"We were on the street corner singing, that's all," Harold Wade said in an interview with Classicbands.com. "Back in the neighborhood, that's all you really ever did. Most of the groups you saw were roaming around the streets. That was the craze back in those days." The reason for the spelling of their name: they used the letter M twice on purpose because they were "high class tramps who could afford more than one M."

In summarizing the effect of having "Disco Inferno" on a great soundtrack, Wade said, "It was the beginning of the end. We've been living off it (for) the past thirty years or so."

"Last Dance" by Donna Summer
Songwriter: Paul Jabara
Peaked at number 3 on *Billboard* Hot 100
August 12, 1978
August 19, 1978

Donna Summer

December 31, 1948-May 17, 2012
Born LaDonna Adrian Gaines in Boston, Massachusetts, and died in Naples, Florida

Donna Summer

Who is the queen of disco, Donna Summer or Gloria Gaynor? Both have been "nominated" for the title. It depends on who you talk to and what websites you consult.

One thing is certain: Summer took a big leap in identifying with disco music with "Last Dance," which she performed as a cast member of the 1978 film *Thank God It's Friday.*

The song has a slow intro before revving up to dancing speed. Co-producer Bob Esty talked about constructing the song on Donnasummer.it:

"Working on the arrangement with Paul (Jabara), I changed some of the chords and extended the hook to repeat three times to finish the last phrase of the chorus. I also added a bridge to build a climax and suggested a ballad intro, a la 'Ain't No Mountain High Enough," and another ballad in the middle of the song, building again to a high note for the last chorus ending.

"To our knowledge, this had never been done in a disco track. I was willing to do this idea and confident that it would work. We did the piano/vocal with Donna and me of the full version, including the two ballad sections and the ending in one pass.

"I recorded the full track in one day, rhythm in the morning, horns and strings during the day. That same night, Giorgio Moroder (Summer's long-time producer) recorded Donna's vocal exactly as she sang the demo, in two takes, and banning me from attending the session.

"In spite of the fact Giorgio didn't like the song and didn't want Donna to sing in a full voice style, I thought I would be at least credited for co-producing the track and cowriting the song with Paul. He ultimately took credit for it. And Paul Jabara took the Oscar. I learned a bitter lesson from that."

The Oscar awarded to Jabara was for best rhythm & blues song. He also won a Golden Globe for best original song.

"Last Dance" held the top spot on *Billboard* Hot Disco Action chart for six weeks.

In the film, Summer plays the role of Nicole Sims, an aspiring singer. At a disco club called the Zoo, she pleads with the disc jockey to let her sing over an instrumental tape she brought with her. After repeated refusals, he gives her that chance at the end of the movie.

Some of the lyrics: "Last dance, last chance for love. Yes, it's my last chance for romance tonight. Oh, I need you by me, beside me to guide me. To hold me, to scold me 'cause when I'm bad I'm so, so bad."

Summer died of lung cancer at her home in Florida.

•••••• ❖ ••••••

"Boogie Oogie Oogie" by A Taste of Honey

Songwriters: Janice Marie Johnson, Perry Kibble
Peaked at number 1 on *Billboard* Hot 100
September 9, 1978
September 16, 1978
September 23, 1978

A Taste of Honey

Janice Marie Johnson (January 18, 1954-?) vocals, bass
Hazel Payne (bio unavailable) vocals, guitar
Perry Kibble (June 10, 1949-February 23, 1999) keyboards
Donald Ray Johnson (1948-?) drums
Formed in 1972 in Los Angeles, California

A Taste Of Honey: (front) Hazel Payne (rear) Donald Johnson, Janice Marie Johnson, Perry Kibble

It took a sour experience for A Taste of Honey to craft one of the funkiest disco smashes.

The band was on a United Service Organizations (USO) tour, playing for airmen at Norton Air Force Base in San Bernardino, Calif., when they were faced with an unresponsive audience. No one seemed to get into the lively music the four-member band was playing.

248

Guitarist/singer Hazel Payne told the servicemen, "If you think you're too cool to boogie, we've got news for you! Everyone here tonight is going to boogie, and you're no exception to the rule."

After the gig, singer/bassist Janice Marie Johnson wrote down what Payne had said. From that thought, she and keyboardist Perry Kibble crafted "Boogie Oogie Oogie," which thrust the veteran band to the top of the disco world for a few weeks.

Almost word-for-word, Payne's quote formed the first verse of the song. The famous, thumping bass part played by J. M. Johnson came from her warm-up exercise in a recording studio, when she didn't even realize the tape was rolling in a recorder.

"We were knocking ourselves out," Johnson told author Fred Bronson, "but (were) getting no reaction from the crowd. In fact, they seemed to have contempt for two women who thought they could front a band."

"Boogie Oogie" sold over two million copies and earned the group a Grammy Award for best new artist.

A Taste of Honey, which was named after a song written by Ric Marlow and Bobby Scott in 1960, polished their act for several years by doing USO shows in countries like Japan, South Korea, Thailand, Philippines, Taiwan, Morocco and Spain. They finally landed a contract with Capitol Records in 1978.

It was the fortieth number 1 single for Capitol, making it the first label to reach that milestone.

A follow-up single, "Do It Good," peaked at number 79 on the Hot 100, and A Taste of Honey would not have another big hit for three years. In 1981, as a J.M. Johnson-Payne duo, they hit number 3 with a remake of "Sukiyaki."

•••••• ❖ ••••••

"Le Freak" by Chic

Songwriters: Nile Rodgers, Bernard Edwards
Peaked at number 1 on *Billboard* Hot 100
December 9, 1978
December 23, 1978
December 30, 1978
January 20, 1979
January 27, 1979
February 3, 1979

As mentioned earlier in this chapter, Chic's breakout recording, "Dance, Dance, Dance (Yowsah, Yowsah, Yowsah)" was popular in many discotheques. In fact, it was on its way up the charts on New Year's Eve 1977.

On that night, Chic's Nile Rodgers and Bernard Edwards were invited by actress/singer Grace Jones to ring in the new year with her at New York's Studio 54. There was just one problem: Jones neglected to notify the club's staff that her guests were coming.

Even though their record was being played inside the discotheque, Rodgers and Edwards were unceremoniously denied entry.

"Somehow, we couldn't give the right password to get in," Rodgers was quoted by Radiox.co.uk. "They slammed the door in our faces and said, 'F—k off.'"

Their anger and humiliation triggered a response, as they wrote the song "Le Freak." Their original lyric was "f—k off," but they wisely changed it to "freak out."

The record was part of a disco tsunami that was about to crest in 1979. And the irrepressible "Le Freak" just wouldn't go away, as it became the first single to take over the number 1 position on the *Billboard Hot 100* three times. Worldwide sales went over seven million, making it Atlantic Records' best-selling single at the time.

Rodgers related to *Melody Maker,* "Right from the start, we had a concept for Chic. The music at the time (1976) was very much a secondary thing. We knew we had to have something that was international and interchangeable with the markets, while at the same time we had to be in with a music that was on the rise. At that time it was rock and roll, and we thought we could make our concept work within its framework.

"When disco came in, it was like a gift from heaven. Discos gave us the perfect opportunity to realize our concept, because it wasn't about being black, white, male or female. Further, it would give us a chance to get into the mainstream. We wanted millions of dollars, Ferraris and planes, and this seemed like the way to get them."

In an interview with *Melody Maker,* Edwards admitted he hated disco music. "I got into it, though, and realized that if we did it our way, it'd be pretty good."

Rodgers said to the *Washington Post,* "We started to use our brains. What we wanted to do was make records. We didn't want to be a small band playing bar mitzvahs the rest of our lives, so we got into disco." Like most disco hits, "Le Freak" was constructed around wispy vocals, guitar, bass and strings.

The lyrics mention the French phrase *c'est chic,* which means "it's stylish." They also reference the dreaded Studio 54: "Now we freak, oh what a joy. Just come on down, to the 54 and find a spot out on the floor."

Nine more disco records would top the pop chart in 1979.

"Goodnight Tonight" by Wings
Songwriter: Paul McCartney
Peaked at number 5 on *Billboard* Hot 100
May 19, 1979
May 26, 1979
June 2, 1979

Wings

Paul McCartney (June 18, 1942-?) lead vocals, bass, electric guitar, drums
Linda McCartney (September 24, 1941-April 17, 1998) backing vocals, keyboards
Denny Laine (October 29, 1944-?) guitar, backing vocals
Laurence Juber (November 12, 1952-?) guitar, backing vocals
Steve Holley (August 24, 1954-?) percussion, backing vocals
Formed in 1971 in London, England

Wings: Laurence Juber, Denny Laine, Linda McCartney,
Steve Holley (seated), Paul McCartney

"Go with the flow," an old saying urges. And that is what Paul McCartney did during the final year of the disco era.

McCartney and his band, Wings, recorded "Goodnight Tonight," a song with a throbbing bass line that fit right in with the disco climate.

And why not go with the flow? The previous year, respected rockers the Rolling Stones took a dip into the disco pool with "Miss You," a song that topped the *Billboard* Hot 100 and peaked at number 6 on the dance club chart.

McCartney, a rock icon who wrote and sang such songs as "Helter Skelter" and "Live And Let Die," turned out to be capable of competing in the disco music arena.

The seventh configuration of Wings played behind McCartney's vocals. Linda McCartney and Denny Laine were veterans of the eight-year-old group, while Steve Holley and Laurence Juber were new additions.

Instrumentation on the track is spiced by some Spanish guitar riffs. A 7-plus-minute version of the song was pressed on 12-inch vinyl, McCartney's first, for dance club play.

"(The song is) based 'round some rhythm," McCartney told *Club Sandwich Magazine.* "I do like dance records. When you listen to records, you're often down a club and want to dance with someone. I like dancin' actually."

With its emphasis on the dance beat, "Goodnight Tonight" has shallow lyrics with a refrain that is repeated over and over. "Don't get too tired for love," the first verse says. "Don't let it end. Don't say goodnight to love, it may never be the same again."

The song was produced during Wings' sessions for the album "Back To The Egg." McCartney later pulled it because he didn't think it fit the theme of the album. It was included in the 2010 film *Grown Ups* starring Adam Sandler.

"Goodnight Tonight" was certified as a million-seller.

••••••• ❖ •••••••

"Ring My Bell" by Anita Ward
Songwriter: Frederick Knight
Peaked at number 1 on *Billboard* Hot 100
June 30, 1979
July 7, 1979

Anita Ward

Born Anita Ward on December 20, 1956, in Memphis, Tennessee

Anita Ward

Sometimes a tweak of the lyrics can turn a song into a big smash. That's how "Ring My Bell" became Anita Ward's contribution to disco mania.

Frederick Knight, owner of Juana Records and Ward's producer, had written "Ring My Bell" for Stacy Lattisaw to record. Lattisaw was only 12 years old at the time, and the song's lyrics were about juveniles talking on the telephone. While Ward was recording her debut album, Knight presented her the song with reworked lyrics that were more adult-oriented, trying to use the dance rhythm to capitalize on the disco trend.

According to author Colin Larkin, Ward didn't like the song, but she consented to recording it.

"(There are) some disadvantages to that," Ward said in an interview for Disco-Disco.com, "because, unfortunately, I didn't get the opportunity for people to hear me sing ballads. I really love ballads. That song is not the type of song that I would have chosen for myself to sing."

In an interview with reporter Paul Grein, Ward revealed, "I had a few doubts about cutting 'Ring My Bell.' It was the last song we recorded. After listening to the completed LP, we felt we needed another up-tempo tune."

Today's culture may cast the adult lyrics in a sexually suggestive light, but Knight told Grein, "Anita is a very clean-cut person, so I went to great pains being picky about lyrical content. We're trying to build a real respectable image for her. The lyrics talk about an everyday situation – it's nothing you'd be ashamed of in front of your kids."

A sample of the lyrics: "I'm glad you're home, now did you really miss me? I guess you did by the look in your eyes. Well, lay back and relax while I put away the dishes, then you and me can rock-a-bye. You can ring my bell."

In 2022 *Billboard* ranked "Ring My Bell" at number 18 on its list of the 60 Sexiest Songs of All Time.

The signature sound of instrumentation on the track is the use of a Synare electronic drum, which has a sound that comes out strong and then fades. At certain parts of the song, it is used on the first beat of every bar.

The song reached number 1 on the *Billboard* Hot Soul Singles and Dance Club Songs charts, and was number 1 in Canada, New Zealand, Norway, Spain and the UK.

Ward earned a degree in psychology from tiny Rust College in Holly Springs, Miss. She served as an elementary school substitute teacher before trying her hand at the recording industry.

She issued several follow-up singles after "Ring My Bell," and the most successful was "Don't Drop My Love," which crested at number 87 on the Hot 100 in 1979.

•••••••• ❖ ••••••••

"Bad Girls" by Donna Summer

Songwriters: Donna Summer, Bruce Sudano, Edward Hokenson, Joe Esposito
Peaked at number 1 on *Billboard* Hot 100
July 14, 1979
July 21, 1979
July 28, 1979
August 4, 1979
August 11, 1979

What a year 1979 was for Donna Summer. She had just finished a three-week stay at number 1 with her rock/dance smash "Hot Stuff," when two weeks later she was on the top of the *Billboard* Hot 100 again with the disco hit "Bad Girls."

The record had the strength to top the *Billboard* Hot Soul Singles and Dance Club Songs charts, as well.

The artwork for an album of the same name carried photos of Summer dressed like a prostitute, which fit the theme of the lyrics.

"Bad girls, talking about the sad girls," the lyrics begin. "Sad girls, talking about bad girls. See them out on the street at night, picking up all kinds of strangers if the price is right. You can score if your pocket's nice. But you want a good time."

Sales of the single soared past the two million mark, making it Summer's biggest hit.

Inspiration for the song came from an assistant of Summer's who was hassled by police, thinking she was a hooker on Sunset Blvd. in Los Angeles. Summer wrote a rough version of the song two years before its release.

Summer was under contract to Neil Bogart's Casablanca Records when he first heard "Bad Girls." He wanted to give it to Cher for her next album. Summer nixed the deal and kept the song for herself.

Members of the vocal group Brooklyn Dreams collaborated with Summer on the songwriting of "Bad Girls." They did backing vocals on her hit "Heaven Knows" in 1978, and the song charted to number 4 on the *Billboard* Hot 100 in March 1979. A year after "Bad Girls" was atop the charts, Brooklyn Dreams member Bruce Sudano married Summer.

According to Songfacts, Summer sang "Bad Girls" on her ABC-TV special, which aired January 27, 1980. Summer appeared dressed like a hooker, performing the song on a studio replica of Sunset Blvd. Her fellow street walkers were played by actresses Debralee Scott, Pat Ast and Twiggy.

Sudano spoke of Summer's songwriting in an interview with Songfacts. "She was very stream-of-consciousness," he said. "Her favorite way to write was to go in the studio, mic the guitar, mic the piano, turn on her microphone, roll tape and flow. That's how 'Bad Girls' was written. That's how many of her songs were written – just flow."

Before 1979 was over, Summer had another number 1 hit on the pop chart, "No More Tears (Enough Is Enough)," which was a duet with Barbra Streisand.

Donna Summer in "Bad Girl" costumes

Stars That Fell from the Sky
Remembering the air crash victims of rock

Overview: Life is fascinating. Death can be fascinating, too.

Despite death's finality and its removal of people from our lives, we are drawn to its details. We know that someday death will claim each one of us.

The rapid expansion of the air travel industry after World War II brought many benefits to society. Inadvertently, it also gave us another way to die.

As mechanical failures, pilot errors and severe weather events began to pile up, the music industry suffered its share of air travel casualties. Music enthusiasts had to grudgingly accept the fact that some of their favorite stars no longer would be making another record.

Rock and Roll, in a way, was losing its innocence. The music may have been fun and pleasure, but the consequences of travel tragedies were just as real for young musicians as for any other air travelers.

All the adoration in the world could not save some of the greatest musicians of all time from the effects of gravity.

Brad Watkins had been a pilot for a major United States airline for thirty years when I spoke with him. He said his training in the 1980s included studying flight mishaps involving small, private aircraft, much like the ones that have taken the lives of more than a dozen musicians.

Watkins added that four of his fellow employees died in air crashes when they were flying small planes for side jobs or for practice. One such casualty involved a pilot repeatedly practicing a maneuver called the *chandelle.* Ironically, the objective of the maneuver is to develop a pilot's coordination, orientation, planning and accuracy of control during maximum performance flight.

While I was writing this chapter, I had the opportunity to take several flights in a small, private plane. I made note of the vulnerability a small aircraft has in the face of severe weather conditions, as well as the paucity of choices a pilot has in making an emergency landing far from an airstrip.

I experienced the helplessness a pilot can feel when a thick cloud cover makes it impossible to find a small airstrip below.

In this chapter, the air crash deaths of several of the most high-profile musicians, and a promoter, will be reviewed. We salute them because they gave their lives while taking to the air to do what they loved.

February 3, 1959

Location: Cerro Gordo County, Iowa, about 5 miles northwest of Mason City
Died:
Buddy Holly, born Charles Hardin Holley on September 7, 1936, in Lubbock, Texas
Ritchie Valens, born Richard Steven Valenzuela on May 13, 1941, in Los Angeles, California
J.P. Richardson, aka The Big Bopper, born Jiles Perry Richardson Jr. on October 24, 1930, in Sabine Pass, Texas
Roger Peterson, pilot for Dwyer Flying Service, born May 24, 1937

Buddy Holly

Ritchie Valens

J.P. Richardson

This might have been the most painful of rock's air crashes, not only because it was the first but also because it took the lives of three of the youngest and most promising stars.

In the years following the tragedy, biographical films were made of the lives of Buddy Holly and Ritchie Valens, and a popular song by Don McLean branded the date as "the day the music died."

The deceased musicians were part of a group that was on a concert extravaganza called the Winter Dance Party. Holly's band consisted of Waylon Jennings, Tommy Allsup and Carl Bunch. Dion & the Belmonts were also on the tour, as well as opening vocalist Frankie Sardo. The tour began in Milwaukee, Wis., on January 23, 1959.

Holly had written and recorded several national hits, including the number 1 smash "That'll Be The Day" and others destined to become classics.

Valens, still a teenager, had a two-sided hit with "Donna" peaking at number 2 and "La Bamba" peaking at number 22.

Richardson, a disc jockey by trade, had a number 6 recording with "Chantilly Lace," which he followed with the number 38 "Big Bopper's Wedding."

The musicians privately called the trip the "tour from hell." Poor planning had the dates scattered across the Midwest on an illogical schedule, using a bus whose heater had broken, making it a breeding ground for flu and frostbite.

Complicating the situation was the fact Holly learned of his wife's pregnancy just before he left New York City for the tour.

Bunch, a drummer, had to be hospitalized for frostbite in Ironwood, Michigan.

By the time the tour played a February 2 stop at the Surf Ballroom in Clear Lake, Iowa, Holly needed rest and relief. He turned to the local Dwyer Flying Service, which had a 1947 V-tailed Beechcraft 35 Bonanza available. There was room for three passengers for a charge of $36 apiece for a flight to Moorhead, Minnesota

Jennings was to be on the flight, but J.P. Richardson was in such poor health that Jennings surrendered his seat to him. That left one seat for either Allsup or Valens. A coin toss gave the seat to Valens.

The last thing Jennings said to Holly, teasingly, was, "I hope your old plane crashes." He had to live with that taunt haunting him until he died in 2002.

Roger Peterson, twenty-one, was assigned to pilot the plane. But, according to Planeandpilotmag.com, he had failed his Instrument Flight Rules (IFR) exam and wasn't qualified to fly in instrument meteorological conditions (IMC).

There was light snow falling with winds of twenty knots, gusting to thirty-two knots. A ceiling of five thousand feet had fallen to three thousand feet, with visibility of 6 miles when the plane took off at 12:55 a.m.

Investigators believe Peterson entered IMC shortly after takeoff and attempted to make an ascending turn to climb over clouds. The plane descended instead. It hit the ground at 170 mph, and the right wing tip hit first, sending the plane into a cartwheel.

Jerry Dwyer, owner of the plane, watched as the plane left the airfield. He saw the plane's lights enter into a descending turn and then vanish. He radioed Peterson but received no response.

At dawn Dwyer got in a plane and retraced the planned path of the Beechcraft. He found the crashed plane in a cornfield, with debris strewn more than 500 feet. Everyone in the Beechcraft died on impact.

The Civil Aeronautics Board determined the cause of the crash was pilot disorientation due to inclement weather.

Holly's widow, Maria Elena, learned of his death from a television news report. The shock and stress caused her to miscarry.

The Winter Dance Party continued for two more weeks, with Bobby Vee & the Shadows, Jimmy Clanton, Frankie Avalon and Fabian joining the entourage to fill in for the deceased musicians.

The Surf Ballroom has a concert each Feb. 3 to celebrate the lives the young stars who died in 1959.

A pair of oversized horn-rimmed eyeglasses marks the spot where Buddy Holly, Ritchie Valens and J.P. Richardson died on February 3, 1959.

This memorial sits outside the Surf Ballroom in Clear Lake, Iowa.

••••••• ❖ •••••••

March 5, 1963

Location: Near Camden, Tennessee
Died:
Patsy Cline, born Virginia Patterson Hensley on September 8, 1932, in Westchester, Virginia
Cowboy Copas, born Lloyd Estel Copas on July 15, 1913, in Blue Creek, Ohio
Hawkshaw Hawkins, born Harold Franklin Hawkins on December 22, 1921, in Huntington, West Virginia
Randy Hughes, pilot, born Ramsey Dorris Hughes on September 11, 1928, in Gum, Tennessee

Patsy Cline

Cowboy Copas

Hawkshaw Hawkins

258

Patsy Cline wasn't a rock singer, but she was one of the first female country music artists to cross over to the pop charts in a big way.

She had two songs that peaked at number 12 on the *Billboard* pop charts, "Walkin' After Midnight" and "I Fall To Pieces."

In 1961, her "Crazy" peaked at number 9 on the Hot 100, and *Billboard* rated it the number 2 song on its year-end list of pop songs. The following year she sent "She's Got You" to number 14 on the Hot 100. Those were the most prolific years of her career.

She found herself on a mission of mercy in March 1963 in Kansas City, Kan., doing three shows at a benefit concert for the family of disc jockey "Cactus Jack" Call, who had died in an automobile crash. She did all three shows despite suffering from a cold virus.

Other country music performers who were on the stage on March 4, 1963, were George Jones, Dottie West, the Clinch Mountain Boys, Billy Walker, Wilma Lee and Stoney Cooper, George Riddle & the Jones Boys, George McCormick, Cowboy Copas and Hawkshaw Hawkins.

On the night of the show, the local airport was fogged in, and Cline was unable to fly home to Nashville. This forced her to spend a night at a hotel. The next day West and her husband offered Cline a ride to Nashville in their car, a 16-hour trip Cline refused.

Cavalierly, Cline told West, "Don't worry about me, Hoss. When it's my time to go, it's my time to go." This may have been a reference to the fact Cline survived a horrific car crash on June 14, 1961. It wasn't her time to go then.

Cline checked out of the hotel on March 5 and went to Fairfax Airport. There she boarded a three-year-old Piper PA-24 Comanche propeller-driven plane with Copas, Hawkins and her manager, Randy Hughes, who was the plane's owner and pilot. Hughes was licensed to fly but was not rated to fly under instrument flight rules (IFR). His total flight time was 160.2 hours.

Hawkins replaced Billy Walker on the flight because Walker took a commercial flight to tend to a sick family member.

Hughes flew the party to Rogers, Ark., where the plane was refueled, then to Dyersburg, Tennesse, for a weather briefing and more refueling. According to author Larry Jordan, the airfield manager warned the travelers of bad weather, and he offered them free meals and overnight accommodations so they could wait for better flying conditions.

This offer was rebuffed, with Hughes saying, "I've already come this far. We'll be there before you know it." They took off at 6:07 p.m.

Apparently, Hughes' plan was to hop from one small airport to another, waiting for storms to clear ahead.

In heavy weather, the plane crashed in a wooded area outside of Camden, Tenn. Investigators determined all four passengers died instantly. Cline's stopped wristwatch was recovered, with the time reading 6:20.

The next day searchers found the plane's engine buried six feet in the mud and a wing embedded in a tree.

Following Cline's death at the young age of thirty, Decca Records re-released many of her recordings, which sold well. In 2005, the *Guinness Book of World Records* cited *Patsy Cline's Greatest Hits* (released in 1967) as the album by a female artist that spent the most weeks on any album chart.

Cline's influence on other artists was extensive. For example, during her country rock period, Linda Ronstadt did covers of "I Fall To Pieces" and "Crazy." Both versions were very true to Cline's style.

In 1985 a motion picture titled *Sweet Dreams,* starring Jessica Lange, chronicled Cline's life.

A large stone memorial marks the spot where Patsy Cline and
her comrades died in the woods of Tennessee.

•••••••• ❖ ••••••••

July 31, 1964

Location: Davidson County, Tennessee, near Brentwood
Died:
Jim Reeves, born James Travis Reeves on August 20, 1923, in Galloway, Texas
Dean Manuel, born Dockie Dean Manuel on January 1, 1934, in Cleveland, Arkansas

Jim Reeves

Dean Manuel

Jim Reeves, known as "Gentleman Jim," was a much-loved and well respected country singer. He released his first single in 1953, and his second single the same year, "Mexican Joe," became his first number 1 hit on the *Billboard* Top Country & Western Records chart.

He endeared himself to pop music fans in 1960, when his number 1 country hit "He'll Have To Go" crossed over to the *Billboard* Hot 100, where it crested at number 2.

Known by his middle name Travis as a child, Reeves was a talented athlete. He won a baseball scholarship to the University of Texas, which he gave up after only six weeks. A right-handed pitcher, he later signed a contract with the St. Louis Cardinals and played three years of minor league baseball. A sciatic nerve injury ended his baseball career.

Reeves appeared headed for service in the U.S. Army, but he failed his induction physical. He then went to work as a radio announcer and sang live on the air between records. This led to a career as a professional singer.

Dean Manuel was Reeves' manager and business partner, and he also played piano in Reeves' backing band, the Blue Boys. On July 31, 1964, he and Reeves were in Batesville, Ark., to buy real estate. Afterward, they headed home to Nashville in Reeves' single-engine Beechcraft Debonair, with Reeves as pilot.

Near Brentwood, Tennesse, the plane encountered a severe thunderstorm, and a resulting crash killed both men in a suburban area south of Nashville.

Evidence uncovered by author Larry Jordan indicates Reeves turned left to follow Franklin Road to the Nashville airport instead of turning right to avoid the rain, as control tower personnel had advised. Concentrating on establishing his ground references, Reeves allowed his speed to decrease and stalled the engine.

A tailspin apparently resulted, with the plane too low for Reeves to correct it. The plane entered heavy rain at 4:51 p.m. and crashed one minute later.

The wreckage was found 42 hours later in a wooded area, with the plane's nose buried deep in the ground.

A powerhouse on the country charts in the 1950s and '60s, Reeves' music continued to appear on the country album and singles charts into the mid-1980s. He had five number 1 singles and two number 1 albums after his death.

A life size statue memorializes Jim Reeves in Carthage, Texas

•••••• ❖ ••••••

Dec. 10, 1967

Location: Lake Monona, Dane County, near Madison, Wisconsin
Died:
Otis Redding, born Otis Ray Redding Jr., on September 9, 1941, in Dawson, Georgia
Jimmy King, born James King on June 8, 1949
Phalon Jones, born Phalon R. Jones Jr. in 1948
Ronnie Caldwell, born Ronald Louis Caldwell on December 27, 1948
Carl Cunningham, born Carl Lee Cunningham in 1948
Matt Kelly, born Matthew Kelly in 1950
Dick Fraser, pilot, born Richard Philip Fraser on October 9, 1941

Otis Redding

The Bar-Kays, clockwise from far right:
James Alexander, Phalon Jones, Ben Cauley,
Ronnie Caldwell, Carl Cunningham, Jimmy King

When Otis Redding, a singer who was dubbed "The King of Soul," met a watery death, the accident took almost an entire band with him.

Seven of the eight men on board Redding's twin engine Beechcraft H18 perished when the airplane, on approach to Truax Field at Madison, Wis., splashed into icy Lake Monona.

The plane originally had a capacity of nine passengers, but the band equipment of the Bar-Kays took up the equivalent of one seat.

That forced one member of the Bar-Kays to take a commercial flight on each leg of the concert tours, on a rotating basis. When the plane left Cleveland, Ohio, to go to Madison, Wis., it was bassist James Alexander's turn to fly commercial.

Besides pilot Dick Fraser and Redding, members of the Bar-Kays who died were guitarist Jimmy King, saxophonist Phalon Jones, organist Ronnie Caldwell, drummer Carl Cunningham and valet/roadie Matt Kelly.

Trumpet player Ben Cauley was the only passenger in the plane who survived. Cauley died in 2015 at the age of sixty-seven.

In the fall of 1967, Redding and the Bar-Kays were playing a series of weekend shows at colleges. On what would be their last trip, they played a gig in Nashville, Tenn., then went to Cleveland. The trip was to end at Madison with two shows at The Factory.

As the band members walked onto the tarmac in Cleveland on the morning of December 10, Cunningham asked an airport attendant to start the plane so the interior could warm up. "But he told us he couldn't crank it up because the battery was kind of low," Cauley told the *Memphis Commercial Appeal.* "He said he'd rather have the pilot do it. "We kinda looked at each other, as young fellows do, and said, 'The battery's low?' Like, what's going on? Five minutes after that, it got started – but we were still thinking about that. But we took off going to Madison with no problems."

The shaking of the plane roused the napping passengers at about 3:30 p.m. Cauley looked over at Jones, who had looked out the window and moaned, "Oh no!"

What Cauley did next may have saved his life.

"I remember I got up, unbuckled my seatbelt to see what it was," Cauley said. "The next thing I remember, I came to and was in all this water."

Cauley, a non-swimmer, latched onto a seat cushion that floated his way. After a few minutes it slipped away from him, but he soon grabbed another that came to him.

"I saw Carl come out of the water, I saw Matt come up on the other side," Cauley said. "I was conscious at that time. I didn't know it, but my head was swollen and bleeding, and I remember I had only one shoe."

A rescue team arrived in about seventeen minutes and plucked Cauley from the water just before hypothermia set in. The other passengers had fatal injuries.

The cause of the crash never has been determined.

Shortly before setting out on his final concert tour, Redding had recorded a song he had written with Stax Records guitarist Steve Cropper, "Dock Of The Bay." The recording hadn't been polished yet, and Redding did some whistling at the end of the song where he planned to insert more lyrics.

Stax released the recording on its Volt subsidiary anyway, and it became the first posthumous number 1 single on the *Billboard* Hot 100. Starting March 16, 1968, "Dock Of The Bay" occupied the top spot for four weeks.

In the aftermath of the crash, Cauley and Alexander rebuilt the Bar-Kays, and they served as backing musicians on many recordings issued by the Stax/Volt labels.

A plaque and bench on the roof of Monona Terrace Community and Convention Center remind visitors of Otis Redding's fatal crash in the nearby water.

•••••• ❖ ••••••

Sept. 20, 1973

Location: Natchitoches, Louisiana
Died:
Jim Croce, born James Joseph Croce on January 10, 1943, in South Philadelphia, Pennsylvania
Maury Muehleisen, born Maurice T. Muehleisen on January 14, 1949, in Trenton, New Jersey
George Stevens, born in 1937
Ken Cortese, born Kenneth Dominick Cortese on October 24, 1945, in Chicago, Illinois
Dennis Rast, born Dennis William Rast on November 27, 1942, in Illinois
Bob Elliott, pilot, born Robert Newton Elliott Jr. on October 2, 1915, in Oklahoma

Jim Croce

Maury Muehleisen

For years Jim Croce fought with the music industry establishment and paid his dues as a folk rock performer, hoping to break through as a mainstream artist.

When success finally came his way, it was ironic that he had only about fifteen months to enjoy it before a plane crash took his life.

While on a concert tour at Natchitoches, La., where he played a show at Northwestern State University, Croce and his entourage died shortly after takeoff in a chartered Beechcraft E18S, a twin-engine, low-wing plane.

Those who died with Croce were his musical partner, Maury Muehleisen; comedian George Stevens, who had opened the show; Croce's manager and booking agent, Ken Cortese; road manager Dennis Rast; and pilot Bob Elliott.

The plane was bound for the next show in Sherman, Texas, as a lengthy tour through Europe and the United States neared its end. Croce's star was on the rise at the time, and "Time In A Bottle," a track from his 1972 album "You Don't Mess Around With Jim," would become a number1 single after his death.

The following day saw the release of Croce's new single, "I Got A Name." It became a number 10 hit in the ensuing weeks. An album by the same name was released December 1, 1973.

According to the *Monroe News-Star*, the travelers had planned to spend the night in Natchitoches, but they called pilot Elliott at the Lakeview Motel and requested an early departure.

A letter Croce wrote to his wife Ingrid, which she received a week after his death, revealed Croce's weariness with touring and a desire to leave the recording business and stay home with his family. Croce's son A.J. was just 2 at the time.

"Remember, it's the first sixty years that count, and I've got thirty to go," he wrote.

Croce told *Rolling Stone Magazine* in 1973, "I've had to get in and out of music a couple of times, because music didn't always mean a living. You don't make that much in bars. I still have memories of those nights, playing for $25 a night, with nobody listening."

According to the VH-1 television documentary *Behind The Music,* when he was recording in New York City, Croce signed a series of contracts with representatives who promised to promote him and his music. He became angry that others were profiting from his music while he was making practically nothing.

By the summer of 1970, Croce was forced to take odd jobs just to make ends meet. He drove a truck, gave guitar lessons and worked construction. On weekends he watched roller derby and stock car racing, which helped him learn about characters who would play prominent roles in his songs.

But he swore off writing for a year, afraid that promoters would take all the money if he did anything of consequence.

After Ingrid announced her pregnancy, Croce began to write again. In a week, he wrote several songs that would help make him famous.

On *Behind The Music,* musician Arlo Guthrie stated, "His music had a lot of depth to it because his life wasn't easy. "I don't know if he thought he was unique. He saw himself as just an ordinary guy."

Croce made it to the top of the singles chart for the first time in July 1973 with "Bad, Bad Leroy Brown."

Back in Natchitoches, with no taxis in town, pilot Elliott had to walk and run most of the three miles to the local airport before police gave him a ride. Jerry Pierce, who was NSU's news bureau director, said Elliott looked disheveled and exhausted.

"He was lost and turned around and went through a cornfield," Pierce told the *News-Star.* "People who saw him said he looked like he'd been hit by a truck – rattled, hot and sweaty. A lot of people think his condition after the walk may have been one of the factors that contributed to the crash."

The plane was airborne when it clipped a pecan tree just off the end of the runway, and all passengers died instantly when the plane hit the ground.

Dan McDonald, who was a sophomore at NSU, told a reporter, "I'd never seen anything like that. It almost looked like a bomb had hit the plane. The debris field gave me an idea of how forceful the crash was."

According to papers filed in the U.S. Court of Appeals, Fifth Circuit, investigators placed total blame for the crash on pilot error because of a downwind takeoff into a "black hole" of darkness, which limited his use of visual references.

Reportedly, Elliott had coronary artery disease and may have suffered a heart attack during the aborted flight.

Also, there were reports of marijuana, hashish and other drugs being found on the bodies and in luggage belonging to some of the travelers. Testing revealed the pilot had no drugs in his system.

As a whiz songwriter, Croce skillfully concocted colorful characters, such as Willie McCoy, Leroy Brown, Rapid Roy and the Roller Derby Queen. But it is Croce who should be memorialized in song for the life he lived.

A photo and plaque on the campus of Northwestern State University commemorate the site of Jim Croce's final performance.

•••••• ❖ ••••••

Aug. 9, 1974

Location: Jackson County, near Jackson, Minnesota
Died:
Bill Chase, born William Edward Chiaiese on October 20, 1934, in Quincy, Massachusetts
John Emma, born John Thomas Emma on April 30, 1952, in Geneva, Illinois
Wally Yohn, born Wallace Keith Yohn on January 12, 1947, in Phoenix, Arizona
Walter Clark, born Walter J. Clark on January 24, 1949, in New Jersey
Dan Ludwig, pilot, age forty-one
Linda Swisher, pilot's secretary

Bill Chase

267

Growing up in Massachusetts, Bill Chase took up the trumpet when he was a teenager. It's the same instrument his father played proficiently.

After freelancing with big bands in Las Vegas showrooms in the 1960s, he formed his own jazz rock band in 1970, calling it Chase. By that time, he had settled in Chicago to avail himself of booking and recording contacts.

Chase's first album yielded the band's biggest hit, "Get It On." It peaked at number 24 on the *Billboard* Hot 100 in the summer of 1971, but it was wildly popular with local fans. On July 19, 1971, the song peaked at number 5 on the WLS radio *Chicagoland Hit Parade* survey.

Terry Richards provided lead vocals on the recording, and Bill Chase played a strong, often soaring trumpet throughout. There were nine members in Chase at that time, including two other trumpeters.

Chase followed the playbook written by the Buckinghams in the 1960s, which featured mainstream rock music accompanied by a brass section.

Fast forward to summer of 1974. With a pared-down lineup, Chase was flying on August 9 from Chicago to Jackson, Minnesota, via Waterloo, Iowa, to play a gig at the Jackson County Fair. Weather conditions included a low, four-foot cloud ceiling with rain falling.

The twin engine Piper PA-30-160 Comanche carrying Bill Chase, guitarist John Emma, keyboardist Wally Yohn and drummer Walter Clark stalled and crashed in a soybean field, about three-eighths of a mile short of the Jackson Municipal Airport runway at around 5:00 p.m.

Searchers discovered the plane at about 8:30 the next morning. There were no survivors.

According to the National Transportation Safety Board, the cause was pilot error and poor radio communication. Pilot Daniel Ludwig, the owner of the airplane, had some 2,600 total flying hours and was instrument rated. His secretary, Linda Swisher, was also a passenger.

The mishap removed one of the trumpet virtuosos from the music world. Before venturing into rock, Chase had played with jazz luminaries such as Maynard Ferguson, Woody Herman and Stan Kenton.

In 1971, Chase received a Grammy nomination for Best New Artist, eventually losing to Carly Simon.

•••••• ❖ ••••••

Oct. 20, 1977

Location: Amite County, Miss., five miles northeast of Gillsburg
Died:
Ronnie Van Zant, born Ronald Wayne Van Zant on January 15, 1948, in Jacksonville, Florida
Steve Gaines, born Steven Earl Gaines on September 14, 1949, in Miami, Oklahoma
Cassie Gaines, born Cassie LaRue Gaines on January 9, 1948, in Miami, Oklahoma
Dean Kilpatrick, born Dean Arthur Kilpatrick on May 30, 1949, in Quebec, Canada
Walter McCreary, pilot, born Walter Wiley McCreary on August 27, 1943, in San Antonio, Texas
William Gray, co-pilot, born William John Gray Jr. on March 7, 1945, in Lubbock, Texas

Ronnie Van Zant   Steve Gaines   Cassie Gaines   Dean Kilpatrick

The crash of a 40-passenger airplane not only took six lives but tore the heart out of one of the greatest American rock bands of the day.

Lynyrd Skynyrd was out on tour, departing Greenville, S.C., for their next stop in Baton Rouge, La. Their Convair CV-240 twin engine, propeller-driven plane had an entourage of 24 passengers aboard, plus pilot Walter McCreary and co-pilot William Gray. The 30-year-old plane had 29,000 flight miles on it and was the third of its kind to be built. The band had obtained it for three payments of $5,000 – a bargain.

But the aircraft had a shady past. According to author Stephen Davis, the flight crew of the band Aerosmith had inspected it for possible use on a concert tour. They rejected it because they felt neither the plane nor its crew were up to standard.

Aerosmith's assistant chief of flight operations said he saw the pilots passing a liquor bottle back and forth in the cockpit during the inspection.

Previously, passengers had been mortified to see flames erupt from an engine while in flight.

As stated in the VH-1 documentary *Behind The Music,* McCreary detected engine trouble as the band prepared to come aboard. But he assured them it was all right for them to get in.

According to guitarist Gary Rossington, guitar player Allen Collins didn't want to get aboard because the plane had been sputtering. But lead singer Ronnie Van Zant said, "If it's your time to go, it's your time. Let's go."

Backup singer JoJo Billingsley was not with the entourage because she was home dealing with health issues brought about by substance abuse. But she'd had a terrifying dream about the plane crashing and had warned Collins about it.

Lynyrd Skynyrd basically was forced off commercial air travel because of the members' penchant for out-of-control drinking and brawling while flying. Hence, the aging Convair became their ride for concert tours.

Throughout their career, the Jacksonville, Florida-based band did not excel on the singles chart. "Sweet Home Alabama" was their top offering with a number 8 showing in 1974. But the public feasted on their albums and concert appearances. "Nuthin' Fancy" topped out at number 9 on the *Billboard* 200, and "Second Helping" peaked at number 12. After the band's infamous crash, "Street Survivors" went to number 5.

After the plane took off without any problems, the passengers relaxed and began their usual card games. About eighty miles from Baton Rouge, however, the cockpit radioed that the plane was low on fuel. It turned out the right engine was using more fuel than usual because it was being operated in "auto-rich mode."

McCreary tried to land at a small airfield, but an engine stalled. Then he tried to transfer fuel from one engine to another, but he panicked and accidentally dumped the fuel. The pilots instructed everyone to sit down and buckle up.

The next option was to make an emergency landing in a swampy area, but the plane descended too fast and began clipping treetops.

"Everybody was sitting down, praying, real silently," keyboardist Billy Powell said. "I thought I was gonna have a heart attack. We were watching the pine trees get bigger and bigger, and then crack! The initial contact was very violent and very sudden."

The plane came down in a wooded area at 6:53 p.m. at about 90 mph.

The pilots were killed on impact, and guitarist Steve Gaines and assistant road manager Dean Kilpatrick also died. Backup singer Cassie Gaines, with her throat cut from ear to ear, died in the arms of Rossington and Powell.

"Ronnie was catapulted when the cockpit buckled under," Powell said, "and he didn't have a scratch on him. He hit a tree with his head, and that's what killed him instantly." Van Zant evidently had declined to protect himself with a seat belt.

The plane broke into three pieces, and passengers were ripped from their seats, dealing them a variety of grisly injuries. The survivor with the worst injuries was Rossington, who suffered two broken arms, a broken leg, a fractured pelvis, a punctured stomach and a punctured liver.

Rossington would recover, and he lived until March 5, 2023.

Despite severe injuries, drummer Artimus Pyle left the wreck to seek help at the nearest farmhouse. He crawled through the darkness, uphill, through mud and over barbed wire fences.

When Pyle reached the farm, the owner had seen helicopters in the distance and feared Pyle was an escaped prisoner. He shot Pyle in the arm, adding to the drummer's misery.

As rescuers attempted to transport victims to local hospitals, souvenir hunters came to the crash site and stole wallets, jewelry, band equipment, etc., from the scene.

A ruling from the NTSB stated the probable cause of the crash was "fuel exhaustion and total loss of power from both engines due to crew inattention to fuel supply."

Van Zant not only was the front man and lead singer of Lynyrd Skynyrd, he also was its primary songwriter. He had a premonition he would die young.

In "Free Bird" he asked, "If I leave here tomorrow, would you still remember me?"

Also, the lyrics of "That Smell" mention "the smell of death surrounds you."

Van Zant's father, Lacy, told *Behind The Music,* "He said to me many times: 'Daddy, I'll never reach 30 years old. Daddy, that's my limit." Ronnie would have turned thirty about three months later.

Bass player Leon Wilkeson said, "The man knew his destiny."

Van Zant left behind a widow, Judy, and a thirteen-month-old daughter, Melody.

"I didn't believe it," Judy Van Zant Jenness said. "It's just one of those things that couldn't be true. There was a lot of frustration, a lot of anger, a lot of denial and a lot of pain. "I knew I had Melody – she was the one thing that kept me going."

There were twenty survivors of the crash. They were following:

- Artimus Pyle, drums
- Allen Collins, guitar
- Leon Wilkeson, bass
- Gary Rossington, guitar
- Billy Powell, keyboards
- Leslie Hawkins, backup singer
- Mark Frank, equipment manager

- Ken Peden, road crew member
- Mark Howard, lighting & rigging technician
- Kevin Elson, sound engineer
- Joe Osborn, road crew member
- James Brace, road crew member
- Don Kretzschmar, road crew member
- Paul Welch, road crew member
- Steve Lawler, lighting technician
- Clayton Johnson, road crew member
- Craig Reed, road crew member
- Gene Odom, security manager
- Ron Eckerman, tour manager
- Bill Sykes, TV crewman accompanying the band

In the aftermath of the tragedy, MCA Records rushed to pull copies of the newly released "Street Survivors" out of stores. The front cover of the album showed the band members standing in front of a wall of flames. MCA replaced that cover with a different photo of Lynyrd Skynyrd in front of a black background.

Two years later, the band members found the strength to appear on stage again, without a vocalist. Out of respect for Van Zant, they renamed themselves the Rossington Collins Band.

"The surviving members of that airplane crash realized that we were still here for a reason," Powell said. "And that reason is to carry on the music that was originally created by the Lynyrd Skynyrd Band."

In 1987 they toured as Lynyrd Skynyrd again, with Johnny Van Zant (Ronnie's younger brother) doing lead vocals.

Pyle commented, "Ronnie Van Zant is Lynyrd Skynyrd. There's nobody else.

"Ronnie asked the question, 'If I leave here tomorrow, will you still remember me?' Well, the world has answered that question with a resounding yes! We will remember the music."

These black granite slabs form a memorial to the Lynyrd Skynyrd plane crash near Gillsburg, Mississippi

March 19, 1982

Location: Leesburg, Florida
Died:
Randy Rhoads, born Randall William Rhoads on December 6, 1956, in Santa Monica, California
Andy Aycock, born Andrew Cotis Aycock on October 30, 1948, in Millen, Georgia
Rachel Youngblood, born Rachel Mae Youngblood on November 10, 1923

Randy Rhoads

A bizarre, senseless accident took the life of one of the most talented hard rock guitarists while he was on tour with Ozzy Osbourne.

After Black Sabbath fired Osbourne as their lead singer in 1979, the shock rocker assembled his own band to carry on as a solo act. He chose Randy Rhoads to be his lead guitarist.

Rhoads was a guitar prodigy who entered a condensed study program at Burbank (California) High School in order to graduate early and begin his music career.

At the top of his résumé was the brilliant work he did on "Crazy Train," a song from the 1980 album *Blizzard Of Ozz,* which also was the name Osbourne gave his band.

Other notable songs Rhoads played on include "Mr. Cowley," "I Don't Know," "Over The Mountain," "Flying High Again," "Diary Of A Madman," "Dee," "Revelation (Mother Earth)," "Laughing Gas" and "Tonight."

In 1973 Rhoads was a founding member of the band Little Women, which changed its name to Quiet Riot.

Osbourne's tour bus left Knoxville, Tennesse, after playing a show on March 18, 1982, and headed for Orlando, Flaorida, for Rock Super Bowl XIV. The troupe stopped in Leesburg, Florida, so that a malfunctioning air conditioning unit could be repaired. They stayed the night at Flying Baron Estates.

There was an airstrip nearby that had light airplanes and helicopters parked on the property. According to a National Transportation Safety Board report, Andy Aycock took one of the planes, a single-engine Beechcraft F35, without permission. Aycock was the tour bus driver and was licensed as a private aircraft pilot.

Keyboard player Don Airey and tour manager Jake Duncan went up with Aycock. The purpose of the flight was to "buzz" the tour bus and wake up drummer Tommy Aldridge.

After landing, Aycock wanted to make another flight for the same purpose. Though he was fearful of flying, Rhoads wanted to go along and snap some aerial photographs to send to his mother. He urged bass player Rudy Sarzo to go along, but Sarzo declined. Rachel Youngblood, a makeup artist and hairdresser for the band, took his place.

Aycock made two close passes over the bus, where Osbourne and band manager Sharon Levy also were sleeping. At about 10 a.m., Aycock made a third pass over the bus. One of the plane's wings clipped the roof, breaking the wing in two places and sending the plane out of control. It cut off the top of a pine tree and crashed into a nearby home.

The contact with the bus sent Rhoads and Youngblood hurtling into the windshield. As the plane burst into flames, all three on board were killed immediately. Their bodies were burned beyond recognition.

Levy, who would marry Osbourne a few weeks later, remarked, "They were all in bits. It was just body parts everywhere."

Aycock had been seen ingesting cocaine the previous night and had not slept. His estranged wife Wanda was in the bus and emerged just before the plane struck it. Sarzo speculated that, although Aycock had been trying to reconcile with Wanda, he may have been aiming for her.

Airy said he saw Rhoads struggling with Aycock over the plane's controls. In doing so, Rhoads may have prevented a direct hit by the plane on the bus.

In a radio interview days later, guitar wizard Eddie Van Halen commented, "You don't fly that low and smash into a crew bus and then hit the house. That's just plain stupidity. I feel so sorry for (Rhoads)."

In Sarzo's memoir, Airey was quoted as saying, "Well, right after we landed, Andy came up and told me he was going to take Rachel up for a ride. And that, being aware of her heart condition, he assured me that he was just going to take it easy, circle the property a couple of times and not pull any crazy stunts. "So, when Randy heard that, he decided to join them so he could take some aerial shots with his camera."

Rhoads, who stood five-foot-seven and weighed 105 pounds, had a girlfriend back in California, Jodi Raskin. She was listening to the radio while driving her car when she heard a disc jockey announce the news of Rhoads' death.

Randy Rhoads' remains are interred in his family's mausoleum in
San Bernardino, California

•••••• ❖ ••••••

Dec. 31, 1985

Location: Bowie County, Texas, near De Kalb
Died:
Rick Nelson, born Eric Hilliard Nelson on May 8, 1940, in Teaneck, New Jersey
Helen Blair, born Helen Blair in September 1957 in South Orange, New Jersey
Andy Chapin, thirty
Rick Intveld, twenty-two
Bobby Neal, thirty-eight
Patrick Woodward, thirty-five
Donald Russell, thirty-five

Rick Nelson

Helen Blair

It isn't often that an in-cabin fire brings down a plane, but that is how veteran singer/songwriter/actor Rick Nelson met his fate.

His fourteen-seat, twin engine Douglas DC-3C, built in 1944, crashed and burned near De Kalb, Texas, killing Nelson and the entire Stone Canyon Band. Helen Blair, Nelson's fiancée, was also a victim. Ironically, pilot Brad Rank, 34, and co-pilot Ken Ferguson, 40, survived.

Nelson and his band were on a tour of Southern states when they departed Guntersville, Ala., the afternoon of December 31. They were scheduled to play a New Year's Eve show in Dallas at the Park Suites Hotel. With the plane nearing De Kalb, the pilots looked for a place to make an emergency landing. A cow pasture, about 135 air miles northeast of Dallas, looked like their best bet.

Texas Public Safety Dept. spokeswoman Marlena Phelps said, "A helicopter flew up alongside the plane, because it saw the plane was in trouble, and asked what the problem was. "They said they had a fire on the plane. There was smoke, and it filled up the cockpit. The plane hit some high wires, then crashed into the ground and exploded."

The wreckage burned for four hours.

United Press International reported John Garner, De Kalb assistant fire chief, said, "The pilot was evidently trying to find a location to land and hit some high-line wires."

The pilots were transported to St. Michael Hospital in Texarkana, Ark. They were able to escape through the cockpit windows but suffered second and third-degree burns on their upper bodies.

274

According to UPI, hospital supervisor Glennette Spears stated, "They are in critical condition but are conscious. They were able to talk."

Nelson reportedly hated to fly, but he declined to tour by bus. He paid $118,000 for the plane, which formerly belonged to the DuPont family, of chemical industry fame, and musician Jerry Lee Lewis.

After Nelson took ownership, the plane was beset by mechanical problems, one of which prevented him from performing at the inaugural Farm Aid concert in Champaign, Ill., on July 13, 1985.

The National Transportation Safety Board stated in a report that, while it could not confirm the fire started in the gasoline-fueled heater, "there is no doubt that the fire did originate in the area of the heater."

A post on Lastflights.com said the NTSB concluded its investigation by saying the pilots failed to follow the emergency checklist procedures for the in-flight fire and by not briefing passengers on evacuation. The exact cause of the fire never was determined, although a heater fuel leak was suspected.

Toxicological tests done on Nelson's body showed he had a small amount of cocaine in his blood, along with the painkiller Darvon. An NTSB spokesman said they found no evidence free-basing cocaine caused the fire, according to the *Los Angeles Times*.

The band members who perished were Andy Chapin, pianist; Rick Intveld, drummer; Bobby Neal, guitarist; and Patrick Woodward, bassist. Sound technician Donald "Clark" Russell also died.

Nelson rose to popularity as a child actor in the early 1950s as part of a family cast on *The Adventures of Ozzie and Harriet*. The ABC-TV sitcom started in 1952 and ran fourteen seasons.

After Ricky, as he was then called, became a teenaged musician, episodes of the show typically would end with him singing a pop song while strumming his guitar. He became the first artist to benefit from regular television exposure of his songs. "A Teenager's Romance" became his first chart success in 1957, climbing to number 2.

Nelson landed more than 40 singles on the pop charts between 1957 and 1963. His status as a teen idol put him, and singers such as Bobby Rydell and Bobby Vee, on the pop music scrapheap when the Beatles began the British Invasion in 1964.

Shifting gears in his career, Nelson took acting roles in the movies *Here Come The Nelsons, Wackiest Ship In The Army, Rio Bravo, A Story Of Three Loves and Love And Kisses*.

Nelson, who shortened his professional name to Rick in 1961, married Kristin Harmon in 1963. By the time they'd had their fourth child in 1975, their relationship had soured.

According to biographer Philip Bashe, Kristin wanted Rick to abandon his music career so he could focus on acting and spend more time at home. But they led a high-flying lifestyle, and Kris's spending habits left Rick with little choice but to keep touring. Their messy divorce was finalized in December 1982.

By that time, Rick had met Helen Blair. She became his personal assistant and liaison for his fan club.

UPI quoted Pat Upton, owner of the Guntersville night club where Nelson played his last show: "He was in good spirits. Music was his whole life. He had no intentions of ever quitting."

The mangled, burned wreckage of Rick Nelson's plane sits in a
stand of trees near De Kalb, Texas

•••••••• ❖ ••••••••

Aug. 27, 1990

Location: East Troy, Wisconsin
Died:
Stevie Ray Vaughan, born Stephen Ray Vaughan on October 3, 1954, in Dallas, Texas
Jeff Brown, born Jeffrey William Brown in 1948
Bobby Brooks, thirty-four
Nigel Browne, thirty
Colin Smythe, forty-eight

Stevie Ray Vaughan

The 1980s were a tough time for a blues-oriented guitarist to make it big in the pop music business. But Stevie Ray Vaughan rose to the top of his craft and was recognized as an elite and influential bluesman.

Vaughan did solo work, played in the trio Double Trouble and also made guest appearances on recordings by other stars.

That all came to an end when the helicopter in which he was riding crashed following a concert. The chopper was one of four transporting musicians and crew from the Alpine Valley Music Theatre.

Vaughan joined Eric Clapton, Robert Cray and his older brother Jimmie Vaughan in the sold-out show attended by thirty-thousand fans. Reports from observers say Stevie Ray stole the show with his performance.

The use of helicopters to fly performers and their support staff in and out of venues is common when heavy ingress and egress clogs the one road serving the venue. The Woodstock Festival of 1969, for example, could not have been held without the use of choppers.

With the final five-passenger Bell 206B Ranger III filling up, Vaughan asked, "Do you mind if I take the seat? I really need to get back." The helicopter's destination was an airport in Chicago.

The helicopter lifted off at 12:40 a.m. in thick, patchy fog. It went about three hundred yards, banked sharply to the southeast and disappeared into the fog. It encountered a 150-foot ski hill, which it struck about fifty feet from the top.

Pilot Jeff Brown and three other passengers were killed along with Vaughan. The passengers, part of Clapton's entourage, were agent Bobby Brooks, assistant tour manager Colin Smythe-Park and bodyguard Nigel Browne.

The Civil Air Patrol was notified of the crash at 4:30 a.m. and located the aircraft almost three hours later. After the victims' bodies underwent toxicology tests, no signs of drugs or alcohol were found.

Brown had an instrument rating for airplanes but not for helicopters. His commercial pilot certificate had been suspended for four days in 1973 for improper marking of an aircraft, according to United Press International. He had helicopter crashes in 1977 and '89.

Federal Aviation Administration spokesman Roland Helwig told UPI it is not unusual for a pilot to be involved in three accidents.

According to the *Orlando Sentinel,* Omniflight Helicopters Inc. of Chicago, the operator of the helicopter charter, agreed to pay undisclosed lifetime annual incomes to the widows of Browne and Smythe-Park. Vaughan's family settled out of court for a monetary award.

In its report, the National Transportation Safety Board attributed blame for the crash to "improper planning/decision by the pilot, and his failure to attain adequate altitude before flying over rising terrain at night. Factors related to the accident were darkness, fog, haze, rising terrain and lack of visual cues that were available to the pilot."

Vaughan, influenced to take up guitar by his brother Jimmie, dropped out of high school and moved from Dallas to Austin, where he honed his skills in the local club scene. In 1978, he formed Double Trouble with Chris Layton and Tommy Shannon. Though he struggled with alcoholism and drug addiction, his career path continued upward. He finally achieved sobriety in 1986.

Vaughan and his wife Lenora divorced in 1988. They had no children together.

In 1983, he released the acclaimed album "Texas Flood," which peaked at number 38 on the *Billboard* 200. That year he also added memorable guitar licks to David Bowie's "Let's Dance," which hit number 1 in the United States and the United Kingdom. The following year saw his album "Couldn't Stand The Weather" ascend to number 31 on the *Billboard* 200. His work on Bowie's singles "China Girl" and "Modern Love" helped both to chart within the top 15 on the pop charts.

Vaughan's single "Crossfire," with Double Trouble, was a number 1 hit on the *Billboard* Mainstream Rock chart in 1989, and the album that spawned it, "In Step," peaked at number 33.

SRV also guested on songs by James Brown and Jennifer Warnes.

After Vaughan's funeral in Dallas on Aug. 31, 1990, approximately 3,000 mourners joined a procession behind his casket.

A bronze statue of Stevie Ray Vaughan stands in Austin, Texas

•••••• ❖ ••••••

Oct. 25, 1991

Location: Solano County, California, west of Vallejo
Died:
Bill Graham, born Wulf Wolodia Grajonca on January 8, 1931, in Berlin, Germany
Steve Kahn, forty-two
Melissa Dilworth Gold, forty-seven

Bill Graham

278

One of rock's premier concert promoters perished on a stormy night when the helicopter in which he was riding flew into an electrical transmission tower.

Bill Graham, an impresario who had fled Nazi Germany as a child during World War II, was killed when the Bell 206B Jet Ranger II helicopter piloted by Steve "Killer" Kahn slammed directly into the tower, causing the craft to explode into a ball of flame. Melissa Gold, Graham's girlfriend, who was a socialite and philanthropist, was also aboard.

Graham gained prominence in the mid-1960s when he began promoting rock, soul and jazz concerts at the Fillmore Auditorium in San Francisco. He proceeded to open a Fillmore East in Manhattan, New York (1968-71) and formed Fillmore Records, which was actually two labels, in 1969.

His scope broadened when he put on concerts at San Francisco venues such as the Cow Palace and Winterland Ballroom, and he also put together stadium shows in the Bay Area. He was a shrewd businessman, but he was also known to look after many of the young artists that made him a success.

Graham was not directly involved with the 1969 Woodstock Festival, but he lent many of his staff and technical crew to the event's producers. He was responsible for the appearance of the Bay Area band Santana, which did not have a record contract at the time.

Many of his events not only delighted music fans but also raised funds for charities. For example, he helped organize the first "Live Aid" concert, which took place in London and Philadelphia in 1985.

Fulfilling an ambition to be an actor, Graham had film roles in *Apocalypse Now, Bugsy, The Doors and Gardens Of Stone.*

On the night he died, Graham was at the Concord Pavilion in Concord, Calif., where he discussed promoting a benefit concert for the victims of the 1991 Oakland hills firestorm. Huey Lewis & the News, who were playing a concert that night, made a commitment to perform at the benefit. Graham and Gold departed the venue at about 9:45 with Kahn, who was Graham's advance man in addition to being a pilot. Their destination was Commodore Center Heliport in Sausalito, twenty-seven miles away.

The copter went up in severe weather with rain and gusty winds. Visibility was about one-half mile, and the cloud ceiling was 200 feet. The aircraft flew off course and traveled at an excessively low altitude over the tidal marshland north of San Pablo Bay.

At 9:56 it hit the 223-foot-high power tower near the point where California Highway 37 crosses Sonoma Creek. A power surge at Concord Pavilion briefly interrupted electricity during the concert. About 23,000 homes in the area were left without electricity until the next morning.

Kahn held certificates for airline transport, flight instruction and commercial flying. He had 4,541 total flying hours. He was not, however, rated to fly helicopters via instruments.

The helicopter, which was exposed to great heat in the explosion, became welded to the tower. It had to remain hanging there until investigators finished their examination.

The National Transportation Safety Board ruled the cause of the tragedy was "the pilot's intentional flight into known adverse weather, continued flight into instrument meteorological conditions and improper altitude. Contributing to the accident were low ceilings, poor visibility, and restricted visual lookout."

It was speculated that Kahn was flying about 200 feet above Highway 37 so he could use the road as a navigation aid.

A concert to celebrate the lives of Graham, Gold and Kahn was held November 3, 1991, in San Francisco's Golden Gate Park. Twenty-two music and show business luminaries performed, many of whom had received Graham's assistance with their careers.

As a memorial and salute to Graham, the San Francisco Civic Auditorium now bears his name.

•••••• ❖ ••••••

Location: Monterey County, California, in Monterey Bay near Pacific Grove
Died:
John Denver, born Henry John Deutschendorf Jr. on December 31, 1943, in Roswell, New Mexico

John Denver

John Denver's heyday as an American music icon was well behind him at the time of his death. His star shone brightest in the mid-1970s.

Over the years, he acquired an affinity for flying. After all, his father had a career in the U.S. Air Force. His hobby as a pilot drew him to the California coast on the second weekend of October 1997.

Denver was practicing touch-and-go landings at Monterey Peninsula Airport when his plane plummeted into Monterey Bay. He was killed instantly.

He was flying solo in an experimental plane, a Rutan Long-EZ. The small craft was assembled from a kit by an amateur.

As a pilot, Denver had 2,700 hours of flying time. He had pilot ratings for single-engine land and sea, multi-engine land, glider and instrument. He also had a type rating in his Learjet.

The day before his death, Denver made a half-hour checkout flight with the Long-EZ. But he was not legally permitted to fly. In 1996 the Federal Aviation Administration learned Denver had failed to refrain from drinking alcoholic beverages and revoked his medical certification. In previous years he had several arrests for driving while intoxicated.

An investigation by the National Transportation Safety Board revealed the leading cause of the crash was Denver's inability to switch fuel tanks after one tank had emptied. The plane was designed to have a fuel switch between the pilot's legs. The assembler put it behind the pilot's left shoulder instead.

Also, the fuel gauge was placed behind the pilot's seat, not visible to the person at the controls. Because of the fuel selector valve's positioning, switching tanks required the pilot to turn his body 90 degrees to access the valve. This body turn created a natural tendency for a pilot to extend his right foot against the right rudder pedal to support himself while turning in his seat. This would cause the aircraft to veer to the right.

A mechanic provided Denver with a mirror so he could check the gauge over his shoulder. Denver said he would use the autopilot to hold the plane level while turning the fuel selector valve.

Denver declined to refuel before taking off, saying he would be flying for only an hour. A mechanic had told him the right tank was less than half full, and the left was at less than one-quarter of its capacity.

Four of the 20 witnesses interviewed by the NTSB said the plane had banked to the right before going down. Eight said they heard a "pop" followed by reduction in engine noise just before the crash.

Drawing audiences of folk, pop and country music fans, Denver used his songwriting skill and smooth tenor voice to build an astonishing career. His most productive years were 1974-75, when he had four number 1 singles on the *Billboard* Hot 100 – "Sunshine On My Shoulders," "Annie's Song," "Thank God I'm A Country Boy" and "I'm Sorry." He had three number 1 singles on the *Billboard* Hot Country Songs chart and back-to-back number 1 albums on the *Billboard* 200.

He expanded his audience even further with a film role opposite George Burns in 1977's *Oh God* and a collaboration with Jim Henson in the 1979 television special *John Denver and the Muppets: A Christmas Together.* A record album of thirteen songs was spun off from that show.

Denver made dozens of TV appearances over the years, from talk shows to variety shows to holiday specials.

Although he is best remembered for the 200 songs he wrote and 300 he recorded, Denver's legacy includes extensive charitable work, mainly in the fight against world hunger, homelessness and environmentalism.

In 2000, CBS aired the made-for-television biographical movie *Take Me Home: The John Denver Story* with Chad Lowe in the title role.

Denver's remains were cremated, and his ashes were scattered over his beloved Colorado Rocky Mountains.

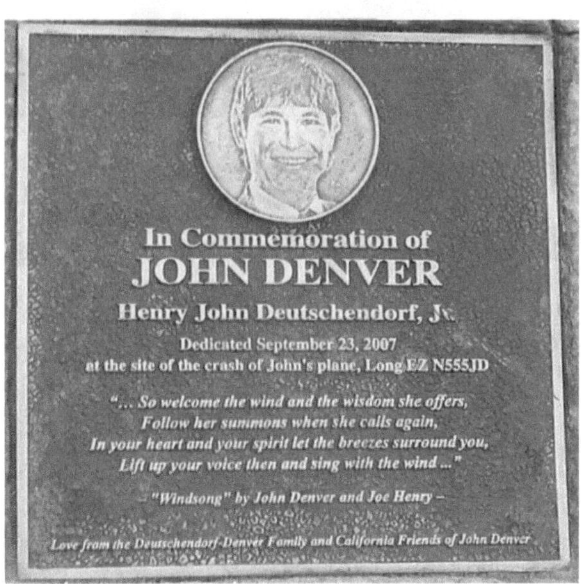

This commemorative plaque is attached to a boulder several yards from the shore of Monterey Bay, near the site where Denver crashed. It was dedicated September 23, 2007

•••••••• ❖ ••••••••

Location: Great Abaco Island, Bahamas
Died:
Aaliyah, born Aaliyah Dana Haughton on January 16, 1979, in Brooklyn, New York
Luis Morales III, thirty
Eric Foreman, twenty-nine
Anthony Dodd, thirty-four
Scott Gallin, forty-one
Christopher Maldonado, thirty-two
Douglas Kratz, twenty-eight
Gina Smith, twenty-nine
Keith Wallace, forty-nine

Aaliyah

The youngest music star to die in an air crash, Aaliyah got her career started at an early age. Her number 1 R&B hit "Back & Forth" peaked at number 5 on the *Billboard* Hot 100 when she was only fifteen.

But her death stands as a tragic example of haste makes waste, and it snuffed what could have been one of the biggest music careers of the twenty-first century. She was twenty-two.

Aaliyah and her entourage were in the Bahamas to shoot a video for her recording of "Rock The Boat." The eight people in the group had an August 26 scheduled departure date back to Florida, but the shooting finished early and some of them were eager to leave Great Abaco Island early. The fact that their plane was two hours late to pick them up only increased their haste to get going.

With Luis Morales as the pilot, the party boarded the twin engine Cessna 402 at 6:50 p.m. at Marsh Harbour Airport. Their destination was Opa-locka Airport in Miami-Dade County, Florida. The plane was smaller than the Cessna 404 that had flown the party to the Bahamas.

The plane took off and rose an estimated sixty to a hundred feet. Then it crashed and caught fire about two hundred feet from the end of the runway.

Five of the passengers, including Aaliyah, died instantly. Others were rushed to a local hospital, where they died.

ABC News reported the plane took off in "perfect weather." But there were other factors involved.

With nine people aboard, plus their gear and heavy camera equipment, an investigation revealed the plane was approximately seven hundred pounds overweight. Morales complained about the heavy load, but the passengers insisted on bringing everything with them. Guardian.ng reported the cargo weight also was unevenly distributed.

Charter pilot Lewis Key told ABC, "He (Morales) tried to convince them the plane was overloaded, but they insisted they had chartered the plane and they had to be in Miami Saturday night (August 25)."

Additionally, Morales was not licensed to fly the plane, and an autopsy revealed he had traces of cocaine and alcohol in his system. Allegedly, his license was suspended.

But there is another complexity to this sad story. Aaliyah was nervous about flying, and she tried to resist boarding the plane.

Music journalist Kathy Iandoli reported thirteen-year-old baggage handler Kingsley Russell said Aaliyah backed out and laid down in the back seat of the taxi his stepmother was driving, while her crew was sorting out problems.

Someone from the entourage went to visit Aaliyah to ask about her concerns. Russell said this person handed her a sleeping pill, which she ingested. She fell into a deep sleep.

In her book, Iandoli quoted Russell: "They took her out of the van. She didn't even know she was getting boarded on a plane. She went on the airplane asleep."

Still strapped in her seat, Aaliyah's body was found about 20 feet from the smoldering wreckage. Head trauma and burns caused her death, an autopsy showed.

The other victims: hairstylist Eric Foreman; hairstylist Anthony Dodd; security guard Scott Gallin; make-up artist Christopher Maldonado; and Blackground Records employees Gina Smith, Douglas Kratz and Keith Wallace.

Iandoli remarked to Guardian.ng, "The only thing I've taken with me is that, after 20 years, I can finally say that Aaliyah didn't want to get on the plane. That makes me feel a little better, but not much. This didn't have to happen. She should still be here, and I think that's the saddest part about it. She deserved better."

For Iandoli, the information from Russell provided "closure … an unfortunate closure."

Nicknamed the "Princess of R&B" and the "Queen of Urban Pop," Aaliyah helped redefine the Rhythm & Blues genre for her generation. She released three albums: "Age Ain't Nothing But A Number" (1994); "One In A Million" (1996); and "Aaliyah" (2001).

Her eponymous third album was released five weeks before her death. It had peaked at number 2 on the *Billboard* 200 and was on its way down the chart, sitting at number 25, the day she died. In the wake of her passing, sales picked up again, and "Aaliyah" hit number 1 for one week on September 15, 2001. Ultimately, it amassed over thirteen million in sales worldwide.

Four of her singles hit number 1 on the *Billboard* Hot R&B/Hip-Hop Songs chart. Her lone number 1 on the *Billboard* Hot 100, "Try Again," spent twenty-nine weeks in the top 40 in 2000.

Aaliyah had acting roles in two movies: *Romeo Must Die* (released in 2000) and *Queen Of The Damned* (released in 2002). Both had lackluster performances at the box office, but they showed Aaliyah's potential as a screen star.

Lifetime Network aired a biopic in 2014, *Aaliyah: The Princess of R&B* with Alexandra Shipp in the title role. Aaliyah's family disapproved of the making of the movie, and it garnered negative reviews. Nonetheless, 3.2 million viewers watched it on opening night.

The Aaliyah Memorial Fund has been established to "provide financial assistance to IRS recognized charities that were important to Aaliyah, such as breast cancer, AIDS, and Alzheimer's disease."

Aaliyah is interred in a mausoleum at Ferncliff Cemetery in Hartsdale, New York

Best Fests

Some concert events that stood above the rest

Overview: When we get tired of playing our vinyl records or compact discs around the house, or if listening to rock music on the car radio gets a little stale, what can we do next to satisfy our thirst for our favorite music?

The obvious answer is to look for a rock concert featuring a popular act – or perhaps several popular acts. Going back to the 1960s, promoters have put together some awesome shows that were so big they began to be known as festivals.

Historically, a festival can have a duration of one day or several days. Or, it can have a multitude of dates spread over an entire season. Practically every possible configuration of formats has been tried over the years.

This chapter will review some of the well-known rock festivals that have drawn thousands to various venues, bringing together rock devotees in an atmosphere of love, comradeship and shared appreciation of a true cultural cornerstone – rock and roll.

Many of these are the festivals where newly prominent artists shared the stage with the legendary performers to whom they listened while growing up.

Monterey International Pop Festival
June 16-18, 1967
Monterey County Fairgrounds, Monterey, California

This was such a ground-breaking event, in many ways it was used as a blueprint for festivals that followed.

Attendance estimates for the three days range from 25,000 to 90,000, although the outdoor venue had an approved capacity of only 7,000 per day. Those unable to enter remained outside the perimeter, where they could hear the music coming from within.

If you were unable to attend, don't be too disappointed. Documentary cinematographer D.A. Pennebaker filmed the festival, so there is audio and video documentation of the festival in *Monterey Pop*.

(Look for Janis Joplin's performance of "Ball and Chain," after which the documentary pans to the audience where we see Mama Cass mouth a great big *wow*!) Planners of the event were John Phillips of the Mamas & the Papas, record producer Lou Adler, publicist Derek Taylor and promoter Alan Pariser.

In a magnanimous gesture, the artists who performed did so on an unpaid basis, save for sitarist Ravi Shankar, who accepted $3,000 for his afternoon-long set on June 18. The artists did receive monetary assistance for their transportation and lodging.

Country Joe & the Fish were paid $5,000 from the revenue that came from Pennebaker's film.

Among the performers who received a serious career boost from the gig were The Who from England and Americans Janis Joplin and Jimi Hendrix.

Although their leader, Brian Wilson, was on the board of the festival, the Beach Boys canceled their spot in the lineup. They announced at the 11th hour they could not appear because of Carl Wilson's ongoing refusal to be drafted into the U.S. Army. The band also cited a commitment to finishing their single "Heroes And Villains" for Capitol Records.

In an interview with Ken Sharp, Beach Boy Bruce Johnston remarked, "... it went from 'here's the money, here's the offer, you're headlining' to 'now this is gonna be a non-profit show,' so we pulled out."

Others on the schedule who had to cancel were the Kinks, the Lovin' Spoonful, Donovan and Dionne Warwick.

Artists who participated were:

Association	Al Kooper
Beverley	Mamas & Papas
Big Brother & the Holding Company	Mar-Keys
Booker T. & the M.G.s	Hugh Masakela
Blues Project	Scott McKenzie
Buffalo Springfield	Steve Miller Band
Eric Burdon & The Animals	Moby Grape
Paul Butterfield	Laura Nyro
Buffalo Springfield Blues Band	Paupers
Byrds	Luo Rawls
Canned Heat	Otis Redding
Country Joe & the Fish	Johnny Rivers
Electric Flag	Quicksilver Messenger Service
Group With No Name	Ravi Shankar
Jimi Hendrix Experirence	Simon & Garfunkel
Jefferson Airplane	

MONTEREY
INTERNATIONAL POP FESTIVAL

Newport Pop Festival
August 3-4, 1968
Orange County Fairgrounds, Costa Mesa, California

Festival organizers still had a lot to learn about logistics when the Newport Pop Festival welcomed huge crowds.

The two-day event became the first music fest to welcome more than 100,000 paying spectators. But it was no picnic for those who braved the spartan conditions.

The number of pre-paid tickets were triple the expected amount for a venue that could hold only about 25,000. That forced a move from an indoor pavilion to a surface parking lot only three days before the event.

Sanitation, food concessions and fencing were arranged hurriedly, which proved to be costly. The perimeter fencing was breached by many, who got to experience the event for free. Food and beverage supplies were exhausted midway through the first day.

In the heat of a southern California summer, attendees got drinking water supplied by garden hoses. However, they had to fill their own containers with the water while giving up their viewing spots among the audience. Portable restrooms appeared to be adequate in number, thankfully.

The stage was under a canopy but, without shade in the viewing area, many concert-goers were sunburned. Those without hotel reservations had nowhere to spend the night, but Costa Mesa designated 32 acres of the fairgrounds as an emergency campsite.

The organizers were father and son Al and Gary Schmidt and Mark Robinson. According to *Rolling Stone Magazine,* their band budget was under $25,000. They hired Harvey "Humble Harve" Miller of Los Angeles radio station KHJ to promote and host the event, along with entertainer/peace activist Wavy Gravy.

The lineup of musicians was top notch and was headed by Jefferson Airplane, Steppenwolf, the Chambers Brothers, Country Joe & the Fish and Tiny Tim.

Rolling Stone reported the sound system was not adequate to provide sound Alice Cooper to all of the viewing area.

At the end of the first day, as Country Joe & the Fish took the stage late into the night, Orange County officials threatened to cut off power to end the show. But they relented and allowed the band to play two songs.

As per plan, David Crosby started a pie fight on stage with the members of Jefferson Airplane. The result was 250 cream pies being tossed, to the crowd's delight.

Artists who participated were:

Alice Cooper	Steppenwolf
Canned Heat	Tiny Tim
Chambers Brothers	Illinois Speed Press
Charles Lloyd Quartet	Iron Butterfly
Country Joe & the Fish	Eric Burdon & the Animals
Electric Flag	Grateful Dead
James Cotton Blues Band	Jefferson Airplane
Sonny & Cher	Quicksilver Messenger Service
Blues Cheer	Things To Come

WESCO-SCENIC PRODUCTIONS 1st. ANNUAL
NEWPORT POP FESTIVAL
SATURDAY, AUG. 3
SUNDAY, AUG. 4
Humble Harve Presents:
TINY TIM
SONNY and CHER
COUNTRY JOE and the FISH
CHAMBERS BROTHERS
CANNED HEAT
ELECTRIC FLAG
BUTTERFIELD BLUES BAND
STEPPENWOLF
JAMES COTTON BLUES BAND
JEFFERSON AIRPLANE
ERIC BURDON and the ANIMALS
THE BYRDS
GRATEFUL DEAD
QUICKSILVER MESSENGER SERVICE
IRON BUTTERFLY
THINGS TO COME
ILLINOIS SPEED PRESS
BLUE CHEER
☆ PLUS MORE STARS TO BE ADDED... ☆
ORANGE COUNTY FAIR GROUNDS
COSTA MESA
10 A.M. to 6 P.M.
To All Craftsmen, Artisans, Concessionaires, etc.—
A NUMBER OF BOOTHS STILL AVAILABLE
CONTACT: WESCO-SCENIC SOUNDS PRODUCTIONS

Newport 69
June 20-22, 1969
Devonshire Downs, Northridge, California

Despite the addition of the Jimi Hendrix Experience and Creedence Clearwater Revival to the lineup, the second incarnation of the Newport Pop Festival was beset by problems in its move from Costa Mesa.

The festival grounds were at Devonshire Downs, a Northridge harness racing track that closed two years later. Cal State University, Northridge now owns the property.

Rioting marred the festival, which was promoted by Mark Robinson. Reportedly, he paid $100,000 to Hendrix alone. Tickets were priced at $6/day in advance, $7 at the gate and $15 in advance for the three days.

Again, gatecrashers were a problem. And traffic was abominable. With an estimated 200,000 in attendance, ingress and egress were slow because of limited parking space. Many resorted to parking in nearby residential neighborhoods.

When police tried to clear the neighborhoods, youths threw rocks and bottles, which resulted in injuries to about 300 and the arrest of some 75 rioters.

According to *LA Observed*, the sound system again was inadequate, as were supplies of food, water and sanitation facilities.

According to reporter Kevin Roderick, Hendrix played so poorly in his set on Friday, reportedly because he ingested a drink spiked with LSD, that he insisted on returning to the stage on Sunday. His set with Buddy Miles and others spanned two hours and inspired Pete Johnson of the *Los Angeles Times* to write that people sitting near the stage "may have heard the best performance of their lives."

Artists who participated were:

Ike & Tina Turner	Buffy Sainte-Marie
Albert King	Charity
Edwin Hawkins Singer	Creedence Clearwater Revival
Joe Cocker	Eric Burdon & War
Southwind	Friends of Distinction
Spirit	Jethro Tull
Don Ellis Orchestra	Lee Michaels
Taj Mahal	Love
Jerry Lauderdale	Steppenwolf
Albert Collins	Sweetwater
Brenton Wood	Booker T & the M.G.s
Flock	Chambers Brothers
Johnny Winter	Grass Roots
Poco	Mother Earth
Rascals	Byrds
	Three Dog Night

Newport
69
AT DEVONSHIRE DOWNS
ALBERT COLLINS
ALBERT KING
BOOKER T. & THE MGS
BRENTON WOOD
BUFFY ST. MARIE
BYRDS
CHAMBERS BROS.
CHARITY
CREEDANCE CLEARWATER
EDWIN HAWKINS SINGERS
ERIC BURDON
FLOCK
FRIENDS OF DISTINCTION
GRASSROOTS
IKE & TINA TURNER
JETHRO TULL
JIMI HENDRIX EXPERIENCE
JOE COCKER
JOHNNY WINTER
LEE MICHAELS
LOVE
MARVIN GAYE
MOTHER EARTH
POCO
RASCALS
SOUTHWIND
SPIRIT
STEPPENWOLF
SWEETWATER
TAJ MAHAL
THREE DOG NITE
THIS PROGRAM HAS NO CONNECTION WITH THE NEWPORT JAZZ OR FOLK FESTIVAL

1968 Pop and Underground Festival
May 18-19, 1968
Gulfstream Park, Hallandale, Florida

For the 1968 Pop and Underground Festival, there was good news and bad news.

The good news was the Jimi Hendrix Experience signed as the headlining act. The bad news was the second day of the fest was rained out.

The event, which drew an estimated 25,000 spectators, often is confused with the Miami Pop Festival, which was held at the same horse race track later in 1968.

Richard O'Barry, Marshall Brevetz and Michael Lang promoted the event. Lang took his experience to the Woodstock festival a year later as one of the four promoters of that event.

As with the aforementioned California festivals, this one had a diverse lineup of players, from the avant-garde rock of the Mothers of Invention to the blues of John Lee Hooker and the ear-splitting psychedelia of Blue Cheer.

The rain-out of the second day is said to have inspired Hendrix to write the song "Rainy Day, Dream Away."

Artists who participated were:

Package	John Lee Hooker
Charles Austin Group	Chuck Berry
Evil	Blue Cheer
Blues Image	Mothers of Invention
Crazy World of Arthur Brown	Jimi Hendrix Experience

Isle of Wight Festival
1968-70
2002-present
Isle of Wight, England

It started out as a counterculture event at the end of the turbulent 1960s, and it took an act of Parliament to shelve the Isle of Wight Festival for thirty-two years.

The event once again is being held annually, as of this writing, and has settled into a three- or four-day format each June. The 2020 festival was canceled, however, because of the COVID-19 pandemic.

The Isle of Wight is four miles off the south coast of the English mainland and is commonly accessed via a forty-five-minute ferry ride. Rail transportation to ferry ports is available from all over England.

Brothers Ron, Ray and Bill Foulk promoted the first three events. The popularity of the fest steadily grew until an enormous crowd estimated at upwards of six hundred thousand attended the five-day 1970 event at Afton Down. Ray Foulk said in an interview he believes that number was greatly inflated. The Doors and Jimi Hendrix were the headliners.

The presence of the horde on the island in '70 led British Parliament to add a section to the Isle of Wight County Council Act in 1971, banning overnight open-air gatherings of more than five thousand people on the island without a special license from the council. That effectively killed the event for decades.

The inaugural event in 1968 had the Jefferson Airplane as its headliner and drew about 10,000 for two days. In 1969, that number swelled to about 150,000 for two days, with Bob Dylan and the Who leading the lineup.

Originally scheduled to coincide with the Summer Bank Holiday at the end of August, the Isle of Wight Festival has settled into a slot in the middle of June. Since its rebirth in 2002, the festival's largest attendance was 72,000 in 2018. The Killers and the Manic Street Preachers headlined on the final day.

As of this writing, Solo Promoters Ltd. promotes the event.

•••••• ❖ ••••••

Miami Pop Festival
December 28-30, 1968
Gulfstream Park, Hallandale, Florida

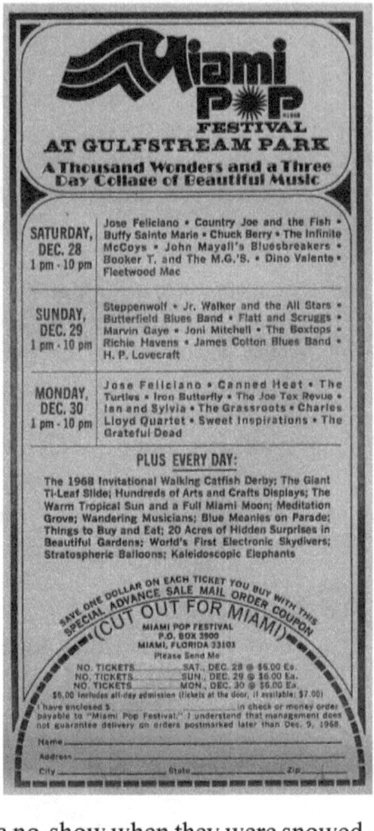

Miami Pop Festival is considered the first major rock music festival on the East Coast of the United States.

The promoters, led by Tom Rounds and Mel Lawrence, made an excellent decision in bringing the event to the Gulfstream thoroughbred horse track.

The infield of horse racing venues has proven to be an excellent locale for large music expositions. The legendary New Orleans Jazz and Heritage Festival, featuring everything from gospel to zydeco to blues to jazz to straight up Rock & Roll, has long been held at the Fair Grounds Race Course in the city's center.

On site parking was plentiful, the perimeter was secure and spectator containment already had been established. Concession stands and restrooms were part of the infrastructure.

One factor that set the festival apart from all others was the set-up of two separate stages at opposite ends of the venue. The Flower Stage and the Flying Stage, several hundred yards apart, had bands playing at the same time.

An attention-getting moment occurred when Joni Mitchell invited her new boyfriend Graham Nash, formerly of the Hollies, to join her and Richie Havens to sing "Get Together."

The McCoys were scheduled to appear but became a no-show when they were snowed-in up in Canada. Booker T. Jones canceled because he was sick with the flu.

Rolling Stone remarked the event was, "… a monumental success in almost every aspect, the first significant and truly festive international pop festival held on the East Coast."

The three-day attendance was estimated to be a hundred thousand.

Artists who participated were:

Amboy Dukes	Fish Ray	Buffy Sainte-Marie
Chuck Berry	Richie Havens	Fleetwood Mac
Blues Image	Ian & Sylvia	Marvin Gaye
Box Tops	Iron Butterfly	Grass Roots
Paul Butterfield Blues Band	Junior Junkaroos	Grateful Dead
Canned Heat	Jr. Walker & the Allstars	Sweet Inspirations
Wayne Cochran & the	Charles Lloyd Quartet	Joe Tex
C.C.Riders	Hugh Masakela	Three Dog Night
Cosmic Drum	Joni Mitchell	Turtles
James Cotton Blues Band	Pacific Gas & Electric	Flatt & Scruggs
Country Joe & the Fish	Procol Harum	Steppenwolf
Jose Feliciano	Terry Reid	

•••••• ❖ ••••••

Atlanta International Pop Festival
July 4-5, 1969
Atlanta International Raceway, Hampton, Gaeorgia

Despite intense heat and humidity, the Atlanta International Pop Festival turned out to be a peaceful event graced by a long and strong roster of music acts.

The infrastructure provided by a NASCAR racing facility was beneficial but, reportedly, the concession setup was inadequate and forced concert goers to endure long waits in line to get food and beverages. With temperatures zooming toward a hundred degrees, spectators found no shade in the viewing area.

The Atlanta International Raceway, twenty miles south of Atlanta, is now called Atlanta Motor Speedway.

One attendee remarked, "The sun reflected off the track and into the infield and made it into an open-air oven."

Another recalled, "I wasn't prepared for the lack of food, drink or shade, but the music was wonderful."

According to Thestripproject.com, Georgia natives the Allman Brothers Band, were not allowed to play because they had signed with a bogus promoter. Yet, another new band, Grand Funk Railroad, was stopped in traffic as they were driving through the area and asked if they could play. And play they did.

Tickets for both days were priced at $16. A promotional team led by Alex Cooley, Chris Cowing and Robin Conant organized the event.

Artists who participated were:

Blood, Sweat & Tears	Tommy James & the Shondells
Booker T. & the M.G.s	Janis Joplin
Paul Butterfield Blues Band	Al Kooper
Canned Heat	Led Zeppelin
Chicago Transit Authority	Pacific Gas & Electric
Joe Cocker	Johnny Rivers
Creedence Clearwater Revival	Spirit
Dave Brubeck Trio/Gerry Mulligan	Staple Singers
Delaney and Bonnie	Sweetwater
Grand Funk Railroad	Ten Wheel Drive
Ian & Sylvia	Johnny Winter

•••••• ❖ ••••••

Woodstock Music & Art Fair
August 15-18, 1969
Max Yasgur's farm, White Lake, New York

Generally speaking, Woodstock is the festival against which all others are measured.

It had the largest attendance at the time and one of the biggest entertainment lineups. The organizers, four men in their mid-twenties, had to scramble twice to find an alternate venue after their original deals were canceled. A dairy farm some 100 miles north of New York City finally hosted the event.

And, against all odds, the team successfully battled adversity and won, pulling off a stellar event that lost money but earned respect for the counterculture.

Estimates of the total attendance run between 400,000 and 500,000. Firm figures were not available because thousands of concertgoers without tickets breached a flimsy perimeter fence on the first day and got in free.

Once again, Jimi Hendrix was on the bill, earning a check for $32,000 and a guarantee of being the last act on the stage. That appearance was supposed to be on Sunday night, August 17. But rain delays pushed back the schedule, and Hendrix played on Monday morning after many attendees had gone home.

Besides intermittent rains, the festival crew found a problem with ingress, since the one road leading to the site was blocked by abandoned cars. Musicians and supplies had to be flown in by helicopter.

The throng of youngsters spent three days on a converted hayfield, sleeping on the ground where they sat to enjoy the music. There were fears that rioting would break out, but the hundreds of thousands remained well behaved throughout the weekend. To avoid confrontations between the audience and law enforcement, the organizers begged the New York governor not to send in national guardsmen.

The organizers – Artie Kornfeld, Michael Lang, John Roberts and Joel Rosenman – were able to recoup some of their losses by having Michael Wadleigh film the festival. Warner Brothers Studio bought the movie and paid $100,000, which Wadleigh used to buy film. In the ensuing years, legions of fans who were unable to attend the event were able to experience it through the documentary.

For a detailed description of the festival, see my first book, *The Coffman Collection,* Chapter 3, "Reality Meets Pop."

Artists who participated were:

Richie Havens	Grateful Dead
Sweetwater	Creedence Clearwater Revival
Bert Sommer	Janis Joplin/Kozmic Blues Band
Tim Hardin	Sly & the Family Stone
Ravi Shankar	Who
Melanie	Jefferson Airplane
Arlo Guthrie	Joe Cocker
Joan Baez	Country Joe & the Fish
Quill	Ten Years After
Keef Hartley Band	The Band
Country Joe McDonald	Johnny Winter
Santana	Blood, Sweat & Tears
John Sebastian	Crosby, Stills, Nash & Young
Incredible String Band	Paul Butterfield Blues Band
Canned Heat	Sha Na Na
Mountain	Jimi Hendrix/Gypsy Sun & Rainbows

★ 3 DAYS OF PEACE, LOVE & MUSIC ★

WOODSTOCK
MUSIC & ART FAIR
AUGUST 1969 - BETHEL, N. Y.

FRIDAY 15th
MELANIE
JOAN BAEZ
ARLO GUTHRIE
RICHIE HAVENS
SLY AND THE
FAMILY STONE
JOHN SEBASTIAN
SHA-NA-NA
SWEETWATER

SATURDAY 16th
CANNED HEAT
CREEDENCE
CLEARWATER
GRATEFUL DEAD
JANIS JOPLIN
JEFFERSON AIRPLANE
SANTANA
THE WHO
COUNTRY JOE
AND THE FISH

SUNDAY 17th
THE BAND
JEFF BECK GROUP
BLOOD, SWEAT AND
TEARS
JOE COCKER
CROSBY, STILLS &
NASH
JIMI HENDRIX
IRON BUTTERFLY
TEN YEARS AFTER
JONNY WINTERS

... THREE DAY TICKETS: $18.00 (NO REFUNDS) ...

2nd Annual Atlanta International Pop Festival
July 3-5, 1970
Middle Georgia Raceway, Byron, Georgia

Politicians in Georgia proved they weren't much different than those in England after the Atlanta International Pop Festival (AIPF) had its second edition on 4th of July weekend in 1970.

Georgia Gov. Lester Maddox had tried to scuttle plans for the festival, which Alex Cooley promoted. After the event, he pressured the state legislators to pass restrictions to make it more difficult for another such event to be held. The legislature complied, and a third AIPF was never held.

The *Atlanta Journal and Constitution* called it "Georgia's Woodstock" and estimated there were 400,000 in attendance. Some estimates went as high as six hundred thousand. Figures were not firm because many attendees got in free after they threatened the security personnel.

Again, heat was a factor at the venue, which was a farm field adjacent to Middle Georgia Raceway, ninety-three miles southeast of Atlanta. Temperatures surpassed 100 degrees Fahrenheit all three days.

Drug use and nudity were rampant among the festival goers. But law enforcement, badly outnumbered, stayed outside the festival perimeter and employed a hands-off policy. There were no reports of violence during the event.

Jimi Hendrix and his band played before the largest audience of his career, according to Prnewswire.com, in a set that began at about midnight on July 4. Other major musicians who performed included Grand Funk Railroad, the Allman Brothers Band, Mountain and B.B. King.

"Agents wouldn't book here back then because they thought we were a bunch of dumb rednecks," Peter Conlon, Cooley's longtime friend and business partner, told the *Journal and Constitution*. "But after the first pop festival in 1969, he showed them. That festival was more successful than Woodstock (the same year), but it didn't get any attention because we weren't a media market in those days. New York gave Woodstock the attention, but Woodstock was a disaster."

Middle Georgia Raceway closed in the late 1980s, but a commemorative plaque has been placed near the site, noting the 1970 festival was "one of the largest such events anywhere in the world during that era" and calling it "one of the largest public gatherings in state history."

Artists who participated were:

Allman Brothers Band	Johnny Jenkins
Ballin' Jack	B.B. King
Bloodrock	Lee Michaels
Bloomsbury People	Mott the Hoople
Cactus	Mountain
Cat Mother & the All Night News-	Poco
boys	Procol Harum
Chakra	Radar
Chambers Brothers	Rare Earth
Goose Creek Symphony	

Grand Funk Railroad	Terry Reid
Gypsy Rig	Rig
Memphis State Univ. cast of "Hair"	Savage Grace
Hampton Grease Band	John Sebastian
Handle	Bob Seger System
Richie Havens	Spirit
Hedge & Donna	Ten Years After
Jimi Hendrix Experience	U.S. Kyds
It's A Beautiful Day	Johnny Winter

•••••• ❖ ••••••

Mississippi River Festival
1969-1980
Southern Illinois University, Edwardsville, Illinois

Like the Isle of Wight Festival, the Mississippi River Festival (MRF) was a recurring event which started in the 1960s and stretched over several years.

Unlike the Isle of Wight Festival, the MRF spread its dates over an entire summer. And it eventually reached its end.

Over its twelve-year life, the fest welcomed an estimated one million visitors.

The venue, not within view of the nearby Mississippi River, was an outdoor bowl on which most viewers sat on a grassy slope atop their blankets. Musicians performed in front of an acoustic shell on the stage.

The shows, which typically numbered about thirty per summer, usually featured a headliner preceded by an opening act. Jackson Browne appeared as both, opening for America in 1973 and headlining in 1977.

When Browne's tour came to MRF in '77, he was in the midst of recording his unique "Running On Empty" album, in which he recorded songs on stage, in hotel rooms and in the tour bus. On Aug. 17, 1977, the same day he played at MRF, he recorded "Cocaine" in his room at the Edwardsville Holiday Inn. The next day, in the same room, he recorded "Shaky Town." The album proved to be the biggest seller in his career.

The festival was a magnet for the biggest stars of the day and drew legendary acts such as Bob Dylan, Janis Joplin, the Eagles, Chicago, Jim Croce, Dolly Parton and Frankie Valli & the 4 Seasons.

I attended the festival three consecutive years. In 1975, I saw Joan Baez and Hoyt Axton; in 1976, Linda Ronstadt and Andrew Gold; and in 1977, Boz Scaggs and Southside Johnny & the Asbury Jukes.

The concert venue was a scant twenty-three miles from St. Louis, Missouri.

Mark Pierce wrote a book memorializing the festival. He told the *Edwardsville Intelligencer,* "The Mississippi River Festival was truly a historic event for the St. Louis area. It built an artistic bridge between the Illinois and Missouri sides of the river and showcased the diverse talents of hundreds of performers, from rock to country to dance to theater, and the list goes on."

The twelve-year series began as a partnership to promote regional confluence of the performing arts. Southern Illinois University-Edwardsville asked the St. Louis Symphony to establish a residence on campus and offer a summer season of concert appearances. To host the symphony, SIU-E created the outdoor venue, according to Djtees.com.

On May 22, 1981, the university announced it would not renew the festival for the upcoming season. The death of SIU-E president John Rendleman in 1976 may have been the beginning of the end for MRF.

"Rendleman worked tirelessly year after year, lobbying in order to keep the festival on campus," SIU-E administrator Lyle Ward told alestelive.com. "The festival was in no way a financial success, but Rendleman knew how important it was to not only students, but the community at large.

"When John died, I suppose the vision of the festival got lost in some way, as well."

The Nederlander Organization had a 10-year contract to book acts for the festival. In 1980, university officials requested bookings of more diverse entertainment, such as symphonies and operas. After Nederlander refused, negotiations broke down, and SIU-E opted to close the venue.

•••••••• ❖ ••••••••

Coachella Valley Music and Arts Festival
1999, 2001-present
Empire Polo Club, Indio, California

As the 20th century melted into the 21st, another major concert event took a toe hold in California. It has proved to be more than a one- or two-shot festival.

The Coachella Valley Music and Arts Festival has blossomed in the desert 130 miles east of Los Angeles and, as of this writing is still returning every spring. The dates in 2020 and 2021 were canceled because of the COVID-19 pandemic.

The festival has grown from a two-day weekend event to a three-day weekend event in 2007 to two consecutive three-day weekends in 2012. The first edition was held in October 1999, but subsequent renewals have been staged in April to take advantage of cooler weather.

With about eighty bands booked each year, Coachella has drawn some of the heaviest hitters in rock music, including Paul McCartney, Prince, Madonna, Roger Waters, Guns N' Roses, AC/DC and Lady Gaga. The Red Hot Chili Peppers have visited three times, as of this writing.

A concert by Pearl Jam at the Empire Polo Club in 1993 lit the fuse for the festival. Pearl Jam was boycotting venues controlled by Ticketmaster, and they chose Empire. Their show revealed the viability of the site for large festivals.

Promoter Paul Tollett and Goldenvoice Presents co-president Rick Van Santen organized the inaugural festival. From a humble beginning with attendance of 37,000, the festival grew to a high-water mark of 579,000 over six days in 2014, according to *Billboard Magazine.*

Tollett found he could not compete for top notch artists with other festivals, so he adopted a strategy to hire trendy artists who weren't necessarily burning up the charts. "Maybe if you put a bunch of them together, that might be a magnet for a lot of people," he told *Desert Sun.*

On-site camping was offered in 2003 for the first time. Through the years, patron shuttles have run from major hotels in the area to alleviate traffic and parking problems.

Empire Polo Club occupies 78 acres, but the land used for parking and camping brings the total size of the venue to about 642 acres.

Attendees also can view art and consume food and beverages when they aren't listening to music acts that appear on some 10 stages. Many stages are contained inside tents. It has been said the event has become just as important for artists as it is for musicians.

Perks for guests include a general store, showers, mobile phone charging stations, an Internet café with free Wi-Fi and garbage recycling.

While the first Coachella event lost hundreds of thousands of dollars, the operation improved to the point where tickets sold out for the first time in 2004, and the festival turned a profit of $114 million in 2017.

It looks like the popular event is here to stay.

Classic West Concert
July 15-16, 2017
Dodger Stadium, Los Angeles, California

Classic East Concert
July 29-30, 2017
Citi Field, Queens, New York

Classic Northwest Concert
September 30, 2017
Safeco Field, Seattle, Washington

They weren't billed as festivals, but the Classic concerts of 2017 brought a lot of festivities when they played at three large baseball stadiums. The first two were two-day affairs.

The series could have been called the "Irving Azoff Festival," since he managed all of the participating bands and organized the shows.

The concerts were marked by two enormous factors. First, the Eagles played for the first time without the late Glenn Frey, who had died from complications following intestinal surgery. His oldest son, Deacon, replaced him in the Eagles lineup. Country/pop artist Vince Gill also joined the band. Deacon Frey and Gill would stay with the Eagles on subsequent lengthy tours.

Secondly, Steely Dan played without Walter Becker for the first time. He missed the shows because of illness, and he died from esophageal cancer at the age of 67 on Sept. 3, 2017. Frey was the same age when he died Jan. 18, 2016. Veteran Los Angeles session guitarist Larry Carlton filled in for Becker.

The first two legs of the series were graced by a star-studded lineup. On the first day at Dodger Stadium, 51,000 packed the house to see the Doobie Brothers open the show, followed by Steely Dan and the Eagles.

When the Eagles played "Heartache Tonight," one of the song's cowriters, Bob Seger, stepped onto the stage to sing lead vocals. The show received rave reviews.

On the second night, Earth, Wind & Fire opened, followed by Journey and Fleetwood Mac. The aging members of Fleetwood Mac struggled with their singing, but they received polite applause for their efforts. Christine McVie, who suffered from cancer and died of a stroke in 2022, was seventy-four at the time.

The same bands congregated at Citi Field, home of the New York Mets, two weeks later to repeat the shows. Seger did not show up there.

The ballparks were nearly perfect venues since they already had parking lots, restrooms and concession stands in place. I paid $150 (plus Ticketmaster fees) per ticket for my two-day seats at Dodger Stadium. VIP packages were priced at $1,750 and $2,000, and a front row seat with all the perks fetched $2,750.

The series wrapped with a one-day, two-band show at the Seattle Mariners' home, now known as T-Mobile Park.

The vaunted six-band original lineup had been boiled down to just the Doobie Brothers and the Eagles. Steely Dan was reeling from the death of Becker, and Fleetwood Mac's Lindsey Buckingham was on a tour with Christine McVie in support of their eponymous album of duets.

Residents of the Emerald City may have been disappointed they didn't get a six-band event. But at least they got the Eagles, who had been off the concert circuit for several years.

JULY 15/16
DODGER STADIUM LOS ANGELES
THE CLASSIC
JULY 29/30
CITI FIELD NEW YORK
SATURDAY
SUNDAY
EAGLES
FLEETWOOD MAC
STEELY DAN
JOURNEY
THE DOOBIE BROTHERS
EARTH, WIND & FIRE

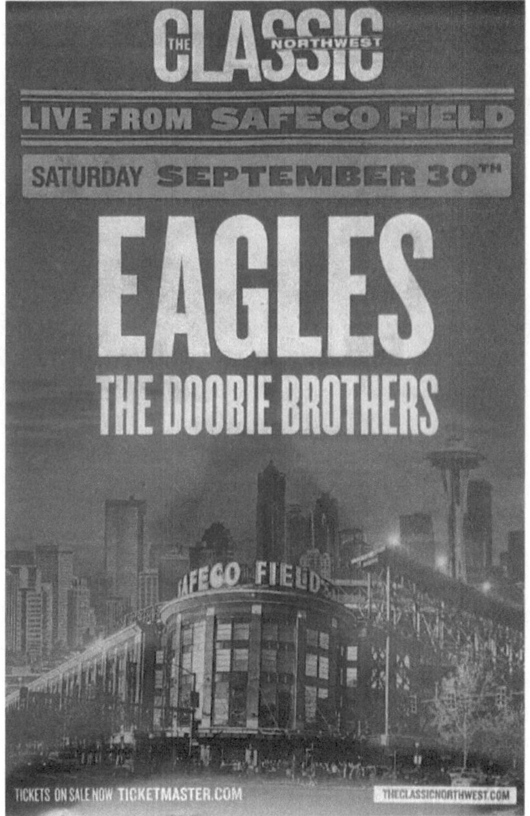

THE CLASSIC NORTHWEST
LIVE FROM SAFECO FIELD
SATURDAY SEPTEMBER 30TH
EAGLES
THE DOOBIE BROTHERS
SAFECO FIELD
TICKETS ON SALE NOW TICKETMASTER.COM
THECLASSICNORTHWEST.COM

The Royalty of Rock
The Buckinghams promoted the 'Chicago Sound'

There are a few things I miss from my youth in the Chicago area. Like watching the Chicago Cubs play baseball, eating a pie at my favorite pizzeria and listening to radio station WLS. And enjoying great rock music that had the "Chicago Sound."

Although the term doesn't get bandied about much, I have been using "Chicago Sound" for decades to describe the brass-rock style that was born in the Windy City in the mid-1960s. My hometown heroes, the Buckinghams, were the first band to employ it as their ticket to Rock & Roll success.

A typical brass section consists of a trumpet, saxophone and trombone. Blended together, those acoustic instruments provide a smooth-yet-potent sound that can replace an electric guitar or organ or be combined with either.

In the early days of the 1960s, James Brown started using a horn section in his funky soul recordings. But the 'Hams were the first to use that feature repeatedly on mainstream rock recordings.

The Buckinghams came from the north side of Chicago and were a coalition of two local bands – the Centuries and the Pulsations. Their big break came in late 1965 when they won a competition to become the house band on WGN-TV's local music show *The All Time Hits.*

The producers of the show wanted the band to have a name that identified with the British Invasion, which was all the rage. A security guard at the TV station suggested "Buckinghams." It didn't hurt that Chicago had a lakefront landmark known as Buckingham Fountain. The moniker came with the slogan "the Royalty of Rock & Roll."

The band members donned fashionable suits reminiscent of those sold on London's Savile Row, playing the part of British musicians who actually were from the American heartland. It had been two years since the Beatles dressed in matching suits for public appearances, but the Buckinghams picked up the trend to cement their English persona.

It wasn't long before the Buckinghams began to record, and they were signed to a minor Chicago label, U.S.A. Records. Their sessions took place at Chess Studios on the south side.

Early in 1966, Chicago radio stations began to play the Buckinghams' "I'll Go Crazy." Penned by James Brown in 1960, Brown recorded a version that went to *Billboard* number 73 on Feb. 26, 1966. After it became a regional hit for the Buckinghams, subsequent single releases were "I Call Your Name" and "I've Been Wrong." John Lennon and Paul McCartney of the Beatles wrote the former, and Allan Clarke, Tony Hicks and Graham Nash of the Hollies wrote the latter.

Carl Bonafede and Dan Belloc can be called the godfathers of the Chicago Sound. They were co-producers of the Buckinghams' early recordings, and Bonafede doubled as the band's manager.

Bonafede and Belloc were not novices in the music industry. Bonafede (born Oct. 16, 1940) is a native Chicagoan who had been a singer, record producer and band promoter. Belloc was a band leader, composer and owner of a Chicago ballroom.

"I would say Belloc and Bonafede were definitely important for the early success we had," said Buckinghams guitar player Carl Giammarese in an exclusive interview for this book. "It was Belloc's idea to add horns in the recording studio.

"It gave the songs a fullness and excitement. Bonafede was relentless in promoting us to the radio stations. He was responsible for getting us a record deal with U.S.A."

Frank Tesinsky arranged the songs and played trombone in the Buckinghams' horn section, alongside Belloc, who played saxophone.

Carl Bonafede

Dan Belloc

James William Guercio

With 1966 coming to a close, U.S.A. released a fourth Buckinghams song, "Kind Of A Drag." Written by Jim Holvay of Brookfield, Illinois, it became much more than a regional hit. It entered the *Billboard* Hot 100 at number 90 on December 31, 1966, and it was the nation's number 1 song on February 18 and February 25, 1967, ending a seven-week stay at the top spot for "I'm A Believer" by the Monkees. According to a fan magazine issued in 1967, "Kind Of A Drag" sold 1.4 million copies. Giammarese is sure the actual figure is higher than that.

With a huge national single in its catalog, U.S.A. quickly assembled an album containing 12 of the Buckinghams' songs and gave it the title *Kind Of A Drag.*

Contract was signed in the air

About that time the band signed a management contract with Chicagoan James William Guercio, who then became the Buckinghams' producer. U.S.A. no longer could hold the red-hot band, as Guercio negotiated a contract termination settlement and found a new recording home at Columbia Records.

"We signed our Columbia contract in the air, flying to New York from Chicago to record 'Don't You Care,'" Giammarese recalled. "I remember a lot of excitement, knowing we would be in the studio in New York City and on a major label. We were amazed at the size of the studio – also recording in a sixteen-track studio.

"We recorded the *Kind Of A Drag* album at Chess on an 8-track. Don't misunderstand me – Chess was an iconic studio. Legends like Muddy Waters, Chuck Berry and the Stones recorded there with the great (engineer) Ron Malo. We were honored to record there and work with Ron.

"Getting to New York was so special, we felt like our music career was really taking off."

How did it feel to be on top of the Hot 100? "It was a tremendous feeling of excitement and accomplishment," Giammarese said. "While 'Kind Of A Drag' was sitting at number 1, the Monkees' 'I'm A Believer' was number 2, and the Stones' 'Ruby Tuesday' was number 3.

"Also, being such a major Beatles fan, I often imagined the Beatles noticing us or talking about us, which was probably pure fantasy on my part."

While local bands like the Shadows of Knight and the Cryan Shames had penetrated the national charts, the Buckinghams were the first Chicago group to hit the top.

"It was a feeling of incredible accomplishment," Giammarese reflected. "We were so busy touring, there wasn't much time to think about it. I don't think I realized we were the first rock band from Chicago to top the national charts. I thought about it years later."

Three singles on the chart at the same time

Before the Buckinghams slipped from their stable, U.S.A. released an earlier recording of "Lawdy Miss Clawdy." The result was three Buckinghams' singles on two different labels in the *Hot 100* at the same time.

Guercio wasted no time in using the brass-rock approach of his predecessors. "Don't You Care" was the first release for Columbia, and it rocketed to number 6.

In all, the Buckinghams placed six singles on the national charts in 1967, prompting *Cash Box Magazine* to name them as "the most promising vocal group in America." *Billboard Magazine* went one better, saying they were "the most listened to band in America" for the year.

There were a couple of earlier personnel changes but, at their peak of popularity, the band consisted of Dennis Tufano (lead vocals), Carl Giammarese (guitar), Nick Fortuna (bass), Jon Poulos (drums) and Marty Grebb (keyboards). Session musicians always comprised the brass section.

Dennis Miccolis was the original keyboardist and left the band in 1966. Larry Nestor replaced him briefly before Grebb came on board. Curtis Bachman was the Buckinghams' founding bass player, and he departed in 1966, forcing Fortuna to move from guitar to bass. George LeGros originally shared lead vocals, but he quit after the Army drafted him in '66.

The influence of Bonafede, Belloc and the Buckinghams soon spread to other Chicago area bands, and brass-rock became the calling card for such groups as the Flock ("Take Me Back"), the American Breed ("Bend Me, Shape Me"), the Ides of March ("Vehicle") and Chase ("Get It On").

Did the Buckinghams influence the Beatles? Perhaps.

The Buckinghams' recording of "I'll Go Crazy" went to radio stations in March 1966 and was getting considerable air play that same month. The Beatles, with ace producer George Martin supervising, held recording sessions between April 7 and June 17, 1966, for "Got To Get You Into My Life," which was the first Beatles' song with full brass instrumentation.

"Got To Get You Into My Life" was placed on the Beatles' album *Revolver,* which became a number 1 LP on the *Billboard* 200. The McCartney composition was finally released as a single by Capital Records in 1976, long after the Beatles had split up.

Another Windy City group was a band that formed in 1967, calling itself the Big Thing. After Guercio left the Buckinghams in 1968, he became manager of this outfit.

Guercio moved the seven-member band to Los Angeles, changed its name to Chicago Transit Authority and signed it to Columbia. They had one album of jazz-rock songs in 1969 before they shortened their name to **Chicago** for their second album.

Unlike the Buckinghams, Chicago had a full-time horn section – Walt Parazaider (saxophone), James Pankow (trombone) and Lee Loughnane (trumpet).

The public acceptance of Chicago's brass-driven style resulted in 35 top 40 singles and thirty-two charted albums. In conjunction with its 60th anniversary, *Billboard* named Chicago as the top American band in its chart history and fourth overall behind the Beatles, Rolling Stones and the Bee Gees.

"Guercio never talked about moving us to L.A.," Giammarese said. "We did spend quite a bit of time there. We rented a house up in the Hollywood hills for several months while recording our 'Portraits' album. I spent more time in L.A. during my Tufano-Giammarese days."

'The Wiz' takes over

Jimmy "The Wiz" Wisner produced the final recordings by the Buckinghams, and their releases after 1968 failed to have much impact. Additionally, the City of Chicago canceled a "Buckinghams Day" fete after word got out that some of the members had been arrested for suspected possession of illegal drugs.

"I give Jim Holvay 100 percent credit for writing the songs," Giammarese told me. "The Buckinghams had a lot of momentum in 1966-67. We had the right mix of personalities, the right look and we were focused.

"Landing the TV variety show The *All Time Hits* got us a lot of exposure on WGN-TV, which was a syndicated station playing in markets all around the country. We were on for 13 weeks. We still needed the hit songs, and Holvay gave us that. "They say timing is everything, and we came along at the right time."

Fame is fleeting in the music business and, when the well of good songs runs dry, any band will have to call it quits. Such was the Buckinghams' fate in 1970.

"There are many reasons for the break-up," Giammarese said. "We had a lack of good management, and they were not looking out for our best interests. Some members wanted to experiment with a different sound, and the upper forces of Columbia were not allowing us to do that. So it became frustrating.

"Dennis Tufano and I were writing songs and going in a totally different musical direction. So was Marty Grebb. I think the main factor was that radio and our audience were changing quickly. Almost overnight, radio went from AM to FM. And there were no more two-minute nineteen- second songs – they became four minutes.

"It wasn't just the Buckinghams that were getting squeezed out. Many pop groups were left behind, like the Turtles, Gary Puckett & the Union Gap, the Association and many more."

As the once proud Royalty of Rock slipped into music history, Tufano and Giammarese continued as a duo and recorded three albums.

"I didn't think about (future plans) much," Giammarese admitted. "When you're young, I don't think you think a lot about the future. I was focused on writing songs. Dennis Tufano and I were committed to getting a record deal as singer/songwriters. We signed with the great Lou Adler and Ode Records. It was a very creative time, working with producer Lou Adler and some of the finest studio musicians at the time.

"Lou gave us a great opportunity. Although my song 'Music Everywhere' made it into the *Billboard* Hot 100, peaking in the 60s, we didn't write songs that were commercial hits. It was a great experience, working with the best in L.A., including Carole King and Tom Scott."

Back together on the nostalgia circuit

The Buckinghams got back together in an altered form in 1980 and got on the nostalgia concert circuit.

"Our brand of pop music came back with a vengeance in 1980," Giammarese said. "All of a sudden, there was a resurgence. Our audience wanted to hear our songs again, and it continues today."

The Buckinghams made a few new recordings and, in 2005, they played at one of the inaugural balls of President George W. Bush. In 2009 they played at an inaugural ball for President Barack Obama.

Celebrity Cruises booked the revamped Buckinghams lineup on a "Flower Power Cruise" to set sail from Miami, Florida, to the southern Caribbean Sea in March 2023. Many other pop musical acts from the 1960s and '70s were scheduled to perform.

The band Chicago was fortunate that their deep roster of hit singles kept them on the charts until 1991. With three original members still on board, Chicago is a top touring act to this day. They released their last album in 2022.

When Guercio left the Buckinghams he became a staff producer for Columbia. In that role he crafted the second album for Blood, Sweat & Tears in late '68. With a heavy brass-rock sound, the record spent seven weeks atop the *Billboard* 200 album chart and sold four million units in the U.S. and Canada.

The Outsiders from Cleveland, Gary Puckett & the Union Gap from San Diego, the Grass Roots from Los Angeles, the Rascals from New Jersey and the Spiral Starecase from Sacramento also parlayed brass-rock into several major hits in the 1960s and '70s.

Here's where the folks at the Rock & Roll Hall of Fame should take notice. The "Chicago Sound" was a brilliant innovation in the evolution of popular music and inspired many. The people responsible for its creation and development should receive recognition for their legitimate contributions to rock.

The artist eligibility requirement of the Hall states: "Besides demonstrating unquestionable musical excellence and talent, inductees will have had a significant impact on the development, evolution and preservation of rock & roll." The Buckinghams and Bonafede, Belloc and Guercio easily meet those qualifications.

Let's move the Royalty of Rock and Roll out of the Windy City so the Hall of Fame can enshrine them in their rightful place in Cleveland.

The Buckinghams classic lineup

Dennis Tufano (September 11, 1946-?) lead vocals
Carl Giammarese (August 21, 1947-?) guitar
Nick Fortuna (May 1, 1946-?) bass
John Poulos (March 31, 1947-March 26, 1980) drums
Marty Grebb (September 2, 1945-January 1, 2020) keyboards
Formed in 1965 in Chicago, Illinois

Dennis Tufano, Marty Grebb, John Poulos, Carl Giammarese, Nick Fortuna

Buckinghams' significant songs:

I'll Go Crazy
I Call Your Name
Makin' Up And Breakin' Up
I've Been Wrong
Kind Of A Drag
You Make Me Feel So Good
Lawdy Miss Clawdy
Don't You Care
Why Don't You Love Me
Hey Baby (They're Playing Our Song)

And Our Love
Susan
Foreign Policy
Back In Love Again
You Misunderstand Me
Where Did You Come From
This Is How Much I Love You
It's A Beautiful Day (For Lovin')
I Got A Feelin'
Difference Of Opinion
You

Remembering Sonny Bono
He reached for the stars, then became one

In January 1998, as Sonny Bono was laid to rest in Cathedral City, California, he left behind a legacy that is both simple and confusing.

On one hand Bono, who died on the Heavenly ski slopes of South Lake Tahoe, Calif., was widely admired as an underdog who beat heavy odds to succeed in the music, television and restaurant industries, as well as the political arena. He was a second-term U.S. Congressman at the time of his death.

But there was a dark side to the man who in the 1960s masterminded the astronomical rise of the Sonny & Cher act. He had three failed marriages, squandered a fortune and died in a peculiar manner – skiing alone through a wooded area and sustaining a massive head injury after hitting a tree. That was not an accident an experienced skier like Bono was likely to have. His widow Mary went on record as saying prescription drug abuse caused his death.

The way he died was not unique. A friend of mine told me of a fraternity brother he had. The man, who was an attorney in his mid-fifties, died when he skied into a tree on the Beaver Creek slopes in Colorado.

If Bono's accident had a Hollywood ending, he would have made a miraculous recovery and continued his political career to become President of the United States. That is the way Bono's life had gone for 62 years – dismal setbacks followed by one incredible success after another.

The youngest of three children, Salvatore Phillip Bono was born in Detroit in 1935 to Sicilian immigrants. After the family relocated to southern California in 1942, he and his father Santo rode a train to Cheyenne, Wyo., to retrieve their car, which had broken down on the drive out West. While driving through a desert, Sonny accidentally fell out of the vehicle, which was traveling at about 70 mph. Recovery from those extensive injuries was his first triumph.

After doctors finished removing gravel from his skin and bandaged him, "I looked like a pint-size mummy, wrapped from head to toe," Bono recalled in his autobiography. "I even bled under each fingernail."

Sonny was not a good student, yet he had the ambition to be an actor. Santo filled his head with the idea that Sonny would be a failure, however, and the young man drifted from job to job for a few years. Technically, he was not supposed to be a successful songwriter since he had no musical training. But that did not stop him from trying. And succeeding.

"I didn't think I had any talent"

Bono confessed in his book, "I didn't think I had any talent. I could barely sing… couldn't play the piano… felt I couldn't do anything. My dad told me I'd be a failure. Everyone believed it, but I fought it, convinced myself to grab any opportunity that came my way."

Bono married Donna Rankin in 1954 and had a daughter, Christy. The marriage was doomed from the start, as the partners drifted apart soon after the wedding. Divorce followed in 1961.

During his marriage to Donna, her father offered Sonny a job with his construction company. It was the mid-1950s, and the young songwriter had been trying to pitch his songs to various artists while working full-time at Douglas Aircraft. Extremely bored with his job operating a tug at Douglas, he accepted the offer immediately and began pouring concrete in Anaheim, building bridges that would lead to Disneyland.

Sonny admitted that it was hard but satisfying work. However, about seven months after he started the job, he was fired, abruptly and mysteriously.

"There was no precipitating incident," Bono wrote. "When I asked my foreman why, he shrugged. None of my superiors came forth with an explanation either. It was incredibly frustrating."

But from that job termination came the chance to sell his songs face-to-face to record executives after he got a job delivering meat on Sunset Boulevard in Hollywood. At the time, that district was the equivalent of New York's Tin Pan Alley with numerous record companies and recording studios making the area their home.

Months later, after having heard that Sonny played one of his songs for Frankie Laine, Donna's father called Bono and admitted that it was he who had him fired from the construction company. The explanation: "I knew your heart was in music, and that you'd never go anywhere if you stayed with the company."

After the breakup of his first marriage, Bono seldom saw Christy and lamented the fact that he wasn't a better father to her. It was an experience that made him an improved parent for children who would come later in his life.

Songwriting really began to pay off for Sonny when, along with musician/producer Jack Nitzsche, he wrote "Needles And Pins." The song launched the career of the British band the Searchers with a number 13 showing in the United States, and it hit number 1 on the English charts in 1964. Several other artists also recorded the song.

He saw his entire world change dramatically when he met aspiring actress Cherilyn LaPierre Sarkisian in the early 1960s, and he became Cher's lover and show business mentor.

Bono made a career leap when he became employed by record producer Phil Spector. Sonny convinced Spector that he needed a West Coast promotions man for his Philles record label, and Spector gave him the position. But Bono was

Sonny & Cher (1965)

a jack of all trades. During this period, he became a recording artist in the simplest of ways: he played tambourine and did background singing, hand claps and finger snaps on recordings by groups like the Crystals, Ronettes and Righteous Brothers.

As he absorbed music industry knowledge from Spector, Bono secretly schemed to produce Cher as a recording artist. They tested the waters as a singing duo under the name of Caesar and Cleopatra before settling on the Sonny & Cher moniker.

The biggest hit from Sonny's pen, "I Got You Babe," launched the duo into musical stardom in 1965. A modest string of releases kept them on the charts for about four years, and they enjoyed the kind of publicity blitz that hadn't been seen since the Beatles were introduced to America 18 months earlier.

Sonny and Cher were more than audio stars. They sent shockwaves through the fashion industry with their over-the-top wardrobe of colors, stripes, patterns and fuzzy vests.

Nasal voice and all, Sonny recorded a few songs by himself. But his only solo album, *Inner Views,* was a commercial failure. He didn't mind because he was focused on making Cher a star.

Between 1967 and 1972, the duo had three hit songs in the *Billboard* Hot 100 top 10. "All I Ever Need Is You" spent five weeks atop the Adult Contemporary chart.

Sonny and Cher were the toast of Hollywood, moving into a Beverly Hills mansion and getting married in 1969 after posing as husband and wife for years. As their stream of recording successes ran dry, Sonny gambled his bankroll on a film he produced called *Chastity*, in which Cher was the star. The film flopped, and they were back to where they had started in early '65. The only difference was that now they had a baby daughter named Chastity.

Hit TV show

TV mogul Fred Silverman helped the pair get back on their feet in 1971 when he created a variety show titled *The Sonny and Cher Comedy Hour* and made it a summer replacement for CBS. It was a tremendous success and ran until 1974. They were ratings winners, with the gorgeous Cher wearing designer outfits and belting out songs while Sonny played the stooge in their comedy skits. The format for the TV show was based on their successful Las Vegas lounge routine.

Amid reports of extramarital affairs, the couple divorced in '74. An attempt to revive their variety show in 1976 was short-lived. Cher then launched her acting career, and Sonny was mostly

The duo in their TV days (1971)

forgotten. He made guest acting appearances on TV series like *The Love Boat, Fantasy Island, Charlie's Angels, The Man From U.N.C.L.E., The Six Million Dollar Man and CHips*.

Model Susie Coelho became Bono's third bride in a ceremony on New Year's Eve 1981, and they divorced in 1984.

Was that marriage cursed? You might conclude that it was when you consider the officiating minister in Aspen, Colo., referred to Susie as "Cherie" at the outset of the ceremony. Concerning the dissolution of his third marriage, Bono wrote, "The problem? If I had to put my finger on one specific thing, I would have to say show business. Our relationship was based more on the pursuit of a career than on romance. Susie wanted to make it as an actress …"

Sonny had no experience in the food service business, but in 1982 he boldly opened his own Italian restaurant on Melrose Ave. in West Hollywood. He entered the business with little more than his mother's recipe for spaghetti sauce and a visual concept for his trattoria. *Bono* was a hit, becoming a trendy hangout for celebrities. He opened a second location in Houston but sold his interest to his partner after the Texas oil industry declined.

He met Mary Whitaker in the Melrose restaurant in 1985 when she was celebrating her graduation from the University of Southern California. A year later she became his fourth bride.

Mary and Sonny had a son and daughter together, Chesare and Chianna.

Bono had fallen in love with the city of Palm Springs around the time he and Cher were breaking up. Having kept a home in the desert town 110 miles east of Los Angeles for fifteen years, he decided to sell his restaurant and move there to open a new *Bono* in January 1986, at the Palm Springs Racquet Club. Again, the business thrived.

The restaurant's fare was strictly Italian in nature, but the menus had a whimsical flair. They were designed to look like 45 rpm records and were categorized by some of Sonny's song titles: "The Beat Goes On" appetizers; "Baby Don't Go" soups and salads; and "Bang Bang" pastas. He also honored his family with "Mary's Favorite" (penne pasta with Italian sausage, artichoke hearts, asparagus and olive oil); "Rigatoni Chesare" (breaded chicken sautéed with spinach, herbs, rigatoni and olive oil; and "Steak Bono" (N.Y. steak crusted with herbs, served with roasted garlic mashed potatoes).

Reinvented one more time

Sonny reinvented himself for the last time in 1988 when he fought with Palm Springs' city hall over his inability to get approval for a larger sign for the restaurant and had "a few silly bureaucratic battles" over the remodeling of his house. Ultimately, he took over city hall after he ran for mayor without any previous political experience and defeated long-time incumbent Frank Bogert. In true Hollywood style, his election came one day after Cher won an Oscar for best actress (*Moonstruck*) and about a year after he had registered to vote for the first time.

Bono, a diminutive five-foot-five, became a popular, high-profile mayor who had time for guest appearances in movies and TV shows. The annual Palm Springs International Film sprang to life under his administration, and a $2.5 million budget deficit was erased without raising taxes.

After one term as mayor, Bono decided to raise the proverbial bar for himself and run for U.S. Senate. Bruce Herschensohn defeated him in the Republican primary of 1992.

But he wasn't finished with politics. Two years later he ran for the U.S. House of Representatives in California's 44 district and won the GOP primary. Ever the bitter loser, Bogert then remarked, "… I sure don't want to see Sonny Bono there, making a fool of himself and us." But Bono defeated Democrat Steve Clute, receiving 56 percent of the vote. He closed his restaurant in 1995, and reelection followed in 1996.

Through all his encounters with the stodgy Washington society, Bono never lost his sense of humor. He told the VH-1 documentary *Behind The Music,* "I walked into my first session as a member of the House Judiciary Committee, and all these faces looked up at me. I could see by the fearful look in their eyes that they were thinking, *Please let him be delivering pizza.*"

He also was a member of the National Security Committee and was active on immigration and Indian gaming issues. He became a popular draw at Republican fundraising events.

A portion of Interstate 10 near Palm Springs has been named the Sonny Bono Freeway. A bronze statue of him depicts the former mayor sitting on a fountain in downtown Palm Springs, and his bronze bust is on display in the Palm Springs International Airport.

Cher, who reached incredible career heights after she split with Sonny, will forever be linked to him. Despite all the acrimony that boiled out of their breakup, his death was a big blow to her. It caused her to reflect on how important he was to her success.

Cher delivered a eulogy

She delivered a tearful eulogy at his funeral. Then, inspired by Sonny, she gathered the strength to record for the first time in three years and ended up with her biggest hit, "Believe" On her website, Cher once stated that the song is "In memory of Son."

"Believe" sold over eleven million units and charted at number 1 in more than twenty countries.

Regardless of whether you liked him, it is important to view Bono's life as an inspiration. He was a diamond in the rough – untrained but not untalented. He took life's pitfalls in stride, and he was not afraid to try something new after he experienced failure.

An everyman who had little but dreams of success in the beginning, he left an indelible fingerprint on the music and television industries and on the city of Palm Springs.

313

What we can learn from Sonny's life, simply, is that seemingly impossible things can be accomplished through sheer determination, hard work, perseverance and passion.

Notable songs written/co-written by Sonny Bono

Needles And Pins
Baby Don't Go
I Got You Babe
Bang Bang (My Baby Shot Me Down)
Just You
Laugh At Me
Little Man
But You're Mine
Where Do You Go
Sing C'est La Vie

The Revolution Kind
Have I Stayed Too Long
Living For You
Love Don't Come
The Beat Goes On
You Better Sit Down Kids
Beautiful Story
It's The Little Things
My Best Friend's Girl Is Out Of Sight
A Cowboy's Work Is Never Done

Congressman Bono (1997)

A souvenir from the *Bono* gift shop

In the summer of 1998, Sonny's widow Mary dedicated a piece of sidewalk artwork in downtown Palm Springs. When he was mayor, he backed a plan for beautification in the city. Mary Bono won a special election in April 1998 to succeed Sonny in Congress, and she was elected to that seat for seven more two-year terms.

A Few Words About the Beatles
Get Back brought them back to us

After the Disney+ television streaming channel released the Beatles documentary *Get Back* late in 2021, viewers finally got to see long-ago film footage of the band at work in their final year as a unit. Viewing it was an experience that had a profound effect on me as a music fan.

Get Back serves as a kind of time machine that takes us back to when the Fab Four were still in their 20s. Ringo Starr and John Lennon were 28, Paul McCartney was 26 and George Harrison was a month shy of 26 when the filming took place. McCartney was fully bearded, and Starr and Harrison wore mustaches. Plagued by poor eyesight, Lennon wore his trademark granny spectacles.

Imagine – the band had enormous, nearly unprecedented success before any of its members turned thirty.

It was pure joy for me to watch the quartet, still in the days of their youth, working together on songs. A few days into the project, keyboardist Billy Preston joined them. The Beatles long have been musical icons for me, and this proverbial turning back of the clock made me ecstatic.

Producer Peter Jackson boiled down sixty hours of tape into 468 minutes of final product.

The camera placements created a vantage point better than being a fly on the wall. I felt as if I were sitting on a chair, sipping a cup of tea, several feet from the Beatles as they went through their creative process.

The original goal of their project in January 1969 was to write and rehearse fourteen songs in the span of twenty-two days to use in a televised show and a concert. A documentary film and a record album were also planned.

George Martin, who was the Beatles' regular record producer, was present at some of the sessions but is not shown in the documentary as giving input on the structure of the new songs. The Beatles chose Phil Spector to produce the album, which was released in 1970 after the Beatles had broken up.

The nature of this goal shifted as the days went by, and a wrench was thrown into the works in the middle of the schedule when George Harrison abruptly quit the band. The others convinced him to return after a three-day absence, but crucial work time was lost.

A sound stage at the Twickenham Film Studios in London's Borough of Richmond upon Thames served as the starting point of the 22-day project. That's where Harrison calmly told Lennon, McCartney and Starr, "I quit. See you 'round the clubs." Days later the band's activities were moved to the Beatles' Apple Corps Studio on Savile Row in central London.

The concert was the climax

The climax of the three-part documentary is the concert the Beatles played with Preston on the rooftop of that building on January 30, 1969. It was the band's first gig since August 29, 1966, when they played a full concert in Candlestick Park in San Francisco, California. And it would be the last time they would play in public as a unit.

The rooftop concert lasted forty-two minutes. Police shut it down after about thirty people complained about the "noise."

It's incredible that some Londoners considered several fresh, new Beatles songs to be offensive racket.

But several cameras were in place on the rooftop, on the ground and across the street on a rooftop. It was a brilliant decision to record the show, aborted though it was. It shows a band of veteran musicians with smiles on their faces, braving the winter cold to present the world with their latest offerings for free.

Paul McCartney, John Lennon and George Harrison play during the rooftop concert on
January 30, 1969. Ringo Starr is at his drumkit behind McCartney,
and Billy Preston is off camera to the left.
(Photo courtesy of Disney)

The album was put on the shelf for a year and finally was released on May 8, 1970. In America it spawned the number 1 singles "Let It Be" and "The Long And Winding Road."

Some of the songs that were in development during the Get Back sessions wound up on the "Abbey Road" LP later in 1969.

The reels of film were turned into a feature-length movie by American director Michael Lindsay-Hogg in 1970. I remember taking a date to see the flick in spring of 1972. I struggled to stay interested in it but, by 2021, I was totally ready for the lengthy documentary.

Decades have gone by, and this time I remained riveted throughout the entirety of *Get Back*. The world has failed to produce a band with the talent of the Beatles since their 1969 break-up, and I reveled in seeing them at work through the time warp of the documentary.

To some viewers, 468 minutes of the Beatles is overkill. But we see a veteran band at work, showing relationships that have been worn thin by time. In a way, it's a good thing the band was on a twenty-two-day schedule, since their interactions may have been quite strained if they'd been together in a studio for much longer.

The music world should never forget the unparalleled feat the Beatles accomplished on April 4, 1964. On that date their songs occupied the top five positions on the *Billboard* Hot 100. That week, the top of the chart looked like this:

1. Can't Buy Me Love
2. Twist And Shout
3. She Loves You
4. I Want To Hold Your Hand
5. Please Please Me

The Greatest

What is obvious is the talent possessed by the Beatles, and that brings me to the person whom I rate as the greatest single talent in the history of rock and roll music. That's **Paul McCartney.**

One day Lennon was late arriving at the *Get Back* sessions. So the camera focused on McCartney strumming his bass guitar, experimenting with a tune and some lyrical phrasing. His kept at it, and Lennon gave some input after he arrived. The song turned out to be "Get Back," and the Beatles played it at the beginning of the rooftop concert. Released April 11, 1969, it became the band's next single.

The single hit number 1 in fourteen countries, including the United Kingdom and United States, where it topped the *Billboard* Hot 100 for five weeks.

It is this kind of talent that has made McCartney the productive musician that he's been as a member of the Beatles, as the leader of Wings and as a solo act. His spontaneity is almost unrivaled. He possesses a great, flexible singing voice. He is a multiple instrumentalist, displaying proficiency on many.

A quip, attributed to Lennon but actually spoken in the BBC comedy *Radio Active* in 1981 claimed, "So maybe Ringo Starr isn't the best drummer in the world. He isn't even the best drummer in the Beatles."

It was a playful slight against Starr that unjustly got legs over time. But the bottom line is that McCartney always has had chops on drums. To wit, he played drums on the recording of "The Ballad Of John And Yoko." He also filled in on drums when Starr briefly quit the band during the recording of the *White Album* in 1968.

Sir Paul played all the instruments on two of his solo albums – *McCartney* (1970) and *McCartney II* (1979) and nearly all instruments on most of the tracks of *McCartney III* (2020). Among the instruments he played just on those three albums were: acoustic guitar, electric guitar, bass, drums, acoustic piano, organ, percussion, wine glasses, Mellotron, electric piano, synthesizer, banjo, sequencer, double bass, harpsichord, harmonium, Fender Rhodes and recorder. Few musicians, living or dead, could play all those instruments with high proficiency.

Thanks to multi-track tape machines, a musician can record one instrument at a time and lay the tracks over one another to create a finished recording. McCartney liked to use this technique when he recorded songs at home.

A concert by Sir Paul as a solo artist fairly well mirrors his recording studio work. I have seen him move from playing bass to acoustic guitar, electric guitar, ukulele and piano while on stage.

Here are some of McCartney's figures from the *Billboard* charts:

- **Twenty** number 1 singles, as a member of the Beatles
- **Nine** number 1 singles, as a solo artist, leader of Wings or in collaboration with Linda McCartney, Stevie Wonder and Michael Jackson
- **Thirty** total weeks at number 1 for those nine songs
- **Fifty-two** top 40 singles, as a member of the Beatles
- **Thirty-seven** top 40 singles, as a solo artist or collaborator
- **Nineteen** number 1 albums, as a member of the Beatles (including anthologies)
- **Eight** number 1 albums, as a solo artist or collaborator

These are impressive numbers, but they do not tell the whole story of McCartney's value as an entertainer. Many of his songs have endured as timeless masterpieces. For evidence, I offer these few:

- I Saw Her Standing There
- Can't Buy Me Love
- And I Love Her
- She's A Woman
- We Can Work It Out
- Drive My Car
- Michelle
- Paperback Writer
- Eleanor Rigby
- I'm Looking Through You
- When I'm Sixty-four
- She's Leaving Home
- Hello Goodbye
- Lady Madonna
- Birthday
- Hey Jude
- Let It Be
- The Long And Winding Road
- My Love
- Live And Let Die
- Band On The Run
- Listen To What The Man Said
- Maybe I'm Amazed
- Ebony And Ivory
- Say Say Say

"Yesterday," with more than 3,000 cover versions (by some estimates), stands as the most-recorded song of all time.

He's got versatility

And what about versatility? McCartney demonstrated that aptly on "The Beatles' White Album of 1968". He balanced a quiet love song, "I Will," with a hard rocker, "Helter Skelter."

Similarly, on "Beatles For Sale (1965) McCartney had both the mellow "I'll Follow The Sun" and the raucous "Kansas City/Hey Hey Hey."

He proved a point with his biggest post-Beatles single, in which he said, "You'd think that people would have had enough of silly loves songs. But I look around me and I see it isn't so. Some people want to fill the world with silly love songs – what's wrong with that?"

It turned out that nothing was wrong with that, as "Silly Love Songs" sat at number 1 on the *Billboard* Hot 100 for five weeks and was rated the top single of 1976.

Heaping praise on McCartney is in no way meant to minimize the talents and accomplishments of the other Beatles. They all proved their worth as members of the band and as solo artists in the 1970s and '80s. I love the music each one has created. It's hard to decide what was better – their work as a band or as individuals.

Lennon often butted heads with McCartney over their individual styles. McCartney preferred to write love songs, which were just plain entertaining. Lennon, on the other hand, had a desire to write songs with messages, displaying his social consciousness.

The two even sniped at each other in their songs shortly after the Beatle break-up. McCartney fired a subtle shot with "Too Many People," and Lennon countered with "How Do You Sleep?"

But that is the factor that sways my preference. McCartney's songs are catchy and fun. Sure, he dabbled in "message" songs with the likes of "Give Ireland Back To The Irish." But, by and large, his songs are light-hearted entertainment – songs I can listen to over and over without having to be concerned about a lyrical message.

As cowriters, Lennon and McCartney published about 180 songs between October 1962 and May 1970.

In an interview with *Playboy Magazine* in 1980, Lennon remarked, "(Paul) provided a lightness, an optimism, while I would always go for the sadness, the discords, the bluesy notes.

"There was a period when I thought I didn't write melodies, that Paul wrote those and I just wrote straight, shouting rock and roll."

It wasn't always easy

In the days following the Beatles' break-up in the fall of 1969, McCartney faced a devastating crisis. "I'd outlived my usefulness," he would remark to biographer Peter Ames Carlin.

In a meeting on September 20, 1969, after the *Abbey Road* album had been completed, McCartney pitched several new projects to the other Beatles, including small, unannounced shows in the U.K. and a TV special. Lennon then announced, "The group is over! I'm leaving!"

The imminent demise of the world's greatest rock band sent McCartney, only 27 years old, reeling for weeks. With wife Linda and their two children, he retreated to his farm on the west coast of Scotland, where he slummed around drinking whiskey and ingesting drugs. McCartney lacked the focus and energy to write new songs.

Finally, in December '69 he moved the family back to London, where he, Harrison and Starr did some overdubs to complete the *Let It Be* album. Then he began writing songs for what essentially became a homemade album that jump-started his solo career.

Some other painful times in McCartney's life: the death of his mother Mary (cancer) when he was fourteen; the death of wife Linda, also a cancer victim, in 1998; his disastrous and brief marriage to Heather Mills; the deaths of Lennon and Harrison, and litigation involving the ex-Beatles. After Linda's death he entered grief therapy with a psychologist.

McCartney also was entangled in the Beatles' financially troubled Apple Corps, which sought a savvy lawyer to save it from ruin. John, Ringo and George favored Allen Klein, who ultimately got the job. But Paul fought hard to give the task to his father-in-law's firm, Eastman & Eastman.

Paul never got over that defeat, knowing that Klein was making a 20 percent commission on profits Paul himself generated. On November 15, 1970, McCartney filed suit demanding that the Beatles be broken up in every conceivable way.

George, Ringo and Yoko Ono sued Paul in the 1980s over escalated Beatles royalties he negotiated for himself from the EMI record label. The case was resolved when EMI agreed to give the others the same rate. But the bad blood kept Paul from joining the others at the Beatles' induction into the rock and roll Hall of Fame in '88.

Paul has used a pseudonym

One of McCartney's songs was involved in a bit of deception in 1966. The Peter and Gordon version of "Woman," released by Capitol in the United States on Jan. 10 and by Columbia in the United Kingdom on Jan. 11, was credited to Bernard Webb.

On the television show *Hullabaloo*, which aired in the U.S. on April 11, 1966, Peter & Gordon performed the song and revealed that McCartney actually was the writer. Label credit for the writer was given to a pseudonym because the parties involved wanted to show the song could succeed on its own merit. It peaked at number 14 on the *Billboard* Hot 100 and number 28 on the *Official Charts Company* survey in the U.K. It was a number 1 hit in Canada.

Gordon Waller would comment later that "Woman" was his personal favorite and the ultimate Peter & Gordon song.

In the *Get Back* documentary, McCartney gives a casual performance of part of the song.

McCartney got Peter and Gordon's career rolling in 1964 when he gave them the song "A World Without Love," which hit number 1 in the U.S. At the time, Peter's sister, Jane Asher, was Paul's girlfriend

He Liked "Road Trips"

McCartney has not been afraid to venture from his home recording studio. Three times he took Wings to exotic locations to record albums.

In 1973, he decided to record "Band On The Run" at EMI's studio in Lagos, Nigeria. Drummer Denny Seiwell and guitarist Henry McCullough quit the band shortly before Wings left England, so McCartney played not only bass but also drums, percussion and most lead guitar parts. Denny Laine and Linda McCartney were the only other band members on the trip.

One day the McCartneys were robbed at knifepoint and lost a bag containing song lyrics and demo tapes. Fortunately, they were able to overcome the theft.

In 1975, Wings recorded three songs for *Venus And Mars* at Abbey Road Studios in London, then hopped on a plane for New Orleans, La. Paul had recruited Jimmy McCullough to play guitar and Geoff Britton to play drums. But a personality clash resulted in Britton quitting the band before the "road trip" began. The remaining Wings finished the album at Sea-Saint Studios, with Paul producing the tracks.

Linda was pregnant with Paul's third child when Wings recorded the album *London Town* in 1977-78. Wings was back to being a trio after drummer Joe English quit and guitarist Jimmy McCulloch left to join the Small Faces.

The main venue for recording was Abbey Road Studios, but McCartney & Co. laid down some of the tracks on board the yacht Fair Carol at Waterlemon Cay in the U.S. Virgin Islands.

Songwriting Credits

As members of the Beatles, Lennon and McCartney had an agreement about songwriting credit. Any song they wrote, be it singly or collaboratively, was credited to

Lennon-McCartney. Hence, they shared royalties equally. Beatle manager Brian Epstein and publisher Dick James hatched the idea of forming Northern Songs, a company that would own the Lennon-McCartney compositions. This muddies the waters a bit when trying to identify which Beatle actually wrote which song or had the most input. A general rule of thumb, however, is the Beatle who sang lead probably was the primary writer.

One notable exception to that rule is "Eight Days A Week." Lennon sang lead on the record, but McCartney is the principal creator.

Nailing down the exact number of songs McCartney has written by himself is tricky. It is safe to say the total exceeds three hundred.

McCartney is the greatest man in rock history, and the Beatles are the greatest band. We're so lucky to have had them making music for us.

Paul McCartney

Born James Paul McCartney on June 18, 1942, in Liverpool, England.
Was made a member of the Order of the British Empire in 1965
Was knighted by Queen Elizabeth II for services to music in 1997
Was appointed Member of the Order of the Companions of Honour (CH) in 2017 for service to music

   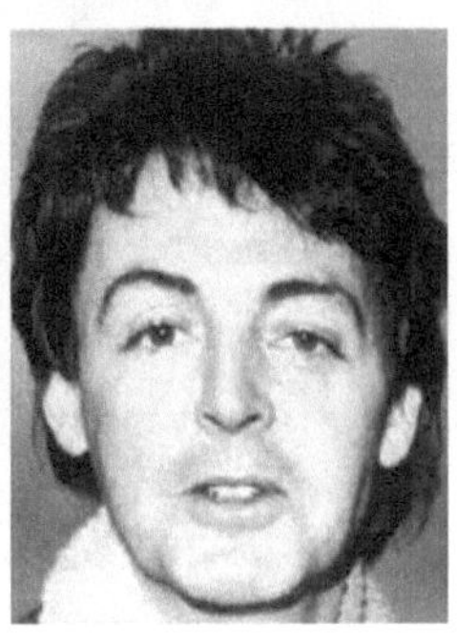

| 1950s | 1960s | 1970s | 1980s |

In 2022, McCartney's
lyrics became
pop culture slogans on T-shirts.

GLOSSARY

Addison's disease – a disorder in which the adrenal glands do not produce enough of the hormones cortisol and, sometimes, aldosterone.

Anorexia nervosa – an eating disorder primarily affecting adolescent girls and young women, characterized by pathological fear of becoming fat, distorted body image, excessive dieting and emaciation.

A-side – the song on a 45 rpm record that gets promotion from a record company.

Boogie woogie – a heavily percussive style of blues piano in which the right hand plays riffs against a driving pattern of repeating eight notes.

Break – an instrumental or percussion section during a song, creating a "break" from the main parts of the song. Breaks usually occur two-thirds to three-quarters of the way through a song.

Bridge – a musical passage that connects two sections of a song. For example, a bridge often connects the verse to the chorus of a song. It can also sit between the last two chorus sections to add variation.

British Invasion – a cultural phenomenon of the mid-1960s, when rock and pop acts from the United Kingdom and other aspects of British culture became overwhelmingly popular in the United States.

B-side – the song on a 45 rpm record that the issuing record company deems to be inferior and occupies the opposite side of the A-side and usually receives no promotion.

Civil Aeronautics Board – an agency of the federal government of the United States, existing from 1938 to 1985, that regulated aviation services and provided air accident investigation.

Crossover hit – a song that appears on two or more of the record charts which track differing musical styles or genres.

Demo – a recording used to demonstrate the capabilities of a musical artist or group as preparation for a full recording.

Double-A release – a 45 rpm record on which both sides get promotion from a record company.

Double bass – the largest and lowest-pitched member of the violin family, providing the bassline of an orchestral string section and also used in some jazz and country music.

Drum machine – a programmable electronic device able to imitate the sounds of a drum kit.

Dubbing – the act of furnishing a tape with a new sound track or adding music, sound effects, etc., to an existing one.

FM radio – a method of broadcasting that uses frequency modulation of the radio broadcast carrier wave. It was invented in 1933 by American engineer Edwin Armstrong.

Freebasing – smoking a purified solid form of cocaine, usually through a small pipe.

Ground effects – an added layer of aerodynamic elements added to an automobile to create a downforce, which helps keep the vehicle firmly on the driving surface.

Hi-hat – a pair of foot-operated cymbals forming part of a drum kit.

Impresario – a producer or sponsor of public entertainment, especially in music or theater.

Intro – the first part of a song structure, used to introduce and establish the song while giving an idea of the song's style and genre and establishing the key and basic rhythm.

Laurel Canyon – a mountainous neighborhood of Los Angeles that became home to many famous rock musicians in the late 1960s and early 1970s.

LSD – lysergic acid diethylamide, a potent psychedelic drug, ingested by mouth, that can trigger intensified thoughts, emotions, and sensory perception, as well as hallucinations.

Musitron – a three octave keyboard-and-slide musical instrument which used a modified clavioline, household appliance parts, resistors, television tubes, an amplifier and a reel-to-reel tape player. A precursor to the synthesizer, it was invented by Max Crook around 1960.

National Transportation Safety Board – an independent federal agency of the United States created by Congress to investigate every civil aviation accident in the U.S. and significant events in other modes of transportation.

Outro – the concluding section of a piece of music, normally short and distinct.

Rockabilly – a hybrid style of popular music combining the elements of

Rock & Roll and hillbilly music.

Royalty – an agreed portion of the income from a musical work paid to its composer, singer, etc., usually a percentage of the retail price of each copy sold.

Scat – vocal improvisation with wordless sounds, nonsense syllables or without words at all.

Spanish guitar – the classic form of the acoustic guitar with six strings, a waisted body and a central sound hole.

String synthesizer – a specialized synthesizer designed specifically to make sounds similar to that of a string orchestra.

Synthesizer – any of various electronic consoles, usually computerized, used to create, modify or reproduce the sounds of musical instruments by controlling voltage patterns, operated by means of keyboards, joysticks, sliders or knobs.

Torch – a sentimental or romantic popular song, usually sung by a woman.

Troubadour – any wandering singer or minstrel.

Uremic pericarditis – a condition that typically occurs in patients with end-stage kidney disease and patients with elevated blood urea nitrogen. Causes include infection, autoimmune processes, malignancy and uremia.

Varietal – in U.S. winemaking, designating a wine made entirely or chiefly from one variety of grape.

Vaudevillian – of, relating to or characteristic of vaudeville, which was theatrical entertainment consisting of a number of individual performances, acts or mixed numbers, as by comedians, singers, dancers, acrobats and magicians.

Zoom call – a communications platform that allows users to connect with video, audio, cellphone and chat. It requires an Internet connection and supported device.

16-track recording studio – an audio recording facility that uses machinery that uses equipment that can record 16 tracks in perfect synchronization, allowing multiple sound sources to be recorded at different times.

About the Author

When he is on vacation, Larry Coffman does not take a vacation from his passion for rock and roll trivia. While traversing the oceans, he has won championships on Carnival and Princess cruise ships for Classic Rock Trivia, 1960s Music Trivia, 1970s Music Trivia, and Through-the-Decades Music Trivia. He also won a Sports Trivia Championship and was on the winning team in a Trivial Pursuit contest on board a ship.

The Rock Doc's first two books are *The Coffman Collection, A History of Distinctive Rock & Roll Hits* (published in 2020), *and Radio Stations & Record Stores, More Distinctive Rock Hits from the Coffman Collection* (2021).

You can visit him at www.LarryCoffman.com.

ARTIST INDEX

H

N

O

P

Seger, Bob 299, 302
Sha Na Na 13, 296
Shames, Cryan 305
Shankar, Ravi 286, 296
Shannon, Del ix, 81, 82, 96, 157
Sherman, Bobby 141
Shirelles 86, 87, 123
Shirley (and Company) 230, 231
Shocking Blue 112, 113
Siegel, Jay 26, 196
Silhouettes 10, 11, 13
Silver Connection 240
Simon, Carly 203, 204, 206
Simon, Joe 232
Sinatra, Frank 121, 136, 166
Smith, Keely 198
Sommers, Joanie 44
Sonny & Cher 47, 288, 310, 311
Soul, Jimmy 159
Souther, J. D. 217
Spector, Phil 16, 31, 311, 316
Spiral Starecase 308
Springfield, Dusty 46, 93, 163, 164, 192
Springfield, Rick 186
Starr, Ringo 78, 169, 316, 317, 318
Steely Dan 61, 179, 180, 234, 302
Steppenwolf 288, 290, 294
Stevens, Dodie 39, 40
Stevens, Ray 175, 189
Storm, Gale 97, 98
Strawberry Alarm Clock 11
Stray Cats 17
Streisand, Barbra 254
Styx 149, 150, 181, 182
Summer, Donna 247, 253, 254
Sunshine Band 234, 235
Supertramp 182 183
Swan, Billy 63
Swinging Blue Jeans 162

T

Taylor, James 81, 82, 145, 203, 204, 205
Teenagers featuring Frankie Lymon 5
Tempchin, Jack 216, 217
Tempos 1, 130
Temptations 92, 93, 172
Terrell, Tammi 93, 94